Peugeot 205 Owners Workshop Manual

A K Legg LAE MIMI

Models covered
All Peugeot 205 models with petrol engines (inc. GTI,
Cabriolet, Automatic & special/limited editions)
954 cc, 1124 cc, 1360 cc, 1580cc & 1905 cc

Covers mechanical features of Vans
Does not cover Diesel engine or T16 Turbo models

(932-5V9)

ABCDE
FGHI

THE
BOOK

Haynes Publishing Group
Sparkford Nr Yeovil
Somerset BA22 7JJ England

Haynes Publications, Inc
861 Lawrence Drive
Newbury Park
California 91320 USA

Acknowledgements
Thanks are due to Champion Spark Plug who supplied the illustrations showing spark plug conditions, to Holt Lloyd Limited who supplied the illustrations showing bodywork repair, and to Duckhams Oils, who provided lubrication data. Certain other illustrations are the copyright of Peugeot Talbot Motor Company Limited, and are used with their permission. Thanks are also due to Sykes-Pickavant, who supplied some of the workshop tools, and to all the staff at Sparkford who assisted in the production of this manual.

© **Haynes Publishing 1993**

A book in the **Haynes Owners Workshop Manual Series**

Printed by J. H. Haynes & Co. Ltd., Sparkford, Nr Yeovil, Somerset BA22 7JJ, England

ISBN 1 85010 915 X

British Library Cataloguing in Publication Data
A catalogue record for this book is available from the British Library

Restoring and Preserving our Motoring Heritage

Few people can have had the luck to realise their dreams to quite the same extent and in such a remarkable fashion as John Haynes, Founder and Chairman of the Haynes Publishing Group.

Since 1965 his unique approach to workshop manual publishing has proved so successful that millions of Haynes Manuals are now sold every year throughout the world, covering literally thousands of different makes and models of cars, vans and motorcycles.

A continuing passion for cars and motoring led to the founding in 1985 of a Charitable Trust dedicated to the restoration and preservation of our motoring heritage. To inaugurate the new Museum, John Haynes donated virtually his entire private collection of 52 cars.

Now with an unrivalled international collection of over 210 veteran, vintage and classic cars and motorcycles, the Haynes Motor Museum in Somerset is well on the way to becoming one of the most interesting Motor Museums in the world.

A 70 seat video cinema, a cafe and an extensive motoring bookshop, together with a specially constructed one kilometre motor circuit, make a visit to the Haynes Motor Museum a truly unforgettable experience.

Every vehicle in the museum is preserved in as near as possible mint condition and each car is run every six months on the motor circuit.

Enjoy the picnic area set amongst the rolling Somerset hills. Peer through the William Morris workshop windows at cars being restored, and browse through the extensive displays of fascinating motoring memorabilia.

From the 1903 Oldsmobile through such classics as an MG Midget to the mighty 'E' Type Jaguar, Lamborghini, Ferrari Berlinetta Boxer, and Graham Hill's Lola Cosworth, there is something for everyone, young and old alike, at this Somerset Museum.

Haynes Motor Museum

Situated mid-way between London and Penzance, the Haynes Motor Museum is located just off the A303 at Sparkford, Somerset (home of the Haynes Manual) and is open to the public 7 days a week all year round, except Christmas Day and Boxing Day.

Contents

Spark plug condition and bodywork repair colour pages between pages 32 and 33

Peugeot 205 GTI

Peugeot 205 Van

About this manual

Its aim

The aim of this manual is to help you get the best value from your vehicle. It can do so in several ways. It can help you decide what work must be done (even should you choose to get it done by a garage), provide information on routine maintenance and servicing, and give a logical course of action and diagnosis when random faults occur. However, it is hoped that you will use the manual by tackling the work yourself. On simpler jobs it may even be quicker than booking the car into a garage and going there twice, to leave and collect it. Perhaps most important, a lot of money can be saved by avoiding the costs a garage must charge to cover its labour and overheads.

The manual has drawings and descriptions to show the function of the various components so that their layout can be understood. Then the tasks are described and photographed in a step-by-step sequence so that even a novice can do the work.

Its arrangement

The manual is divided into Chapters, each covering a logical sub-division of the vehicle. The Chapters are each divided into Sections, numbered with single figures, eg 5; the Sections are divided into paragraphs, or into sub-sections and paragraphs.

It is freely illustrated, especially in those parts where there is a detailed sequence of operations to be carried out. There are two forms of illustration: figures and photographs. The figures are numbered in sequence with decimal numbers, according to their position in the Chapter – eg Fig. 6.4 is the fourth drawing/illustration in Chapter 6. Photographs carry the same number (either individually or in related groups) as the Section and paragraph to which they relate.

There is an alphabetical index at the back of the manual as well as a contents list at the front. Each Chapter is also preceded by its own individual contents list.

References to the 'left' or 'right' of the vehicle are in the sense of a person in the driver's seat facing forwards.

Unless otherwise stated, nuts and bolts are removed by turning anti-clockwise, and tightened by turning clockwise.

Vehicle manufacturers continually make changes to specifications and recommendations, and these, when notified, are incorporated into our manuals at the earliest opportunity.

We take great pride in the accuracy of information given in this manual, but vehicle manufacturers make alterations and design changes during the production run of a particular vehicle of which they do not inform us. No liability can be accepted by the authors or publishers for loss, damage or injury caused by any errors in, or omissions from, the information given.

Introduction to the Peugeot 205

The Peugeot 205 was introduced in the UK in September 1983 as a five-door Hatchback with a transversely-mounted engine and transmission assembly driving the front wheels. The suspension is of front coil springs and rear transverse torsion bars.

Three engine sizes were originally available, featuring a chain driven overhead camshaft design mounted directly over the transmission. The GTI was introduced in the Spring of 1984 and was fitted with a belt-driven overhead camshaft engine with a side-mounted transmission. The GTI engine is equipped with an electronically-controlled fuel injection system.

In October 1984 three-door versions became available, with an X series designation, in addition to the three-door GTI. Van versions were introduced in June 1985, together with the limited edition Lacoste, based on the GT version. In September 1985 the XT was introduced, being a three-door version of the GT, and at the same time the 954 cc XL three-door was introduced, having a higher specification than the XE. The 1580 cc Automatic was introduced in April 1986 at the same time as the Cabriolet CTI. The XS replaced the XT in July 1986, at which time the limited edition Junior, based on the XE, became available. The 1.9 GTI was introduced in August 1986, and at the same time dim-dip headlights and rear seat belts were fitted as standard. In December 1987 the new TU engines and MA gearboxes were fitted to all except fuel injection, diesel and automatic models.

General dimensions, weights and capacities

Dimensions
Overall length	3705 mm (145.9 in)
Overall width:	
Basic, GL, GE and Van	1562 mm (61.5 in)
All other models except Cabriolet	1572 mm (61.9 in)
Cabriolet	1589 mm (62.6 in)
Overall height	1372 to 1381 mm (54.0 to 54.4 in)
Wheelbase	2420 mm (95.35 in)
Front track:	
All models except SR, GT, Cabriolet and GTI	1350 mm (53.19 in)
SR and GT models	1364 mm (53.74 in)
1.6 GTI and Cabriolet models	1392 mm (54.8 in)
1.9 GTI models	1383 mm (54.4 in)
Rear track:	
All models except SR, GT, Cabriolet and GTI	1300 mm (51.22 in)
SR and GT models	1314 mm (51.77 in)
1.6 GTI and Cabriolet models	1328 mm (52.3 in)
1.9 GTI models	1344 mm (52.9 in)

Weights
Kerb weight*	740 to 935 kg (1628 to 2057 lbs)
Maximum towing weight:	
TU9 and TU1 engines	700 kg (1540 lbs)
All other engines	800 kg (1760 lbs)
Maximum roof rack load	50 kg (110 lbs)

* Exact kerb weight varies depending on model – refer to VIN plate for details

Capacities
Engine/transmission oil:	
954 cc and 1124 cc engines	4.5 litres (8.0 pints)
1360 cc engines	5.0 litres (8.9 pints)
Engine oil:	
TU engines (with filter)	3.5 litres (6.2 pints)
XU engines	5.0 litres (8.8 pints)
Transmission:	
BE 1/5, BE 3/5 and MA	2.0 litres (3.5 pints)
ZF4 HP14:	
From dry	6.2 litres (10.9 pints)
Drain and refill	2.4 litres (4.25 pints)
Cooling system:	
XV8 and XW7 engines	5.8 litres (10.2 pints)
XY7 and XY8 engines	6.0 litres (10.6 pints)
XU engines (except Automatic models)	6.6 litres (11.6 pints)
XU engines (Automatic models)	6.7 litres (11.8 pints)
TU9 and TU3 series engines	5.8 litres (10.2 pints)
TU1 series engine (except Van)	7.0 litres (12.3 pints)
TU1 series engine (Van)	5.8 litres (10.2 pints)
Fuel tank	50.0 litres (11.0 gallons)

Jacking and towing

Jacking

The jack supplied with the car is designed for use only when changing a wheel. The jack engages in one of the two holes provided below each sill on either side of the car.

If you are going to carry out work under the car it is preferable to position the car over an inspection pit. If this is not available use a workshop trolley jack or substantial screw or bottle type hydraulic jack. *Always supplement a jack with axle stands.* The sill jacking points or their adjacent re-inforced areas should be used as jacking points for raising the car. A beam may be placed under the front subframe and the front end jacked up under that. The side-members of the front subframe should be used as axle stand support points. The rear side-members may be used in a similar way.

Towing and being towed

Front and rear anchorage points are provided for securing the car during transportation on a car transporter, boat, train and so on. These points can also be used for towing the car (all wheels on the ground) or for towing another in an emergency (photos). For permanent towing requirements a tow-bar is necessary, properly attached to the vehicle.

Do not tow BH type gearbox models with the front wheels on the ground for long distances, as the engine lubrication system also supplies pressure-fed oil to the gears and differential bearings. Unnecessary wear may occur if the car is towed with the engine stopped.

Similarly, automatic transmission models should not be towed with the front wheels on the ground for more than 30 miles, or at speeds over 30 mph. See Chapter 13, Section 12.

Front towing eye

Front jacking point

Position front part of jack (1) directly under the jacking point (2)

Rear towing eye

Buying spare parts
and vehicle identification numbers

Buying spare parts

Spare parts are available from many sources. Peugeot have many dealers throughout the UK, and other dealers, accessory stores and motor factors will also stock some spare parts suitable for Peugeot cars.

Our advice regarding spare part sources is as follows:

Officially appointed vehicle main dealers – This is the best source for parts which are peculiar to your vehicle and are otherwise not generally available (eg, complete cylinder heads, internal transmission components, badges, interior trim etc). It is also the only place you should buy parts if your vehicle is still under warranty. To be sure of obtaining the correct parts it will always be necessary to give the storeman your vehicle's engine and chassis number, and if possible, to take the 'old' part along for positive identification. Remember that many parts are available on a factory exchange scheme – any parts returned should always be clean. It obviously makes good sense to go straight to the specialists on your vehicle for this type of part, for they are best equipped to supply you.

Other dealers and auto accessory stores – These are often very good places to buy materials and components needed for the maintenance of your vehicle (eg, oil filters, spark plugs, bulbs, drivebelts, oils and greases, touch-up paint, filler paste etc.) They also sell general accessories, usually have the convenient opening hours, charge lower prices and can often be found not far from home.

Motor factors – Good factors will stock all the more important components which wear out relatively quickly (eg, clutch components, pistons, valves, exhaust systems, brake cylinders/pipes/hoses/seals/shoes and pads etc). Motor factors will often provide new or reconditioned components on a part exchange basis – this can save a considerable amount of money.

Vehicle identification numbers

Modifications are a continuing and unpublicised process in vehicle manufacture. Spare parts manuals and lists are compiled on a numerical basis, the individual vehicle numbers being essential to identify correctly the component required.

The *vehicle identification plate* is located on the right-hand front wing valance in the engine compartment (photo).

Vehicle identification plate (1) and body serial number (2)

The *body serial number* is stamped on the scuttle crossmember above the vehicle identification plate.

The *engine number* is riveted on the cylinder block at the flywheel housing flange on non-XU engine models or on the left-hand side of the cylinder block on XU engine models.

The *body colour reference plate* is located on the left-hand end of the radiator grille crossmember.

General repair procedures

Whenever servicing, repair or overhaul work is carried out on the car or its components, it is necessary to observe the following procedures and instructions. This will assist in carrying out the operation efficiently and to a professional standard of workmanship.

Joint mating faces and gaskets

Where a gasket is used between the mating faces of two components, ensure that it is renewed on reassembly, and fit it dry unless otherwise stated in the repair procedure. Make sure that the mating faces are clean and dry with all traces of old gasket removed. When cleaning a joint face, use a tool which is not likely to score or damage the face, and remove any burrs or nicks with an oilstone or fine file.

Make sure that tapped holes are cleaned with a pipe cleaner, and keep them free of jointing compound if this is being used unless specifically instructed otherwise.

Ensure that all orifices, channels or pipes are clear and blow through them, preferably using compressed air.

Oil seals

Whenever an oil seal is removed from its working location, either individually or as part of an assembly, it should be renewed.

The very fine sealing lip of the seal is easily damaged and will not seal if the surface it contacts is not completely clean and free from scratches, nicks or grooves. If the original sealing surface of the component cannot be restored, the component should be renewed.

Protect the lips of the seal from any surface which may damage them in the course of fitting. Use tape or a conical sleeve where possible. Lubricate the seal lips with oil before fitting and, on dual lipped seals, fill the space between the lips with grease.

Unless otherwise stated, oil seals must be fitted with their sealing lips toward the lubricant to be sealed.

Use a tubular drift or block of wood of the appropriate size to install the seal and, if the seal housing is shouldered, drive the seal down to the shoulder. If the seal housing is unshouldered, the seal should be fitted with its face flush with the housing top face.

Screw threads and fastenings

Always ensure that a blind tapped hole is completely free from oil, grease, water or other fluid before installing the bolt or stud. Failure to do this could cause the housing to crack due to the hydraulic action of the bolt or stud as it is screwed in.

When tightening a castellated nut to accept a split pin, tighten the nut to the specified torque, where applicable, and then tighten further to the next split pin hole. Never slacken the nut to align a split pin hole unless stated in the repair procedure.

When checking or retightening a nut or bolt to a specified torque setting, slacken the nut or bolt by a quarter of a turn, and then retighten to the specified setting.

Locknuts, locktabs and washers

Any fastening which will rotate against a component or housing in the course of tightening should always have a washer between it and the relevant component or housing.

Spring or split washers should always be renewed when they are used to lock a critical component such as a big-end bearing retaining nut or bolt.

Locktabs which are folded over to retain a nut or bolt should always be renewed.

Self-locking nuts can be reused in non-critical areas, providing resistance can be felt when the locking portion passes over the bolt or stud thread.

Split pins must always be replaced with new ones of the correct size for the hole.

Special tools

Some repair procedures in this manual entail the use of special tools such as a press, two or three-legged pullers, spring compressors etc. Wherever possible, suitable readily available alternatives to the manufacturer's special tools are described, and are shown in use. In some instances, where no alternative is possible, it has been necessary to resort to the use of a manufacturer's tool and this has been done for reasons of safety as well as the efficient completion of the repair operation. Unless you are highly skilled and have a thorough understanding of the procedure described, never attempt to bypass the use of any special tool when the procedure described specifies its use. Not only is there a very great risk of personal injury, but expensive damage could be caused to the components involved.

Tools and working facilities

Introduction

A selection of good tools is a fundamental requirement for anyone contemplating the maintenance and repair of a motor vehicle. For the owner who does not possess any, their purchase will prove a considerable expense, offsetting some of the savings made by doing-it-yourself. However, provided that the tools purchased meet the relevant national safety standards and are of good quality, they will last for many years and prove an extremely worthwhile investment.

To help the average owner to decide which tools are needed to carry out the various tasks detailed in this manual, we have compiled three lists of tools under the following headings: *Maintenance and minor repair*, *Repair and overhaul*, and *Special*. The newcomer to practical mechanics should start off with the *Maintenance and minor repair* tool kit and confine himself to the simpler jobs around the vehicle. Then, as his confidence and experience grow, he can undertake more difficult tasks, buying extra tools as, and when, they are needed. In this way, a *Maintenance and minor repair* tool kit can be built-up into a *Repair and overhaul* tool kit over a considerable period of time without any major cash outlays. The experienced do-it-yourselfer will have a tool kit good enough for most repair and overhaul procedures and will add tools from the *Special* category when he feels the expense is justified by the amount of use to which these tools will be put.

It is obviously not possible to cover the subject of tools fully here. For those who wish to learn more about tools and their use there is a book entitled *How to Choose and Use Car Tools* available from the publishers of this manual.

Maintenance and minor repair tool kit

The tools given in this list should be considered as a minimum requirement if routine maintenance, servicing and minor repair operations are to be undertaken. We recommend the purchase of combination spanners (ring one end, open-ended the other); although more expensive than open-ended ones, they do give the advantages of both types of spanner.

> Combination spanners - 10, 11, 12, 13, 14 & 17 mm
> Adjustable spanner - 9 inch
> Engine sump/gearbox/drain plug key
> Spark plug spanner (a deep reaching one is required)
> Spark plug gap adjustment tool
> Set of feeler gauges
> Brake bleed nipple spanner
> Screwdriver - 4 in long x ¼ in dia (flat blade)
> Screwdriver - 4 in long x ¼ in dia (cross blade)
> Combination pliers - 6 inch
> Hacksaw (junior)
> Tyre pump
> Tyre pressure gauge
> Oil can
> Fine emery cloth (1 sheet)
> Wire brush (small)
> Funnel (medium size)

Repair and overhaul tool kit

These tools are virtually essential for anyone undertaking any major repairs to a motor vehicle, and are additional to those given in the *Maintenance and minor repair* list. Included in this list is a comprehensive set of sockets. Although these are expensive they will be found invaluable as they are so versatile - particularly if various drives are included in the set. We recommend the ½ in square-drive type, as this can be used with most proprietary torque wrenches. If you cannot afford a socket set, even bought piecemeal, then inexpensive tubular box spanners are a useful alternative.

The tools in this list will occasionally need to be supplemented by tools from the *Special* list.

> Sockets (or box spanners) to cover range in previous list
> Reversible ratchet drive (for use with sockets)
> Extension piece, 10 inch (for use with sockets)
> Universal joint (for use with sockets)
> Torque wrench (for use with sockets)
> 'Mole' wrench - 8 inch
> Ball pein hammer
> Soft-faced hammer, plastic or rubber
> Screwdriver - 6 in long x 56 in dia (flat blade)
> Screwdriver - 2 in long x 56 in square (flat blade)
> Screwdriver - 1½ in long x ¼ in dia (cross blade)
> Screwdriver - 3 in long x ⅛ in dia (electricians)
> Pliers - electricians side cutters
> Pliers - needle nosed
> Pliers - circlip (internal and external)
> Cold chisel - ½ inch
> Scriber
> Scraper
> Centre punch
> Pin punch
> Hacksaw
> Valve grinding tool
> Steel rule/straight-edge
> Allen keys
> Selection of files
> Wire brush (large)
> Axle-stands
> Jack (strong trolley or hydraulic type)

Special tools

The tools in this list are those which are not used regularly, are expensive to buy, or which need to be used in accordance with their manufacturers' instructions. Unless relatively difficult mechanical jobs are undertaken frequently, it will not be economic to buy many of these tools. Where this is the case, you could consider clubbing together with friends (or joining a motorists' club) to make a joint purchase, or borrowing the tools against a deposit from a local garage or tool hire specialist.

The following list contains only those tools and instruments freely available to the public, and not those special tools produced by the vehicle manufacturer specifically for its dealer network. You will find occasional references to these manufacturers' special tools in the text of this manual. Generally, an alternative method of doing the job without the vehicle manufacturers' special tool is given. However, sometimes, there is no alternative to using them. Where this is the case and the relevant tool cannot be bought or borrowed, you will have to entrust the work to a franchised garage.

> Valve spring compressor
> Piston ring compressor
> Balljoint separator
> Universal hub/bearing puller
> Impact screwdriver
> Micrometer and/or vernier gauge
> Dial gauge
> Stroboscopic timing light
> Dwell angle meter/tachometer
> Universal electrical multi-meter
> Cylinder compression gauge
> Lifting tackle
> Trolley jack
> Light with extension lead

Buying tools

For practically all tools, a tool factor is the best source since he will have a very comprehensive range compared with the average garage or accessory shop. Having said that, accessory shops often offer excellent quality tools at discount prices, so it pays to shop around.

There are plenty of good tools around at reasonable prices, but always aim to purchase items which meet the relevant national safety standards. If in doubt, ask the proprietor or manager of the shop for advice before making a purchase.

Care and maintenance of tools

Having purchased a reasonable tool kit, it is necessary to keep the tools in a clean serviceable condition. After use, always wipe off any dirt, grease and metal particles using a clean, dry cloth, before putting the tools away. Never leave them lying around after they have been used. A simple tool rack on the garage or workshop wall, for items such as screwdrivers and pliers is a good idea. Store all normal wrenches and sockets in a metal box. Any measuring instruments, gauges, meters, etc, must be carefully stored where they cannot be damaged or become rusty.

Take a little care when tools are used. Hammer heads inevitably become marked and screwdrivers lose the keen edge on their blades from time to time. A little timely attention with emery cloth or a file will soon restore items like this to a good serviceable finish.

Working facilities

Not to be forgotten when discussing tools, is the workshop itself. If anything more than routine maintenance is to be carried out, some form of suitable working area becomes essential.

It is appreciated that many an owner mechanic is forced by circumstances to remove an engine or similar item, without the benefit of a garage or workshop. Having done this, any repairs should always be done under the cover of a roof.

Wherever possible, any dismantling should be done on a clean, flat workbench or table at a suitable working height.

Any workbench needs a vice: one with a jaw opening of 4 in (100 mm) is suitable for most jobs. As mentioned previously, some clean dry storage space is also required for tools, as well as for lubricants, cleaning fluids, touch-up paints and so on, which become necessary.

Another item which may be required, and which has a much more general usage, is an electric drill with a chuck capacity of at least 56 in (8 mm). This, together with a good range of twist drills, is virtually essential for fitting accessories such as mirrors and reversing lights.

Last, but not least, always keep a supply of old newspapers and clean, lint-free rags available, and try to keep any working area as clean as possible.

Spanner jaw gap comparison table

Jaw gap (in)	Spanner size
0.250	$\frac{1}{4}$ in AF
0.276	7 mm
0.313	$\frac{5}{16}$ in AF
0.315	8 mm
0.344	$\frac{11}{32}$ in AF; $\frac{1}{8}$ in Whitworth
0.354	9 mm
0.375	$\frac{3}{8}$ in AF
0.394	10 mm
0.433	11 mm
0.438	$\frac{7}{16}$ in AF
0.445	$\frac{3}{16}$ in Whitworth; $\frac{1}{4}$ in BSF
0.472	12 mm
0.500	$\frac{1}{2}$ in AF
0.512	13 mm
0.525	$\frac{1}{4}$ in Whitworth; $\frac{5}{16}$ in BSF
0.551	14 mm
0.563	$\frac{9}{16}$ in AF
0.591	15 mm
0.600	$\frac{5}{16}$ in Whitworth; $\frac{3}{8}$ in BSF
0.625	$\frac{5}{8}$ in AF
0.630	16 mm
0.669	17 mm
0.686	$\frac{11}{16}$ in AF
0.709	18 mm
0.710	$\frac{3}{8}$ in Whitworth; $\frac{7}{16}$ in BSF
0.748	19 mm
0.750	$\frac{3}{4}$ in AF
0.813	$\frac{13}{16}$ in AF
0.820	$\frac{7}{16}$ in Whitworth; $\frac{1}{2}$ in BSF
0.866	22 mm
0.875	$\frac{7}{8}$ in AF
0.920	$\frac{1}{2}$ in Whitworth; $\frac{9}{16}$ in BSF
0.938	$\frac{15}{16}$ in AF
0.945	24 mm
1.000	1 in AF
1.010	$\frac{9}{16}$ in Whitworth; $\frac{5}{8}$ in BSF
1.024	26 mm
1.063	$1\frac{1}{16}$ in AF; 27 mm
1.100	$\frac{5}{8}$ in Whitworth; $\frac{11}{16}$ in BSF
1.125	$1\frac{1}{8}$ in AF
1.181	30 mm
1.200	$\frac{11}{16}$ in Whitworth; $\frac{3}{4}$ in BSF
1.250	$1\frac{1}{4}$ in AF
1.260	32 mm
1.300	$\frac{3}{4}$ in Whitworth; $\frac{7}{8}$ in BSF
1.313	$1\frac{5}{16}$ in AF
1.390	$\frac{13}{16}$ in Whitworth; $\frac{15}{16}$ in BSF
1.417	36 mm
1.438	$1\frac{7}{16}$ in AF
1.480	$\frac{7}{8}$ in Whitworth; 1 in BSF
1.500	$1\frac{1}{2}$ in AF
1.575	40 mm; $\frac{15}{16}$ in Whitworth
1.614	41 mm
1.625	$1\frac{5}{8}$ in AF
1.670	1 in Whitworth; $1\frac{1}{8}$ in BSF
1.688	$1\frac{11}{16}$ in AF
1.811	46 mm
1.813	$1\frac{13}{16}$ in AF
1.860	$1\frac{1}{8}$ in Whitworth; $1\frac{1}{4}$ in BSF
1.875	$1\frac{7}{8}$ in AF
1.969	50 mm
2.000	2 in AF
2.050	$1\frac{1}{4}$ in Whitworth; $1\frac{3}{8}$ in BSF
2.165	55 mm
2.362	60 mm

Safety first!

Professional motor mechanics are trained in safe working procedures. However enthusiastic you may be about getting on with the job in hand, do take the time to ensure that your safety is not put at risk. A moment's lack of attention can result in an accident, as can failure to observe certain elementary precautions.

There will always be new ways of having accidents, and the following points do not pretend to be a comprehensive list of all dangers; they are intended rather to make you aware of the risks and to encourage a safety-conscious approach to all work you carry out on your vehicle.

Essential DOs and DON'Ts

DON'T rely on a single jack when working underneath the vehicle. Always use reliable additional means of support, such as axle stands, securely placed under a part of the vehicle that you know will not give way.

DON'T attempt to loosen or tighten high-torque nuts (e.g. wheel hub nuts) while the vehicle is on a jack; it may be pulled off.

DON'T start the engine without first ascertaining that the transmission is in neutral (or 'Park' where applicable) and the parking brake applied.

DON'T suddenly remove the filler cap from a hot cooling system – cover it with a cloth and release the pressure gradually first, or you may get scalded by escaping coolant.

DON'T attempt to drain oil until you are sure it has cooled sufficiently to avoid scalding you.

DON'T grasp any part of the engine, exhaust or catalytic converter without first ascertaining that it is sufficiently cool to avoid burning you.

DON'T allow brake fluid or antifreeze to contact vehicle paintwork.

DON'T syphon toxic liquids such as fuel, brake fluid or antifreeze by mouth, or allow them to remain on your skin.

DON'T inhale dust – it may be injurious to health (see *Asbestos* below).

DON'T allow any spilt oil or grease to remain on the floor – wipe it up straight away, before someone slips on it.

DON'T use ill-fitting spanners or other tools which may slip and cause injury.

DON'T attempt to lift a heavy component which may be beyond your capability – get assistance.

DON'T rush to finish a job, or take unverified short cuts.

DON'T allow children or animals in or around an unattended vehicle.

DO wear eye protection when using power tools such as drill, sander, bench grinder etc, and when working under the vehicle.

DO use a barrier cream on your hands prior to undertaking dirty jobs – it will protect your skin from infection as well as making the dirt easier to remove afterwards; but make sure your hands aren't left slippery. Note that long-term contact with used engine oil can be a health hazard.

DO keep loose clothing (cuffs, tie etc) and long hair well out of the way of moving mechanical parts.

DO remove rings, wristwatch etc, before working on the vehicle – especially the electrical system.

DO ensure that any lifting tackle used has a safe working load rating adequate for the job.

DO keep your work area tidy – it is only too easy to fall over articles left lying around.

DO get someone to check periodically that all is well, when working alone on the vehicle.

DO carry out work in a logical sequence and check that everything is correctly assembled and tightened afterwards.

DO remember that your vehicle's safety affects that of yourself and others. If in doubt on any point, get specialist advice.

IF, in spite of following these precautions, you are unfortunate enough to injure yourself, seek medical attention as soon as possible.

Asbestos

Certain friction, insulating, sealing, and other products – such as brake linings, brake bands, clutch linings, torque converters, gaskets, etc – contain asbestos. *Extreme care must be taken to avoid inhalation of dust from such products since it is hazardous to health.* If in doubt, assume that they *do* contain asbestos.

Fire

Remember at all times that petrol (gasoline) is highly flammable. Never smoke, or have any kind of naked flame around, when working on the vehicle. But the risk does not end there – a spark caused by an electrical short-circuit, by two metal surfaces contacting each other, by careless use of tools, or even by static electricity built up in your body under certain conditions, can ignite petrol vapour, which in a confined space is highly explosive.

Always disconnect the battery earth (ground) terminal before working on any part of the fuel or electrical system, and never risk spilling fuel on to a hot engine or exhaust.

It is recommended that a fire extinguisher of a type suitable for fuel and electrical fires is kept handy in the garage or workplace at all times. Never try to extinguish a fuel or electrical fire with water.

Note: *Any reference to a 'torch' appearing in this manual should always be taken to mean a hand-held battery-operated electric lamp or flashlight. It does NOT mean a welding/gas torch or blowlamp.*

Fumes

Certain fumes are highly toxic and can quickly cause unconsciousness and even death if inhaled to any extent. Petrol (gasoline) vapour comes into this category, as do the vapours from certain solvents such as trichloroethylene. Any draining or pouring of such volatile fluids should be done in a well ventilated area.

When using cleaning fluids and solvents, read the instructions carefully. Never use materials from unmarked containers – they may give off poisonous vapours.

Never run the engine of a motor vehicle in an enclosed space such as a garage. Exhaust fumes contain carbon monoxide which is extremely poisonous; if you need to run the engine, always do so in the open air or at least have the rear of the vehicle outside the workplace.

If you are fortunate enough to have the use of an inspection pit, never drain or pour petrol, and never run the engine, while the vehicle is standing over it; the fumes, being heavier than air, will concentrate in the pit with possibly lethal results.

The battery

Never cause a spark, or allow a naked light, near the vehicle's battery. It will normally be giving off a certain amount of hydrogen gas, which is highly explosive.

Always disconnect the battery earth (ground) terminal before working on the fuel or electrical systems.

If possible, loosen the filler plugs or cover when charging the battery from an external source. Do not charge at an excessive rate or the battery may burst.

Take care when topping up and when carrying the battery. The acid electrolyte, even when diluted, is very corrosive and should not be allowed to contact the eyes or skin.

If you ever need to prepare electrolyte yourself, always add the acid slowly to the water, and never the other way round. Protect against splashes by wearing rubber gloves and goggles.

When jump starting a car using a booster battery, for negative earth (ground) vehicles, connect the jump leads in the following sequence: First connect one jump lead between the positive (+) terminals of the two batteries. Then connect the other jump lead first to the negative (–) terminal of the booster battery, and then to a good earthing (ground) point on the vehicle to be started, at least 18 in (45 cm) from the battery if possible. Ensure that hands and jump leads are clear of any moving parts, and that the two vehicles do not touch. Disconnect the leads in the reverse order.

Mains electricity and electrical equipment

When using an electric power tool, inspection light etc, always ensure that the appliance is correctly connected to its plug and that, where necessary, it is properly earthed (grounded). Do not use such appliances in damp conditions and, again, beware of creating a spark or applying excessive heat in the vicinity of fuel or fuel vapour. Also ensure that the appliances meet the relevant national safety standards.

Ignition HT voltage

A severe electric shock can result from touching certain parts of the ignition system, such as the HT leads, when the engine is running or being cranked, particularly if components are damp or the insulation is defective. Where an electronic ignition system is fitted, the HT voltage is much higher and could prove fatal.

For information applicable to later models, see Supplement at end of manual

Maintenance is essential for ensuring safety and is desirable for the purpose of getting the best in terms of performance and economy from the car. Over the years the need for periodic lubrication – oiling and greasing – has been drastically reduced, if not totally eliminated. This has unfortunately tended to lead some owners to think that because no such action is required the components either no longer exist or will last for ever. This is a serious delusion. If anything, there are now more places, particularly in the steering and suspension, where joints and pivots are fitted. Although you do not grease them any more you still have to look at them – and look at them just as often as you may previously have had to grease them. The largest initial element of maintenance is visual examination. This may lead to repairs or renewal.

Under-bonnet view (GT/1360 cc)

1	Right-hand front engine mounting	10	Brake fluid reservoir filler cap
2	Jack	11	Vehicle identification plate
3	Drivebelt	12	Choke cable
4	Oil filter	13	Heater hose
5	Bottom hose	14	Oil filler cap/crankcase ventilation filter
6	Water pump	15	Windscreen wiper arm
7	Throttle cable	16	Hydraulic brake lines
8	Fuel pump	17	Cooling fan motor resistor
9	Brake master cylinder	18	Front suspension shock absorber top mounting nut

18	Front suspension shock absorber top mounting nut	26	Ignition timing aperture
19	Ignition coil cover	27	Diagnostic socket
20	Distributor	28	Radiator filler cap
21	Bottom hose	29	Air cleaner
22	Clutch release fork	30	Bonnet lock
23	Clutch housing	31	Oil pressure switch
24	Washer reservoir	32	Alternator
25	Battery	33	Cooling system expansion bottle

View of front underside of car (GT/1360 cc)

1 Bottom hose	5 Gear linkage
2 Reverse lamp switch	6 Clutch housing and transfer
3 Engine/transmission oil drain	gear assembly
plug	7 Washer reservoir
4 Radiator	8 Disc caliper

9 Lower suspension arm	14 Fuel feed and return pipes
10 Anti-roll bar	15 Hydraulic brake lines
11 Track rod	16 Subframe
12 Guide bar	17 Driveshaft
13 Exhaust front pipe	18 Front towing eye

View of rear underside of car (GT/1360 cc)

1	Exhaust front pipe	5	Brake hydraulic flexible hose	9	Exhaust rubber mounting
2	Handbrake cables	6	Rear shock absorber	10	Exhaust rear silencer
3	Heatshield	7	Trailing arm	11	Spare wheel
4	Rear suspension cross-tube	8	Side-member		

12	Rear towing eye
13	Torsion bars
14	Fuel tank

At weekly intervals

Engine
Check the oil level. Top up if necessary (photo)

Cooling system
Check the coolant level. Top up if necessary

Braking system
Check the brake fluid level. Top up if necessary

General
Check the tyres for condition and pressure
Check all systems for operation leaks and security
Check the washer fluid level. Top up if necessary, adding a screen wash such as Turtle Wax High Tech Screen Wash

Topping-up the engine oil

After first 1000 to 1500 miles (1500 to 2250 km) – new cars

Engine
Renew the oil and filter

Transmission
Renew the oil (pre-1988 models only)

Every 5000 miles (7500 km) on models up to July 1984
Every 6000 miles (9000 km) on models from July 1984 on – or six monthly, if sooner

In addition to the weekly maintenance

Engine
Renew the oil
Renew the filter (first 5000/6000 miles only)

Automatic transmission
Check the fluid level. Top up if necessary

Braking system
Check the brake pads for wear. Renew if necessary (Chapter 8, Section 3)

Electrical system
Check the battery electrolyte level. Top up if necessary (not usually required on low maintenance type)

Every 10 000 miles (15 000 km) on models up to July 1984 only

Engine
Renew the oil filter (every second oil change)

Every 15 000 miles (22 500 km) on models up to July 1984
Every 12 000 miles (18 000 km) on models from July 1984 on – or annually, if sooner

In addition to the six monthly maintenance

Engine
Renew the oil filter (models July 1984 on only)
Renew the spark plugs

Fuel system
Check and, if necessary, adjust the throttle cable
Lubricate the throttle and choke cables

Clutch
Check and, if necessary, adjust the clutch cable (Chapter 5, Section 2)

Braking system
Check the brake shoes for wear. Renew if necessary (Chapter 8, Section 4)
Check the operation of the handbrake. Adjust if necessary (Chapter 8, Section 14)

Steering system
Check power steering fluid level

Bodywork
Check the bodywork for condition. Repair as necessary

Electrical system
Check the alternator drivebelt tension. Adjust if necessary (Chapter 12, Section 2)

Every 30 000 miles (45 000 km) on models up to July 1984
Every 24 000 miles (36 000 km) on models from July 1984 on – or two yearly, if sooner

In addition to the annual maintenance

Cooling system
Renew the coolant

Fuel system
Renew the air cleaner element

Ignition system
Check the ignition timing. Adjust if necessary (not July 1984 on models)

Manual transmission (BE 1/5 – pre-1988 models only)
Renew the oil

Automatic transmission
Renew the fluid

Braking system
Renew the brake fluid (Chapter 8, Section 2)

Suspension and steering
Check the wheel bearings for wear and damage
Check the steering and suspension balljoints for wear and damage
Check the shock absorbers for operation and leaks

Every 36 000 miles (58 000 km)

Engine (XU and TU series only)
Renew the camshaft drivebelt. **Note:** *Although not specified by the manufacturers, the author advises renewal as a precautionary measure against possible high mileage failure*

Every 48 000 miles (80 000 km) all models – or five yearly, if sooner

Fuel system
Renew the fuel filter (injection models only)

BH gearbox models

BE and MA manual gearbox and automatic transmission models

Recommended lubricants and fluids

Component or system	Lubricant type/specification	Duckhams recommendation
Engine (1)	Multigrade engine oil, viscosity SAE 10W/40 or 15W/40	Duckhams QXR, Hypergrade, or 10W/40 Motor Oil
Manual gearbox:		
BH3 type (1)	As above (integral with engine)	As above
BE1 type (2) (pre-1988 models)	Multigrade engine oil, viscosity SAE 10W/40 or 15W/40	Duckhams QXR, Hypergrade, or 10W/40 Motor Oil
BE1, BE3 and MA type (2) (1988-on models)	Gear oil, viscosity SAE 75W/80	Duckhams Hypoid PT 75W/80
Automatic transmission (3)	Dexron II type ATF	Duckhams Uni-Matic or D-Matic
Wheel bearings (4)	Multi-purpose lithium-based grease	Duckhams LB 10
Steering rack (5)	Multi-purpose lithium-based grease with molybdenum disulphide	Duckhams LBM 10
Brake fluid reservoir (6)	Hydraulic fluid to SAE J1703 or DOT 3	Duckhams Universal Brake and Clutch Fluid
Driveshaft CV joints (7)	Special lubricant supplied in repair kit	
Power steering (8)	Dexron II type ATF	Duckhams Uni-Matic or D-Matic

Conversion factors

Length (distance)

Inches (in)	X 25.4	= Millimetres (mm)	X 0.0394	= Inches (in)
Feet (ft)	X 0.305	= Metres (m)	X 3.281	= Feet (ft)
Miles	X 1.609	= Kilometres (km)	X 0.621	= Miles

Volume (capacity)

Cubic inches (cu in; in³)	X 16.387	= Cubic centimetres (cc; cm³)	X 0.061	= Cubic inches (cu in; in³)
Imperial pints (Imp pt)	X 0.568	= Litres (l)	X 1.76	= Imperial pints (Imp pt)
Imperial quarts (Imp qt)	X 1.137	= Litres (l)	X 0.88	= Imperial quarts (Imp qt)
Imperial quarts (Imp qt)	X 1.201	= US quarts (US qt)	X 0.833	= Imperial quarts (Imp qt)
US quarts (US qt)	X 0.946	= Litres (l)	X 1.057	= US quarts (US qt)
Imperial gallons (Imp gal)	X 4.546	= Litres (l)	X 0.22	= Imperial gallons (Imp gal)
Imperial gallons (Imp gal)	X 1.201	= US gallons (US gal)	X 0.833	= Imperial gallons (Imp gal)
US gallons (US gal)	X 3.785	= Litres (l)	X 0.264	= US gallons (US gal)

Mass (weight)

Ounces (oz)	X 28.35	= Grams (g)	X 0.035	= Ounces (oz)
Pounds (lb)	X 0.454	= Kilograms (kg)	X 2.205	= Pounds (lb)

Force

Ounces-force (ozf; oz)	X 0.278	= Newtons (N)	X 3.6	= Ounces-force (ozf; oz)
Pounds-force (lbf; lb)	X 4.448	= Newtons (N)	X 0.225	= Pounds-force (lbf; lb)
Newtons (N)	X 0.1	= Kilograms-force (kgf; kg)	X 9.81	= Newtons (N)

Pressure

Pounds-force per square inch (psi; lbf/in²; lb/in²)	X 0.070	= Kilograms-force per square centimetre (kgf/cm²; kg/cm²)	X 14.223	= Pounds-force per square inch (psi; lbf/in²; lb/in²)
Pounds-force per square inch (psi; lbf/in²; lb/in²)	X 0.068	= Atmospheres (atm)	X 14.696	= Pounds-force per square inch (psi; lbf/in²; lb/in²)
Pounds-force per square inch (psi; lbf/in²; lb/in²)	X 0.069	= Bars	X 14.5	= Pounds-force per square inch (psi; lbf/in²; lb/in²)
Pounds-force per square inch (psi; lbf/in²; lb/in²)	X 6.895	= Kilopascals (kPa)	X 0.145	= Pounds-force per square inch (psi; lbf/in²; lb/in²)
Kilopascals (kPa)	X 0.01	= Kilograms-force per square centimetre (kgf/cm²; kg/cm²)	X 98.1	= Kilopascals (kPa)
Millibar (mbar)	X 100	= Pascals (Pa)	X 0.01	= Millibar (mbar)
Millibar (mbar)	X 0.0145	= Pounds-force per square inch (psi; lbf/in²; lb/in²)	X 68.947	= Millibar (mbar)
Millibar (mbar)	X 0.75	= Millimetres of mercury (mmHg)	X 1.333	= Millibar (mbar)
Millibar (mbar)	X 0.401	= Inches of water (inH₂O)	X 2.491	= Millibar (mbar)
Millimetres of mercury (mmHg)	X 0.535	= Inches of water (inH₂O)	X 1.868	= Millimetres of mercury (mmHg)
Inches of water (inH₂O)	X 0.036	= Pounds-force per square inch (psi; lbf/in²; lb/in²)	X 27.68	= Inches of water (inH₂O)

Torque (moment of force)

Pounds-force inches (lbf in; lb in)	X 1.152	= Kilograms-force centimetre (kgf cm; kg cm)	X 0.868	= Pounds-force inches (lbf in; lb in)
Pounds-force inches (lbf in; lb in)	X 0.113	= Newton metres (Nm)	X 8.85	= Pounds-force inches (lbf in; lb in)
Pounds-force inches (lbf in; lb in)	X 0.083	= Pounds-force feet (lbf ft; lb ft)	X 12	= Pounds-force inches (lbf in; lb in)
Pounds-force feet (lbf ft; lb ft)	X 0.138	= Kilograms-force metres (kgf m; kg m)	X 7.233	= Pounds-force feet (lbf ft; lb ft)
Pounds-force feet (lbf ft; lb ft)	X 1.356	= Newton metres (Nm)	X 0.738	= Pounds-force feet (lbf ft; lb ft)
Newton metres (Nm)	X 0.102	= Kilograms-force metres (kgf m; kg m)	X 9.804	= Newton metres (Nm)

Power

Horsepower (hp)	X 745.7	= Watts (W)	X 0.0013	= Horsepower (hp)

Velocity (speed)

Miles per hour (miles/hr; mph)	X 1.609	= Kilometres per hour (km/hr; kph)	X 0.621	= Miles per hour (miles/hr; mph)

Fuel consumption*

Miles per gallon, Imperial (mpg)	X 0.354	= Kilometres per litre (km/l)	X 2.825	= Miles per gallon, Imperial (mpg)
Miles per gallon, US (mpg)	X 0.425	= Kilometres per litre (km/l)	X 2.352	= Miles per gallon, US (mpg)

Temperature

Degrees Fahrenheit = (°C x 1.8) + 32

Degrees Celsius (Degrees Centigrade; °C) = (°F - 32) x 0.56

*It is common practice to convert from miles per gallon (mpg) to litres/100 kilometres (l/100km), where mpg (Imperial) x l/100 km = 282 and mpg (US) x l/100 km = 235

Fault diagnosis

Introduction

The vehicle owner who does his or her own maintenance according to the recommended schedules should not have to use this section of the manual very often. Modern component reliability is such that, provided those items subject to wear or deterioration are inspected or renewed at the specified intervals, sudden failure is comparatively rare. Faults do not usually just happen as a result of sudden failure, but develop over a period of time. Major mechanical failures in particular are usually preceded by characteristic symptoms over hundreds or even thousands of miles. Those components which do occasionally fail without warning are often small and easily carried in the vehicle.

With any fault finding, the first step is to decide where to begin investigations. Sometimes this is obvious, but on other occasions a little detective work will be necessary. The owner who makes half a dozen haphazard adjustments or replacements may be successful in curing a fault (or its symptoms), but he will be none the wiser if the fault recurs and he may well have spent more time and money than was necessary. A calm and logical approach will be found to be more satisfactory in the long run. Always take into account any warning signs or abnormalities that may have been noticed in the period preceding the fault – power loss, high or low gauge readings, unusual noises or smells, etc – and remember that failure of components such as fuses or spark plugs may only be pointers to some underlying fault.

The pages which follow here are intended to help in cases of failure to start or breakdown on the road. There is also a Fault Diagnosis Section at the end of each Chapter which should be consulted if the preliminary checks prove unfruitful. Whatever the fault, certain basic principles apply. These are as follows:

Verify the fault. This is simply a matter of being sure that you know what the symptoms are before starting work. This is particularly important if you are investigating a fault for someone else who may not have described it very accurately.

Don't overlook the obvious. For example, if the vehicle won't start, is there petrol in the tank? (Don't take anyone else's word on this particular point, and don't trust the fuel gauge either!) If an electrical fault is indicated, look for loose or broken wires before digging out the test gear.

Cure the disease, not the symptom. Substituting a flat battery with a fully charged one will get you off the hard shoulder, but if the underlying cause is not attended to, the new battery will go the same way. Similarly, changing oil-fouled spark plugs for a new set will get you moving again, but remember that the reason for the fouling (if it wasn't simply an incorrect grade of plug) will have to be established and corrected.

Don't take anything for granted. Particularly, don't forget that a 'new' component may itself be defective (especially if it's been rattling round in the boot for months), and don't leave components out of a fault diagnosis sequence just because they are new or recently fitted. When you do finally diagnose a difficult fault, you'll probably realise that all the evidence was there from the start.

Electrical faults

Electrical faults can be more puzzling than straightforward mechanical failures, but they are no less susceptible to logical analysis if the basic principles of operation are understood. Vehicle electrical wiring exists in extremely unfavourable conditions – heat, vibration and chemical attack – and the first things to look for are loose or corroded connections and broken or chafed wires, especially where the wires pass through holes in the bodywork or are subject to vibration.

All metal-bodied vehicles in current production have one pole of the battery 'earthed', ie connected to the vehicle bodywork, and in nearly all modern vehicles it is the negative (–) terminal. The various electrical components – motors, bulb holders etc – are also connected to earth, either by means of a lead or directly by their mountings. Electric current flows through the component and then back to the battery via the bodywork. If the component mounting is loose or corroded, or if a good path back to the battery is not available, the circuit will be incomplete and malfunction will result. The engine and/or gearbox are also earthed by means of flexible metal straps to the body or subframe; if these straps are loose or missing, starter motor, generator and ignition trouble may result.

Assuming the earth return to be satisfactory, electrical faults will be due either to component malfunction or to defects in the current supply. Individual components are dealt with in Chapter 12. If supply wires are broken or cracked internally this results in an open-circuit, and the easiest way to check for this is to bypass the suspect wire temporarily with a length of wire having a crocodile clip or suitable connector at

Crank engine and check for spark. Hold lead with an insulated tool

A simple test lamp is useful for checking electrical faults

each end. Alternatively, a 12V test lamp can be used to verify the presence of supply voltage at various points along the wire and the break can be thus isolated.

If a bare portion of a live wire touches the bodywork or other earthed metal part, the electricity will take the low-resistance path thus formed back to the battery: this is known as a short-circuit. Hopefully a short-circuit will blow a fuse, but otherwise it may cause burning of the insulation (and possibly further short-circuits) or even a fire. This is why it is inadvisable to bypass persistently blowing fuses with silver foil or wire.

Spares and tool kit

Most vehicles are supplied only with sufficient tools for wheel changing; the *Maintenance and minor repair* tool kit detailed in *Tools and working facilities,* with the addition of a hammer, is probably sufficient for those repairs that most motorists would consider attempting at the roadside. In addition a few items which can be fitted without too much trouble in the event of a breakdown should be carried. Experience and available space will modify the list below, but the following may save having to call on professional assistance:

> *Spark plugs, clean and correctly gapped*
> *HT lead and plug cap – long enough to reach the plug furthest from the distributor*
> *Distributor rotor*
> *Drivebelt(s) – emergency type may suffice*
> *Spare fuses*
> *Set of principal light bulbs*
> *Tin of radiator sealer and hose bandage*
> *Exhaust bandage*
> *Roll of insulating tape*
> *Length of soft iron wire*
> *Length of electrical flex*
> *Torch or inspection lamp (can double as test lamp)*
> *Battery jump leads*
> *Tow-rope*
> *Ignition water dispersant aerosol*
> *Litre of engine oil*
> *Sealed can of hydraulic fluid*
> *Emergency windscreen*
> *Worm drive clips*

If spare fuel is carried, a can designed for the purpose should be used to minimise risks of leakage and collision damage. A first aid kit and a warning triangle, whilst not at present compulsory in the UK, are obviously sensible items to carry in addition to the above.

When touring abroad it may be advisable to carry additional spares which, even if you cannot fit them yourself, could save having to wait

Carrying a few spares can save a long walk!

while parts are obtained. The items below may be worth considering:

Clutch and throttle cables
Cylinder head gasket
Alternator brushes
Fuel pump repair kit (if available)
Tyre valve core

One of the motoring organisations will be able to advise on availability of fuel etc in foreign countries.

**Jump start lead connections for negative earth vehicles –
connect leads in order shown**

Engine will not start

Engine fails to turn when starter operated
Flat battery (recharge, use jump leads, or push start)
Battery terminals loose or corroded
Battery earth to body defective
Engine earth strap loose or broken
Starter motor (or solenoid) wiring loose or broken
Ignition/starter switch faulty
Major mechanical failure (seizure)
Starter or solenoid internal fault (see Chapter 12)

Starter motor turns engine slowly
Partially discharged battery (recharge, use jump leads, or push start)
Battery terminals loose or corroded
Battery earth to body defective
Engine earth strap loose
Starter motor (or solenoid) wiring loose
Starter motor internal fault (see Chapter 12)

Engine turns normally but fails to start
Damp or dirty HT leads and distributor cap (crank engine and check for spark) – try moisture dispersant such as Holts Wet Start
No fuel in tank (check for delivery at carburettor or fuel filter, as applicable)
Excessive choke (hot engine) or insufficient choke (cold engine)
Fouled or incorrectly gapped spark plugs (remove and regap, or renew)

Other ignition system fault (see Chapter 4)
Other fuel system fault (see Chapter 3)
Poor compression
Major mechanical failure (eg camshaft drive)

Engine fires but will not run
Insufficient choke (cold engine)
Air leaks at carburettor or inlet manifold
Fuel starvation (see Chapter 3)
Ignition fault (see Chapter 4)

Engine cuts out and will not restart

Engine cuts out suddenly – ignition fault
Loose or disconnected LT wires
Wet HT leads or distributor cap (after traversing water splash)
Coil failure (check for spark)
Other ignition fault (see Chapter 4)

Engine misfires before cutting out – fuel fault
Fuel tank empty
Fuel pump defective or filter blocked (check for delivery)
Fuel tank filler vent blocked (suction will be evident on releasing cap)
Carburettor needle valve sticking, where applicable
Carburettor jets blocked (fuel contaminated), where applicable
Other fuel system fault (see Chapter 3)

Engine cuts out – other causes
Serious overheating
Major mechanical failure (eg camshaft drive)

Engine overheats

Ignition (no-charge) warning light illuminated
Slack or broken drivebelt – retension or renew (Chapter 12)

Ignition warning light not illuminated
Coolant loss due to internal or external leakage (see Chapter 2)
Thermostat defective
Low oil level
Brakes binding
Radiator clogged externally or internally
Electric cooling fan not operating correctly
Engine waterways clogged
Ignition timing incorrect or automatic advance malfunctioning
Mixture too weak

Note: *Do not add cold water to an overheated engine or damage may result*

Low engine oil pressure

Gauge reads low or warning light illuminated with engine running
Oil level low or incorrect grade
Defective gauge or sender unit
Wire to sender unit earthed
Engine overheating
Oil filter clogged or bypass valve defective
Oil pressure relief valve defective
Oil pick-up strainer clogged
Oil pump worn
Worn main or big-end bearings
Note: *Low oil pressure in a high-mileage engine at tickover is not necessarily a cause for concern. Sudden pressure loss at speed is far more significant. In any event, check the gauge or warning light sender before condemning the engine.*

Engine noises

Pre-ignition (pinking) on acceleration

Incorrect grade of fuel
Ignition timing incorrect
Distributor faulty or worn
Worn or maladjusted carburettor, where applicable
Excessive carbon build-up in engine

Whistling or wheezing noises

Leaking vacuum hose
Leaking carburettor or manifold gasket, as applicable
Blowing head gasket

Tapping or rattling

Incorrect valve clearances
Worn valve gear
Worn timing chain or belt
Broken piston ring (ticking noise)

Knocking or thumping

Unintentional mechanical contact
Peripheral component fault (alternator, water pump etc)
Worn big-end bearings (regular heavy knocking, perhaps less under load)
Worn main bearings (rumbling and knocking, perhaps worsening under load)
Piston slap (most noticeable when cold)

Chapter 1 Engine

For modifications, and information applicable to later models, see Supplement at end of manual

Contents

Specifications

XV8, XW7, XY7 and XY8 engines
General

Type .... Four-cylinder in-line overhead camshaft. All alloy with wet cylinder liners. Mounted transversely with transmission and inclined to rear at 72° from vertical

Code and displacement:
XV8 (108C) .... 954 cc (58.2 cu in)
XW7 (109F) .... 1124 cc (68.5 cu in)
XY7 (150D) .... 1360 cc (82.9 cu in)
XY8 (150B) .... 1360 cc (82.9 cu in)

Bore:
954 cc .... 70.0 mm
1124 cc .... 72.0 mm
1360 cc .... 75.0 mm

Stroke:
954 cc .... 62.0 mm
1124 cc .... 69.0 mm
1360 cc .... 77.0 mm

Compression ratio:
954 cc .... 9.3 : 1
1124 cc .... 9.7 : 1
1360 cc .... 9.7 : 1

Maximum power (DIN):
954 cc .... 44.5 bhp at 6000 rpm
1124 cc .... 49.0 bhp at 4800 rpm
1360 cc (XY7) .... 59.0 bhp at 5000 rpm
1360 cc (XY8) .... 79.0 bhp at 5800 rpm

Maximum torque (DIN):
954 cc .... 50.6 lbf ft at 2750 rpm
1124 cc .... 62.9 lbf ft at 2800 rpm
1360 cc (XY7) .... 78.8 lbf ft at 2500 rpm
1360 cc (XY8) .... 81.0 lbf ft at 2800 rpm

Firing order .... 1–3–4–2 (No 1 at clutch end)

Crankshaft

Number of main bearings	5
Journal diameter	49.965 to 49.981 mm
Regrind undersize	0.30 mm
Crankpin diameter	44.975 to 44.991 mm
Regrind undersize	0.30 mm
Endfloat	0.07 to 0.27 mm
Thrust washer thicknesses	2.30; 2.40; 2.45; 2.50 mm

Cylinder liners

Type .... Cast-iron, wet type

Grades:

	Liner
Piston	
A	One file mark
B	Two file marks
C	Three file marks

Paper type gasket seals:

	Thickness
Identification	
Blue	0.087 mm
White	0.102 mm
Red	0.122 mm
Yellow	0.147 mm

Cylinder liner projection above block:

With paper gasket	0.11 to 0.18 mm
With O-ring	0.10 to 0.17 mm

Pistons

Type .... Aluminium alloy, bulged skirt and oval cross-section. Two compression rings and one oil control ring. Gudgeon pin free in piston, interference fit in connecting rod

Running clearance .... 0.07 to 0.09 mm

Valve and valve gear

Clearance (cold):

Inlet	0.10 mm (0.004 in)
Exhaust	0.25 mm (0.010 in)

Seat angle (inclusive):

Inlet	120°
Exhaust	90°

Stem diameter .... 8.0 mm

Head diameter:

	XV8	XW7, XY7 and XY8
Inlet	34.8 mm	37.0 mm
Exhaust	27.8 mm	29.5 mm

Oil capacity (engine/transmission)

954 and 1124 cc engines	4.5 litres (8.0 pints)
1360 cc engines	5.0 litres (8.8 pints)

Oil type/specification

.... Multigrade engine oil, viscosity SAE 10W/40 or 15W/40 (Duckhams QXR, Hypergrade, or 10W/40 Motor Oil)

Oil filter

.... Champion C204 (UNF thread)

Oil pump

Endfloat	0.02 to 0.10 mm
Maximum lobe-to-body clearance	0.064 mm

Torque wrench settings

	Nm	lbf ft
Engine mounting nuts	34	25
Main bearing bolts:		
Stage 1	36	27
Stage 2	51	38
Big-end cap nuts	36	27
Oil pump screws	7	5
Cylinder head bolts (cold):		
Stage 1	50	37
Stage 2	77	57
Chain tensioner bolts	7	5
Camshaft sprocket bolt	73	54
Oil pick-up strainer bolts	10	7
Sump plate bolts	12	9
Engine/transmission connecting bolts	9	7
Timing chain cover bolts	7	5
Crankshaft pulley nut	88	65
Coolant pump bolts	13	10
Carburettor nuts	17	13
Clutch cover bolts	9	7
Transfer gear plate bolts	9	7
Starter motor mounting nuts	12	9
Starter motor mounting bolts	16	12

	Nm	lbf ft
Flywheel bolts	66	49
Rocker cover bolts	7	5
Alternator pivot bolt	45	33
Alternator adjuster link bolt	17	13
Oil drain plug	27	20
Flywheel housing bolts	11	8

XU5J engine
General
Type ....
Four-cylinder in-line overhead camshaft. All alloy with wet cylinder liners. Mounted transversely and inclined 30° to rear. Transmission mounted on left-hand end of engine.

Code and displacement:
XU5J (180A) .... 1580 cc (96.4 cu in)
Number of cylinders 4
Bore x stroke .... 83 x 73 mm
Compression ratio .... 9.8 : 1
Maximum power (DIN) .... 104 bhp at 6250 rpm
Maximum torque (DIN) .... 13.7 kgf m at 4000 rpm
Firing order .... 1-3-4-2 (No 1 at clutch end)

Camshaft
Drive .... Toothed belt
Action .... Directly onto bucket tappets
Endfloat (not adjustable) .... 0.07 to 0.16 mm
Lift:
Early models .... 10.4 mm
Later models .... 9.7 mm

Connecting rods
Type .... Forged steel
Big-end bore .... 48.655 to 48.671 mm
Small-end bore .... 21.959 to 21.971 mm

Crankshaft and main bearings
Number of main bearings 5
Main bearing bore in crankcase .... 63.708 to 63.727 mm
Main journal diameter:
New .... 59.981 to 60.000 mm
After regrinding .... 59.681 to 59.700 mm
Crankpin diameter:
New .... 44.971 to 44.990 mm
After regrinding .... 44.671 to 44.690 mm
Journal or crankpin out-of-round .... 0.007 mm max
Endfloat .... 0.07 to 0.27 mm
Thrust washer thicknesses available .... 2.30, 2.35, 2.40, 2.45 and 2.50 mm

Cylinder liners
Type .... Wet, removable, matched to piston
Protrusion from block (without seal) .... 0.08 to 0.15 mm
Protrusion difference between liners .... 0.05 mm max
Coding mark.. One, two or three slashes, or letter A, B or C

Pistons
Type .... Aluminium alloy with three compression rings and one scraper; matched to liner

Coding marks:
For gudgeon pin .... Figure 1 (blue), 2 (white) or 3 (red)
For liner.. One, two or three slashes, or letter A, B or C

Gudgeon pins
Nominal diameter .... 22 mm
Coding mark .... Coloured paint (see piston specs)
Fit .... Clearance in piston, interference in connecting rod

Cylinder head
Material .... Aluminium alloy
Warp limit .... 0.05 mm
Number of camshaft bearings 5

Valves
Head diameter:
Inlet .... 40 mm

Exhaust .... 32 mm (early models), 32.95 mm (later models)

Stem diameter:
  Inlet .... 7.965 to 7.980 mm
  Exhaust .... 7.945 to 7.960 mm

Length:
  Inlet .... 109.29 mm
  Exhaust .... 108.72 mm

Valve clearances (cold):
  Inlet .... 0.15 to 0.25 mm (0.006 to 0.010 in)
  Exhaust .... 0.35 to 0.45 mm (0.014 to 0.018 in)
  Adjustment method .... Shims between tappet and valve stem

Valve springs:
  Identification:
    Early type (high lift camshaft) .... Blue marking
    Later type (reduced lift camshaft) .... Black marking

Valve timing:
  Nominal clearance .... 1 mm
  Inlet opens .... 5°5' BTDC
  Inlet closes .... 34°3' ABDC
  Exhaust opens .... 38°3' BBDC
  Exhaust closes .... 0°5' ATDC

Lubrication system

Type .... Wet sump, pressure feed and splash
Filter type .... Full flow, disposable cartridge (Champion F104)
Sump capacity .... 5.0 litres (8.8 pints)
Oil type/specification .... Multigrade engine oil, viscosity SAE 10W/40 or 15W/40 (Duckhams QXR, Hypergrade, or 10W/40 Motor Oil)
Pressure .... 3.5 bar at 4000 rpm
Warning light sender operates at .... 0.44 to 0.58 bar
Oil pump drive .... Chain from crankshaft

Torque wrench settings

	Nm	lbf ft
Camshaft cover bolts	10	7
Camshaft bearing caps	15	11
Camshaft sprocket bolt (M12)	80	59
Crankshaft pulley bolt	109	80
Sump bolts	20	15
Main bearing cap nuts and bolts	49	36
Main bearing cap side bolts	24	18
Big-end cap nuts:		
Stage 1	40	30
Stage 2	Slacken fully	
Stage 3	20	15
Stage 4	Tighten a further 70°	
Flywheel bolts (renew bolts and use thread locking compound)	49	36
Cylinder head bolts (see text):		
Stage 1	58	43
Stage 2 (after slackening)	20	15
Stage 3	One third of a turn (120°) further	
Distributor and thermostat housing	15	11
Spark plugs	18	13
Engine mounting bracket bolts:		
M8	34	25
M10	45	33
Oil pump-to-block bolts	20	15
Oil seal carrier plate bolts	15	11
Camshaft drivebelt tensioner nuts	15	11
Coolant outlet housing bolt	20	15
Oil pressure switch	24	18
Alternator pivot bolt	39	29
Alternator strap bolt	20	15
Engine-to-transmission bolts	45	33
Starter motor bolts	34	25
Inlet manifold nuts	20	15
Exhaust manifold nuts	20	15
Coolant pump securing bolts	15	11
Engine mountings:		
RH nut	27	20
LH nut	35	26
Battery tray/bracket	18	13
Lower mounting centre bolt	34	25
Lower mounting to subframe	45	33
Driveshaft intermediate bearing bracket	23	17

PART A: GENERAL DESCRIPTION AND ROUTINE MAINTENANCE

1 General description

XV8, XW7, XY7 and XY8 engines

One of three different capacity engines may be fitted, the difference in displacement being achieved by increasing the bore and stroke. The engine, which has four cylinders and an overhead camshaft, is mounted transversely, driving the front wheels, and it is inclined to the rear at an angle of 72° from vertical.

The manual gearbox is also mounted transversely in line with and below the engine, and the final drive to the roadwheels is via the differential unit which is integral with the gearbox. Drive from the engine to the transmission is by means of transfer gears which are separately encased in the clutch housing.

The crankcase, cylinder head, gearcase and clutch housing are all manufactured from aluminium alloy. Removable wet cylinder liners are fitted; the aluminium pistons each have two compression rings and one oil control ring. The valves are operated by the single overhead camshaft

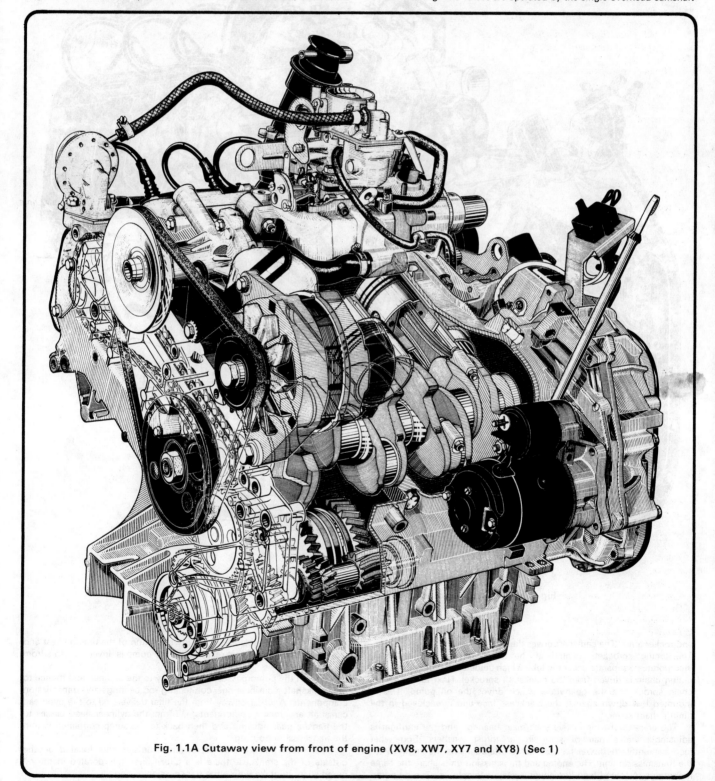

Fig. 1.1A Cutaway view from front of engine (XV8, XW7, XY7 and XY8) (Sec 1)

Fig. 1.1B Cutaway view from rear of engine (XV8, XW7, XY7 and XY8) (Sec 1)

and rocker arms. The camshaft drives the distributor at the flywheel end. The timing sprocket, located at the other end of the camshaft, incorporates a separate eccentric lobe which actuates the fuel pump. The timing chain is driven from the crankshaft sprocket. Next to the timing chain sprocket is the gearwheel which drives the oil pump. This is mounted low down against the crankcase face and is enclosed in the timing chain cover.

The crankshaft runs in five shell main bearings and the endfloat is adjustable via a pair of semi-circular thrust washers. Somewhat inconveniently, the lower half crankcase interconnects the engine with the transmission unit. The engine and transmission units share the same mountings. A forced feed lubrication system is employed. The oil pump

is attached to the crankcase in the lower section of the timing chest and it incorporates the pressure relief valve. The pump is driven by gears from the crankshaft.

Oil from the pump passes via an oilway to the oil filter, and thence to the crankshaft main bearings, connecting rod bearings and transmission components. Another oilway from the filter delivers oil to the overhead camshaft and rocker components. Oil from the cylinder head passes to the transfer gear housing and then back to the sump contained within the transmission housing.

Apart from the standard replaceable canister filter located on the outside of the crankcase there is a gauze filter incorporated in the oil pump suction intake within the transmission casing.

XU5J engine

The engine, which has four cylinders and an overhead camshaft, is mounted transversely, driving the front wheels, and it is inclined to the rear at an angle of 30° from vertical.

The manual gearbox is also mounted transversely in line with and on the left-hand end of the engine. The final drive unit is integral with the gearbox and transmits drive to the front wheels via driveshafts.

The engine has four wet liner cylinders, a five-bearing crankshaft and an overhead camshaft.

Camshaft drive is by toothed belt. The belt is tensioned by a spring loaded wheel and also drives the coolant pump. The camshaft operates directly on bucket tappets; valve clearance adjustment is by shims inserted between the tappet and the valve stem. The distributor is driven directly from the tail of the camshaft.

The oil pump is located in the sump and is chain driven from the crankshaft. A forced feed lubrication system is employed. Oil from the pump passes to the oil filter then to the oil gallery, crankshaft and camshaft. The valve stems are lubricated by oil returning from the camshaft to the sump. The oil pump chain and sprockets are lubricated by oil in the sump.

Fig. 1.2 Cutaway view of the engine (XU5J) (Sec 1)

Fig. 1.3 Lubrication system
(Sec 1)

A   XV8, XW7, XY7 and XY8
    engines
B   XU5J engine

2 Routine maintenance

Carry out the following procedures at the intervals given in Routine Maintenance at the beginning of the manual.

1 The oil level should be checked preferably when the engine is cold.

2 Withdraw the dipstick, wipe it clean, re-insert it and then withdraw it for the second time. The oil level should be between the high and low marks. If it is too low, top up through the filler cap.

3 The quantity of oil required to raise the oil level from the low to the high mark is 1.0 litre (1.75 pints).

4 To drain the engine oil it is preferable for the engine to be hot. First raise the front of the car on ramps or with a jack. Unscrew the socket-headed plug in the sump, remove the filler cap and allow the oil to drain into a suitable container (photos).

5 When the oil has drained, wipe clean the drain plug then refit and tighten it.

6 The oil filter is of disposable cartridge type. Unscrew it with an oil filter wrench, but first wrap it in cloth as some oil will run out. If a proper wrench is not available a large worm drive hose clip can be fitted to the filter and the screw used as a gripping point. If all else fails, a screwdriver can be driven right through the cartridge and this used as a lever to unscrew it (photo).

7 It is very important to purchase and fit the correct type of filter as some engines have a bypass valve incorporated in the filter mounting base of the crankcase whilst others have the valve incorporated in the filter cartridge.

8 No problem will arise if genuine Peugeot filters are used as they all incorporate a bypass valve. This will have no bearing upon the fact that a valve may already be built into the crankcase.

9 Clean the filter mounting ring on the crankcase and apply engine oil to the rubber seal on the cartridge. Do not use grease as it may make the filter difficult to unscrew.

10 Check that the threaded sleeve is tight on the crankcase, offer up the new filter and screw it on using hand pressure only.

11 Lower the car to the ground then fill the engine with the specified quantity and grade of oil.

12 Start the engine. There will be a short delay before the oil warning lamp goes out. This is normal and is caused by the new filter having to fill with oil.

13 Switch off the engine, wait ten minutes and check the oil level and top up if necessary.

14 Periodically, particularly on an engine which has covered a high mileage, remove the engine oil filler cap and check the filter mesh incorporated in the cap (photo). The filter is a breather for the crankcase ventilation system and should be cleaned or renewed if it is blocked with sludge.

15 It is possible for the filter mesh to corrode due to water vapour, or to freeze in very cold weather. Should these symptoms occur, discard the mesh and do not replace it.

2.4B Sump drain plug (GTI models)

2.6 Bottom view of the oil filter (GTI models)

2.4A Sump drain plug (non-GTI models)

2.14 Oil filler cap (non-GTI models) showing filter mesh

Fig. 1.4 Bypass valve built into oil filter mounting base (Sec 2)

Fig. 1.5 Oil filter cartridge with integral bypass valve (Sec 2)

PART B: XV8, XW7, XY7 AND XY8 ENGINES

3 Operations possible without removing the engine from the car

The following operations can be carried out without having to remove the engine from the car:

(a) Valve clearances – adjustment
(b) Timing chain – removal and refitting
(c) Cylinder head – removal and refitting
(d) Engine mountings – renewal

4 Valve clearances – adjustment

1 Disconnect the spark plug HT leads and remove the oil filler/crankcase ventilation cap from the rocker cover.
2 The engine can be turned by using a spanner on the crankshaft pulley nut – rotation is made easier if the spark plugs are removed.
3 Remove the rocker cover (photo) and then turn the engine until the valves on No 1 cylinder are rocking (ie inlet valve opening and exhaust valve closing). The rocker arm clearances of both valves of No 4 cylinder can now be checked and, if necessary, adjusted. Remember that No 1 cylinder is at the flywheel/clutch end of the engine.
4 The feeler gauge of the correct thickness is inserted between the valve stem and rocker arm. When the clearance is correctly set the feeler gauge should be a smooth stiff sliding fit between the valve stem and rocker arm.
5 If the feeler gauge is a tight or loose fit then the clearance must be adjusted. To do this, loosen the locknut of the adjustment stud and screw the adjuster stud in or out until the feeler gauge blade can be felt to drag slightly when drawn from the gap.
6 Hold the adjuster firmly in this position and tighten the locknut. Recheck the gap on completion to ensure that it has not altered when locking the nut and stud (photo).
7 Check each valve clearance in turn in the following sequence remembering that the clearances for inlet and exhaust valves are different. The valves are numbered from the flywheel end of the engine.

Valves rocking	Valves to adjust
1 In 2 Ex	7 In 8 Ex
5 In 6 Ex	3 In 4 Ex
7 In 8 Ex	1 In 2 Ex
3 In 4 Ex	5 In 6 Ex

8 Fit the rocker cover using a new gasket, then refit the spark plugs, HT leads and oil filler/crankcase ventilation cap.

Are your plugs trying to tell you something?

Normal.
Grey-brown deposits, lightly coated core nose. Plugs ideally suited to engine, and engine in good condition.

Heavy Deposits.
A build up of crusty deposits, light-grey sandy colour in appearance.
Fault: Often caused by worn valve guides, excessive use of upper cylinder lubricant, or idling for long periods.

Lead Glazing.
Plug insulator firing tip appears yellow or green/yellow and shiny in appearance.
Fault: Often caused by incorrect carburation, excessive idling followed by sharp acceleration. Also check ignition timing.

Carbon fouling.
Dry, black, sooty deposits.
Fault: over-rich fuel mixture.
Check: carburettor mixture settings, float level, choke operation, air filter.

Oil fouling.
Wet, oily deposits. Fault: worn bores/piston rings or valve guides; sometimes occurs (temporarily) during running-in period.

Overheating.
Electrodes have glazed appearance, core nose very white – few deposits. Fault: plug overheating. Check: plug value, ignition timing, fuel octane rating (too low) and fuel mixture (too weak).

Electrode damage.
Electrodes burned away; core nose has burned, glazed appearance. Fault: pre-ignition. Check: for correct heat range and as for 'overheating'.

Split core nose.
(May appear initially as a crack). Fault: detonation or wrong gap-setting technique. Check: ignition timing, cooling system, fuel mixture (too weak).

WHY DOUBLE COPPER IS BETTER FOR YOUR ENGINE.

Unique Trapezoidal Copper Cored Earth Electrode — 50% Larger Spark Area — Copper Cored Centre Electrode

Champion Double Copper plugs are the first in the world to have copper core in both centre _and_ earth electrode. This innovative design means that they run cooler by up to 100°C – giving greater efficiency and longer life. These double copper cores transfer heat away from the tip of the plug faster and more efficiently. Therefore, Double Copper runs at cooler temperatures than conventional plugs giving improved acceleration response and high speed performance with no fear of pre-ignition.

Champion Double Copper plugs also feature a unique trapezoidal earth electrode giving a 50% increase in spark area. This, together with the double copper cores, offers greatly reduced electrode wear, so the spark stays stronger for longer.

 FASTER COLD STARTING

 FOR UNLEADED OR LEADED FUEL

 ELECTRODES UP TO 100°C COOLER

 BETTER ACCELERATION RESPONSE

 LOWER EMISSIONS

 50% BIGGER SPARK AREA

 THE LONGER LIFE PLUG

Plug Tips/Hot and Cold.
Spark plugs must operate within well-defined temperature limits to avoid cold fouling at one extreme and overheating at the other.
Champion and the car manufacturers work out the best plugs for an engine to give optimum performance under all conditions, from freezing cold starts to sustained high speed motorway cruising.
Plugs are often referred to as hot or cold. With Champion, the higher the number on its body, the hotter the plug, and the lower the number the cooler the plug.

Plug Cleaning
Modern plug design and materials mean that Champion no longer recommends periodic plug cleaning. Certainly don't clean your plugs with a wire brush as this can cause metal conductive paths across the nose of the insulator so impairing its performance and resulting in loss of acceleration and reduced m.p.g.
However, if plugs are removed, always carefully clean the area where the plug seats in the cylinder head as grit and dirt can sometimes cause gas leakage.
Also wipe any traces of oil or grease from plug leads as this may lead to arcing.

DOUBLE **CC** COPPER

This photographic sequence shows the steps taken to repair the dent and paintwork damage shown above. In general, the procedure for repairing a hole will be similar; where there are substantial differences, the procedure is clearly described and shown in a separate photograph.

First remove any trim around the dent, then hammer out the dent where access is possible. This will minimise filling. Here, after the large dent has been hammered out, the damaged area is being made slightly concave.

Next, remove all paint from the damaged area by rubbing with coarse abrasive paper or using a power drill fitted with a wire brush or abrasive pad. 'Feather' the edge of the boundary with good paintwork using a finer grade of abrasive paper.

Where there are holes or other damage, the sheet metal should be cut away before proceeding further. The damaged area and any signs of rust should be treated with Turtle Wax Hi-Tech Rust Eater, which will also inhibit further rust formation.

For a large dent or hole mix Holts Body Plus Resin and Hardener according to the manufacturer's instructions and apply around the edge of the repair. Press Glass Fibre Matting over the repair area and leave for 20-30 minutes to harden. Then ...

... brush more Holts Body Plus Resin and Hardener onto the matting and leave to harden. Repeat the sequence with two or three layers of matting, checking that the final layer is lower than the surrounding area. Apply Holts Body Plus Filler Paste as shown in Step 5B.

For a medium dent, mix Holts Body Plus Filler Paste and Hardener according to the manufacturer's instructions and apply it with a flexible applicator. Apply thin layers of filler at 20-minute intervals, until the filler surface is slightly proud of the surrounding bodywork.

For small dents and scratches use Holts No Mix Filler Paste straight from the tube. Apply it according to the instructions in thin layers, using the spatula provided. It will harden in minutes if applied outdoors and may then be used as its own knifing putty.

Use a plane or file for initial shaping. Then, using progressively finer grades of wet-and-dry paper, wrapped round a sanding block, and copious amounts of clean water, rub down the filler until glass smooth. 'Feather' the edges of adjoining paintwork.

Protect adjoining areas before spraying the whole repair area and at least one inch of the surrounding sound paintwork with Holts Dupli-Color primer.

Fill any imperfections in the filler surface with a small amount of Holts Body Plus Knifing Putty. Using plenty of clean water, rub down the surface with a fine grade wet-and-dry paper – 400 grade is recommended – until it is really smooth.

Carefully fill any remaining imperfections with knifing putty before applying the last coat of primer. Then rub down the surface with Holts Body Plus Rubbing Compound to ensure a really smooth surface.

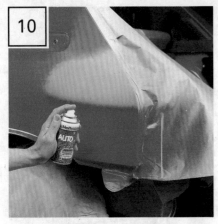

Protect surrounding areas from overspray before applying the topcoat in several thin layers. Agitate Holts Dupli-Color aerosol thoroughly. Start at the repair centre, spraying outwards with a side-to-side motion.

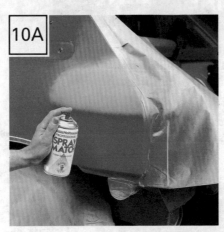

If the exact colour is not available off the shelf, local Holts Professional Spraymatch Centres will custom fill an aerosol to match perfectly.

To identify whether a lacquer finish is required, rub a painted unrepaired part of the body with wax and a clean cloth.

If *no* traces of paint appear on the cloth, spray Holts Dupli-Color clear lacquer over the repaired area to achieve the correct gloss level.

The paint will take about two weeks to harden fully. After this time it can be 'cut' with a mild cutting compound such as Turtle Wax Minute Cut prior to polishing with a final coating of Turtle Wax Extra.

When carrying out bodywork repairs, remember that the quality of the finished job is proportional to the time and effort expended.

HAYNES No1 for DIY

Haynes publish a wide variety of books besides the world famous range of *Haynes Owners Workshop Manuals*. They cover all sorts of DIY jobs. Specialist books such as the *Improve and Modify* series and the *Purchase and DIY Restoration Guides* give you all the information you require to carry out everything from minor modifications to complete restoration on a number of popular cars. In addition there are the publications dealing with specific tasks, such as the *Car Bodywork Repair Manual* and the *In-Car Entertainment Manual*. The *Household DIY* series gives clear step-by-step instructions on how to repair everyday household objects ranging from toasters to washing machines.

Whether it is under the bonnet or around the home there is a Haynes Manual that can help you save money. Available from motor accessory stores and bookshops or direct from the publisher.

4.3 Removing the rocker cover

4.6 Adjusting a valve clearance

5 Timing chain – removal and refitting

1 Support the engine/transmission on a trolley jack with a block of wood as an insulator.

2 Release the nuts on the right-hand flexible engine mounting at the base of the timing chain cover.

3 Raise the engine just enough to clear the side-member and anti-roll bar.

4 Release the drivebelt tension, remove the belt. Remove the fuel pump.

5 Unscrew and remove the crankshaft pulley nut. To do this the crankshaft must be held against rotation by jamming the starter ring gear. Remove the starter, as described in Chapter 12. Alternatively, if an assistant is available, apply the brakes fully with a gear engaged. Withdraw the pulley.

6 Unbolt and remove the rocker cover, and disconnect the spark plug HT leads.

7 Unscrew and remove the timing chain cover bolts. Take off the cover and extract the fuel pump operating rod.

8 Turn the crankshaft either by temporarily refitting the pulley nut or by engaging a gear and turning a front wheel (raised) until the timing marks are located in the following positions. Camshaft sprocket mark between two bright links on chain. Crankshaft sprocket mark opposite centre of single bright link.

9 Remove the crankshaft oil pump drivegear and its Woodruff key.

10 Unbolt the oil pump. Some socket-headed screws are accessible through the holes in the driven gear.

11 Jam the camshaft sprocket and unscrew the sprocket retaining bolt. Take off the fuel pump operating eccentric.

12 Turn the lock on the chain tensioner anti-clockwise to lock it in its retracted state.

13 Remove the camshaft sprocket with timing chain.

14 Commence reassembly by engaging the chain around the crankshaft sprocket so that the timing mark on the sprocket is in the centre of the single bright link on the chain.

15 Now engage the upper loop of the chain over the camshaft sprocket so that the timing mark is between the two bright links on the chain.

16 Now offer the camshaft sprocket to the shaft. Adjust the position of the camshaft so that the sprocket keyway aligns with the key.

17 Push the camshaft sprocket into position. Insert and tighten its retaining bolt with the fuel pump eccentric correctly located.

18 Using a very thin screwdriver blade, turn the lock on the chain tensioner fully clockwise to release the slipper.

19 Refit the oil pump with its spacer plate.

20 Fit the oil pump drivegear to the crankshaft.

21 Bolt on the timing chain cover using a new gasket. The bolt nearest the coolant pump pulley must be located in the cover before offering it up, otherwise the pulley will prevent the bolt entering its cover hole. Do not tighten the cover bolts until the crankshaft pulley has been pushed into place to centralise the cover. Fit the coolant hose safety rod under its cover bolts. This rod prevents the coolant hose being cut by the rim of the coolant pump pulley should the hose sag.

Fig. 1.6 Timing marks (Sec 5)

a Camshaft sprocket   b Crankshaft sprocket

25 Refit the starter, if removed.
26 Refit and tension the drivebelt.
27 Lower the engine, reconnect the mounting.

6 Cylinder head – removal and refitting

Note: *The following paragraphs describe the removal and refitting of the cylinder head with the engine in the car. If the home-made tool described in paragraph 28 is used note that it will not be possible to turn the engine for cleaning the tops of the pistons or checking bore wear. However, the engine can be turned when using the special Peugeot tool but if this is not available the timing chain and sprockets should be removed, as described in Section 5.*

1 Disconnect and remove the battery, as described in Chapter 12.
2 Remove the air cleaner, complete with mounting brackets, hot air hose and inlet hose, with reference to Chapter 3. Also remove the inlet cowl.
3 Drain the cooling system, as described in Chapter 2.
4 Remove the engine oil filler/crankcase ventilation cap and disconnect the hoses from the inlet cowl and carburettor.
5 Jack up the front of the car and support on axle stands. Apply the handbrake.
6 Disconnect the gearchange selector and engagement rods with reference to Chapter 6 (photo). Unscrew the engagement rod nut. Make sure that the gears are in neutral.

Fig. 1.7 Removing oil pump screw with Allen key (Sec 5)

6.6 Removing a gearchange rod retaining clip (arrowed)

Fig. 1.8 Timing chain tensioner lock (2) (Sec 5)

Turn in direction of arrow to release slipper

22 Fit the fuel pump operating rod and fuel pump.
23 Tighten the timing chain cover bolts to the specified torque and then trim the upper ends of the gasket flush. Fit the rocker cover using a new gasket. Do not overtighten the securing bolts.
24 Tighten the crankshaft pulley nut to the specified torque, again jamming the flywheel to prevent the crankshaft rotating.

7 Unscrew the bolt and nuts, and disconnect the exhaust downpipe from the exhaust manifold. An Allen key will be required to unscrew the bolt.
8 Loosen the left-hand engine mounting nuts beneath the battery tray so that the mounting is lowered by approximately 4.0 mm (0.16 in).
9 Disconnect the heater hoses from the bulkhead, water pump and cylinder head outlet (photo).
10 Remove the fuel pump, as described in Chapter 3.
11 Disconnect the top hose from the thermostat housing.
12 Disconnect the temperature sender wiring.
13 Remove the distributor, as described in Chapter 4.
14 Disconnect the spark plug HT leads and remove them from the rocker cover.
15 Disconnect the throttle and choke cables, as described in Chapter 3.
16 Disconnect the brake servo vacuum hose from the inlet manifold (if applicable) and place to one side.

6.9 Heater hoses at the bulkhead

6.18 Lever up the engine and support with a block of wood

17 Unscrew and remove the two bolts securing the right-hand rear engine mounting to the subframe (photo).
18 Using a suitable long bar inserted through the right-hand rear engine mounting bracket, lever up the rear of the engine as far as possible, without damaging the radiator, and support with a block of wood (photo). If necessary, loosen the left-hand engine mounting to gain extra height. Make sure that the right-hand front mounting is not damaged by excessive twisting.
19 Unbolt the rocker cover and remove the gasket.
20 Turn the engine on the crankshaft pulley nut until the key slot in the camshaft is facing upwards, then remove the ignition timing aperture cover and turn the engine as necessary until the mark on the flywheel is aligned with the TDC mark on the timing plate (refer to Chapter 4 if necessary). Pistons No 2 and 3 will be at TDC.
21 Extract the fuel pump plunger from the timing cover (photo).
22 Unbolt the access plate from the top of the timing cover.
23 Unscrew and remove the camshaft sprocket retaining bolt from the end of the camshaft using an Allen key (retain the sprocket with a suitable bar) (photo).

6.21 Removing the fuel pump plunger

6.17 Right-hand rear engine mounting

6.23 Removing the camshaft sprocket retaining bolt

6.24 Loosening the timing cover-to-cylinder head bolts

6.26 Removing the rocker shaft assembly

24 Loosen only the four bolts securing the timing cover to the cylinder head (photo).

25 Progressively unscrew the cylinder head bolts in the order shown in Fig. 1.9, and recover the nuts from their channels in the crankcase.

26 Remove the head bolts and lift off the rocker shaft assembly (photo). It may be necessary to leave one or two bolts in the assembly if they foul the bulkhead due to insufficient engine height.

27 Loosen the camshaft thrust plate bolt, pull out the plate and temporarily retighten the bolt (photos).

28 The camshaft sprocket must now be supported in its normal position while the cylinder head is removed. If it is allowed to drop it will be possible to lift it again without releasing the timing chain tensioner which will necessitate removal of the timing cover. Peugeot dealers use a special mandrel, tool number 70132, but as this is unlikely to be available to the home mechanic it is suggested that a plate and bolt are used, together with the access plate, as shown (photo). Tighten the bolt on the plate with a nut and use a further nut to prevent the sprocket coming off the end of the bolt.

6.27A Loosening the camshaft thrust plate bolt

Fig. 1.9 Sequence for tightening or loosening cylinder head bolts (Sec 6)

6.27B The camshaft thrust plate and elongated hole (cylinder head removed)

Fig. 1.10 Special Peugeot tool 70132 for use when removing the cylinder head (Sec 6)

6.28 Using a home-made plate to support the camshaft sprocket

6.29A The fuel pump eccentric (arrowed)

6.29B End of camshaft removed from sprocket

29 Slide the camshaft from the fuel pump eccentric and camshaft sprocket and let it rest in the cylinder head (photos).
30 Before removing the cylinder head the following must be noted. The cylinder head is positioned during assembly by means of two dowels. When removing the cylinder head it is most important not to lift it directly from the cylinder block; it must be twisted slightly. This action prevents the cylinder liners from sticking to the cylinder head face and being lifted with it, thus breaking their bottom seals. Before the cylinder head can be twisted, the dowel at the flywheel end must be tapped down flush with the top of the cylinder block, using a drift as shown in Fig. 1.11.
31 Remove the four timing cover-to-cylinder head bolts then move the flywheel end of the cylinder head sideways slightly to release the gasket.
32 Lift the cylinder head from the block and remove the gasket without disturbing the liners (photo). Do not turn the engine over as this also will break the liner bottom seals. If further work is to be carried out on the engine, such as cleaning the tops of the cylinder liners, they should be clamped in position using two cylinder head bolts, metal tubing, and large washers (photo).
33 Before refitting the head, the nuts must be retained in their channels. The use of rubber or plastic tubing is very effective, or wooden wedges may be used (photo).
34 Commence refitting by lifting the location dowel (paragraph 30) and retaining it by inserting a short pin in the hole provided – leaving room for the bolt to pass through (photo).
35 Locate a new cylinder head gasket on the cylinder block, making sure that all the holes are aligned (photos).
36 Apply a silicone sealing compound to the timing cover mating surface (photo).
37 Lower the cylinder head into position over the dowels.
38 Fit the four timing cover-to-cylinder head bolts finger tight.
39 Slide the camshaft into the sprocket and fuel pump eccentric.

Fig. 1.11 Driving cylinder head dowel down flush with block (Sec 6)

Slight rotation of the eccentric may be necessary in order to align its key with the camshaft slot.
40 Push the thrust plate fully into the camshaft groove then tighten the bolt.
41 Unbolt and remove the sprocket retaining tool.
42 Insert the sprocket retaining bolt and tighten it with an Allen key while holding the sprocket with a bar through one of the holes resting on packing pieces (photo).

6.32A Lifting the cylinder head (complete with carburettors on GT model) from the block

6.32B One method of clamping the cylinder liners

6.33 Using rubber tubing to hold the cylinder head nuts in position

6.34 Using a pop rivet to retain the head location dowel

6.35 Cylinder head gasket located on the block

6.36 Applying sealing compound to the timing cover

6.42 Tightening the camshaft sprocket retaining bolt

6.43 Refitting the access plate

6.45 Tightening the cylinder head bolts

43 Apply a silicone sealing compound to the access plate then refit it and tighten the bolts (photo).

44 Refit the rocker shaft assembly with the two location pegs towards the front.

45 Insert the head bolts (threads and heads oiled) and tighten them in two stages to the specified torques and in the sequence shown in Fig. 1.9 (photo). Note that washers must be fitted beneath the bolt heads on XY7 and XY8 engines.

46 Remove the nut retainers (paragraph 33) from the cylinder block.

47 Tighten the four timing cover-to-cylinder head bolts.

48 Insert the fuel pump plunger in the timing cover.

49 Adjust the valve clearances, with reference to Section 4.

50 Refit the rocker cover with a new gasket.

51 Remove the block of wood and lower the engine to its normal position.

52 Insert and tighten the right-hand rear engine mounting bolts, also tighten the left-hand mounting bolts.

53 Reconnect the brake servo vacuum hose to the inlet manifold (if applicable).

54 Reconnect the throttle and choke cables (Chapter 3).

55 Refit the distributor and spark plug HT leads (Chapter 4).

56 Reconnect the temperature sender wiring.

57 Refit the top hose to the thermostat housing.

58 Refit the fuel pump (Chapter 3).

59 Reconnect the heater hoses.

60 Refit the exhaust downpipe to the exhaust manifold.

61 Reconnect the gearchange rods (Chapter 6).
62 Lower the car to the ground.
63 Refit the oil filler/crankcase ventilation cap and hoses.
64 Refill the cooling system (Chapter 2).
65 Refit the air cleaner, inlet cowl and inlet hoses.
66 Refit the battery.
67 After the engine has been started and run to full operating temperature, it should be switched off and allowed to cool for at least two hours. Remove the rocker cover.
68 Unscrew the first cylinder head bolt one half a turn and then retighten it to the Stage 2 torque. Repeat the operation on the remaining bolts, one at a time in the sequence specified (Fig. 1.9).
69 Check the valve clearances and readjust if necessary.

7 Engine mountings – renewal

1 The engine/transmission is supported by three mountings, two at the timing chain end and one at the transfer gear end.
2 It is recommended that one mounting is renewed at a time after the weight of the unit has been taken on a jack with a block of wood as an insulator.
3 The battery and tray must be removed when renewing the left-hand mounting.
4 Tighten the bolts to the specified torque after renewing the mountings.

8 Engine/transmission – removal

1 The engine and transmission assembly is removed by lifting upwards from the engine compartment. The transmission is separated from the engine on the bench.
2 Jack up the front of the car and support on axle stands. Apply the handbrake.
3 Remove the drain plug and drain the engine/transmission oil. Clean and refit the drain plug on completion.
4 Drain the cooling system, as described in Chapter 2.
5 Unscrew the bolt and nuts, and disconnect the exhaust downpipe from the exhaust manifold. An Allen key will be required to unscrew the bolt.
6 Disconnect the gearchange selector and engagement rods, with reference to Chapter 6. Unscrew the engagement rod nut. Make sure that the gears are in neutral.
7 Unscrew the nut and detach the bonnet stay from the right-hand front suspension tower then raise the bonnet to vertical and retain by inserting two suitable U-bolts in the special holes provided in the bonnet hinges. Alternatively use welding rod or bend metal dowel rod.
8 Disconnect and remove the battery, as described in Chapter 12.
9 Remove the air cleaner, complete with mounting brackets, hot air hose and inlet hose, with reference to Chapter 3. Also remove the inlet cowl.
10 Disconnect and remove the radiator top and bottom hoses.
11 Disconnect and remove the heater hoses.
12 Disconnect and plug the fuel pump hoses.
13 Disconnect all wiring from the engine and transmission noting the correct routing for reassembly (photos).
14 Disconnect the throttle and choke cables, as described in Chapter 3.
15 Disconnect the brake servo vacuum hose from the inlet manifold (if applicable) and place to one side.
16 Disconnect the clutch cable and remove the pushrod, with reference to Chapter 5.
17 Connect a suitable hoist to the engine lifting eyes and take the weight of the assembly.
18 Unscrew and remove the right-hand engine mounting bolts and the top left-hand mounting nut.
19 Unbolt and remove the battery tray and the right-hand front and left-hand mounting brackets.
20 Lift the assembly slightly, then move to the left to disconnect the right-hand driveshaft and to the right to disconnect the left-hand driveshaft. Let the driveshafts rest on the subframe.
21 Lift the assembly from the engine compartment and also disconnect the speedometer cable from the gearbox.

8.13A Oil pressure switch and cable

8.13B Reverse lamp switch leads

9 Engine/transmission – separation

1 With the power unit out of the car, clean away external dirt using paraffin and a stiff brush, or a water soluble solvent.
2 Unscrew and remove the flywheel housing-to-engine connecting bolts and nuts.
3 There are thirteen bolts and two nuts altogether. Note that an engine lifting lug and earth strap are fitted under some of the bolts.
4 Refer to Chapter 5 and remove the clutch assembly.
5 Unbolt and remove the flywheel. Remove the starter motor (Chapter 12).
6 Unscrew and remove the two bolts and the nut close to the crankshaft oil seal.
7 Unscrew the engine-to-transmission flange connecting bolts. Unbolt the right-hand rear engine mounting.
8 Unscrew and remove the crankshaft pulley nut. In order to hold the crankshaft against rotation, temporarily screw in two bolts into the holes in the flywheel mounting flange and place a long lever between them.
9 Remove the crankshaft pulley.

Fig. 1.12 Flange connecting bolts and nuts adjacent to crankshaft oil seal (Sec 9)

10 Remove the rocker cover.
11 Remove the timing chain cover and extract the fuel pump operating plunger.
12 Unscrew and remove the remaining connecting bolts and nuts which are located on the final drive casing side near the driveshaft oil seals.
13 Using a length of wood, prise the engine and transmission apart.

10 Engine dismantling – general

1 As the engine is stripped, clean each part in a bath of paraffin.
2 Never immerse parts with oilways in paraffin (eg crankshaft and rocker shaft). To clean these parts, wipe down carefully with a petrol-dampened rag. Oilways can be cleaned out with wire. If an air line is available, all parts can be blown dry and the oilways blown through as an added precaution.
3 Re-use of old gasket or oil seals is false economy. To avoid the possibility of trouble after the engine has been reassembled always use new items throughout.
4 Do not throw away the old gaskets, for sometimes it happens that an immediate replacement cannot be found and the old gasket is then very useful as a template. Hang up the gaskets as they are removed.
5 If this is the first time that you have dismantled your engine/transmission unit then special attention should be given to the location of the various components and sub-assemblies. This is especially necessary due to the slightly unconventional layout of the model.
6 Many of the component casings are manufactured in aluminium alloy and special care must therefore be taken not to knock, drop or put any unnecessary pressure on these components.
7 Whenever possible, refit nuts, bolts and washers from where they were removed in order not to mix them up. If they cannot be reinstalled lay them out in such a way that it is clear where they came from.
8 Do not remove or disturb the timing plate on the clutch housing if this can be avoided. To reset, refer to Chapter 4.

11 Engine – complete dismantling

1 Support the engine on the bench or strong table. If such facilities are not available then it will have to be dismantled on the floor, but at least cover the floor with a sheet of hardboard.
2 Unbolt and remove the exhaust manifold (three bolts and two nuts) with hot air box.
3 Unbolt the spring-loaded throttle reel (if applicable) from the cylinder head and the thermostat housing. Remove the carburettor(s).
4 Unscrew the oil pressure switch from the crankcase. Unscrew and discard the oil filter.
5 Unbolt and remove the alternator adjuster link and the water pump (Chapter 2).
6 Remove the spark plugs using the special spanner supplied with the car. Remove the distributor.
7 Retract the chain tensioner by turning the lock in an anti-clockwise direction. Unbolt the tensioner and remove it.
8 Unscrew the camshaft sprocket bolt which is of socket-headed type. The crankshaft must be held against rotation for this operation. Do this by screwing two bolts into the flange and passing a long lever between them.
9 Remove the fuel pump eccentric cam.
10 Remove the oil pump socket-headed screws. Some of these are accessible through the holes in the oil pump driven gear.
11 Remove the oil pump and backplate.
12 Remove the camshaft sprocket with the timing chain.
13 Remove the Woodruff key and take off the crankshaft oil pump gear.
14 Remove the second Woodruff key and take off the crankshaft timing chain sprocket.
15 Reposition the engine and unbolt and remove the exhaust manifold and hot air box for the air cleaner.
16 Remove the cylinder head bolts by unscrewing them in the order shown in Fig. 1.9.
17 Lift off the rocker assembly.
18 Drive down the cylinder head positioning dowel, as described in Section 6, so that the cylinder head can be swivelled rather than lifted

Fig. 1.13 Separating transmission from engine (Sec 9)

from the block. This is to prevent breaking the cylinder liner base seals. If the liners are to be removed then obviously this precaution is not necessary, neither is the need to fit cylinder liner clamps to hold the liners down once the cylinder head has been removed.

19 Dismantling the cylinder head and removal of the camshaft is covered in Section 14.

20 Unscrew and remove the bolts which hold the crankcase half sections together. Split the crankcase and keep the main bearing shells with their crankcase web recesses if the shells are to be used again.

21 Remove the crankshaft oil seal.

22 Mark the rim of the cylinder liners in respect of position in the block and orientation.

23 Mark the big-end caps and the connecting rods so that they can be refitted in their original sequence and the correct way round. A centre punch or hacksaw blade is useful for this purpose.

24 Unscrew the big-end nuts and remove the caps. If the bearing shells are to be used again, keep them taped to their respective cap or connecting rod.

25 Lift the crankshaft from its crankcase half section, keep the shell bearings in their original web recesses if they are to be used again and retrieve the semi-circular thrust washers from either side of Number 2 web.

26 Remove each liner/piston/connecting rod as an assembly from the crankcase. Use a plastic-faced or wooden mallet to tap the liners out if necessary. Make sure that the liners and their respective piston rod assemblies are marked as to position in the block and orientation. A spirit marker is useful for this purpose.

27 Discard the liner base seals which may be of paper or rubber O-ring type.

12 Crankcase ventilation system – description

The system is designed to extract oil, fuel and exhaust gas from the engine crankcase, the latter having passed the piston rings (blow-by gas) particularly when the rings have worn.

The system consists of an intake for fresh air in the oil filler cap with connecting hoses to the carburettor air intake.

The crankcase gases are drawn up into the rocker cover, out through the filler cap hoses and into the manifold where they are burned during the normal engine combustion process.

13 Engine components – examination and renovation

1 With the engine dismantled, all components must be thoroughly cleaned and examined for wear, as described in the following Sections.

2 If a high mileage has been covered since new or the last engine rebuild, and general wear is evident, consideration should be given to renewing the engine with a reconditioned one.

3 If a single component has malfunctioned and the rest of the engine is in good condition endeavour to find out the cause of its failure if not readily apparent. For example, if a bearing has failed, check that the adjoining oilways are clear; the new bearing will not last long if it is not being lubricated.

4 If uncertain about the condition of any components, seek a second opinion, preferably from a Peugeot Talbot dealer/mechanic who will obviously have an expert knowledge of your model and be able to advise on the best course of action.

5 Check on the availability of replacement parts before discarding the old ones. Check the new part against the old to ensure that you have the correct replacement.

6 Some of the measurements required will need the use of feeler blades or a micrometer, but in many instances wear will be visually evident or the old component can be compared with a new one.

14 Cylinder head – dismantling, decarbonising and reassembly

1 Having removed the cylinder head, place it onto a clean workbench where it can be dismantled and examined. Unbolt the retaining plate (if necessary) and withdraw the camshaft (photos).

2 Remove each valve and spring assembly using a valve spring compressor. Extract the split collets from between the spring retaining cup washer and valve stem (photo).

3 Progressively release the tension of the compressor until it can be removed, the spring and retainer withdrawn, and the valve extracted from the guide (photos).

4 As the valves are removed, keep them in order by inserting them in a card having suitable holes punched in it, numbered from 1 to 8. Discard the valve stem oil seals.

5 Wash the cylinder head clean and carefully scrape away the carbon build-up in the combustion chambers and exhaust ports, using a scraper which will not damage the surfaces to be cleaned. If a rotary wire brush and drill is available this may be used for removing the carbon. Take care to prevent foreign matter entering the inlet manifold; it is cast into the cylinder head and cleaning is difficult.

6 The valves may also be scraped and wire-brushed clean in a similar manner.

7 With the cylinder head cleaned and dry, examine it for cracks or damage. In particular inspect the valve seat areas for signs of hairline cracks, pitting or burning. Check the head mating surfaces for distortion, the maximum permissible amount being 0.05 mm (0.002 in).

8 Minor surface wear and pitting of the valve seats can probably be removed when the valves are reground. More serious wear or damage should be shown to your Peugeot Talbot dealer or a competent automotive engineer who will advise you on the action necessary.

9 Carefully inspect the valves, in particular the exhaust valves. Check the stems for distortion and signs of wear. The valve seat faces must be in reasonable condition and if they have covered a high mileage they will probably need to be refaced on a valve grinding machine; again, this is a job for your Peugeot Talbot dealer or local garage/automotive machine shop.

10 Insert each valve into its respective guide and check for excessive side play. Worn valve guides allow oil to be drained past the inlet valve stem causing a smoky exhaust, while exhaust leakage through the exhaust valve guide can overheat the valve guide and cause sticking valves.

14.1A Camshaft retaining/thrust plate

14.1B Removing camshaft

14.2 Compressing a valve spring

14.3A Valve spring cup retainer

14.3B Removing a valve spring

14.3C Removing a valve

14.14 Valve stem oil seal

14.15 Valve spring seating washer

14.16 Cylinder head cleaned and reassembled

11 If the valve guides are to be renewed this is a job best left to your Peugeot Talbot agent who will have the required specialist equipment.

12 Assuming the valves and seats are in reasonable condition they should be reseated by grinding them using valve grinding carborundum paste. The grinding process must also be carried out when new valves are fitted.

13 The carborundum paste used for this job is normally supplied in a double-ended tin with coarse paste at one end and fine at the other. In addition, a suction tool for holding the valve head so that it may be rotated is also required. To grind in the valve, first smear a trace of the coarse paste onto the seat face and fit the suction grinder to the valve head. Then with a semi-rotary motion grind the valve head into its seat, lifting the valve occasionally to redistribute the grinding paste. When a dull matt continuous line is produced on both the valve seat and the valve then the paste can be wiped off. Apply a little fine paste and finish off the grinding process, then remove all traces of the paste. If a light spring is placed over the valve stem behind the head this can often be of assistance in raising the valve from time to time against the pressure of the grinding tool so as to redistribute the paste evenly round the job. The width of the line which is produced after grinding indicates the seat width, and this width should not exceed about 2 mm (0.08 in). If, after a moderate amount of grinding, it is apparent that the seating line is too wide, it probably means that the seat has already been cut back one or more times previously, or else the valve has been ground several times. Here again, specialist advice is best sought.

14 Examine all the valve springs to make sure that they are in good condition and not distorted. If the engine has covered 30 000 miles (45 000 km) then fit new springs at reassembly. Renew the valve stem oil seals. Earlier models are fitted with seals on the inlet valves only, later models have seals on all valves (photo).

15 At the same time renew the valve spring seating washers which sit directly on the cylinder head (photo). These wear fairly quickly.

16 Before reassembling the valve and springs to the cylinder head make a final check that everything is thoroughly clean and free from grit (photo), then lightly smear all the valve stems with engine oil prior to reassembly. The camshaft can now be refitted in the cylinder head and located with the retaining plate. This is then secured with its bolt and a new shakeproof washer. If the cylinder head is being refitted with the engine already in the car leave the camshaft loose in the head without fitting the retaining/thrust plate.

15 Examination and renovation of dismantled components

Crankshaft and main bearings

1 Carefully examine the crankpin and main journal surfaces for signs of scoring or scratches, and check the ovality and taper of each journal in turn. Use a dial gauge and V-blocks and check the main bearing journals for ovality. If any journals are found to be more than 0.02 mm (0.001 in) out of round then they will have to be reground. If the crankpins are scored or scratched, don't bother measuring them as they will have to be reground.

2 If a bearing has failed after a short period of operation look for the cause and rectify before reassembly.

3 If the crankshaft is to be reground this will have to be done by your Peugeot Talbot dealer or a competent automotive engineer. The regrinder will also be able to supply the new shell bearings to suit the undersize requirement. New thrust washers to control endfloat will also be supplied.

Big-end bearings

4 The main bearing shells themselves are normally a matt grey in colour all over and should have no signs of pitting or ridging or discolouration as this usually indicates that the surface bearing metal has worn away and the backing material is showing through. It is worthwhile renewing the main bearing shells anyway if you have gone to the trouble of

removing the crankshaft, but they *must,* of course, be renewed if there is any sign of damage to them or if the crankshaft has been reground.

5   If the crankshaft is not being reground, yet bearing shells are being renewed, make sure that you check whether or not the crankshaft has been reground before. This will be indicated by looking at the back of the bearing shells and will show whether it is undersize or not. The same type of shell bearing must be used when they are renewed.

6   The big-end bearings are subject to wear at a greater rate than the crankshaft journals. A sign that one or more big-end bearings are getting badly worn is a pronounced knocking noise from the engine, accompanied by a significant drop in oil pressure due to the increased clearance between the bearing and the journal permitting oil to flow more freely through the resultantly larger space. If this should happen quite suddenly and action is taken immediately, and by immediately is meant within a few miles, then it is possible that the bearing shell may be renewed without any further work needing to be done.

7   If this happens in an engine which has been neglected, and oil changes and oil filter changes have not been carried out as they should have been, it is most likely that the rest of the engine is in a pretty terrible state anyway. If it occurs in an engine which has been recently overhauled, then it is almost certainly due to a piece of grit or swarf which has got into the oil circulation system and finally come to rest in the bearing shell and scored it. In these instances renewal of the shell alone accompanied by a thorough flushing of the lubrication system may be all that is required.

Cylinder liners

8   The liner bores may be examined for wear either in or out of the engine block; the cylinder head must, of course, be removed in each case.

9   First of all examine the top of the cylinder about a quarter of an inch below the top of the liner and with a finger feel if there is any ridge running round the circumference of the bore. In a worn cylinder bore a ridge will develop at the point where the top ring on the piston comes to the uppermost limit of its stroke. An excessive ridge indicates that the bore below the ridge is worn. If there is no ridge, it is reasonable to assume that the cylinder is not badly worn. Measurement of the diameter of the cylinder bore both in line with the piston gudgeon pin and at right angles to it, at the top and bottom of the cylinder, is another check to be made. A cylinder is expected to wear at the sides where the thrust of the piston presses against it. In time this causes the cylinder to assume an oval shape. Furthermore, the top of the cylinder is likely to wear more than the bottom of the cylinder. It will be necessary to use a proper bore measuring instrument in order to measure the differences in bore diameter across the cylinder, and variations between the top and bottom ends of the cylinder. As a general guide it may be assumed that any variation more than 0.25 mm (0.010 in) indicates that the liners should be renewed. Provided all variations are less than 0.25 mm (0.010 in) it is probable that the fitting of new piston rings will cure the problem of piston-to-cylinder bore clearances. Once again it is difficult to give a firm ruling on this as so much depends on the amount of time, effort and money which the individual owner is prepared, or wishes to spend, on the task. Certainly if the cylinder bores are obviously deeply grooved or scored, the liners must be renewed, regardless of any measurement differences in the cylinder diameter.

10   If new liners are to be fitted, new pistons will be required also, as they are supplied as matched sets.

11   Examine the piston surface and look for signs of any hairline cracks especially round the gudgeon pin area. Check that the oil drain holes below the oil control ring groove are clear, and, if not, carefully clean them out using a suitably sized drill, but don't mark the piston.

12   If any of the pistons are obviously badly worn or defective they must be renewed. A badly worn top ring land may be machined to accept a wider, stepped ring, the step on the outer face of this type of ring being necessary to avoid fouling the unworn ridge at the top of the cylinder bore.

13   Providing the engine has not seized up or suffered any other severe damage, the connecting rods should not require any attention other than cleaning. If damage has occurred or the piston/s show signs of irregular wear it is advisable to have the connecting rod alignment checked. This requires the use of specialised tools and should therefore be entrusted to a Peugeot Talbot agent or a competent automotive engineer, who will be able to check and realign any defective rods.

14   New Peugeot Talbot rings are supplied with their gaps already preset, but if you intend to use other makes the gaps should be checked and adjusted if necessary. Before fitting the new rings on the pistons,

each should be inserted approximately 75 mm (3 in) down the cylinder bore and the gap measured with a feeler gauge. This should be between 0.38 mm (0.015 in) and 0.97 mm (0.038 in). It is essential that the gap should be measured at the bottom of the ring travel, as if it is measured at the top of a worn bore and gives a perfect fit, it could easily seize at the bottom. If the ring gap is too small, rub down the ends of the ring with a very fine file until the gap, when fitted, is correct. To keep the rings square in the bore for measurement, line each up in turn by inserting an old piston in the bore upside down, and use the piston to push the ring down. Remove the piston and measure the piston ring gap.

Gudgeon pins

15   The gudgeon pins float in the piston and are an interference fit in the connecting rods. This interference fit between gudgeon pin and connecting rod means that heat is required (230 to 260°/446°C to 500°F) before a pin can be satisfactorily fitted in the connecting rod. If it is necessary to renew either the piston or connecting rod, we strongly recommend that the separation and assembly of the two be entrusted to someone with experience. Misapplied heat can ruin one, or all, of the components very easily.

16   Never re-use a piston if the original gudgeon pin has been removed from it.

Connecting rod/piston

17   With the pistons removed from the liners, carefully clean them and remove the old rings, keeping them in order and the correct way up. The ring grooves will have to be cleaned out, especially the top, which will contain a burnt carbon coating that may prevent the ring from seating correctly. A broken piston ring will assist in groove cleaning. Take care not to scratch the ring lands or piston surface in any way.

18   The top ring groove is likely to have worn the most. After the groove has been cleaned out, refit the top ring and any excessive wear will be obvious by a sloppy fit. The degree of wear may be checked by using a feeler gauge.

Timing chain, sprocket and tensioner

19   Examine the teeth of both sprockets for wear. Each tooth on a sprocket is an inverted V-shape and wear is apparent when one side of the tooth becomes more concave in shape than the other. When badly worn, the teeth become hoop-shaped and the sprockets must be renewed.

Fig. 1.14 Cutaway view of timing chain tensioner (Sec 15)

1	Ratchet screw	5	Rack
2	Piston	6	Washer
3	Oil supply	7	Slipper
4	Spring		

20 If the sprockets need to be renewed then the chain will have worn also and should also be renewed. If the sprockets are satisfactory, examine the chain and look for play between the links. When the chain is held out horizontally, it should not bend appreciably. Remember, a chain is only as strong as its weakest link and, being a relatively cheap item, it is worthwhile fitting a replacement anyway.

21 Check the condition of the tensioner slipper. If it is worn, renew it.

22 Inspect the oil pump drive gears for wear or damage and renew if necessary. Always fit a new timing cover oil seal (photo).

15.31A Rocker shaft end circlip

15.22 Timing cover oil seal

Transfer gears (refer also to Chapter 5)

23 The condition of the transfer gears, their bearings and the input and output shafts, is obviously critical as they transmit the power of the engine to the transmission unit, and are liable to be a source of noise if worn.

24 Clean the input and output shaft ball-bearings and check them for excessive play and/or signs of damage. Inspect the intermediate shaft needle roller bearings. Renew any suspect or worn bearings. If a bearing has collapsed due to general wear and fatigue, then the chances are that the other bearings are close to failure and it is therefore advisable to renew all the bearings.

25 Carefully inspect the transfer gears. If excessive transmission noise has been experienced it may be reduced by changing the transfer gears. If the teeth are worn or damaged, then the gears should be renewed. Renew the gear set rather than a single gear; it is not good practice to mesh new gears with old as the wear rate of both is increased and they will be noisy in operation.

26 Check the input and output shafts, and inspect their splines for wear or damage. Renew them if necessary.

Camshaft and rocker gear

27 The camshaft lobes should be examined for signs of flats or scoring or any other form of wear or damage. At the same time the rocker arms should also be examined, particularly on the faces where they bear against the camshaft, for signs of wear. Very slight wear may be removed by rubbing with an oilstone but maintain the original contour.

28 The camshaft bearing journals should be in good condition and show no signs of pitting or scoring as they are relatively free from stress.

29 If the bearing surfaces are scored or discoloured it is possible that the shaft is not running true, and in this case it will have to be renewed. For an accurate check get your Peugeot Talbot agent to inspect both the camshaft and cylinder head.

30 Worn camshaft bearings in the cylinder head can only be rectified by renewal of the head, an expensive business, as the bearings are machined directly in the head.

31 The rocker arm assembly can be dismantled on removing the circlip from the end of the rocker shaft (photos).

15.31B Dismantling the rocker shaft assembly

32 When removing the various rocker components from the shaft take careful note of the sequence in which they are removed. In particular note that the No 2 and No 4 rocker bearings are identical, keep the components in order as they are removed from the shaft for inspection. The final rocker bearing (timing chain end) is secured to the rocker shaft by the rocker cover stud, or an Allen screw under that stud.

33 Check the rocker shaft for signs of wear. Check it for straightness by rolling it on a flat surface. It is unlikely to be bent but if this is the case it must either be straightened or renewed. The shaft surface should be free of wear ridges caused by the rocker arms. Check the oil feed holes and clear them out if blocked or sludged-up.

34 Check each rocker arm for wear on an unworn part of the shaft. Check the end of the adjuster screw and the face of the rocker arm where it bears on the camshaft. Any signs of cracks or serious wear will necessitate renewal of the rocker arm.

Flywheel and starter ring gear

35 There are two areas in which the flywheel may have been worn or damaged. The first is on the driving face where the clutch friction plate bears against it. Should the clutch plate have been permitted to wear down beyond the level of the rivets, it is possible that the flywheel will have been scored. If this scoring is severe it may be necessary to have it refaced or even renewed.

36 Evidence of tiny cracks on the flywheel driving face will indicate that overheating has occurred.

37 The other part to examine is the teeth of the starter ring gear around the periphery of the flywheel. If several of the teeth are broken or missing, or the front edges of all teeth are obviously very badly chewed up, then it would be advisable to fit a new ring gear.

38 The old ring gear can be removed by cutting a slot with a hacksaw down between two of the teeth as far as possible, without cutting into the flywheel itself. Once the cut is made a chisel will split the ring gear which can then be drawn off. To fit a new ring gear requires it to be heated first to a temperature of 220°C (428°F), no more. This is best done in a bath of oil or an oven, but not with a naked flame. It is much more difficult to heat evenly and to the required temperature with a naked flame. Once the ring gear has attained the correct temperature it can be placed onto the flywheel; making sure that it beds down properly onto the register. It should then be allowed to cool down naturally. If by mischance, the ring gear is overheated, it should not be used. The temper will have been lost, thereby softening it, and it will wear out in a very short space of time.

39 Although not actually fitted into the flywheel itself, there is a bush in the centre of the crankshaft flange onto which the flywheel fits. Whilst more associated with gearbox and clutch, it should always be inspected when the clutch is removed. The main bearing oil seal is revealed when the flywheel is removed. This can be prised out with a screwdriver but must always be renewed once removed. The spigot bush is best removed using a suitable extractor. Another method is to fill the recess with grease and then drive in a piece of close fitting steel bar. This should force the bush out. A new bush may be pressed in, together with a new seal. Make sure that the chamfered end of the bush abuts the seal. The bush is self-lubricating.

Oil pump

40 The oil pump gears are exposed once the spacer plate is removed.

41 Side movement of the gear spindles will indicate wear in the bushes and the pump should be renewed complete.

42 Worn or chipped gearteeth must be rectified by renewal of the gear.

43 Check the endfloat of the gears using a straight-edge and feeler blades (photo).

15.44 Checking oil pump lobe tip clearance

15.46 Oil pump relief valve components

15.43 Checking oil pump gear endfloat

44 Check the clearance between the tip of the gear lobes and the oil pump body (photo).

45 If any of these clearances exceed the specified limit, renew the pump.

46 Remove the retaining pin from the relief valve housing and withdraw the cup, spring, guide and piston. Renew any worn components (photo).

16 Engine reassembly – general

1 It is during the process of engine reassembly that the job is either made a success or a failure. From the word go there are certain basic rules which is folly to ignore, namely:

(a) *Absolute cleanliness. The working area, the components of the engine and the hands of those working on the engine must be completely free of grime and grit. One small piece of carborundum dust or swarf can ruin a big-end in no time, and nullify all the time and effort you have spent.*

(b) *Always, no matter what the circumstances may be, use new gaskets, locking tabs, seats, nyloc (self-locking) nuts and any other parts mentioned in the Sections in this Chapter. It is pointless to dismantle an engine, spend considerable money and time on it and then waste all this for the sake of something as small as a failed oil seal. Delay the rebuilding if necessary.*

(c) *Don't rush it. The most skilled and experienced mechanic can easily make a mistake if he is rushed.*

(d) Check that all nuts and bolts are clean and in good condition and ideally renew all spring washers, lockwashers and tab washers as a matter of course. A supply of clean engine oil and clean cloths (to wipe excess oil off your hands) and a torque spanner are the only things which should be required in addition to all the tools used in dismantling the engine.

(e) The torque wrench is an essential requirement when reassembling the engine (and transmission) components. This is because the various housings are manufactured from aluminium alloy and whilst this gives the advantage of less weight, it also means that the various fastenings must be accurately tightened as specified to avoid distortion and/or damage to the components.

17 Engine – preparation for reassembly

1 Assuming that the engine has been completely stripped for reconditioning and that the block is now bare, before any reassembly takes place it must be thoroughly cleaned both inside and out.

2 Clean out the oilways using a bottle brush, wire or other suitable implement, and blow through with compressed air. Squirt some clean engine oil through to check that the oilways are clear.

3 If the core plugs are defective and show signs of weeping, they must be renewed at this stage. To remove, carefully drive a punch through the centre of the plug and use the punch to lever the plug out. Clean the aperture thoroughly and prior to fitting the new plug, smear the orifice with sealant. Use a small-headed hammer and carefully drive the new core plug into position with the convex side outwards. Check that it is correctly seated on completion.

4 As the components are assembled, lubricate them with clean engine oil and use a suitable sealant where applicable.

5 Make sure that all blind tapped holes are clean, with any oil mopped out of them. This is because it is possible for a casting to fracture when a bolt is screwed in owing to hydraulic pressure.

18 Cylinder liners – checking projection

Paper type gasket seals

1 If the cylinder liners had paper type base seals, the first thing to do is to check the liner projection and select new paper seals (photo).

2 If rubber O-rings are used, no checking or measurement of liner projection is required, simply renew the O-rings.

3 Paper gaskets are available in four different thicknesses:

Blue 0.087 mm
White 0.102 mm
Red 0.122 mm
Yellow 0.147 mm

Fig. 1.15 Cylinder liner and block match marks (a) (Sec 18)

4 The correct projection for each liner above the surface of the cylinder block is between 0.13 and 0.18 mm, preferably nearer to the greater projection.

5 Fit the liners without gaskets into their original locations. If new liners are being fitted, they of course can be fitted in any order.

6 Using a dial indicator or feeler gauges and a straight-edge, measure the projection of each liner.

7 It is now a simple matter to select a paper gasket which, when its thickness is added to the recorded projection, will equal the specified projection.

8 Make sure that the difference in projection between adjacent liners does not exceed 0.04 mm. If it does, reduce the gasket thickness on the greater projecting liner.

9 If new liners are being fitted, the projection differences can be eliminated by changing the position of the liner in the block or by twisting it on its base.

10 Once selected, mark each liner's position in the block, then remove them and place with their paper gaskets ready for final assembly.

O-ring type seals

11 If the original liners are being refitted then the projection should be correct once new O-ring seals have been fitted.

12 If new liners are being fitted, then measure the projection of each

18.1 Liner with paper gasket

18.12 Measuring cylinder liner projection

liner without its seal. This should be between 0.10 and 0.17 mm, with a maximum difference between liners of 0.05 mm (photo).

13 If the difference between adjacent liners exceeds 0.05 mm, rotate the liners through half a turn or interchange the liner position in the block.

14 Once correctly located, mark their sequence in the block and withdraw them so that their piston/rods can be fitted.

19 Engine – complete reassembly

1   Fit the piston rings to the pistons. Always fit the rings from the piston crown end. Use three old feeler blades equally spaced behind the ring so that it will slide down to the lower grooves without dropping into the higher ones (photo).

2   Make sure that the rings are correctly located and the right way up. If genuine Peugeot Talbot piston rings are being used, refer to Fig. 1.16. If special proprietary rings are being fitted, follow the manufacturer's instructions.

3   Twist the piston rings so that the gap in the oil control ring expander aligns with the gudgeon pin and the gaps in the rails are offset from the gudgeon pin by between 20.0 and 50.0 mm (0.79 and 1.97 in). The gaps in the top two compression rings should be equally spaced (120°) from the gap in the oil control expander around the piston.

4   If new piston/liner assemblies have been supplied, the identification marks on the piston and liner should be:

Piston	Liner
A	One file mark on rim
B	Two file marks on rim
C	Three file marks on rim (photo)

5   All four pistons should be of the same grading.

6   Fit the liners to the piston/connecting rod assemblies so that when installed in the cylinder block, the rim mark on the liner will be towards the oil gallery side and the arrow on the piston crown facing towards the timing chain cover end of the engine (photo). Piston-to-rod relationship is not important.

7   Oil the piston rings liberally and fit a compressor to the piston and compress the rings fully.

19.1 Method of fitting piston rings

19.4 Piston/liner grading mark

Fig. 1.16 Piston ring identification (Sec 19)

1	Oil control ring	3	Compression ring
2	Compression ring	b	Oil control expander gap
	(tapered)	c	Oil control rail gaps

19.6 Piston crown directional arrow

8 Lubricate the bore of the liner and insert the piston. As this is done, the compressor will be pushed off (photo).

9 Push the piston right into the liner.

10 Fit either the selected paper gasket seals so that their tabs are diametrically opposite to the liner rim marks or locate the O-ring seals making sure that they are not twisted (photo).

11 Remove the big-end caps, wipe the recesses in rod and cap absolutely clean and fit the bearing shells. If the original shells are being used again, make sure that they are being returned to their original locations.

12 Push the liner/rod assemblies into the block, without disturbing the seals and aligning the location marks (photo).

13 Fit clamps to hold the liners in the block.

14 Place the block so that it rests on its top face and wipe out the recesses and fit the main bearing shells (photo).

15 Fit the semi-circular thrust washers which control crankshaft endfloat. The oil grooves of the thrust washers must be against the machined face of the crankshaft (photo).

16 Oil the shell bearings and lower the crankshaft into position (photo).

17 Now check the crankshaft endfloat. Do this by first pushing the crankshaft fully in one direction and then in the other. A dial gauge or feeler blades should be used to measure the endfloat (photo). If the endfloat is outside the specified tolerance, change the thrust washers for ones of different thickness, from the four thicknesses available.

18 Fit the big-end caps complete with bearing shells, well lubricated. Make sure that the cap/rod matching marks are in alignment. This will ensure that both tongues of the shells are on the same side (photo).

19 Tighten the big-end nuts to the specified torque (photo).

20 Into the crankcase flange fit a new O-ring seal and check that the locating dowels are in position (photo).

21 Apply jointing compound to the flange.

22 Clean the recesses in the remaining crankcase housing section and fit the main bearing shells. Note that the grooved shells are located in positions 2 and 4.

Fig. 1.17 Crankshaft thrust washers (Sec 19)

R   Oil grooves

23 Locate the housing, taking care not to displace the bearing shells (photo).

24 Screw in the ten main bearing/casing bolts with flat washers; noting that the two longer bolts are at the flywheel housing end and the very long one at the crankshaft pulley end on the oil pump side (photo).

19.8 Inserting piston in liner

19.10 Cylinder liner O-ring seal

19.12 Installing piston/liner assembly

19.14 Main bearing shells in position

19.15 Crankshaft thrust washers

19.16 Lowering crankshaft into place

19.17 Checking crankshaft endfloat

19.18 Fitting a big-end cap

19.19 Tightening a big-end cap nut

19.20 Crankcase flange O-ring seal

19.23 Fitting crankcase housing

19.24 Tightening main bearing bolts

Fig. 1.18 Main bearing bolt tightening sequence (Sec 19)

19.26 Crankcase housing flange bolts

19.27 Fitting crankshaft oil seal

19.29A Chain tensioner filter

19.29B Fitting chain tensioner

25 Tighten the bolts in the sequence given in two stages to the specified torque (see Fig. 1.18).

26 Now screw in and tighten the seven housing flange bolts with their spring washers (photo).

27 Grease the lips of a new crankshaft oil seal and drive it squarely into position (photo).

28 Fit the cylinder head, as described in Section 6.

29 Fit the timing chain tensioner oil filter and the crankshaft sprocket Woodruff key. Bolt the chain tensioner into position (photos).

30 Rotate the crankshaft by temporarily screwing in two flywheel bolts and placing a bar between them until the key is in alignment with the crankcase joint (Fig. 1.19).

31 Temporarily fit the camshaft sprocket and rotate the camshaft until the keyway is positioned as shown in Fig. 1.19.

32 Fit the crankshaft sprocket (photo).

33 Loop the chain around the crankshaft sprocket so that the bright link on the chain is centred on the timing mark on the sprocket (photo).

34 Now loop the chain around the camshaft sprocket so that the two bright links are positioned one on each side of the sprocket timing mark (photo). Push the sprocket with chain onto the camshaft, if necessary move the camshaft a fraction to align the keyway.

35 Screw in the camshaft sprocket bolt with fuel pump eccentric and tighten to the specified torque (photos).

36 Turn the key in the chain tensioner fully clockwise to release the slipper (photo).

37 Check that the locating dowel is in position and fit the oil pump with spacer plate; no gasket is used (photo). If the pump driven sprocket is hard to turn, release the pump mounting bolts and turn the pump slightly on its locating dowel. Re-tighten the bolts.

38 Fit the oil pump drive sprocket and Woodruff key to the crankshaft (photo).

39 Fit the spark plugs. Do not overtighten them.

40 Fit the alternator adjuster link and coolant pump.

41 Screw in the oil pressure switch (photo).

42 Fit a new oil filter.

43 Bolt on the throttle reel with return spring (where applicable).

Fig. 1.19 Crankshaft and camshaft keyway positions when fitting the timing chain (Sec 19)

19.32 Crankshaft sprocket

19.33 Timing chain bright link at crankshaft sprocket (arrowed)

19.34 Timing chain bright links (arrowed) at camshaft sprocket

19.35A Fuel pump eccentric

19.35B Tightening camshaft sprocket bolt

19.36 Releasing timing chain tensioner

19.37 Fitting oil pump with spacer plate

19.38 Oil pump drive sprocket

19.41 Oil pressure switch

19.44A Fitting the exhaust manifold ...

19.44B ... and hot air box

20.6 O-ring seal on transmission casing

44 Bolt on the exhaust manifold using new gaskets. Leave the end nuts loose until the hot air collector has been fitted and then tighten them (photos).
45 Fit the fuel pump and operating rod.
46 Fit the distributor (Chapter 4).
47 Fit the carburettor(s) with a new gasket.
48 Fit the thermostat and thermostat housing cover using a new gasket.
49 The engine is now ready for connecting to the transmission, as described in the next Section.

20 Engine/transmission – reconnection

1 Check that the oil pick-up strainer is in position within the transmission casing.

2 Fit the sump cover using a new gasket.
3 Tighten the fixing bolts and drain plug to the specified torque.
4 Fit the cover plate.
5 Apply jointing compound to the mating surfaces on the engine and transmission.
6 On the transmission, locate a new O-ring seal and check that the locating dowels and the studs are in position (photo).
7 Offer the transmission to the engine, screw in the connecting bolts and nuts and tighten to the specified torque (photo).
8 Locate a new timing chain cover gasket and fit the cover.
9 Before offering the cover to the engine, put the bolt nearest the coolant pump pulley into its cover hole otherwise the pulley will prevent it from being fitted later. Do not tighten the cover bolts yet (photo).
10 Fit the coolant hose safety rod under its cover bolts (photo).
11 Use the crankshaft pulley to centralise the timing chain cover and then tighten the cover bolts.

20.7 Offering transmission to engine

20.9A Fitting timing chain cover and gasket

20.9B Timing cover bolt nearest coolant pump pulley

20.10 Coolant hose safety support rod

20.13 Tightening crankshaft pulley nut

20.14A Inserting flywheel bolts

20.14B Tightening flywheel bolts

20.16 Offering up flywheel housing

12 Cut the upper ends of the cover gasket off flush.
13 Apply grease to the crankshaft pulley oil seal contact surface and push it onto its key. Fit a new lockplate, tighten the nut to the specified torque and then bend up the lockplate (photo).
14 Fit the flywheel. Apply thread locking fluid to clean threads and screw in the flywheel bolts to the specified torque (photos). The flywheel holes are offset so it will only go onto the crankshaft flange in one position.
15 Fit the clutch and centralise the driven plate, as described in Chapter 5.
16 Fit a new gasket and offer up the flywheel housing (Chapter 5), complete with transfer gears (photo). Make sure that the engine lifting lug and earth strap are correctly located under their respective bolts (photo).
17 If they were removed, bolt the engine mountings to the flywheel housing.
18 Fit the starter motor. Tighten the bolts and nuts in the following order:

1   Starter drive end flange to flywheel housing
2   Brush end bracket to engine crankcase
3   Brush end bracket to starter motor

19 Adjust the valve clearances. Use a new gasket and fit the rocker cover.
20 Fit the alternator.
21 The engine/transmission is now ready for refitting to the car.

21 Engine/transmission – refitting

1   Refitting is a reversal of the removal procedure given in Section 8 with particular attention to the following points:

(a) To assist engagement of the driveshafts, turn the front wheels as necessary until the splines engage

(b) Adjust the clutch cable, as described in Chapter 5
(c) Adjust the throttle and choke cables, as described in Chapter 3
(d) Fill the engine/transmission with oil
(e) Fill the cooling system, as described in Chapter 2

22 Engine – initial start-up after overhaul

1   Make sure that the battery is fully charged and that all lubricants, coolant and fuel are replenished.
2   It will require several revolutions of the engine on the starter motor to pump the petrol up to the carburettor(s).
3   As soon as the engine fires and runs, keep it going at a fast tickover only (no faster) and bring it up to the normal working temperature.
4   As the engine warms up there will be odd smells and some smoke from parts getting hot and burning off oil deposits. The signs to look for are leaks of water or oil which will be obvious if serious. Check also the exhaust pipe and manifold connections, as these do not always 'find' their exact gastight position until the warmth and vibration have acted on them, and it is almost certain that they will need tightening further. This should be done with the engine stopped.
5   When normal running temperature has been reached, adjust the engine idling speed, as described in Chapter 3. Run the engine until the fan cuts in and then switch off. Check that no oil or coolant is leaking with the engine stationary.
6   Allow at least two hours for the engine to cool down and then retighten the cylinder head bolts after removing the rocker cover. Follow the bolt tightening sequence and, starting with the first, slacken the bolt and retighten it to the specified final tightening torque before loosening the second bolt. Repeat until all bolts have been retightened.
7   Check and adjust the valve clearances.
8   Check the ignition timing.
9   Road test the car to check that the timing is correct and that the

engine is giving the necessary smoothness and power. Do not race the engine – if new bearings and/or pistons have been fitted it should be treated as a new engine and run in at a reduced speed.
10 Change the engine oil at 1000 miles (1500 km) if many of the engine internal components have been renewed. At the same mileage, check the tension of the drivebelt.

PART C: XU5J engine

23 Operations possible without removing the engine from the car

The following items can be removed and refitted with the engine in the car:

(a) Cylinder head
(b) Camshaft drivebelt and camshaft
(c) Sump and oil pump
(d) Clutch and flywheel (after removal of transmission)

Since the sump and cylinder head can be removed *in situ*, it is possible to renew the pistons, liners and big-end bearings without removing the engine. Such work is not recommended, however, since it can be performed more easily with the engine on the bench.

24 Cylinder head – removal and refitting

1 Remove the camshaft drivebelt (Section 25).
2 Drain the cooling system (Chapter 2).
3 Slacken, but do not remove, the engine lower mounting rubber centre nut and bolt (photo).

24.3 Engine lower mounting

4 Remove the air cleaner, its pipes and trunking, and the crankcase breather and its pipes.
5 Remove the nut which secures the engine right-hand mounting rubber.
6 Carefully raise the engine 60 to 80 mm (say 3 inches) using a hoist or a well-protected jack. Remove the two bolts which secure the right-hand mounting bracket to the cylinder head, then lower the engine back into position.
7 Remove the airflow sensor, inlet manifold, injectors and associated components with reference to Chapter 3.
8 Disconnect all coolant and vacuum hoses.
9 Disconnect the electrical leads.

10 Disconnect the exhaust downpipes at the manifold flange.
11 Remove the coolant pipe from the pump inlet housing. Also remove the diagnostic socket from its bracket and unbolt the oil filler pipe from the inlet manifold, if applicable.
12 Remove the camshaft cover, at the same time removing the distributor cap and HT leads.
13 Slacken the cylinder head bolts in the reverse sequence to that used when tightening (Fig. 1.20). Remove the bolts.
14 Remove the cylinder head, using a couple of bars through two of the bolt holes and 'rocking' it towards the front of the car. Do not lift the head directly from the block, as this will disturb the liners. Remove the gasket and recover any loose dowels.
15 Fit cylinder liner clamps, or large washers secured with nuts and bolts, to keep the liners in position (photo). *If the liners are disturbed, the engine will have to be removed for new seals to be fitted.*

Fig. 1.20 Cylinder head bolt tightening sequence (Sec 24)

24.15 Cylinder liners clamped with washers and bolts

16 Commence refitting by fitting the dowels to the cylinder block. Keep the flywheel-end dowel raised by inserting a 5 mm punch or large nail through the hole in the front of the block (photo). Remove the liner clamps.
17 Fit the new gasket, dry, with the tab at the flywheel end. Lower the cylinder head into position, making sure that it mates with the dowels. Remove the punch or nail.
18 Fit the cylinder head bolts, their threads clean and lightly oiled. Remember to fit the spacer to the bolt above the coolant pump.
19 Progressively tighten the bolts in the order shown in Fig. 1.20 to the Stage 1 specified torque.

24.16 Dowel is kept raised by inserting a nail beneath it

24.21 Home-made disc for measuring tightening angle. Disc is fixed and pointer rotates

20 Raise the engine slightly and refit the two bolts which secure the right-hand mounting bracket to the cylinder head. Tighten these bolts and slacken the one which holds the same bracket to the engine block. Lower the engine and tighten the right-hand mounting nut and the lower mounting rubber nut and bolt.

21 Slacken cylinder head bolt No 1, then immediately retighten it to the Stage 2 specified torque. Tighten further by the angle specified for Stage 3 (photo). Repeat for all the bolts, following the tightening sequence.

22 Check the valve clearances and adjust, if necessary.

23 Refit the remaining components in the reverse order of removal. Make sure that the correct inlet manifold gasket is fitted. A gasket for carburettor versions is included in the gasket overhaul set which is not the same as the one for fuel injection models.

24 Refill and bleed the cooling system (Chapter 2).

25 Start the engine and warm it up until the cooling fan cuts in, then switch off and allow it to cool for at least two hours.

26 Retighten the cylinder head bolts, as described in paragraph 21, then recheck the valve clearances.

27 If a new camshaft drivebelt has been fitted, retension it as described in Section 25.

28 Tighten the engine mounting bracket bolt.

25 Camshaft drivebelt – removal and refitting

1   Disconnect the battery earth lead.

2   Remove the alternator drivebelt.

3   Remove the inner shield from the right-hand wheel arch (photo) and wedge the radiator bottom hose under the sump.

4   Remove the shield from the camshaft sprocket.

5   Turn the crankshaft until the dowel hole in the pulley is at about 12 o'clock and the hole in the camshaft sprocket is at about 7 o'clock. In this position a 10 mm dowel should pass through each hole and into the timing recess behind. Verify this and then remove the dowels (photo).

6   Remove the clutch bottom shield. Have an assistant jam the starter ring gear while the crankshaft pulley bolt is undone. This bolt is very tight. **Do not** jam the pulley by means of the timing dowel: damage will result. Remove the bolt and washer.

7   Check that the 10 mm dowels will still enter the timing holes: adjust the crankshaft position if necessary by means of the starter ring gear. Remove the crankshaft pulley, retrieving the Woodruff key if it is loose.

8   Remove the plastic covers from the front of the camshaft drivebelt. Note the location of the various bolts.

25.3 Removing the inner shield

25.5 Timing dowels in position – engine removed for clarity

9 Slacken the two nuts on the front of the drivebelt tensioner and the single nut at the rear. Use a spanner on the square end of the tensioner cam spindle to turn the cam to the horizontal position and so compress the tensioner spring (photo). Tighten the cam locknut.

10 Remove the camshaft drivebelt, taking care not to kink it or contaminate it with oil if it is to be re-used.

11 Commence refitting by positioning the belt on the crankshaft sprocket, then refitting the pulley and verifying the correct position of the crankshaft by means of the dowel. (Observe the arrows on the belt showing the direction of rotation, and the timing lines which align with marks on the crankshaft and camshaft sprockets) (photo).

12 Fit the belt to the camshaft sprocket, round the tensioner and to the coolant pump sprocket.

13 Release the tensioner cam locknut and turn the cam downwards to release the spring. Tighten the locknut and the tensioner front nuts (photo).

14 Remove the timing dowels and turn the crankshaft through two full turns in the normal direction of rotation. Turn the crankshaft further to bring No 1 piston to TDC on the firing stroke.

15 Slacken the tensioner front nuts and the cam locknut, then retighten them.

25.13 Drivebelt tensioner front nuts

25.9 Turning the tensioner cam spindle

16 Turn the crankshaft further and make sure that the timing dowels can still be inserted. If not, remove the drivebelt and start again.

17 If a new belt has been fitted, it must be run in and retensioned, as follows.

18 Tighten the crankshaft pulley bolt to the specified torque, then refit and tension the alternator drivebelt. Temporarily refit the camshaft sprocket cover.

19 Run the engine up to operating temperature, indicated by the cooling fan operating, then stop it and allow it to cool for at least two hours.

20 Rotate the crankshaft to the TDC position, No 1 cylinder firing, then slacken and retighten the tensioner nuts once more.

21 Remove the alternator drivebelt and the crankshaft pulley. Refit and secure the plastic covers, then refit the pulley and tighten its bolts to the specified torque. Refit and tension the alternator drivebelt.

22 Check the ignition timing and adjust if necessary.

26 Camshaft – removal and refitting

1 Remove the camshaft drivebelt as previously described in Section 25.

2 Remove the camshaft cover. For ease of access, remove the distributor cap and HT leads, air cleaner and brake servo vacuum hose.

3 Remove the distributor, as described in Chapter 4.

4 Remove the camshaft lubrication manifold.

5 Lock the camshaft sprocket (eg with a timing dowel) and remove the sprocket retaining bolt. Remove the sprocket and the cover plate behind it. Remove the thrust plate (photos).

6 Progressively slacken the camshaft bearing cap securing nuts. Make identifying marks if necessary, then remove the caps. Be prepared for the camshaft to spring upwards. Remove the camshaft.

7 Commence refitting by making sure that the crankshaft is in the correct (dowelled) position – if not, move it to this position to avoid possible piston/valve contact.

8 Refit the camshaft, then oil and fit its bearing caps. Tighten the cap nuts progressively to the specified torque. Refit and secure the thrust plate.

9 Fit a new oil seal to the sprocket end of the camshaft.

10 Refit the sprocket rear cover plate, locate it correctly with a 10 mm dowel and tighten its fastenings (photo). Fit the camshaft sprocket, dowel it and tighten its securing bolt to the specified torque.

11 Refit the lubrication manifold and distributor.

12 Refit the camshaft cover, HT leads and distributor cap, air cleaner, and brake servo vacuum hose.

13 Refit the camshaft drivebelt (Section 25).

25.11 Line on belt aligns with mark on sprocket

26.5A Removing the camshaft thrust plate screw

26.5B Removing the camshaft thrust plate

26.10 Locating the cover plate with a 10 mm dowel

27 Valve clearances – checking and adjustment

1 Remove the air cleaner and trunking, and the brake servo vacuum hose.
2 Remove the camshaft cover, trying not to damage the gasket.
3 Prepare to rotate the crankshaft, either by jacking up one front wheel and turning the wheel with 4th or 5th gear engaged, or with a spanner on the crankshaft pulley bolt. The crankshaft will be easier to rotate if the spark plugs are first removed.
4 Have ready a pencil and paper to record the measured clearances.
5 Turn the crankshaft until the cam lobe nearest the pulley end of the engine is pointing vertically upwards. Use feeler gauges to measure the clearance between the base of the cam and the tappet (photo). Record the clearance.
6 Repeat the measurement for the other seven valves, turning the crankshaft as necessary so that the cam lobe in question is always vertically upwards.

7 Calculate the difference between each measured clearance and the desired value (see Specifications). Note that the value for inlet valves is different from that for exhaust. Counting from either end of the engine, the valve sequence is:

Exhaust – Inlet – Inlet – Exhaust – Exhaust – Inlet – Inlet – Exhaust

8 If any clearance measured is outside the specified tolerance, adjustment must be carried out as described below. If all clearances are within tolerance, refit the camshaft cover, using a new gasket if necessary. Note the diagnostic socket and copper washer under the bolt at the timing belt end.
9 To adjust the clearances remove the camshaft as described in Section 26.
10 Lift off a tappet and its shim. Be careful that the shim does not fall out of the tappet. Clean the shim and measure its thickness with a micrometer (photos).
11 Refer to the clearance recorded for the valve concerned. If the

Fig. 1.21 Valve clearance is measured at point J and altered by shim (4) (Sec 27)

27.5 Measuring a valve clearance

27.10A Lift off the tappet

27.10B Measuring the thickness of a shim

clearance was larger than specified, a thicker shim must be fitted; if the clearance was too small, a thinner shim must be fitted.

Sample calculation – clearance too large:

Desired clearance (A) 0.20 mm
Measured clearance (B) 0.28 mm
Difference (B – A) = +0.08 mm
Original shim thickness 2.62 mm
Required shim thickness 2.62 + 0.08 = 2.70 mm

Sample calculation – clearance too small:
Desired clearance (A) 0.40 mm
Measured clearance (B) 0.23 mm
Difference (B-A) = −0.17 mm
Original shim thickness 2.86 mm
Required shim thickness 2.86 − 0.17 = 2.69 mm

12 Shims are available in thicknesses from 1.650 to 4.000 mm, in steps of 0.025 mm in the middle of the range and at the ends in steps of 0.075 mm. Clean new shims before measuring or fitting them.
13 Repeat the operations on the other tappets and shims, keeping each tappet identified so that it can be refitted in the same position.
14 When reassembling, oil the shim and fit it on the valve stem, then oil the tappet and lower it smoothly into position. If the tappet is raised at any stage the shim may be dislodged.
15 When all the tappets are in position with their shims, refit the camshaft. Check the valve clearances before refitting the camshaft drivebelt in case a mistake has been made and the camshaft has to be removed again. With the drivebelt disconnected the camshaft will not be moved by rotation of the crankshaft. Before rotating the camshaft alone, position all the pistons halfway down the bores to avoid piston-to-valve contact.

28 Engine – removal

1 The engine and transmission assembly is removed by lifting upwards from the engine compartment. The transmission is separated from the engine on the bench.
2 Unscrew the nut and detach the bonnet stay from the right-hand front suspension tower, then raise the bonnet vertical and retain by inserting two suitable U-bolts in the special holes provided in the bonnet hinges. Alternatively use welding rod or bend metal dowel rod.
3 Jack up the front of the car and support on axle stands. Apply the handbrake.
4 Remove the drain plug and drain the engine oil. Clean and refit the drain plug on completion.
5 Drain the cooling system, as described in Chapter 2.
6 Disconnect the coolant hoses by the water pump.
7 Disconnect the exhaust downpipe from the manifold.
8 Disconnect the gear linkage (Chapter 6) and speedometer cable (Chapter 12).
9 Unscrew and remove both front clamp bolts securing the hub carriers to the bottom of the front suspension struts.
10 Pull the lower suspension arms down from the hub carriers and unbolt the balljoint guard plates.
11 Pull the left-hand hub carrier outwards and at the same time withdraw the inner end of the driveshaft from the final drive unit.
12 Refer to Chapter 7 and fit the special tool to the differential side gear in order to prevent it from falling into the final drive housing.
13 Unbolt the right-hand rear engine mounting link then loosen the two nuts retaining the right-hand driveshaft intermediate bearing in the bracket bolted to the rear of the cylinder block and turn the bolt heads through 90°.
14 Pull the right-hand hub carrier outwards and at the same time withdraw the inner end of the driveshaft from the final drive unit. Unbolt the intermediate bearing bracket from the cylinder block.
15 Disconnect the wiring from the oil temperature sensor (photo).
16 Remove the air cleaner and trunking, airflow sensor, inlet manifold, injectors and associated components, with reference to Chapter 3.
17 Remove the battery (Chapter 12) and radiator (Chapter 2).
18 Disconnect all coolant and vacuum hoses.
19 Disconnect all electrical leads.
20 Disconnect the throttle cable (Chapter 3) and clutch cable (Chapter 5).
21 Connect a suitable hoist to the engine lifting eyes and take its weight.

28.15 Oil temperature sensor and wiring

29.1A Starter motor is secured by three Allen bolts ...

22 Unscrew the left-hand engine mounting upper nut in the battery tray aperture.
23 Lower the engine slightly, then unbolt and remove the battery tray and bracket.
24 Unscrew the right-hand engine mounting upper nut (photo).
25 Lift the assembly from the engine compartment.

28.24 Right-hand engine mounting

29.1B ... and a mounting bracket

30 Engine dismantling – general

Refer to Section 10.

31 Engine – complete dismantling

1 Remove the ancillary components still on the engine:

    (a) *Alternator and drivebelt (Chapter 10)*
    (b) *Oil filler and breather pipes*
    (c) *Clutch (Chapter 5)*
    (d) *Oil filter*
    (e) *Oil pressure switch*

29 Engine – separation from transmission

1 Remove the starter motor, which is secured by three Allen bolts and a mounting bracket (photos).
2 Remove the remaining engine-to-transmission bolts.
3 Support the engine and pull the transmission away from it. Do not allow the weight of the transmission to hang on the input shaft. Recover any loose dowels.

2 The exhaust manifold may be removed now, or it can be left in place to serve as a handle until the head is removed.
3 Unbolt and remove the crankshaft pulley. Jam the flywheel teeth when undoing the pulley bolt to stop the crankshaft rotating.
4 Remove the camshaft drivebelt covers, noting the location of the various sizes of bolt.

5   Unbolt and remove the camshaft cover.

6   Rotate the crankshaft by means of the flywheel until a 10 mm diameter rod can be passed through the hole in the camshaft sprocket and into the timing recess. The pistons are now at mid-stroke so piston/valve contact cannot occur.

7   Release the camshaft drivebelt tensioner by slackening its nuts (two at the front and one behind the front plate) and using the square end of the cam spindle to bring the cam into a horizontal position.

8   Remove the camshaft drivebelt, taking care not to kink it and noting its direction of travel if it is to be re-used.

9   Unbolt and remove the camshaft drivebelt tensioner.

10   Remove the belt side covers and the crankshaft sprocket. Recover the Woodruff key.

11   Unbolt and remove the camshaft sprocket. Restrain the sprocket from turning if necessary using the 10 mm diameter rod inserted through the timing hole in the sprocket (photo).

12   Unbolt and remove the engine mounting bracket, the camshaft sprocket backplate and the coolant pump.

13   Slacken the ten cylinder head bolts, working in the reverse sequence of that used when tightening (Fig. 1.20). Remove the bolts and washers, noting the spacer under the No 8 bolt (directly above the coolant pump) (photo).

31.11 Lock the sprocket with a 10 mm rod

31.13 Removing the cylinder head bolts – note spacer (arrowed)

14   Remove the cylinder head. If it seems to be stuck, use a couple of metal rods in two of the bolt holes to rock it free. Do not attempt to hammer, lever it off or to lift the head directly upwards otherwise the cylinder liner base seals may be broken. Retrieve the two locating dowels if they are loose.

15   Fit liner clamps if it is not proposed to remove the pistons and liners (see Section 24). Invert the engine.

16   Unbolt and remove the flywheel. It is dowelled so it can only be refitted one way.

17   Remove the suction drain pipe (photo).

18   Unbolt and remove the sump. Note the location of the three Allen-headed bolts (photo).

31.17 Removing the suction drain pipe

31.18 The three Allen-headed bolts are fitted here

19   Remove the bolts which secure the oil pump, noting the special centering bolt at the rear.

20   Unbolt and remove the oil seal carrier plate.

21   Lower the oil pump into the engine so that its chain can be removed. Withdraw the pump and recover the spacer, the dowel and the chain.

22   Pull the oil pump sprocket off the crankshaft and recover the Woodruff key.

23 Unbolt the connecting rod big-end caps and push the pistons out through the tops of the liners. (If it is intended to re-use the pistons, it is prudent to remove the wear ridge at the top of the liner bores first, using a ridge reamer or scraper). Make identification marks on the pistons, rods and caps so that they can be refitted in their original positions.

24 Remove the bolts from main bearing caps, 1, 2, 4 and 5. Also remove the two nuts and the two side bolts from the centre cap. Make alignment marks on the bearing caps and remove them. Keep the bearing shells with their caps if they are to be re-used. Recover the thrust washer segments from either side of No 2 bearing cap.

25 Remove the oil seal from the flywheel end of the crankshaft.

26 Lift the crankshaft out of the crankcase. Recover the upper half main bearing shells and the other two thrust washer segments.

27 Make alignment marks on the cylinder liners if they are to be re-used, then release the liner clamps and remove the liners. Dismantling of the engine is now complete.

32 Cylinder head – dismantling, decarbonising and reassembly

1 If not already done, remove the spark plugs and exhaust manifold.

2 Unbolt and remove the coolant outlet housing. Do not overlook the recessed securing screw in the end (photo). Remove the thermostat elbow from the housing and withdraw the thermostat.

3 Lift out the camshaft lubrication manifold (photo).

4 Unbolt and remove the camshaft thrust fork.

5 Progressively slacken the camshaft bearing cap nuts. Remove the caps – be prepared for the camshaft to spring upwards. Remove the oil seal from the sprocket end, then remove the camshaft (photo).

6 Remove the tappets and shims, identifying their locations if they are to be re-used.

7 Extract the oil filter gauze from the oilway (photo).

8 Use a universal type valve spring compressor to compress a valve spring. Remove the collets, carefully release the compressor and extract the valve and spring. Repeat for the other seven valves.

9 Using long-nosed pliers, carefully remove the valve stem oil seals from their locations in the head. Dismantling of the cylinder head is now complete.

10 Decarbonise the cylinder head with reference to Section 14.

11 The makers state that no machining of the cylinder head surface is permitted. A warped head must therefore be renewed.

12 Factory exchange cylinder heads may have had 0.2 mm machined off the mating face. These heads are identified by the letter 'R' stamped on a boss at the distributor end of the head. A gasket 0.2 mm thicker than normal must be used with such a head; the thicker gasket is identified by a cut-out in the tab at the clutch end.

32.3 Lifting out the camshaft lubrication manifold

32.5 Removing the camshaft

32.2 Undoing the recessed securing screw in the coolant outlet housing

32.7 Oil filter gauze in the cylinder head oilway

13 Commence reassembly by fitting new valve stem oil seals, then fit the valves, springs and collets. Oil the valve stems liberally; a smear of of grease will hold the collets in position while the spring is compressed. The valve springs can be fitted either way up.

14 Lubricate the tappet bores. Secure each shim to its valve stem with a dab of grease and carefully fit the tappets. If new components have been fitted so that the valve clearances are unknown, fit the thinnest possible shims to all valves.

15 Fit the camshaft to the head and oil its lobes and journals. Fit the bearing caps, making sure that the middle ones are the right way round. Progressively tighten the bearing cap nuts to the specified torque (photo).

3 Inspect the camshaft lobes and bearing journals for wear and damage: if evident, renewal is probably necessary. Also inspect the bearing surfaces in the cylinder head and bearing caps.

4 Clean the camshaft lubrication manifold with solvent and then blow through it with compressed air. All the holes must be clear (photo).

5 Inspect the tappets for wear and scuffing; renew them as necessary. New tappets **must** be fitted if the camshaft is renewed; it is also advisable to renew the valve springs.

6 The camshaft drivebelt tensioner should be examined for roughness of the wheel bearing and wear or distortion of the spring. Renew as necessary – the wheel, bearing and backplate must be renewed as an assembly (photo).

32.15 Tightening the camshaft bearing nuts

34.4 The pinholes in the lubrication manifold must be clear

16 Fit the camshaft thrust plate and tighten its securing bolt.

17 Press the lubrication manifold into position.

18 Fit a new filter gauze in the oilway.

19 Fit the coolant outlet housing, using a new gasket.

20 Fit the exhaust manifold with a new gasket and tighten the bolts.

21 Fit a new oil seal to the sprocket end of the camshaft, using a piece of tube to drive it home.

22 If valve clearance adjustment is to be carried out now, temporarily fit the camshaft sprocket and stand the cylinder head on wooden blocks so that open valves do not strike the work surface.

33 Engine components – examination and renovation

Refer to Section 13.

34 Examination and renovation of dismantled components

1 Refer to Section 15 for the examination and renovation of the following components:

(a) Crankshaft and main bearings
(b) Big-end bearings
(c) Cylinder liners
(d) Gudgeon pins
(e) Connecting rod/pistons
(f) Flywheel and starter ring gear

34.6 Camshaft drivebelt tensioner components

Camshaft and drivebelt

2 Renew the camshaft drivebelt as a matter of course unless it is in perfect condition and is known to have covered only a nominal mileage. Renew the sprockets if they are damaged.

Crankshaft spigot bush

7 Later engines have no spigot bush in the crankshaft tail; the diameter of the gearbox input shaft is correspondingly increased.

8 If fitting a new style crankshaft to mate with an old style input shaft, obtain and insert a spigot bush. If the reverse situation applies (new input shaft and old crankshaft), extract the spigot bush.

Oil pump – dismantling, inspection and reassembly

9 Remove the six bolts which hold the two halves of the oil pump together. Separate the halves; being prepared for the release of the relief valve spring and plunger (photo).

10 Inspect the rotors and their housing for wear and damage. No wear limits are published for this pump; any visible wear on the moving parts suggests that renewal is necessary. With the exception of the relief valve spring and plunger, individual components are not available (photos).

11 Lubricate the pump components well before reassembly. Bolt the two halves together, being careful not to trap the spring.

12 If the pump is to be renewed it is wise to renew the chain and the crankshaft sprocket also.

Cylinder liner protrusion – checking

13 Liner protrusion is determined by the dimensions of the block and liners and is not adjustable. Nevertheless it should be checked as follows.

14 Make sure that the liners and their seats in the block are clean. Fit the liners without their seals, observing the marks made during dismantling if the old liners are being refitted.

15 Using a straight-edge and feeler blades, or a dial gauge, measure the protrusion of each liner above the block and the relative difference in

34.10B Oil pump relief valve spring and plunger

protrusion between adjacent liners. Desired values are given in the Specifications.

16 New liners can be rotated half a turn (180°), and/or fitted in a different position in the block, to bring protrusion within tolerance. Old liners which will not produce the desired results are best scrapped. Consult a Peugeot dealer for advice.

17 When the liners are correctly positioned, mark each one so that it may be refitted in the same position, then remove the liners from the block.

35 Engine reassembly – general

Refer to Sections 16 and 17.

36 Engine – complete reassembly

1 Position the block for access to the bottom end and fit the main bearing upper shells. Also fit the thrust washer segments to No 2 bearing, grooved sides outwards (photo); retain them with a smear of grease. Note that the recommended placement of grooved (G) and plain (P) bearing shells varies according to model:

Early models (up to Serial No 9 207 534)

Bearing No	1	2	3	4	5
Top	P	G	P	G	P
Bottom	P	P	P	P	P

Later models (from Serial No 9 207 535)

Bearing No	1	2	3	4	5
Top	G	P	P	P	G
Bottom	G	P	P	G	G

The arrangement of shells on the engine dismantled did not agree with either of the above schemes; no harm seemed to have resulted. Consult the supplier of the bearings if in doubt.

2 Oil the bearing shells and lower the crankshaft into position, taking care not to dislodge the thrust washer segments (photo). Inject some oil into the crankshaft oilways.

3 Fit new side seals to No 1 main bearing cap. Carefully fit the cap with its bearing shell; lubricate the shell, the sides of the cap and the locating surfaces in the block. There is a risk of displacing or distorting the side seals as the cap is fitted, so protect them with a couple of feeler blades or thin strips of tin which can be withdrawn rearwards after fitting the cap (photos).

34.9 Separating the two halves of the oil pump

34.10A Inspect the pump gears for wear

36.1 Fitting the thrust washer upper segments

36.3B Protecting the side seals with feeler blades

36.2 Fitting the crankshaft

4 Fit the shells to the other main bearing caps, lubricate them and fit the caps. Fit the thrust washer segments, grooved side outwards, to No 2 cap. Observe the mating marks when dismantling; the lug on each bearing cap points towards the timing sprockets.

5 Fit the main bearing cap nuts and bolts and tighten them to the specified torque. Tighten the side bolts on No 3 cap last (photo).

6 Check the protrusion of No 1 cap side seals above the sump mating face: it should be 2 mm. Trim off any excess.

7 Now check the crankshaft endfloat by first pushing it in one direction and using a feeler blade between the thrust washer and crankshaft. Alternatively a dial gauge may be used. If the endfloat is outside the specified tolerance, change the thrust washers for ones of different thicknesses.

36.3A Fitting a side seal to No 1 main bearing cap

36.5 Tightening the side bolts on No 3 main bearing

36.8 Crankshaft oil seal – flywheel end

36.9 Arrow on piston crown points to camshaft sprocket end. Letter and number show liner and gudgeon pin grade

36.10A Fitting the oil pump drive sprocket – the chain must be engaged first

36.10B Oil pump drive chain

36.11A Fitting the oil pump – the chain must be engaged first

36.11B Sliding in the oil pump spacer

8   Fit a new oil seal, lips inwards and lubricated, to the flywheel end of the crankshaft (photo). Drive it into place with a piece of tube.

9   Fit new O-rings seals to the cylinder liners, then fit the pistons and liners and big-end caps, as described in Section 19, paragraphs 1 to 13, 18 and 19. The arrow on the piston crown should point to the timing belt end (photo).

10 Fit the Woodruff key and oil pump drive sprocket to the crankshaft nose. Fit the chain over the sprocket (photos).

11 Make sure that the locating dowel is in position, then engage the oil pump sprocket in the chain and offer the pump to the block (photo). Engage the pump on the dowel, then lift it up far enough to slide the L-shaped spacer in underneath it (photo).

12 Fit the oil pump securing bolts, remembering that the special centering bolt is nearest the flywheel (photo), and tighten them to the specified torque. Generously lubricate the pump and the chain.

13 Refit the pulley oil seal carrier plate, using silicone jointing compound on the block mating faces. Fit a new oil seal, lubricated lips inwards and drive it home with a piece of tube.

14 Fit the sump, using a new gasket, and tighten its securing bolts progressively to the specified torque. Remember the correct location of the three Allen-headed bolts, and note that the two shortest bolts must be fitted to No 1 main bearing cap.

15 Refit the suction drain pipe, using a new O-ring. Do not overtighten the securing nuts – 5 Nm (say 3.5 lbf ft) is the maximum allowed.

16 Fit the flywheel to the crankshaft flange and secure with new bolts, using thread locking compound. Tighten the bolts progressively to the specified torque.

17 Fit the clutch disc and pressure plate, as described in Chapter 5.

18 Position the engine for access to the cylinder head face. Rotate the crankshaft to bring the pistons to mid-stroke (none at TDC), then remove the liner clamps.

19 Check that the head mating surface is clean and that the two locating dowels are present. Place a 5 mm diameter rod in the hole beneath the dowel at the flywheel end to stop the dowel being displaced downwards.

20 Fit a new cylinder head gasket, dry, with the protruding tab at the flywheel end (photo).

21 Lower the assembled cylinder head into position, making sure that it engages with the dowels.

22 Fit the cylinder head bolts, with their threads clean and lightly oiled. Remember to fit the spacer to the bolt above the coolant pump.

23 Tighten the cylinder head bolts progressively in the order shown in Fig. 1.20 to the Stage 1 specified torque.

24 Slacken bolt No 1 and then retighten it to the Stage 2 specified torque. Tighten the bolt further through the angle specified for Stage 3. Repeat this operation on the other bolts in sequence.

25 Fit the camshaft sprocket backplate, using a 10 mm rod through the timing hole to locate it precisely before tightening its securing bolts.

26 Fit the camshaft sprocket, washer and bolt. Use the 10 mm rod to lock the sprocket in the correct position and tighten the bolt to the specified torque. Remove the rod.

27 Fit the engine mounting bracket and tighten its bolts (photo).

28 Fit and secure the coolant pump, using a new gasket. Tighten the bolts to the specified torque.

29 Fit the covers around the coolant pump, noting the locations of the various special bolts (Fig. 1.22).

30 Fit the Woodruff key and the crankshaft sprocket.

31 Fit the camshaft drivebelt tensioner, but leave the nuts slack. Compress the spring by locking the cam in the horizontal position.

32 Temporarily fit the crankshaft pulley, its washer and bolt; lightly tighten the bolt. Carefully turn the crankshaft until a 10 mm rod will pass through the timing hole in the pulley and into the timing recess. If piston/valve contact occurs, back off and try again with the camshaft in a slightly different position. **Do not** try to force the crankshaft if a piston contacts a valve.

36.12 Special bolt fits here

36.20 Head gasket correctly fitted

36.27 Fitting the engine mounting bracket

33 Use the 10 mm rod to position the camshaft sprocket, then remove the crankshaft pulley and fit the camshaft drivebelt. Be careful not to kink the belt as it is fitted, and observe the arrows showing the correct direction of rotation. The white stripes on the belt should align with the timing marks on the sprockets.

34 Withdraw the timing rod. Tension the belt by turning the tensioner cam so that it points downwards; secure it with its locknut. Tighten the two nuts at the front of the tensioner.

35 Turn the crankshaft through two full turns in the normal direction of rotation; rotate it further to bring Nos. 1 and 4 pistons to TDC with the valves on No 1 cylinder both partially open (ie 'rocking').

36 Slacken the two nuts and the cam locknut on the drivebelt tensioner, then retighten them.

37 Temporarily refit the crankshaft pulley, rotate the crankshaft and check that the timing rods can be inserted simultaneously in the crankshaft pulley and camshaft sprocket holes. If not, remove the belt and try again. Remove the pulley.

38 Fit the drivebelt covers in the sequence shown in Fig. 1.23. (Note, however, that they will have to be removed to retension the drivebelt if a new one has been fitted).

39 Fit the crankshaft pulley, washer and bolt, making sure that the Woodruff key is still in position. Jam the starter ring gear teeth and tighten the bolt to the specified torque.

40 Refit the camshaft cover, noting the copper washer and diagnostic socket at the sprocket end bolt, and using a new gasket.

41 Refit the ancillary components listed below:

    (a) Oil pressure switch
    (b) New oil filter
    (c) Oil filler and breather pipes (photo)
    (d) Alternator and drivebelt

Fig. 1.22 Drivebelt cover special bolts (Sec 36)

Apply sealant to bolt threads A

H.2511/2

Fig. 1.23 Fit the covers in numerical sequence (Sec 36)

36.41 Oil filler and breather pipes

37 Engine – reconnection to transmission

1 Check that the clutch release components are correctly fitted in the gearbox and that the pressure plate and friction disc are fitted to the flywheel.

2 Smear a little anti-seize compound on the nose and splines of the transmission input shaft, then offer the transmission to the engine. Do not allow the weight of the transmission to hang on the input shaft. If the input shaft does not wish to pass the clutch, it is possible that the clutch disc is not centred. Check also that the transmission input shaft is compatible with the spigot recess in the crankshaft (Section 34 paragraphs 7 and 8).

3 Engage the engine-to-transmission dowels and loosely fit the bolts. Also fit the starter motor, which is secured by three Allen bolts and a bracket. Tighten the bolts to the specified torque.

38 Engine – refitting

Refitting is a reversal of the removal procedure given in Section 28 with particular attention to the following points:

- (a) Use a final drive oil seal protector (photo) when inserting the right-hand driveshaft. Remove the protector when the driveshaft is fitted
- (b) Adjust the clutch cable, with reference to Chapter 5, and the throttle cable, with reference to Chapter 3
- (c) Tighten the exhaust flange bolts, as described in Chapter 3
- (d) If necessary, adjust the right-hand engine mounting side buffers with spacers to give the clearances shown in Fig. 1.24
- (e) Fill the engine with oil
- (f) Fill the cooling system, as described in Chapter 2
- (g) Route the wiring as shown in Fig. 1.25

38.1 Right-hand driveshaft oil seal protector

Fig. 1.24 Engine right-hand mounting (Sec 38)

a = 1.0 mm (0.04 in)

4 Spacer
5 Spacer

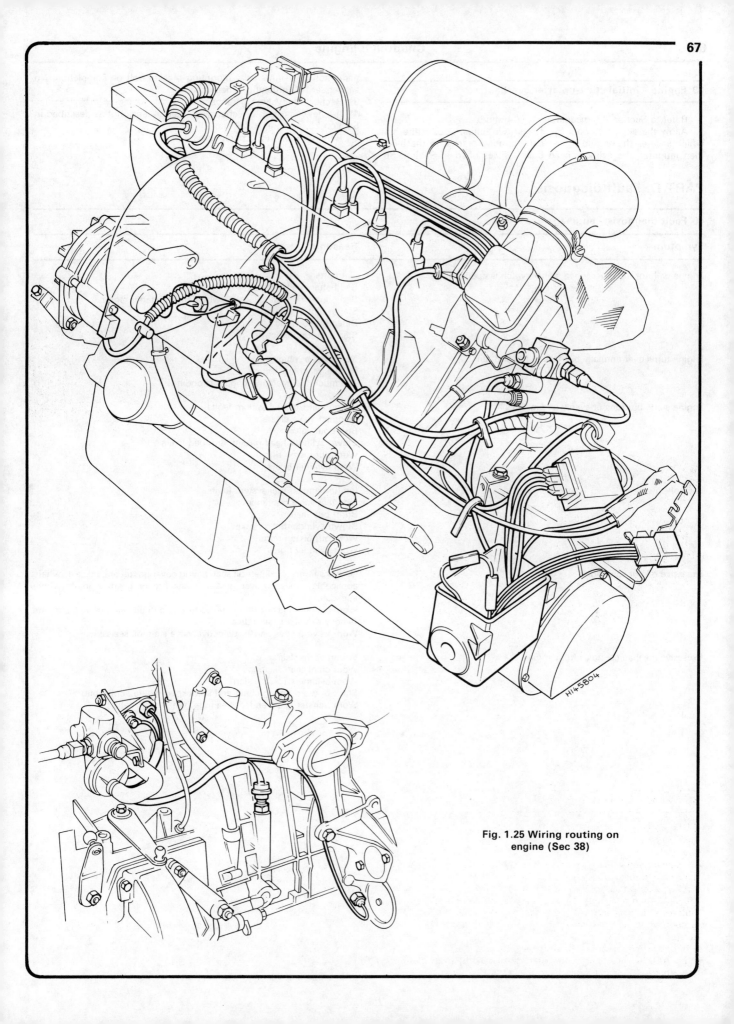

Fig. 1.25 Wiring routing on engine (Sec 38)

39 Engine – initial start-up after overhaul

1 Refer to Section 22, paragraphs 1, 3, 4 and 5.
2 Allow the engine to cool for at least two hours. Loosen the bolt which secures the engine right-hand mounting bracket to the block then retighten the cylinder head bolts, as described in Section 36, paragraph 24. Tighten the mounting bracket bolt on completion. No subsequent retightening is necessary.
3 Recheck the valve clearances.
4 If a new camshaft drivebelt was fitted, retension it as described in Section 25, paragraphs 20 and 21.
5 Refer to Section 22, paragraphs 8, 9, and 10.

PART D: Fault diagnosis

40 Fault diagnosis – engine

Symptom	Reason(s)
Engine will not turn over when starter switch is operated	Flat battery Bad battery connections Bad connections at solenoid switch and/or starter motor Starter motor jammed Defective solenoid Starter motor defective
Engine turns over normally but fails to fire and run	No sparks at plugs No fuel reaching engine Too much fuel reaching engine (flooding)
Engine starts but runs unevenly and misfires	Ignition and/or fuel system faults Incorrect valve clearance Burnt out valves Blown cylinder head gasket, dropped liners Worn out piston rings Worn cylinder bores
Lack of power	Ignition and/or fuel system faults Incorrect valve clearance Burnt out valves Blown cylinder head gasket Worn out piston rings Worn cylinder bores
Excessive oil consumption	Oil leaks from crankshaft oil seal, timing cover gasket and oil seal (where applicable), rocker cover gasket, crankcase or gearbox joint (where applicable) Worn piston rings or cylinder bores resulting in oil being burnt by engine (smoky exhaust is an indication) Worn valve guides and/or defective valve stem oil seals
Excessive mechanical noise from engine	Wrong valve clearance Worn crankshaft bearings Worn cylinders (piston slap) Slack or worn timing chain and sprockets (where applicable) Worn transfer gears and/or bearings (where applicable)

Chapter 2 Cooling system

For modifications, and information applicable to later models, see Supplement at end of manual

Contents

Specifications

General

System type	Pressurised with expansion tank/bottle and front-mounted radiator, electric cooling fan, water pump and thermostat

System capacity:
XV8 and XW7 engines	5.8 litres (10.2 pints)
XY7 and XY8 engines	6.0 litres (10.6 pints)
XU5J engine	6.6 litres (11.6 pints)

Pressure cap setting:
XU5J engine	1.0 bar (14.5 lbf/in²)
Except XU5J engine	0.8 bar (11.6 lbf/in²)

Thermostat:
Starts to open	79° to 82° (174° to 180°F)
Fully open (7.5 mm/0.296 in)	93°C (199°F)
Warning lamp switch cut-in temperature	102 to 108°C (216 to 226°F)

Electric coolant fan operating temperatures:

	Cut-in	Cut-out
XV8 and XW7 engines	87 to 89.5°C (189 to 193°F)	77.5 to 81°C (172 to 178°F)
XY engine (up to engine 5065000)	87 to 89.5°C (189 to 193°F)	77.5 to 81°C (172 to 178°F)
XY engine (from engine 5065001):		
1st stage	82 to 86°C (180 to 187°F)	77 to 81°C (171 to 178°F)
2nd stage	86 to 90°C 187 to 194°F)	81 to 85°C (178 to 185°F)
XU5J engine:		
1st stage	82 to 86°C (180 to 187°F)	77 to 81°C (171 to 178°F)
2nd stage	86 to 90°C (187 to 194°F)	81 to 85°C (178 to 185°F)

Temperature sensor (XU5J engine):
Resistance at 40°C (104°F)	1045 to 1215 ohm
Resistance at 95.6°C (206°F)	136 to 150 ohm
Antifreeze type/specification	Ethylene glycol based antifreeze (Duckhams Universal Antifreeze and Summer Coolant)

Antifreeze mixture:
Protection to −15°C (5°F)	27% antifreeze
Protection to −35°C (−31°F)	50% antifreeze

Torque wrench settings

	Nm	lbf ft
Water pump:		
XU5J engine	15	11
Except XU5J engine	13	10
Thermostat elbow	15	11

1 General description

The cooling system is of pressurised type incorporating an expansion bottle on non-GTI models and an expansion tank on GTI models. The system includes a front-mounted cross-flow radiator, thermoswitch controlled electric cooling fan, water pump and thermostat. The car interior heater matrix is supplied with a continuous supply of coolant since there is no water valve and the hot air supply is controlled by an air flap.

On GTI models the water pump is driven by the engine camshaft drivebelt, but on non-GTI models it is driven by the alternator drivebelt.

The cooling system functions in the following way. After a cold start the thermostat valve is shut and coolant circulation is restricted to the engine and heater matrix. When the coolant reaches the normal engine operating temperature the thermostat starts to open and coolant circulation also flows through the radiator. The engine temperature is then controlled by the thermostat and the electric cooling fan located on the front of the radiator.

Fig. 2.1 Cooling system layout for non-GTI models (Sec 1)

1 Radiator	4 Electric cooling fan thermoswitch	7 Expansion bottle
2 Thermostat	5 Electric cooling fan and motor	8 Radiator filler plug
3 Coolant temperature switch	6 Heater matrix	9 Water pump

Fig. 2.2 Cooling system layout for GTI models (Sec 1)

1 Radiator	4 Temperature gauge sensor	7 Expansion tank
2 Thermostat	5 Electric cooling fan thermoswitch	8 Water pump
3 Coolant temperature switch	6 Heater matrix	9 Electric cooling fan and motor

2 Routine maintenance

Carry out the following procedures at the intervals given in Routine Maintenance at the beginning of the manual.

1 Check the level of coolant in the expansion bottle/tank with the engine cold and top up to the maximum mark if necessary (refer to Section 3, paragraph 14).

2 Check the cooling system hoses, thermostat housing and water pump for leakage and rectify as necessary.

3 Drain the coolant, flush the cooling system and fill with fresh coolant, as described in Section 3.

3 Cooling system – draining, flushing and refilling

1 Unscrew the filler cap from the expansion bottle located on the front right (non-GTI models) or rear left (GTI models) of the engine compartment (photos). **Do not** remove the cap if the engine is hot, but allow it to cool first otherwise pressurised steam and boiling water may be forced out.

2 On non-GTI models unscrew and remove the filler plug fom the top left-hand side of the radiator.

3.1A Expansion bottle on non-GTI models

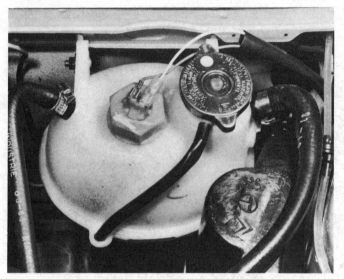

3.1B Expansion tank on GTI models

3.9A Cooling system bleed screw located in the heater return hose

3.3 Radiator drain plug (arrowed)

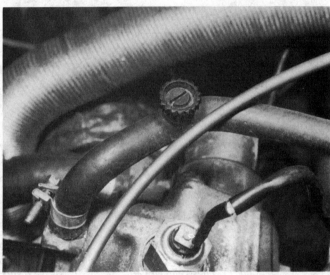

3.9B Cooling system bleed screw located in the inlet manifold
coolant hose (non-GTI models)

3 Place a suitable container beneath the left-hand side of the radiator
then unscrew the drain plug and drain the coolant (photo).

4 Drain the cylinder block by removing the plug located above the
right-hand driveshaft (non-GTI models) or above the right-hand
driveshaft intermediate bearing (GTI models).

5 On non-GTI models remove the expansion bottle and invert it to
drain the remaining coolant if necessary.

6 Provided the coolant has been renewed at the specified intervals
there should be no need to flush the system. If the system has been
neglected and the coolant contains excessive amounts of sediment,
disconnect the radiator top hose and use cold water to flush the
radiator until the water runs clear from the radiator and cylinder block.

7 In severe cases, remove the radiator and reverse flush it, or alternatively use a proprietary chemical cleaner such as Holts Radflush or Holts
Speedflush.

8 With the system clean, refit the hoses and drain plugs as necessary.

9 To refill the system, first loosen the bleed screw(s) located in the
heater return hose and, on non-GTI models only, also in the inlet
manifold coolant hose (photos).

10 On non-GTI models the manufacturers recommend that the
expansion bottle is raised as high as possible (see Fig. 2.3) to prevent
an air trap; however, in practice, the system can be refilled satisfactorily
with the bottle in its normal position.

11 Fill the system with the correct quantity of coolant (photo) and
close the bleed screw(s) when the water runs clear of air bubbles. On
non-GTI models the radiator should be first completely filled and the
filler plug retightened before the expansion bottle is refilled.

12 With the system full, refit the expansion bottle filler cap.

13 Run the engine at a fast idle speed until it reaches the normal
operating temperature indicated by the electric cooling fan cutting in.
Run it for several more minutes then switch off and allow to cool for
approximately 2 hours.

14 Top up the coolant level in the expansion bottle and refit the cap.
On non-GTI models the bottle incorporates maximum and minimum
level marks visible from the outside, but on GTI models a stepped tube
is fitted in the filler neck.

Fig. 2.3 Tie up the expansion bottle when refilling the cooling system (Sec 3)

3.11 Filling the expansion bottle on non-GTI models

Fig. 2.4 Fill the radiator full on non-GTI models (Sec 3)

Fig. 2.5 Expansion bottle level marks on non-GTI models (Sec 3)

Fig. 2.6 Level indicators in the expansion tank on GTI models (Sec 3)

a   Maximum   b   Minimum

4 Coolant mixture – general

1   Plain water should never be used in the cooling system. Apart from giving protection against freezing, an antifreeze mixture protects the engine internal surfaces and components against corrosion. This is very important in an alloy engine.
2   Always use a top quality glycol-based antifreeze which is recommended for alloy engines.
3   Ideally a 50% mixture of antifreeze and soft or demineralised water should be used to maintain maximum protection against freezing and corrosion. On no account use less than 25% antifreeze.

4 Renew the coolant at the specified intervals as the inhibitors contained in the antifreeze gradually lose their effectiveness.
5 Even when operating in climates where antifreeze is not required never use plain water, but add a corrosion inhibitor to it.

5 Thermostat – removal, testing and refitting

1 The thermostat housing is located on the cylinder head adjacent to the distributor.
2 Drain the cooling system as previously described.
3 Disconnect the radiator top hose from the thermostat housing (photo). On GTI models first remove the air inlet duct from the air cleaner.
4 Unscrew and remove the two thermostat housing cover bolts and remove the cover. This may need a little persuasion with a wooden or plastic-faced hammer (photo).
5 Remove the thermostat. If it is stuck, do not lever it out under its bridge piece, but cut around its edge with a sharp knife.
6 Remove the rubber ring(s) and clean the mating faces of the housing and cover.

5.3 Thermostat housing on non-GTI models (arrowed)

5.4 Removing the thermostat housing cover on non-GTI models

7 If the thermostat is suspected of being faulty, suspend it in a container of water which is being heated. Using a thermometer, check that the thermostat starts to open at the specified temperature and is fully open also at the specified temperature.
8 Remove the thermostat from the water and allow it to cool. The valve plate should close smoothly.
9 If the unit fails to operate as described or is stuck open or shut, renew it with one of similar temperature rating (photo).

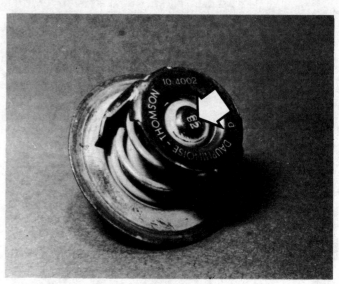

5.9 Thermostat, showing temperature rating (arrowed)

10 Fit the thermostat and new rubber ring(s). Bolt on the cover.
11 Reconnect the coolant hose and refill and bleed the system, as described in Section 3.

6 Radiator – removal, repair and refitting

1 Drain the cooling system, as described in Section 3.
2 Remove the front grille (Chapter 12) then unbolt the engine compartment front crossmember (photos).
3 Disconnect the top and bottom hoses from the radiator and, on GTI models, disconnect and unclip the vent hose for the expansion tank (photo).
4 Disconnect the wiring from the electric cooling fan, the thermo-switch and, where applicable, the low level sensor.
5 Disconnect the top mountings, as applicable, then lift the radiator, complete with cooling fan, from the car – taking care not to damage the matrix. The base of the radiator incorporates pins which locate in rubber mountings.
6 If necessary separate the cooling fan, with reference to Section 7.
7 The radiator side tanks are plastic on non-GTI models or a copper core on GTI models. If the radiator is leaking it must either by renewed or exchanged for a reconditioned unit. However, in an emergency repairs may be possible by adding a proprietary product to the coolant such as Holts Radweld with the radiator in situ.
8 Refitting is a reversal of removal; fill the cooling system as described in Section 3.

7 Cooling fan and thermoswitch – removal and refitting

1 The electric cooling fan may be removed with the radiator, as described in the preceding Section, and then separated. Alternatively it may be unbolted or unclipped (as applicable) from the radiator after having removed the front grille and crossmember. The motor can be

6.2A Engine compartment front
crossmember mounting bolts (arrowed)

6.2B View of radiator with front grille and
crossmember removed (GTI models)

6.3 Vent hose for the expansion tank (GTI
models)

7.1A Clip for retaining the electric cooling
fan assembly to the radiator (GTI models)

7.1B Electric cooling fan motor and
mounting bolts

7.1C Cooling fan motor resistor on wing
valance

7.2 Electric cooling fan thermoswitch and
wiring

8.1 Coolant temperature switch – arrowed
(non-GTI models)

unbolted from the frame and then the fan removed from the motor
(photos). No spare parts are available for the motor.
2 The thermostatically controlled switch for the cooling fan is
screwed into the radiator. Before this can be removed, the system must
be drained and the switch leads disconnected (photo).
3 When refitting the switch, use a new sealing ring.

8 Coolant temperature switch, gauge and level switch – general

1 The coolant temperature switch is located in the left-hand end of

the cylinder head on non-GTI models and beneath the thermostat
housing on GTI models (photo).
2 It is difficult to test a temperature switch without special equipment
and the best method to use if a fault develops is to substitute a new
switch, but only after the wiring to the gauge has been thoroughly
checked.
3 When refitting the switch, make sure that the seal is in good
condition and do not overtighten it.
4 If the switch is changed and the gauge still does not register, then
the gauge should be checked by a competent auto-electrician. Access
to the gauge is obtained after removing the instrument panel, as
described in Chapter 12.
5 On non-GTI models, the coolant level switch is located in the

Fig. 2.7 Cutaway diagram of the coolant level switch (Sec 8)

   1   Body
   2   Terminal connections
   3   Float
   4   Magnet
   5   Reed contact (inside glass
      bulb)
   a   Off position (float lifts magnet above reed contact)
   b   On position (magnetic field switches on reed contact)

radiator right-hand side tank, but on GTI models it is located in the expansion tank. The switch is float-operated and actuates a warning lamp in the event of a low coolant level. If the switch malfunctions it must be renewed as no repair is possible.

---

9   Water pump – removal and refitting

1   Drain the cooling system, as described in Section 3.

Non-GTI models
2   Remove the drivebelt, as described in Chapter 12.
3   Disconnect the radiator bottom hose, heater return hose, and inlet manifold return hose from the water pump (photo). For better access, remove the air cleaner and inlet cowl, with reference to Chapter 3.
4   Unscrew the mounting bolts and remove the water pump from the cylinder block. Remove the O-ring (photos).

GTI models
5   Remove the camshaft drivebelt, as described in Chapter 1, followed by the tensioner.
6   Remove the plastic shield, noting the locations of the different types of bolt.
7   Unscrew the five mounting bolts and remove the water pump from the cylinder block. Remove the gasket.

All models
8   If the water pump is worn, noisy or leaks coolant it must be renewed, as repair is not possible. However, on non-GTI models, if either of the

half casings is individually damaged it may be renewed, together with the central gasket.
9   Refitting is a reversal of removal, but clean the mating faces and always fit a new O-ring or gasket, as applicable. Fill the cooling system, as described in Section 3, and on non-GTI models tension the drivebelt, as described in Chapter 12.

Fig. 2.8 Water pump fitted to non-GTI models (Sec 9)

   1   Pulley and vane assembly   *3   End casing*
   2   Gasket   *4   O-ring*

Fig. 2.9 Water pump fitted to GTI models (Sec 9)

   1   Gasket   *2   Water pump*

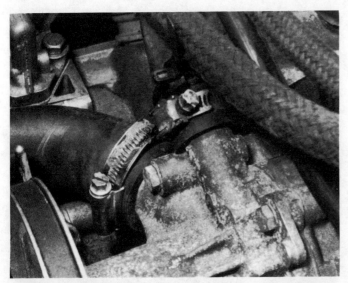

9.3 Bottom hose and heater return hose locations on the water pump (non-GTI models)

9.4B Withdrawing the water pump from the cylinder block (non-GTI models)

9.4A Removing the water pump mounting bolts (non-GTI models)

9.4C The water pump O-ring in the cylinder block- non-GTI models

10 Fault diagnosis – cooling system

Symptom	Reason(s)
Overheating	Insufficient coolant in system Loose drivebelt (non-GTI models only) Radiator blocked either internally or externally Thermostat not opening Electric cooling fan or thermoswitch faulty Pressure cap faulty
Overcooling	Faulty, incorrect or missing thermostat Electric cooling fan thermoswitch not switching off
Loss of coolant	Damaged hoses or loose clips Leaking water pump O-ring or gasket, as applicable

Chapter 3 Fuel and exhaust systems

For modifications, and information applicable to later models, see Supplement at end of manual

Contents

Specifications

Carburettor engines
General

System type	Rear-mounted fuel tank, mechanical fuel pump, single or twin carburettor
Fuel tank capacity	50 litres (11.0 gallons)
Fuel octane rating	97 (4-star)

Air cleaner
Champion W138

Carburettor

Type	Fixed jet, downdraught
Application:	
XV8 (954 cc)	Solex 32 PBISA
XW7 (1124 cc)	Solex 32 PBISA
XY7 (1360 cc)	Solex 34 PBISA
XY8 (1360 cc)	Solex 35 PBISA 8

Calibrations and settings:

	XV8	XW7	XY7	XY8
Choke	25 mm	25 mm	26 mm	28 mm
Main jet	120 ± 5	125 ± 5	130 ± 25	145 ± 10
Air correction jet	155 ± 20	175 ± 20	160 ± 20	175 ± 10
Idling fuel jet	44 ± 5	42 ± 5	45 ± 5	47 ± 5
Acceleration pump injector	35 ± 5	32 ± 5	40 ± 5	40 ± 10
Enricher calibration	55 ± 20	60 ± 20	75 ± 20	–
Needle valve	1.6 mm	1.6 mm	1.6 mm	1.5 mm*
Initial throttle opening	20°40′ ± 30′	20°40′ ± 30′	20°40′ ± 30′	15°
Normal idling position	–	–	–	7° 45′
Choke opening after starting	–	–	–	2.5mm ± 0.3
Idling speed	650 ± 50 rpm	650 ± 50 rpm	650 ± 50 rpm	950 to 1000 rpm**
CO percentage	1.5 ± 0.5	1.5 ± 0.5	1.5 ± 0.5	2.0 ± 0.5

* 1.2 from serial number 5043526
** 850° to 900 rpm from serial number 5043526

Torque wrench settings

	Nm	lbf ft
Exhaust manifold	20	15
Inlet manifold	18	13
Carburettor nuts	18	13
Fuel pump	18	13

Fuel injection engine
General

System type .... Rear-mounted fuel tank, Bosch LE2-Jetronic fuel injection system, electric fuel pump

Application .... XU5J/A (1580 cc), XU9JA (1905 cc)
Fuel tank capacity .... 50 litres (11 gallons)
Fuel octane rating 97 (4-star)
Idling speed .... 850 to 900 rpm
CO% at idling .... 1 to 2
CO_2% at idling .... 10 minimum
Fuel pressure .... 2.9 to 3.1 bar (42.1 to 45.0 lbf/in²)
Fuel pump delivery .... 540 cc/15 sec
Tachometric relay cut-out speed .... 6600 rpm
Fuel cut-off speed (decelerating) .... Above 1600 rpm

Fuel filter .... Champion L205

Air cleaner .... Champion W175

Torque settings .... As carburettor engines (as applicable)

PART A: GENERAL DESCRIPTION AND ROUTINE MAINTENANCE

1 General description

The fuel system comprises a rear-mounted fuel tank, single downdraught Solex carburettor on XV8, XW7 and XY7 engines, twin downdraught Solex carburettors on the XY8 engine, and a Bosch LE2-Jetronic fuel injection system on the XU5J and XU9J engines.

On carburettor versions the fuel pump is mounted on the cylinder head and driven by a plunger from an eccentric on the camshaft. On the fuel injection system the electric fuel pump is located in the fuel tank.

The air cleaner incorporates a dry element and the inlet air is temperature controlled.

2 Routine maintenance

Carry out the following procedures at the intervals given in Routine Maintenance at the beginning of the manual.
1 Check all fuel lines and hoses for damage and security, including those located on the underbody.
2 Check the accelerator pedal operation and the throttle cable for correct adjustment.
3 Renew the air filter element (Section 3 or 18).
4 On carburettor engines, clean the fuel pump filter (Section 5).
5 On fuel injection engines, to renew the fuel filter first unscrew the union bolt from the top of the unit (photo) then place the bolt union and washers to one side and cover to prevent ingress of dirt. Unscrew

the clamp bolt, then lift the filter and unscrew the bottom union. Fit the new filter using a reversal of the removal procedure; making sure that dust and dirt is prevented from entering the fuel lines.

2.5 Fuel filter canister on fuel injection models

PART B: CARBURETTOR ENGINES

3 Air cleaner element – renewal

1 Unscrew the wing nut on the air cleaner casing end-face (photo).
2 Withdraw the end cover with element (photo).
3 Discard the element and wipe the casing interior clean.
4 Fit the new element and the cover, tighten the wing nut.

3.1 Air cleaner and wing nut

3.2 Removing the air cleaner element

4 Air cleaner – removal and refitting

1 Disconnect the intake and warm air hoses.
2 Release the rubber straps from the mounting brackets (photo).
3 Lift the air cleaner from the brackets then disconnect the outlet hose and, where fitted, the crankcase ventilation hose.
4 If necessary, unbolt the mounting brackets – noting the location of the diagnostic socket and cable retaining brackets (photos).
5 Refitting is a reversal of removal.

4.2 Air cleaner rubber strap

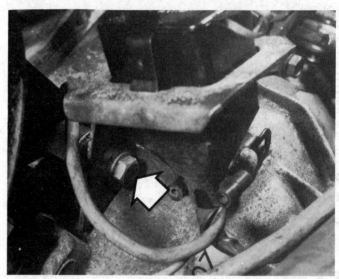

4.4A Air cleaner bracket bolt (arrowed) also retaining diagnostic socket

4.4B Cable retaining bracket on air cleaner bracket

5.1 Removing the fuel pump cover

5.2 Removing the fuel pump filter

6.2 Removing the fuel pump

5 Fuel pump – cleaning

1 The fuel pump may be one of several types. On one type, the filter cover is simply unbolted and removed. On another, the pump cover is removed (two screws). With some pumps, the fuel outlet hose must be removed in order to be able to withdraw the pump cover. Inspection will determine (photo).
2 With the cover removed, take out the filter screen and wash it in fuel until it is free from fluff and dirt (photo).
3 Mop out the fuel from the pump body and wipe out any sediment.
4 Refit the filter screen and cover, making sure that the gasket is in good condition.

6 Fuel pump – removal, overhaul and refitting

1 Disconnect the fuel hoses from the pump. Plug the inlet hose.
2 Unscrew the pump mounting bolts and lift the pump away (photo).
3 Remove the gasket.
4 Once the pump is removed, the pushrod may be withdrawn.
5 If the pump is to be dismantled, remove the cover, gasket and filter screen.
6 Scribe a mark across the edges of the upper and lower body flanges and extract the flange screws.
7 Remove the upper body.
8 Drive out the operating arm pivot pin, withdraw the arm and lift out the diaphragm.
9 Obtain a repair kit which will contain a new diaphragm and the necessary gaskets.
10 If the valves are damaged, reassemble the pump and obtain a new one complete.
11 If the valves are in good condition, locate the diaphragm, push the operating arm into position so that its forked end engages with the groove in the end of the diaphragm rod, with the coil springs in position.
12 Fit the pivot pin and stake around the holes to secure both ends of the pin.
13 Fit the upper body so that the alignment marks are opposite and then fit the screws and tighten evenly.
14 Fit the filter screen and cover with gasket.
15 Refitting to the cylinder head is a reversal of removal, but fit a new gasket.

7 Fuel level transmitter – removal and refitting

1 Disconnect the battery earth lead.
2 Raise the rear seat cushion.

Fig. 3.1 Exploded view of the fuel pump (Sec 6)

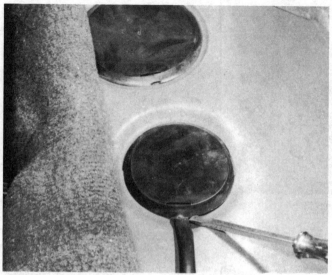

7.3A Prise up the cover ...

8.6 Fuel tank mounting bolt

7.3B ... for access to the fuel level transmitter (fuel supply and
return pipes also shown)

3   Remove the circular plastic cover to expose the fuel level
transmitter (photos).
4   Disconnect the electrical lead.
5   Using a suitable tool, unscrew the transmitter mounting plate to
release it from the securing tabs.
6   Withdraw the transmitter unit, taking care not to damage the float
as it passes through the hole in the tank.
7   Refitting is a reversal of removal, but use a new sealing ring if there
is any doubt about the condition of the original one.

8   Fuel tank – removal, repair and refitting

1   As a drain plug is not fitted, the tank must be syphoned empty of
fuel using a length of plastic or rubber tubing.
2   Either remove the complete exhaust system or on later models
release the support band on the silencer, and lower the system using a

jack under the tailpipe.
3   Release the handbrake cables from their fuel tank and other guide
sleeves. there is no need to disconnect the cables.
4   Unbolt and remove the heat shield.
5   Disconnect the wiring from the fuel level transmitter (Section 7).
6   Unscrew the mounting and safety strap bolts (photo) and nuts,
then lower the tank – at the same time disconnecting the filler, breather
and supply hoses.
7   As the tank is of plastic construction, any leak due to damage can
only be rectified by renewal of the assembly.
8   If the tank contains sediment, pour in some paraffin, remove the
fuel level transmitter and shake the tank vigorously. Repeat as
necessary and finally rinse out with clean fuel.
9   Refitting is a reversal of removal.

9   Carburettors – description

A Solex carburettor is fitted to all models as listed in the
Specifications, but the XY8 engine (GT) has two carburettors linked
together. All carburettors are of single choke fixed jet design with a
manually-operated choke. On the XY8 engine the choke is automatically opened after starting by a vacuum device.

10 Carburettor – idle speed and mixture adjustment

Solex 32 and 34 PBISA
1   The following adjustments must be made with the ignition timing
correctly adjusted, the air cleaner and filter element fitted, and the engine
at normal operating temperature.
2   Connect a tachometer to the engine and where necessary remove the
tamperproof cap from the mixture adjustment screw.
Without an exhaust gas analyser
3   Turn the throttle stop screw to adjust the engine speed to 650 rpm.
4   Turn the mixture adjustment screw to obtain the highest idling speed.
5   Repeat the procedure given in paragraphs 3 and 4 until the engine
speed is 650 rpm (ie after adjusting the mixture screw).
6   Screw in the mixture adjustment screw slightly until the engine
speed starts to decrease.
With an exhaust gas analyser
7   Turn the throttle stop screw to adjust the engine speed to 650 rpm.
8   Turn the mixture adjustment screw to obtain the specified CO
reading.
9   Repeat the procedure in paragraphs 7 and 8 until the idle speed is
650 rpm.

H14.5811

Fig. 3.2 Fuel tank components (Sec 8)

1 Access cover
2 Fuel level transmitter
3 Outlet assembly and filter
4 Fuel tank
5 Heat shield
6 Safety strap

Fig. 3.3 Throttle stop screw (A) on Solex 32 and 34 PBISA carburettors (Sec 10)

Fig. 3.4 Mixture adjustment screw (B) on Solex 32 and 34 PBISA carburettors (Sec 10)

Fig. 3.5 Adjustment screw locations on the Solex 35 PBISA 8 carburettor (Sec 10)

1 Mixture screw	3 Combined idle speed screw	5 Pipe	a Vacuum gauge pipe
2 Mixture screw	4 Pipe	6 Screw	b Vacuum gauge pipe

Solex 35 PBISA 8

10 Before attempting to adjust the idle speed and mixture ensure that the carburettors are synchronised. Refer to Fig. 3.5 for screw locations.

Synchronising with a vacuum gauge

11 Have the engine at working temperature with the air cleaner removed.

12 Turn the mixture screws (1) and (2) in until they lightly seat and then unscrew them four complete turns.

13 With the engine running, set the idle speed screw (3) until the speed is 1000 rpm.

14 Disconnect the pipes (4) and (5) and connect the gauge pipe (a).

15 Turn the screw (3) to obtain a reading on the gauge of 100 mmHg (150 mbar).

16 Transfer the gauge pipe to (b). If the reading is not as previously recorded, turn the screw (6) in or out until it is.

17 Blip the throttle once or twice and check that both vacuum readings are as previously indicated.

Synchronising with a synchroniser

18 These are available at most motor stores and should be used as directed by the manufacturers.

19 These instruments are basically airflow meters and should show identical readings when moved from one venturi to the other. Adjust where necessary by turning screws (3) and (6).

Idle speed and mixture adjustment without an exhaust gas analyser

20 Have the engine at normal operating temperature.

21 Disconnect the twin wiring plug from the rear face of the alternator.

22 Turn the mixture screws (1) and (2) in until they lightly seat and then unscrew them four complete turns.

23 Obtain the highest idle speed by turning the mixture screws (1) and (2) by equal amounts.

24 Reset the idle speed to 1000 rpm by means of screw (3).

25 Repeat the operations with screws (1) and (2) and then reset once again by using screw (3).

26 With the engine idling at 1000 rpm reduce its speed by screwing in screws (1) and (2) equally until the engine speed drops to 970 rpm.

27 Reconnect the alternator wiring plug and, where originally fitted, fit new tamperproof caps to screws (1) and (2).

Idle speed and mixture adjustment with an exhaust gas analyser

28 Follow the procedure given in paragaphs 20 to 22.

29 Set the idle speed to 950 rpm by means of screw (3).

30 Turn the mixture screws (1) and (2) until the CO level is as specified.

31 Reset the idle speed to specified level using screw (3).

32 Reconnect the alternator wiring plug and, where originally fitted, fit new tamperproof caps to screws (1) and (2).

11 Carburettor – removal and refitting

1 Remove the air cleaner, as desribed in Section 4.

2 Unscrew the bolts or nuts and remove the air intake duct from the top of the carburettor(s).

3 Remove the short hose which runs between the oil filler cap and the carburettor. Disconnect the solenoid valve wiring, where fitted.

4 Disconnect the distributor vacuum hose from the carburettor. Disconnect the vacuum gauge hoses (where applicable).

5 Disconnect the fuel intake hose(s) from the carburettor(s) (photo).

6 Disconnect the balljointed throttle control rod from the carburettor(s) (photo).

7 Disconnect the choke cable (Section 15).

8 Disconnect and plug the carburettor coolant hose(s).

9 Disconnect the brake servo vacuum hose (if applicable).

10 Unscrew the mounting nuts and lift the carburettor(s) from the inlet manifold. Remove the gasket(s).

11 Refitting is a reversal of removal, but renew the gasket(s) and bleed the cooling system, as described in Chapter 2.

12 Carburettor (Solex 32 and 34 PBISA) – dismantling, reassembly and adjustment

1 Remove the screws and lift off the float chamber cover (photo).

2 Unscrew the air correction jet, followed by the main jet and idling fuel jet.

3 Unscrew the accelerator pump valve and remove the pump injector.

11.5 Hoses attached to carburettor

11.6 Throttle control rod – arrowed (XY8 engine)

12.1 Removing the float chamber cover on the Solex PBISA carburettor

4   Remove the enricher valve.
5   Unscrew the needle valve.
6   Clean the float chamber and removed components with fuel and blow through the internal channels using an air line if possible.
7   Obtain a repair kit of gaskets then reassemble the carburettor in reverse order. The float level is not adjustable.
8   The only adjustment possible is the fast idle setting of the throttle valve. To adjust this accurately it will be necessary to measure the angular movement of the throttle valve. The use of a piece of card with the angle drawn on it will provide the necessary setting.
9   Fully close the choke valve then check that the throttle valve has opened by 20° 40′ ± 30′.
10 If necessary turn the fast idle adjustment screw as required.

H145812

Fig. 3.6 Exploded view of the Solex 32 PBISA carburettor (Sec 12)

1 Float chamber cover	4 Accelerator pump injector	7 Main jet	10 Idling fuel jet
2 Needle valve	5 Air correction jet	8 Idle mixture screw	11 Throttle stop screw
3 Float	6 Main body	9 Enricher device	

Fig. 3.7 Exploded view of the Solex 34 PBISA carburettor (Sec 12)

1	Float chamber cover	4	Accelerator pump injector
2	Needle valve	5	Air correction jet
3	Float	6	Main body

7	Main jet	9	Enricher device
8	Idle mixture screw	10	Idling fuel jet

13 Carburettor (Solex 35 PBISA 8) – dismantling, reassembly and adjustment

1   The dismantling and reassembly procedure is identical to that for the carburettor described in Section 12, but there is no enricher valve. The adjustment procedure is as follows.

2   To adjust the initial throttle valve opening, fully unscrew the adjustment screw then, using a piece of card as described in Section 12, turn the screw until the valve is opened by 7° 45'.

3   The fast idle setting is only made on the LH carburettor with the reference number 346. First close the choke valve then check that the throttle valve has opened by 15°. If not, turn the adjustment screw as required.

4   To adjust the choke opening after starting first close the choke then pull the vacuum opener rod and, using a suitable twist drill, check that the gap between the bottom edge of the throttle valve and the carburettor wall is 2.5 ± 0.3 mm. If not, turn the nut on the end of the vacuum opener as required.

**Fig. 3.8 Exploded view of the
Solex 35 PBISA 8 carburettor
(Sec 13)**

*1   Float chamber cover
2   Needle valve
3   Accelerator pump injector
4   Air correction jet
5   Float
6   Main body
7   Idling fuel jet
8   Idling shut-off solenoid
    (deleted from serial number
    5043526)
9   Idle mixture screw
10 Main jet*

14 Throttle cable – removal and refitting

1   The throttle cable is connected to a spring-loaded reel which pivots on the face of the cylinder head. The reel then operates the throttle lever on the carburettor through a plastic balljointed control rod.
2   Extract the spring clip from the adjustment ferrule at the cable bracket on the cylinder head.
3   Working inside the car, disconnect the cable end fitting from the top of the accelerator pedal arm (photo).
4   Release the cable from the bracket on the carburettor intake cowl (photo).
5   Withdraw the throttle cable through the bulkhead grommet.
6   Refitting is a reversal of removal, but adjust the cable at the ferrule to remove all but the slightest amount of play. Check that full throttle can be obtained with the accelerator pedal fully depressed.

15 Choke cable – removal and refitting

1   Remove the carburettor intake cowl.
2   Unscrew the pinch bolts and disconnect the inner and outer cables from the lever and bracket (photo).
3   Release the cable from the clips in the engine compartment.

14.3 Throttle pedal and cable end fitting (arrowed)

14.4 Throttle cable bracket on the intake cowl

16.2A Removing the exhaust manifold

15.2 Choke cable connection (XY8 engine)

16.2B Exhaust manifold gaskets

4   Working inside the car, disconnect the warning lamp wiring and detach the cable from the support bracket.
5   Refitting is a reversal of removal, but adjust the cable at the carburettor end so that, when the control knob is pushed fully in, the choke valve plate is fully open.

16 Manifolds and exhaust system – general

1   The inlet and exhaust manifolds are located on opposite sides of the cylinder head.
2   The exhaust manifold is simply bolted into position with separate flange gaskets for each port (photos).
3   The inlet manifold has coolant connections and before it can be removed, the cooling system should be at least partially drained to avoid any coolant running into the cylinder bores as the manifold is removed.
4   The exhaust system is in two main sections with a short extension

16.4A Exhaust silencer front joint

16.4B Exhaust rear flexible mounting

16.6 Exhaust front flange showing compression springs

connecting the exhaust manifold to the twin front section. The mountings are of flexible rubber type (photos).

5   Even if only one section of the system is to be renewed, it is recommended that the complete system is removed from under the car with the car supported on axle stands.

6   When fitting the exhaust system tighten the flange mounting nuts evenly so that the special springs are compressed equally; approximately four threads of the bolt should be visible and the springs should be compressed to 22.0 mm/0.866 in (photo) (Fig. 3.9).

7   Holts Flexiwrap and Holts Gun Gum exhaust repair systems can be used for effective repairs to exhaust pipes and silencer boxes, including ends and bends. Holts Flexiwrap is an MOT approved permanent exhaust repair.

PART C: FUEL INJECTION ENGINE

17 Fuel injection system – general description and precautions

The fuel injection system components are shown in Fig. 3.10. A roller type electric pump located in the fuel tank pumps fuel through

Fig. 3.9 Exhaust flange components showing spring compression dimension (Sec 16)

| A Exhaust downpipe | C Collar | E Chamfered edge |
| B Extension | D Ring | F Parallel faces |

Fig. 3.10 Fuel injection system components (Sec 17)

A	Securing screw	2	Fuel pump	7	Throttle switch unit	11	Tachometric relay and engine
B	Securing screw	3	Fuel filter	8	Airflow sensor		speed limiter
C	Securing screw	4	Distribution pipe	9	Supplementary air device	12	Electric control unit (LHD
D	ECU connector	5	Injectors	10	Temperature sensor		model shown)
1	Fuel pump housing	6	Fuel pressure regulator			13	Connector

17.1 Injectors and distribution pipe

18.2 Removing the air cleaner end cover

the filter to the injectors via a distribution pipe (photo). The electronic control unit which is triggered by the ignition circuit sends impulses to the injectors which operate simultaneously and inject fuel in the vicinity of the inlet valves. The electronic control unit is provided with sensors to determine engine temperature, speed and load, and the quantity of air entering the engine. This information is computed to determine the period of injection.

For cold starting, additional fuel is provided and, to compensate for this, additional air is provided by a supplementary air device.

The following Sections describe procedures which can be carried out by the home mechanic. Work involving the use of pressure gauges is not included.

In order to prevent damage to the electrical components of the system the battery must **never** be disconnected with the engine running, the electronic control unit must not be disconnected with the ignition on, and a test lamp must not be used for checking the circuits.

18.3 Removing the element

18 Air cleaner element – renewal

1   Disconnect the air duct from the end of the air cleaner.
2   Unscrew the nuts and remove the end cover (photo).
3   Extract the element (photo).
4   Discard the element and wipe the casing interior clean.
5   Insert the new element then refit the end cover and air duct.

19 Air cleaner – removal and refitting

1   Disconnect the inlet and outlet ducts.
2   Unscrew the mounting bolts and lift the air cleaner from the engine.
3   Refitting is a reversal of removal.

20 Throttle initial position – checking and adjustment

1   Run the engine to normal operating temperature – indicated when the electric cooling fan has cut in and out twice. The ignition timing must be correctly adjusted, as described in Chapter 4.
2   Connect a vacuum gauge to the test point (Fig. 3.11) in the distributor vacuum advance line.
3   Check that the throttle movement is smooth.
4   With the engine stopped turn the air screw fully in (photo).
5   Prise the tamperproof cap from the throttle stop screw (photo).

20.4 Air (volume) adjustment screw

20.5 Throttle stop screw (arrowed)

Fig. 3.11 Vacuum gauge test point (1) (Sec 20)

6 Loosen the two screws on the throttle switch unit.
7 Unscrew the throttle stop screw then retighten it until it just touches the throttle lever. Tighten the screw a further four complete turns.
8 Adjust the idling speed and mixture, as described in the following Section.

21 Idle speed and mixture – adjustment

Note: *Fine adjustment of the idle speed should be done using the air screw (photo 20.4)*

1 Connect a tachometer and an exhaust gas analyser to the engine.
2 With the throttle initial position set, as described in Section 20, run the engine at idle speed.
3 Turn the throttle stop screw to obtain an idle speed of 650

rpm. Check that the vacuum reading does not exceed 50 mmHg (65 mbar) and if necessary adjust the throttle stop screw.
4 Stop the engine and adjust the throttle switch, as described in Section 22.
5 With the engine at normal operating temperature, unscrew the air screw to set the idling speed between 850 and 900 rpm.
6 Check that the CO reading is between 1 and 2% and the CO_2 reading is more than 10%.
7 If adjustment is necessary, prise out the tamperproof cap on the airflow sensor (photo) and use an Allen key to adjust the mixture. Turn the screw in to richen the mixture and out to weaken it.
8 Blip the throttle two or three times and then recheck that the idle speed and mixture is correct.
9 If the CO_2 reading is less than 10% check that the air filter is clean and that there are no leaks in the inlet or exhaust systems. It is important that the engine oil level dipstick is pushed fully into its guide tube after having checked the oil level. If left partially withdrawn, the fuel mixture strength will be upset.

21.7 The mixture adjustment screw is located below this tamperproof cap (arrowed)

Fig. 3.12 Mixture adjustment screw (2) (Sec 21)

22 Throttle switch – checking and adjustment

1 Pull the connector from the throttle switch (photo).
2 Connect a voltmeter between the middle terminal on the connector and earth.
3 Pull the connector from the ignition control module (see Chapter 4), then operate the starter motor and check that there is a reading of at least 9 volts.
4 Disconnect the air hose from the throttle housing.
5 Position a 0.30 mm (0.012 in) feeler blade between the throttle stop screw and the throttle lever.
6 Loosen the two throttle switch screws.
7 Connect an ohmmeter between terminals 18 and 2 on the throttle switch, then rotate the switch until the internal contacts close and the reading is zero ohms. Tighten the screws with the switch in this position.
8 Remove the feeler blade and insert in its place a 0.70 mm (0.028 in) feeler blade. The internal contacts should now be separated and the reading on the ohmmeter infinity. If not, repeat the procedure in paragraph 7.
9 Remove the feeler blade.
10 Check the full throttle operation by connecting an ohmmeter between terminals 18 and 3, then fully opening the throttle so that dimension X (Fig. 3.14) is 4.0 mm (0.158 in). The internal contacts should close and the ohmmeter reading be zero.
11 If the switch does not operate correctly it should be renewed.

Fig. 3.14 Full throttle dimension X (Sec 22)

4   Throttle lever   X = 4.0 mm (0.158 in)
7   Throttle housing

22.1 Removing the throttle switch connector

Fig. 3.13 Adjusting the throttle switch (Sec 22)

3   Idle speed adjustment screw   4   Throttle lever

23 Air intake system – checking for leaks

1 For the correct operation of the airflow sensor there must be no air entering the system upstream of the sensor.
2 Check that there is no leakage at the points arrowed in Fig. 3.15 or at the inlet manifold gasket.
3 If an air line is available, disconnect the airflow sensor inlet hose and use an adaptor to blow air through the intake system while fully opening the throttle, blocking the exhaust pipe and pinching the crankcase breather hose. If the points indicated in paragraph 2 are then brushed with soapy water any bad seals will be immediately evident.

24 Fuel pump – removal and refitting

1 Raise the rear seat cushion.
2 Prise up the right-hand plastic cover then disconnect the wiring, and the fuel supply and return pipes, noting their location (photo).
3 Unscrew the retaining screws and lift the fuel pump housing from the fuel tank.
4 Release the filter from the bottom of the housing, followed by the collar.
5 Disconnect the wiring and release the fuel pump from the upper collar.
6 Refitting is a reversal of removal, but fit new collars and make sure that the wiring terminals are positioned away from the pump terminals. Always fit a new gasket between the pump housing and fuel tank.

25 Supplementary air device (cold start) – removal and refitting

1 Remove the battery (Chapter 12).
2 Disconnect the air hoses then unbolt the airflow sensor and bracket. Disconnect the wiring.
3 Unscrew the supplementary air device bracket nuts and disconnect the wiring.
4 Tilt the assembly and coolant outlet housing (without disconnecting the coolant hoses) and remove the concealed mounting bolt.
5 Disconnect the air hoses, then remove the remaining mounting bolt and withdraw the unit.
6 Refitting is a reversal of removal.

Fig. 3.15 Areas (arrowed) for checking air intake leakage (Sec 23)

1	Airflow sensor	4	Throttle housing
2	Cylinder head	5	Brake vacuum servo

6	Fuel pressure regulator	10	Air distribution manifold
7	Crankcase breather hose	11	Injectors

Fig. 3.16 Fuel pump components (Sec 24)

1	Bleed tube	4	Collar
2	Bracket	5	Fuel pump
3	Collar	6	Filter

24.2 Fuel pump location and connections

26 Fuel injection system – complete test

1   Pull the connector from the airflow sensor and connect a voltmeter between wire 18A and earth (photos).
2   Disconnect the ignition control unit then operate the starter motor and check that a minimum of 9 volts is obtained.
3   Disconnect the battery negative lead.
4   Connect an ohmmeter between wire M18 and earth and check that the reading is less than 1 ohm.
5   Disconnect the airflow sensor inlet hose (photo) and use a screwdriver to open and close the sensor flap. The movement should be free. Clean the interior of the sensor if necessary.

26.1A Removing the connector from the airflow sensor

26.1B Showing terminals 18A (1) and M18 (2) on the airflow sensor connector

26.5 Disconnecting the airflow sensor inlet hose

6 Connect an ohmmeter between terminals 5 and 8 on the airflow sensor (Fig. 3.17) and check that a reading of 340 to 450 ohms is obtained.

7 Connect the ohmmeter between terminals 9 and 8 and check that the reading is now between 160 and 300 ohms.

8 Connect the ohmmeter between terminals 5 and 7, then move the flap with a screwdriver. The resistance should vary between 60 and 1000 ohms.

9 Connect the ohmmeter between the terminal on the engine temperature sensor (above the supplementary air device) and earth (photo). The reading should be less than 1 ohm.

10 Pull off the temperature sensor connector and connect the ohmmeter across the two terminals on the sensor. If the reading is infinity, renew the sensor.

11 Connect a voltmeter between wire 48 on the supplementary air device connector and earth.

12 Disconnect the ignition control unit then operate the starter motor and check that the reading is at least 9 volts.

13 With the battery disconnected, connect an ohmmeter between wire M24 on the connector and earth. The reading should be less than 1 ohm.

14 Remove the supplementary air device (Section 25) and check that, at an ambient temperature of 20°C (68°F), the opening in the diaphragm is visible through the end of the unit.

15 Connect an ohmmeter across the terminals of the unit and check that a reading of 45 to 55 ohms is obtained at an ambient temperature of 20°C (68°F).

16 Connect a 12 volt supply to the terminals of the unit. After five minutes the diaphragm must completely block the airflow aperture.

Fig. 3.17 Airflow sensor terminals (Sec 26)

26.9 Engine temperature sensor (1) and supplementary air device (2)

Fig. 3.18 Checking the supplementary air device wiring
(Sec 26)

28.1 Fuel tank vent valve

29.1 Throttle cable adjustment ferrule (arrowed)

30.5 Exhaust system flange nuts

27 Fuel level transmitter – removal and refitting

Refer to Section 7.

28 Fuel tank – removal, repair and refitting

Refer to Section 8. Note that there is an additional vent valve located near the rear towing eye (photo).

29 Throttle cable – removal and refitting

The procedure is similar to that described in Section 14, but the adjustment ferrule is located beneath the inlet manifold (photo).

30 Manifolds and exhaust system – general

1 The inlet manifold is combined with an air distribution chamber. A single gasket seals the assembly to the cylinder head.
2 The exhaust manifold is similar in design to that described in Section 16.
3 The exhaust system is in three main sections with flexible rubber mountings.
4 Since removal is easy it is recommended that the complete system is removed even when renewing a single section.
5 When fitting the exhaust system observe the procedure for tightening the flange nuts given in Section 16 (photo).

Fig. 3.19 Exhaust system (Sec 30)

PART D: FAULT DIAGNOSIS

31 Fault diagnosis – fuel and exhaust systems

Symptom	Reason(s)
Difficult starting from cold	Choke control inoperative (carburettor) Fuel pump fault Blocked fuel line or filter Needle valve sticking (carburettor) Supplementary air device fault (fuel injection) Temperature sensor faulty or disconnected (fuel injection)
Difficult starting when hot	Choked air filter Choke control sticking (carburettor) Fuel pump faulty
Excessive fuel consumption	Mixture setting incorrect Excessive fuel pressure (fuel injection) Temperature sensor faulty (fuel injection) Airflow sensor faulty (fuel injection)
Uneven idling	Mixture setting incorrect Air leak in intake system Throttle switch out of adjustment (fuel injection) Loose electronic control unit connector (fuel injection)

Chapter 4 Ignition system

For modifications, and information applicable to later models, see Supplement at end of manual

Contents

Specifications

System type .... Electronic (breakerless)

Distributor
Rotor rotation	Anti-clockwise
Firing order	1 – 3 – 4 – 2 (No 1 at clutch end)
Pulse generator resistance	990 to 1210 ohms

Ignition timing (vacuum hose disconnected)
XV8 and XW7 engines	6° BTDC at 650 rpm
XY7 engine	8° BTDC at 650 rpm
XY8 engine:	
Early with M152E curve	0° BTDC at 950 rpm
Later with M159E curve	8° BTDC at 850 to 950 rpm
XU5J engine	30° BTDC at 3500 rpm or 6° BTDC at 700 rpm

Spark plugs
Type:	
XV8, XW7, and XY7 engines	Champion S9YCC, S9YC or S281YC
XY8 and XU5J engines	Champion S7YCC, S7YC or S279YC
Electrode gap (S9YCC, S7YCC)	0.8 mm (0.032 in)
Electrode gap (S9YC, S7YC, S281YC, S279YC)	0.6 mm (0.024 in)

HT leads
Carburettor models..	Champion LS04
Fuel injection models...	Champion LS12

Ignition coil
Primary resistance	0.85 ohm
Secondary resistance	6000 ohms

Torque wrench settings
	Nm	lbf ft
Spark plugs	17.5	13
Timing plug (non-GTI models)	27.5	20
Timing plate bolt (non GTI models)	7.0	5

1 General description

The ignition system is of electronic breakerless type incorporating a control module (located near the ignition coil), pulse generator (located in the distributor), ignition coil and distributor. The spark plugs have taper seats without sealing washers.

In order that the engine may run correctly it is necessary for an electrical spark to ignite the fuel/air mixture in the combustion chamber at exactly the right moment in relation to engine speed and load.

Basically the ignition system functions as follows. Low tension voltage from the battery is fed to the ignition coil, where it is converted into high tension voltage. The high tension voltage is powerful enough to jump the spark plug gap in the cylinder many times a second under high compression pressure, providing that the ignition system is in good working order.

The ignition system consists of two individual circuits known as the low tension (LT) circuit and high tension (HT) circuit.

The low tension circuit (sometimes known as the primary circuit) comprises the ignition switch, primary ignition coil windings, and control module. The high tension circuit (sometimes known as the secondary circuit) comprises the secondary ignition coil windings, distributor cap, rotor arm, spark plugs and HT leads.

The primary circuit is initially switched on by the control module and a magnetic field is formed within the ignition coil. At the precise point of ignition the pulse generator causes the control module to switch off the primary circuit, and high tension voltage is then induced in the secondary circuit and fed to the spark plug via the distributor cap and rotor arm.

The ignition is advanced and retarded automatically by centrifugal weights and a vacuum capsule to ensure that the spark occurs at the correct instant in relation to engine speed and load.

Note: When working on the ignition system remember that the high tension voltage can be considerably higher than on a conventional system and in certain circumstances could prove fatal.

2 Routine maintenance

Carry out the following procedures at the intervals given in Routine Maintenance at the beginning of the manual.
1   Remove the spark plugs and renew them, with reference to Section 10. Do not forget to set the electrode gaps on the new plugs.
2   Check and, if necessary, adjust the ignition timing, as described in Section 7.

3 Distributor – removal and refitting

1   On GTI models, remove the air cleaner and inlet duct, as described in Chapter 3.
2   Identify the HT leads for position then disconnect them from the spark plugs.
3   Slide off the ignition coil cover and disconnect the HT lead from the coil.
4   Pull back the plastic cover then unclip and remove the distributor cap (photo).
5   Disconnect the wiring at the connector, where necessary pulling out the spring clip first.
6   Pull the hose from the vacuum advance unit.
7   Mark the distributor mounting flange in relation to the cylinder head (non-GTI models) or thermostat housing (GTI models).
8   Unscrew the mounting nuts, remove the small plates, and withdraw the distributor (photos).
9   Check the condition of the O-ring on the mounting flange and renew it if necessary.
10 Refitting is a reversal of removal, but turn the rotor arm as required to align the lugs with the offset slot in the camshaft (photo). If the old distributor is being refitted, align the previously made marks before tightening the mounting nuts. If fitting a new distributor, initially set the distributor in the middle of the slotted holes or follow the procedure given in Section 7, then finally adjust the ignition timing (Section 7).

4 Distributor – overhaul

1   Clean the exterior of the distributor.
2   Pull off the rotor arm and remove the plastic cover, where fitted.

3.4 The distributor cap on a GTI model

3.8A Unscrew the mounting nuts ...

3.8B ... and remove the distributor (non-GTI models)

3.8C Removing the distributor on a GTI model

3.10 The offset slot in the end of the camshaft

Ducellier

3 Extract the screw and remove the clamp and wiring plug (photo).
4 Extract the three body screws. The lugs are offset so the body sections cannot be misaligned when reassembled. Separate the body sections (photo).
5 Invert the body upper section, pull out the plastic ring and lift out the magnetic coil (photo).
6 From the body upper section, extract the circlip and the thrust washer (photo).
7 Extract the vacuum unit screw and then lift out the baseplate at the same time unhooking the vacuum link (photos).
8 Extract the circlip and shim from the body lower section (photo).
9 Lift out the counterweight assembly.
10 The drive dog is secured to the shaft by a pin.
11 Reassembly is a reversal of dismantling, but note that one baseplate hole is marked by engagement of the vacuum unit link rod (photo).

Bosch

12 The procedure is similar to that for the Ducellier distributor but the body is in one piece. Refer to Fig. 4.2 (photos).

4.3 Clamp and wiring plug (Ducellier)

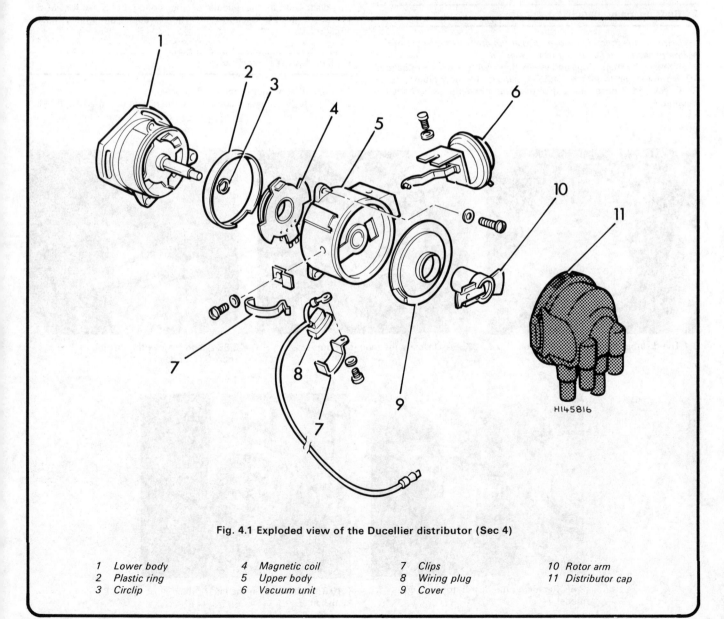

Fig. 4.1 Exploded view of the Ducellier distributor (Sec 4)

1 Lower body	4 Magnetic coil	7 Clips	10 Rotor arm
2 Plastic ring	5 Upper body	8 Wiring plug	11 Distributor cap
3 Circlip	6 Vacuum unit	9 Cover	

4.4 Separating body sections (Ducellier)

4.5A Remove the plastic ring (Ducellier)

4.5B ... and magnetic coil (Ducellier)

4.6 Removing the circlip and thrust washer (Ducellier)

4.7A Vacuum unit and screw (Ducellier)

4.7B Removing the baseplate (Ducellier)

4.8 View of reluctor, centrifugal weights and securing circlip – arrowed (Ducellier)

4.11 Hole marked for engagement of vacuum unit link (Ducellier)

4.12A Removing the clamp (Bosch) ...

4.12B ... and wiring connector (Bosch)

4.12C View of the bearing plate (Bosch)

4.12D View of reluctor with bearing plate removed (Bosch)

Fig. 4.2 Exploded view of the Bosch
distributor (Sec 4)

1 Wiring plug
2 Connector
3 Clip
4 Body
5 Vacuum unit
6 Distributor cap
7 Rotor arm
8 Cover
9 Bearing plate
10 Ring
11 Circlip
12 Reluctor
13 Magnetic coil
14 Stator
15 Baseplate
16 Clip
17 Shaft assembly

H145817

5 Ignition module – removal and refitting

1 Slide the cover off the ignition coil and module (photo).
2 Disconnect the battery negative lead.
3 Disconnect the wiring harness.
4 Remove the screws and withdraw the module from the mounting plate.
5 Refitting is a reversal of removal.

5.1 Removing the coil and module cover

6 Timing plate (non-GTI models) – setting

1 The timing plate which is located in the aperture under the plastic cover at the top of the flywheel housing can be moved within the limits of its elongated slot.
2 The plate is set during production and should not be disturbed

Fig. 4.3 Timing components on non-GTI models (Sec 6)

1 Diagnostic socket   3 Timing plate
2 Cover

unless a new flywheel, flywheel housing or other associated components have been fitted.
3 To set the timing plate, carry out the following operations.
4 Remove the plastic cover.
5 Using the crankshaft pulley nut, turn the crankshaft until the mark on the flywheel is at the start of the timing plate.
6 Remove the plug from behind the crankshaft pulley using an Allen key. Note that if the hole in the pulley is not over the plug, the crankshaft should be turned exactly half a turn. This is because there are two diametrically opposite timing marks on the flywheel, and the mark corresponding to TDC on No 2 and 3 cylinders must be used to bring the slot in the crankshaft counterbalance in line with the plug hole.
7 Insert the special tool 80133 into the plug hole and turn the crankshaft until the tool is felt to drop into the cut-out in the counterbalance weight of the crankshaft.
8 If the special tool is not available, use a rod 8.00 mm diameter x 100.0 mm long (photo).
9 The pistons 2 and 3 are now located at TDC.
10 Release the timing plate bolt and move the plate to align the flywheel, and 0 (TDC) mark on the plate. Tighten the bolt to the specified torque. Apply a blob of paint on the edge of the bolt so that any subsequent movement can be recognised.
11 Withdraw the pin, fit a new sealing ring to the plug and tighten to the specified torque.

6.8 Substitute rod for setting crankshaft position on non-GTI models

7 Ignition timing – checking and adjustment

Note: *The ignition timing may be checked and adjusted using the engine diagnosis socket, but the special Peugeot instrument necessary will not normally be available to the home mechanic.*

Non-GTI models (XV8, XW7, XY7 and XY8 engines)

1 To set the ignition timing statically so that the engine can be started first remove No 2 spark plug and turn the engine in the normal rotational direction until pressure is felt – indicating that the piston is commencing the compression stroke. The pressure can be felt using a suitable wooden rod or a piece of cork placed over the spark plug hole.
2 Remove the plastic cover from the timing aperture then continue turning the crankshaft until the mark on the flywheel is opposite the BTDC mark on the timing plate (photo).
3 Check that the distributor rotor arm is facing the No 2 HT lead segment position in the distributor cap. To do this, remove the cap and mark the outside in line with the segment, then put it back on the distributor noting which way the rotor arm is facing.

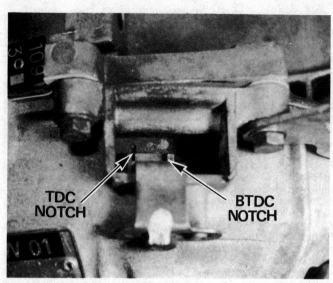

7.2 Timing plate marks on non-GTI models

the timing aperture. The single mark on the flywheel should be aligned with the BTDC mark on the timing plate. If the ignition coil HT lead has been used (see paragraph 5), and there is wear in the distributor, there will be two marks visible on the flywheel close to each other. In this case the mid-point between the two marks should be aligned with the BTDC mark on the timing plate.

8   If adjustment is necessary, loosen the distributor mounting nuts and rotate the distributor body as required. Tighten the nuts on completion.

9   The operation of the centrifugal advance weights in the distributor can be checked by increasing the engine speed with the timing light pointing in the timing aperture and observing that the mark on the flywheel advances from its initial position.

10 To check the vacuum advance unit, run the engine at a fast idle speed and reconnect the vacuum pipe. The flywheel mark should again advance.

11 Stop the engine, disconnect the tachometer and timing light and reconnect the vacuum pipe. Refit the timing aperture cover.

GTI models (XU5J engine)

12 To set the ignition timing statically so that the engine can be started, first remove No 1 spark plug (nearest clutch) and turn the engine in the normal rotational direction until pressure is felt – indicating that the piston is commencing the compression stroke. The pressure can be felt using a suitable wooden rod or piece of cork placed over the spark plug hole.

13 While looking into the timing aperture in the clutch housing/gearbox casing, continue turning the crankshaft until the single mark on the flywheel is opposite the BTDC mark on the timing plate.

14 Check that the distributor rotor arm is facing the No 1 HT lead segment position in the distributor cap. To do this, remove the cap and mark the outside in line with the segment, then put it back on the distributor noting which way the rotor arm is facing.

15 If necessary, loosen the mounting nuts and turn the distributor body to bring the segment and rotor arm in line, then tighten the nuts. Refit No 1 spark plug.

16 Run the engine to normal operating temperature then stop it and connect a tachometer to it.

17 Disconnect and plug the vacuum pipe at the distributor vacuum advance unit.

18 Disconnect and remove the air cleaner inlet duct then connect a stroboscopic timing light to the engine using the HT pick-up lead connected to No 1 spark plug HT lead.

4   If necessary, loosen the mounting nuts and turn the distributor body to bring the segment and rotor arm in line, then tighten the nuts. Refit No 2 spark plug.

5   Run the engine to normal operating temperature then stop it and connect a tachometer and stroboscopic timing light to it. If the HT pick-up lead of the timing light is connected to the HT lead on the ignition coil it is possible to detect any discrepancy between the firing of Nos 1 and 4 and Nos 2 and 3 cylinders since there are two diametrically opposite timing marks on the flywheel. However, the pick-up lead may be connected to any one of the spark plug HT leads, in which case only one of the flywheel timing marks will be used.

6   Disconnect and plug the vacuum pipe at the distributor vacuum advance unit.

7   Run the engine at the specified speed and point the timing light into

Fig. 4.4 Ignition timing adjustment on non-GTI models (Sec 7)

A   Using spark plug HT lead   *B   Using ignition coil HT lead*

Fig. 4.5 Initial static ignition timing on GTI models (Sec 7)

a   Single flywheel mark   *b   BTDC mark on timing plate*

Fig. 4.6 Dynamic ignition timing on GTI models (Sec 7)

a   *Double flywheel mark*   b   *TDC mark on timing plate*

9.1 TDC sensor on non-GTI models

19 Run the engine at 3500 rpm and point the timing light into the timing aperture. The double mark on the flywheel should be aligned with the TDC mark on the timing plate; indicating that the ignition is advanced by 30°. If the car is an early model, without the double timing marks, adjust the engine speed to 700 rpm and check that the single mark on the flywheel is aligned with the BTDC mark on the timing plate – indicating that the ignition is advanced by 6°.
20 If adjustment is necessary, loosen the distributor mounting nuts and rotate the distributor body as required. Tighten the nuts on completion.
21 Check the centrifugal and vacuum advance characteristics of the distributor, as described in paragraphs 9 and 10.
22 Stop the engine, disconnect the tachometer and timing light then reconnect the vacuum pipe and air cleaner inlet duct.

8 Ignition coil – general

1 The maintenance of the coil is minimal and is limited to periodically wiping its surfaces clean and dry and ensuring that the lead connectors are secure. High voltages generated by the coil can easily leak to earth over its surface and prevent the spark plugs from receiving the electrical pulses. Water repellent sprays are now available to prevent dampness causing this type of malfunction.
2 Wipe clean and spray the HT leads and distributor cap also.
3 Special equipment is required to test a coil and is best left to an auto-electrician. Substitution of another coil is an alternative method of fault tracing.

9 TDC sensor – removal and refitting

1 The TDC sensor (photo) is for use with the diagnostic socket located on the clutch housing. As a special instrument and adaptor are required it will normally be used only by a Peugeot garage.
2 To remove the sensor, unscrew the mounting screw (non-GTI models) or release the clamp (GTI models).
3 The sensor forms part of the diagnostic socket assembly so, if it is to be completely removed, the socket must be unclipped from its bracket and the remaining wiring and earth leads disconnected.
4 Refitting is a reversal of removal, but the adjustment procedure for new and used sensors differs. New sensors have three extensions on the inner face and the unit should be inserted through the clamp until the extensions just touch the flywheel. The clamp screw is then tightened and clearance is provided as the flywheel rotates and wears the ends of the extensions. This method should not be used when refitting a used sensor. In this case, cut off the extensions completely

then temporarily insert the sensor until it touches the flywheel, remove it and reposition it in the clamp 1.0 mm (0.04 in) further out.

10 Spark plugs, HT leads and distributor cap – general

1 The correct functioning of the spark plugs is vital for the correct running and efficiency of the engine. It is essential that the plugs fitted are appropriate for the engine, and the suitable type is specified at the beginning of this chapter. If this type is used and the engine is in good condition, the spark plugs should not need attention between scheduled replacement intervals. Spark plug cleaning is rarely necessary and should not be attempted unless specialised equipment is available as damage can easily be caused to the firing ends.
2 To remove the plugs, first open the bonnet and pull the HT leads from them. Grip the rubber end fitting not the lead otherwise the lead connection may be fractured. Also remove the extensions.
3 The spark plugs are deeply recessed in the cylinder head and it is recommended that dirt is removed from the recesses using a vacuum cleaner or compressed air, before removing the plugs, to prevent dirt dropping into the cylinders.

10.4 Removing a spark plug with the special box spanner

4 Unscrew the plugs using the special box wrench supplied with the car and located in the front left-hand corner of the engine compartment by the washer bottle (photo).

5 Examination of the spark plugs will give a good indication of the condition of the engine. If the insulator nose of the spark plug is clean and white, with no deposits, this is indicative of a weak mixture, or too hot a plug (a hot plug transfers heat away from the electrode slowly, a cold plug transfers heat away quickly).

6 If the top and insulator nose are covered with hard black-looking deposits, then this is indicative that the mixture is too rich. Should the plug be black and oily, then it is likely that the engine is fairly worn, as well as the mixture being too rich.

7 If the insulator nose is covered with light tan to greyish brown deposits, then the mixture is correct and it is likely that the engine is in good condition.

8 The spark plug gap is of considerable importance as, if it is too large or too small, the size of the spark and its efficiency will be seriously impaired. For the best results the spark plug gap should be set in accordance with the Specifications at the beginning of this Chapter.

9 To set it, measure the gap with a feeler gauge, and then bend open, or close, the outer plug electrode until the correct gap is achieved. The centre electrode should never be bent, as this may crack the insulation and cause plug failure, if nothing worse.

10 Special spark plug electrode gap adjusting tools are available from most motor accessory shops.

11 Before fitting new spark plugs check that the threaded connector sleeves are tight.

12 Screw in the spark plugs by hand where possible, then tighten them to the specified torque. Take extra care to enter the plug threads correctly as the cylinder head is of aluminium.

13 Refit the extensions followed by the HT leads, making sure that the latter are in their correct order of 1–3–4–2 (No 1 nearest the clutch end of engine) in relation to the anti-clockwise direction of the rotor arm.

14 The HT leads and their connections should always be kept clean and dry and arranged neatly in the special holder. If any lead shows signs of cracking or chafing of the insulation it should be renewed.

15 Check the distributor cap whenever it is removed. If there are any very thin black lines running between the electrodes this indicates tracking and a new cap should be fitted. Check the rotor arm in a similar way. Where applicable check that the spring-tensioned carbon brush in the centre of the cap is free to move and is not worn excessively.

11 Fault diagnosis – ignition system

1 If the engine fails to start and the car was running normally when it was last used, first check that there is fuel in the fuel tank. If the engine turns over normally on the starter motor and the battery is evidently well charged first check the HT (high tension) circuit.

2 A common reason for bad starting is wet or damp spark plug leads and distributor cap. Holts Wet Start can be very effective to combat this. To prevent the problem recurring, Holts Damp Start can be used to provide a sealing coat, so excluding any further moisture from the ignition system. In extreme difficulty, Holts Cold Start will help to start a car when only a very poor spark occurs.

3 If the engine still fails to start, disconnect an HT lead from any spark plug and, using a nail inserted into the end fitting, hold the lead approximately 5.0 mm (0.2 in) away from the cylinder head with well-insulated pliers. While an assistant spins the engine on the starter motor, check that a regular blue spark occurs. If so the spark plugs are probably the cause of the engine's not starting and they should therefore be cleaned and regapped.

4 If no spark occurs, disconnect the main feed HT lead from the distributor cap and check for a spark as in paragraph 3. If sparks now occur, check the distributor cap, rotor arm, and HT leads, as described in Section 10, and renew them as necessary.

5 Check the security of the wiring to the ignition coil, distributor and electronic module.

6 Using an ohmmeter, check the resistance of the distributor pulse generator coil and the ignition coil windings. Renew them if the readings are not as given in the Specifications.

7 If necessary, dismantle the distributor and check that the gaps between the reluctor arms and the stator posts are all equal.

8 Using a voltmeter, check that there is battery voltage at the ignition coil low tension positive terminal with the ignition switched on. Connect the voltmeter across the coil LT terminals and check that the reading is zero. If it is not zero the module may be defective or the coil-to-module wire earthed.

Chapter 5 Clutch

For modifications, and information applicable to later models, see Supplement at end of manual

Contents

Specifications

General

Type	Diaphragm spring, single dry plate, cable operation
Driven plate diameter:	
All models except GTI	180.0 mm
GTI	200.0 mm
Release bearing	Sealed ball-bearing
Clutch pedal stroke..	140.0 ± 5.0 mm

Torque wrench settings

	Nm	lbf ft
Clutch cover	10	7
Clutch housing	12	9

1 General description

The clutch is of diaphragm spring, single dry plate type with cable actuation.

The clutch pedal pivots in a bracket mounted under the facia and operates a cable to the clutch release arm (or fork). The release lever operates a thrust bearing (clutch release bearing) which bears on the diaphragm spring of the pressure plate, and releases the clutch driven plate from the flywheel. The driven plate (or disc) is splined to a shaft which transmits the drive to the gearbox. On non-GTI models with the BH 3 gearbox the shaft is part of the transfer gear assembly, but on GTI models with the side-mounted BE 1 gearbox the shaft is the gearbox input shaft.

The clutch release mechanism consists of a fork and bearing which are in permanent contact with release fingers on the pressure plate assembly. The fork pushes the release bearing forwards to bear against the release fingers, so moving the centre of the diaphragm spring inwards. The spring is sandwiched between two rings which act as fulcrum points. As the centre of the spring is pushed in, the outside of the spring is pushed out, so moving the pressure plate backwards and disengaging it from the clutch driven plate.

When the clutch pedal is released, the diaphragm spring forces the pressure plate into contact with the friction linings on the driven plate and at the same time pushes the driven plate a fraction of an inch forwards on its splines so engaging it with the flywheel. The driven plate is now firmly sandwiched between the pressure plate and the flywheel, so the drive is taken up.

As wear takes place on the driven plate friction linings the diaphragm fingers move outwards and the pedal stroke decreases; the cable mechanism incorporates an adjustment to compensate for this wear.

Fig. 5.1 Cross-section of the clutch and transfer gears (Sec 1)

1 Clutch housing	4 Gasket	7 Intermediate gear	10 Flywheel
2 Guide sleeve	5 Cover plate	8 Input shaft	11 Pressure plate assembly
3 Intermediate plate	6 Output (clutch) shaft	9 Driven plate	

AH145821

2 Routine maintenance

Carry out the following procedures at the intervals given in Routine Maintenance at the beginning of the manual.
1 Depress the clutch pedal fully three times then, using a rule, measure the total stroke of the pedal pad.
2 If the stroke is not as given in the Specifications it will be necessary to adjust the pushrod bolt on the intermediate lever on non-GTI models or adjust the cable on GTI models.
3 On non-GTI models, loosen the locknut, then the pushrod bolt in the lever as required, then retighten the locknut (photo).
4 On GTI models, loosen the locknut at the gearbox end of the cable, turn the adjusting nut as required, then retighten the locknut.
5 Before checking the adjustment, fully operate the clutch pedal three times.

3 Clutch cable – removal and refitting

1 Working in the engine compartment, loosen the locknut and slacken the cable adjustment.
2 Release the cable end fitting from the intermediate lever. Recover the pushrod on non-GTI models.
3 Working inside the car, remove the lower facia panel from the steering column.
4 Pull off the spring clip and remove the clevis pin from the top of the pedal to disconnect the cable end.
5 Release the cable from the bulkhead and withdraw it into the engine compartment.
6 Refitting is a reversal of removal, but finally adjust the pedal stroke, as described in Section 2.

4 Clutch pedal – removal and refitting

1 Working in the engine compartment, loosen the locknut and slacken the cable adjustment.
2 Working inside the car, remove the lower facia panel from the steering column.
3 Pull off the spring clip and remove the clevis pin from the top of the pedal to disconnect the cable end.
4 Unhook the cable tension spring from the pedal.
5 Unscrew the nut from the pivot bolt, pull out the bolt and lower the clutch pedal from the bracket.
6 Examine the pedal bushes for wear and renew them if necessary.
7 Refitting is a reversal of removal, but lightly grease the bushes and clevis pin; finally adjust the pedal stroke, as described in Section 2.

Fig. 5.2 Clutch pedal stroke (X) adjustment diagram for GTI models (Sec 2)

1 Adjustment nut and locknut

Fig. 5.3 Clutch pedal components (Sec 4)

1 *Pivot bolt*	6 *Clevis pin*
2 *Bush*	7 *Pedal*
3 *Spacer*	8 *Bush*
4 *Tension spring (circular type on some models)*	9 *Nut*
	10 *Pad*
5 *Clip*	

2.3 Clutch intermediate lever and adjustment bolt (arrowed) on non-GTI models

5   Clutch – removal

Non-GTI models with BH 3 gearbox

1   Remove the battery and starter motor, as described in Chapter 12.

2   Jack up the front of the car and drain the oil from the gearbox/engine assembly. Also disconnect the gear selector rod with reference to Chapter 6. Use stands to support the car and apply the handbrake.

3   Disconnect the bonnet stay from the right-hand suspension tower and use suitable U-brackets in the bonnet hinge holes to hold the bonnet in a vertical position.

4   Remove the complete air cleaner and brackets, as described in Chapter 3.

5   Disconnect the vacuum advance pipe from the distributor to prevent damage to it.

6   Disconnect the clutch cable at the gearbox end with reference to Section 3.

7   Working through the hole in the battery tray, unscrew and remove the top nut from the left-hand engine mounting. If necessary remove the splash guard from the wheel housing (photos).

8   Using a trolley jack and block of wood, support the left-hand side of the engine beneath the gearbox.

9   Unscrew the two nuts securing the left-hand engine mounting to the bottom of the battery tray (photo). Remove the mounting.

10   Lower the engine and gearbox until the left-hand driveshaft rests on the subframe.

11   Unclip the starter motor wiring from the clutch housing (photo).

12   Unscrew the bolts securing the clutch housing to the gearbox and engine noting the location of the lifting eye and earth cable. Do not forget to remove the bolt located in the bottom recess of the housing (photos).

13   If necessary for additional working room, unbolt and remove the battery tray (photo).

5.7A Splash guard screw in left-hand wheel housing

5.7B View of transfer gear housing with splash guard removed

5.9 Bottom view of left-hand engine mounting

5.11 Starter motor wiring clip (arrowed)

5.12A Lower clutch housing mounting bolts (arrowed)

5.12B Engine lifting eye

5.12C Earth cable location

5.12D Mounting bolt located in the clutch housing recess (arrowed)

5.13 Unbolting the battery tray

5.14A Remove the clutch housing and transfer gear assembly ...

5.14B ... and the gasket

5.17 Removing the clutch pressure plate assembly and driven plate

14 Withdraw the clutch housing and transfer gear assembly from the engine and gearbox. Remove the gasket (photos).

GTI models with BE 1 gearbox
15 Remove the gearbox from the engine, as described in Chapter 6.

All models
16 Mark the clutch pressure plate in relation to the flywheel then progressively loosen the bolts. If necessary hold the flywheel stationary using a screwdriver engaged with the starter ring gear.
17 With all the bolts removed lift the pressure plate assembly from the location dowels followed by the driven plate (photo).

6 Clutch – inspection and renovation

1 The clutch driven plate should be inspected for wear and for contamination by oil. Wear is gauged by the depth of the rivet heads below the surface of the friction material. If this is less than 0.6 mm (0.024 in) the linings are worn enough to justify renewal.
2 Examine the friction faces of the flywheel and clutch pressure plate. These should be bright and smooth. If the linings have worn too much it is possible that the metal surfaces may have been scored by the rivet heads. Dust and grit can have the same effect. If the scoring is very severe it could mean that even with a new clutch driven plate, slip and juddering and other malfunctions will recur. Deep scoring on the flywheel face is serious because the flywheel will have to be removed and machined by a specialist, or renewed. If the pressure plate is worn excessively it must be renewed. If the driven plate friction linings are contaminated with oil, the plate must be renewed and the source of the oil traced and rectified.
3 If the reason for removal of the clutch has been because of slip and the slip has been allowed to go on for any length of time, it is possible that the heat generated will have adversely affected the diaphragm spring in the cover with the result that the pressure is now uneven and/or insufficient to prevent slip, even with a new driven plate. Where this occurs, the friction surfaces on the flywheel and pressure plate will often show a blue discolouration necessitating the renewal of the pressure plate.
4 With the clutch removed, the release bearing should be checked for excessive wear and noise, and renewed if necessary. Also check the spigot bush in the crankshaft rear flange for wear and, if necessary, renew it, as described in Chapter 1.

7 Clutch – refitting

1 Locate the driven plate on the flywheel with the cushioning spring hub facing outwards (see Fig. 5.1), then place the pressure plate assembly over it with the dowels and holes correctly aligned and fit the bolts finger tight.
2 It is now necessary to align the centre of the driven plate with that

of the flywheel. To do this, use a special alignment tool located in the flywheel spigot bearing, or alternatively a suitable diameter bar or wooden dowel can be used. If the transfer gears have been removed (non-GTI models) or the gearbox dismantled (GTI models) the relevant shaft can be used (photo).
3 With the driven plate centralized, the cover bolts should be tightened diagonally and evenly to the specified torque. Ideally new spring washers should be used each time a replacement clutch is fitted. When the bolts are tight remove the centralizing tool.

7.2 Using the transfer gear shaft to centralise the clutch driven plate

GTI models with BE 1 gearbox
4 Refit the gearbox, as described in Chapter 6.

Non-GTI models with BH 3 gearbox
5 Clean the mating surfaces, then locate a new gasket on the dowels on the cylinder block.
6 Refit the clutch housing and transfer gear assembly to the engine and gearbox. If the splines on the shafts do not line up correctly move the flywheel fractionally. Make sure that the clutch cable intermediate lever is in its working position.
7 Insert the bolts, together with the lifting eye and earth cable, and tighten them progressively to the specified torque.
8 If removed, refit the battery tray and tighten the bolts.
9 Clip the starter motor wiring to the clutch housing.
10 Using a trolley jack and block of wood, raise the engine and gearbox,

locate the left-hand mounting and tighten the two nuts on the bottom of the battery tray.

11 Refit and tighten the mounting top nut.

12 Refer to Section 3 and reconnect the clutch cable. Also adjust the pedal stroke, as described in Section 2.

13 Reconnect the vacuum advance pipe.

14 Refit the air cleaner, with reference to Chapter 3, and refit the bonnet stay.

15 Reconnect the gear selector rod and lower the car to the ground.

16 Refit the starter motor and battery, with reference to Chapter 12.

17 Refill the gearbox/engine assembly with oil.

8 Clutch release mechanism – overhaul

Non-GTI models with BH 3 gearbox

1 Remove the clutch housing and transfer gear assembly, as described in Section 5.

2 Release the spring clips and slide the bearing from the guide sleeve (photos).

3 Remove the foam ring (photo).

4 Withdraw the release fork from the ball-stud (photo).

8.3 Foam cushion ring located behind the release bearing on non-GTI models

8.2A The release bearing and spring clips

8.4 Release fork disconnected from the ball-stud on non-GTI models

8.2B Reverse side of release bearing and fork

Fig. 5.4 Removing clutch release fork ball-stud (Sec 8)

Fig. 5.5 Clutch release fork spring blade (1) and rubber cup (2) (Sec 8)

5 Do not clean the bearing with solvent as it will harm the bearing. Wipe it clean and check for excessive wear or play. Always renew if in doubt.

6 Inspect the fork retaining ball-stud and, if obviously distorted or worn, renew it. Drift the ball-stud from the housing using a suitable diameter drift. Fit the new one, together with a new rubber cup, by driving it carefully into position using a soft-faced hammer. Support the housing during this operation to prevent it from being damaged.

7 Before reassembly, check the output (clutch) shaft oil seal. If it is leaking then the complete guide sleeve/seal assembly must be renewed as the seal is not supplied separately.

8 Press the guide sleeve out of the clutch housing.

9 Press the new sleeve/seal assembly fully into its recess so that it seats firmly.

10 Any wear in the spigot bush which is located in the centre of the crankshaft rear flange (flywheel mounting) and supports the output shaft can be rectified by renewal of the bush, as described in Chapter 1.

11 Refit the components using a reversal of the removal procedure. Lubricate the ball-stud and guide sleeve with suitable high melting-point grease. When fitting the release fork, locate the spring blade **under** the rubber cap.

GTI models with BE 1 gearbox

12 Remove the gearbox, as described in Chapter 6.

13 Release the spring clips and slide the bearing from the guide sleeve.

14 Withdraw the release fork from the ball-stud.

15 Where applicable, the pivot bush may be removed as follows. First drill out the rivets which secure the old bush. Remove the bush and discard it. Position the new bush on the fork and pass its rivets through the holes. Heat the rivets with a cigarette lighter or a low powered blowlamp, then peen over their heads while they are still hot.

16 Lightly coat the bush with grease, then refit the release fork. Press it onto the ball-stud until it snaps home.

17 If the ball-stud requires renewal, remove it with a slide hammer having a suitable claw. Support the casing and drive in the new stud using a soft metal drift.

18 Refit the remaining components using a reversal of the removal procedure.

9 Transfer gears (non-GTI models) – removal and refitting

1 The transfer gears are located under a cover plate at the end of the clutch/flywheel housing. Their purpose is to transmit power from the engine crankshaft and clutch to the transmission input shaft which lies below the engine.

2 Remove the clutch housing and transfer gear assembly, as described in Section 5.

3 Unbolt the cover plate then unbolt and remove the transfer gear intermediate plate. The plate will probably require tapping off with a plastic-faced hammer. Take care that the intermediate gear does not drop out as the plate is removed.

4 Remove the intermediate gear.

5 Clean away all old gasket material and obtain a new one.

6 Examine the gearteeth for wear or damage, and the bearings for wear or 'shake'.

7 If a ball-bearing is to be renewed, use a pair of circlips pliers to fully expand the circlip before pressing the shaft out of the bearing or the shaft/bearing out of the intermediate plate.

8 When reassembling, remember that the shorter shaft is located at the narrower end of the intermediate plate. Always use new circlips and support the plate adequately during the pressing operation.

9 Always use a new Belleville washer under the circlip so that its concave face is towards the bearing.

Fig. 5.6 Removing the intermediate plate (Sec 9)

1 Intermediate plate	a Casting boss (impact point)
2 Intermediate gear	b Casting boss (impact point)

Fig. 5.7 Intermediate plate and gear removed (Sec 9)

Fig. 5.8 Expanding circlip (1) and pressing out ball-bearing
from intermediate plate (Sec 9)

Fig. 5.9 Bearing circlip (2) and Belleville washer (3) (Sec 9)

Fig. 5.10 Shaft identification (Sec 9)

1 Output (clutch) shaft

Fig. 5.11 Using intermediate shaft to press needle roller
bearing (3) into intermediate plate (Sec 9)

Fig. 5.12 Assembling transfer gears and cover plate (Sec 9)

2   Gasket

10 If the intermediate gear needle race if to be renewed in the
intermediate plate, press the old one out and use the intermediate gear
as an installation tool, but make sure that the gearteeth do not lock
with those of the other gears during the pressing operation.
11 Lubricate the bearings and fit the intermediate gear.
12 Offer the transfer gears with intermediate plate to the clutch
housing. No gasket is used (photo).
13 Locate the cover plate and its gasket (photo).
14 Fit the cover plate bolts and tighten to the specified torque setting.
15 Refit the clutch housing and transfer gear assembly, as described in
Section 7.

10 Fault diagnosis – clutch

Symptom	Reason(s)
Judder when taking up drive	Loose engine/gearbox mountings Badly worn friction linings or contaminated with oil Worn splines on transfer/input shaft or driven plate hub Worn spigot bush in crankshaft flange
Clutch drag (failure to disengage so that gears cannot be meshed)	Incorrect cable adjustment Rust on splines (may occur after vehicle standing idle for long periods) Damaged or misaligned pressure plate assembly Cable stretched or broken
Clutch slip (increase in engine speed does not result in increase in vehicle road speed – particularly on gradients)	Incorrect cable adjustment Friction linings worn out or oil contaminated
Noise evident on depressing clutch pedal	Dry, worn or damaged release bearing Excessive play between drive plate hub splines and shaft splines
Noise evident as clutch pedal released	Distorted driven plate Broken or weak driven plate cushion coil springs Release bearing loose on retainer hub

Chapter 6 Transmission

For modifications, and information applicable to later models, see Supplement at end of manual

Contents

Specifications

BH 3/4 and BH 3/5 gearboxes

Type .... Four (BH 3/4) or five (BH 3/5) forward speeds all with synchromesh, and one reverse

    Application .... XV, XW and XY series engines

Gear ratios

1st	3.882:1
2nd:	
XV8 and XW7 engines	2.074:1
XY7 and XY8 engines	2.296:1
3rd:	
XV8 and XW7 engines	1.377:1
XY7 and XY8 engines	1.502:1
4th:	
XV8 and XW7 engines	0.944:1
XY7 and XY8 engines	1.124:1
5th (XY7 and XY8 engines)	0.904:1
Reverse	3.568:1
Final drive:	
XV8 engine	3.563:1
XW7 engine	3.354:1
XY7 engine	3.177:1
XY8 engine	3.501:1

Lubrication .... Common supply with engine

Torque wrench settings

	Nm	lbf ft
Primary shaft nut	45	33
Secondary shaft nut:		
4-speed	23	17
5-speed	95	70
Crownwheel bolt	65	48
Reverse lockplate (5-speed)	10	7
Detent ball plug	12	9
Oil filter screen bolt	10	7
Sump plate bolts	12	9
Drain plug	27	20
Reverse lamp switch	27	20
Selector lever bolt	13	10
Half casing bolts (refer to Section 10)		
Primary shaft bearing preload on 4-speed transmission (refer to Section 10)		

BE 1/5 gearbox

Type .... Five forward speeds all with synchromesh, and one reverse

Application .... XU5J (1580 cc) engine

Gear ratios

1st	3.308:1
2nd	1.882:1
3rd	1.360:1 or 1.280:1 (close ratio)
4th	1.069:1 or 0.969:1 (close ratio)
5th	0.865:1 or 0.757:1 (close ratio)
Reverse	3.333:1 or 4.063:1 (close ratio)
Final drive	4.063:1

Lubrication

Oil capacity .... 2.0 litres (3.5 pints)
Oil type/specification (pre-1988 models) .... Multigrade engine oil, viscosity SAE 10W/40 or 15W/40 (Duckhams QXR, Hypergrade, or 10W/40 Motor Oil)

Torque wrench settings

	Nm	lbf ft
Rear cover bolts (use thread locking compound)	12	9
Input and output shaft nuts	54	40
Rear bearing retainer bolts	15	11
Selector rod backplate bolt	15	11
End casing-to-main casing bolts	12	9
Reverse idle spindle bolt	20	15
Selector shaft spring bracket	15	11
Reverse selector spindle nut	20	15
Breather	15	11
Reversing lamp switch	24	18
Drain plug (gearbox)	10	7
Drain plug (final drive)	30	22
Speedometer pinion adaptor	12	9
Final drive extension housing bolts	15	11
Crownwheel securing bolts	65	48
Final drive half housing bolts, 10 mm	41	30
Final drive half housing bolts, 7 mm	12	9
Clutch release bearing guide tube bolts	12	9
Mounting stud nut	34	25

PART A: GENERAL DESCRIPTION AND ROUTINE MAINTENANCE

1 General description

BH 3/4 and BH 3/5 gearboxes

The transmission is mounted transversely directly under and to the rear of the engine with which it shares a common lubrication system.

The transmission casing is constructed in light alloy and incorporates the final drive and differential.

Power from the engine crankshaft is transmitted through the output shaft then the transfer gears to the transmission input shaft.

Drive to the front roadwheels is transmitted through open driveshafts from the differential side gears.

The transmission may be of four or five-speed type, depending upon the vehicle model. Both types are similar except for the 5th gear located on the ends of the primary and secondary shafts.

The transmission is of conventional two shaft constant-mesh layout. There are four pairs of gears, one for each forward speed. The gears on the primary shaft are fixed to the shaft, while those on the secondary or pinion shaft float, each being locked to the shaft when engaged by the synchromesh unit. The reverse idler gear is on a third shaft.

On five-speed units, the 5th gears are of fixed type with an extra synchromesh assembly.

The gear selector forks engage in the synchromesh unit; these slide axially along the shaft to engage the appropriate gear. The forks are mounted on selector shafts which are located in the base of the gearbox.

The helical gear on the end of the pinion shaft drives directly onto the crownwheel mounted on the differential unit. The latter differs from normal practice in that it runs in shell bearings and the end thrust is taken up by thrust washers in a similar manner to the engine crankshaft.

Fig. 6.1 Sectional view of the BH 3/5 gearbox (Sec 1)

1 Casing
2 Input (clutch) shaft
3 Primary shaft
4 Selector dogs
5 Final drive pinion
6 Reverse gear (secondary shaft)
7 1st gear (secondary shaft)
8 2nd gear (secondary shaft)
9 3rd gear (secondary shaft)
10 4th gear (secondary shaft)
11 5th gear
12 5th gear (secondary shaft)
13 1st/2nd synchro
14 3rd/4th synchro
15 5th gear synchro
16 Crownwheel
17 Differential pinion gears
18 Pinion shaft
19 Differential side gears
20 Differential case
21 Speedometer drivegear

Fig. 6.2 Sectional view of the BE 1/5 gearbox (Sec 1)

1	Input shaft	8	5th gear (driving)	14	1st gear (driven)
2	Release bearing guide tube	9	5th synchro	15	Output shaft
3	Casings	10	5th gear (driven)	16	Crownwheel
4	Reverse idler gear	11	3rd/4th gears (driven)	17	Differential gear
5	3rd gear (driving)	12	2nd gear (driven)	18	Side gear
6	3rd/4th synchro	13	1st/2nd synchro	19	Differential carrier
7	4th gear (driving)				

20	Speedo driving gear
21	Extension housing
a	Selective shim – input shaft bearing preload
b	Selective shim – differential bearing preload

BE 1/5 gearbox

The transmission is mounted on the left-hand side of the engine and may be removed separately leaving the engine in the car.

The gearbox has five forward gears, all with synchromesh, and one reverse. As is common practice in five-speed units, the 5th gear components are on the far side of an intermediate plate which carries one pair of shaft bearings.

The differential (final drive) unit is contained in its own housing which is bolted to the gearbox casing. The gearbox and differential share the same lubricant.

2 Routine maintenance

Carry out the following procedures at the intervals given in Routine Maintenance at the beginning of the manual.

1 Using a suitable container beneath the transmission, remove the drain plug and drain the oil. On BH 3/4 and BH 3/5 gearboxes the engine uses the same oil, but on the BE 1/5 gearbox the oil is separate and two drain plugs are provided: one for the main gearbox, the other for the differential.

2 Clean the drain plug(s) then refit and tighten.

3 Refill the transmission with the correct quantity and grade of oil. On BH 3/4 and BH 3/5 gearboxes the level can be checked using the engine oil dipstick, but on the BE 1/5 gearbox there is no provision for checking the oil level so the correct quantity must be measured out before pouring into the top filler/breather plug aperture (depending on model). On the latter gearbox it is therefore important to completely drain the old oil. Refit and tighten the filler plug on completion.

4 There is no routine maintenance interval for checking and topping-up the transmission oil level on the BE 1/5 gearbox. The BH 3/4 and BH 3/5 gearboxes are automatically checked when checking the engine oil level.

PART B: BH 3/4 AND BH 3/5 GEARBOXES

3 Gearchange linkage – adjustment

1 The gearchange linkage does not normally require adjustment. Problems with gear selection are likely to be due to worn gearbox internal components, or worn gearchange link rod balljoints.

2 If a link rod is to be renewed, check that the length of the new rod supplied is the same as the old rod removed. If necessary, the rod length can be adjusted by loosening the locknut and turning the balljoint as required. Note the relative alignment of the balljoints before carrying out adjustments, as incorrect positioning can lead to premature wear. No adjustment dimensions are specified by the manufacturers.

Fig. 6.4 Gearchange link rods (Sec 3)

1 *Upper rod*   2 *Lower rod*

3.1 Bottom view of gearchange linkage rod 2 (arrowed)

2 If the linkage is not already fitted with a tension spring, fit one as shown (Fig. 6.5).

3 The gear lever can be removed after withdrawal of the centre console (photos).

Fig. 6.3 Drain and filler plug locations on the BE 1/5 gearbox (Sec 2)

a Gearbox drain plug   *c Filler/breather plug*
b Final drive drain plug   *(depending on model)*

3.3A View of a link rod attached to the bottom of the gear lever

3.3B Centre console rear screw

3.3C Removing the gear lever surround

Fig. 6.5 Location of gearchange link rod tension spring (2) (Sec 3)

4 Transmission overhaul – general

1 No work can be carried out to the transmission until the engine/transmission has been removed from the car, as described in Chapter 1, and cleaned externally.
2 Remove the clutch/flywheel housing and transfer gears, as described in Chapters 1 and 5. Drain the lubricating oil.
3 Unbolt and remove the timing chain cover and the flywheel, as described in Chapter 1.
4 Unscrew and remove all the engine-to-transmission connecting bolts, making sure that the two bolts and one nut are removed from the flange joint adjacent to the flywheel mounting flange on the end of the crankshaft.
5 Prise the transmission from the engine using a length of wood as a lever.

5 Transmission – dismantling into major units

1 With the transmission on the bench unbolt and remove the protective plate and sump cover (bolts).
2 Unbolt and remove the oil pick-up screen (photo).
3 Remove the speedometer drivegear (photo).
4 Unscrew and remove the reverse lamp switch (photo).
5 Release, but do not remove, the nineteen bolts which hold the two transmission half casing sections together.

Four-speed unit
6 Unscrew and remove the primary shaft bearing ring nut by engaging a suitable tool in the nut cut-outs (photo).

5.1A Sump protective plate

5.1B Sump cover and gasket

5.2 Oil pick-up screen

5.3 Speedometer drivegear

5.4 Reverse lamp switch

5.6 Primary shaft bearing ring nut cut-outs – arrowed (four-speed)

5.7 Removing primary shaft (five-speed)

5.8 Removing secondary shaft

5.10 Transmission shaft bearing shells

All units

7   Remove the casing bolts, separate the casing sections and lift out the primary shaft (photo).

8   Lift out the secondary shaft (photo).

9   Lift out the final drive/differential.

10 Remove the bearing shells, identifying them in respect of location if they are used again (photo).

11 Examine all components for wear or damage and carry out further dismantling as necessary and as described in the following Sections.

12 If it is intended to renew the casing sections then they must both be renewed at the same time as a pair.

13 Clean old gasket material from the original casings without scoring the metal and clean out the oilways.

---

6   Primary shaft – overhaul

1   Only the bearings can be renewed as the gears cannot be removed from the shaft.

Four-speed unit

2   Either support the bearing and press the shaft from it or draw the bearing form the shaft using a two legged puller (photo).

3   When fitting the bearing, apply pressure to the inner track only.

Five-speed unit

4   Mark the position of the 5th gear synchro sleeve in relation to the hub.

5   Grip the shaft in a vice fitted, with jaw protectors.

6   Unscrew the nut (photo).

7   Withdraw 5th gear synchro sleeve from the shaft (photo).

8   Support the gear and press the shaft out of the synchro-hub. Alternatively use a suitable puller (photo).

9   Remove 5th gear, bush and washer (photos).

Fig. 6.6 Pressing primary shaft out of bearing (four-speed) (Sec 6)

Fig. 6.7 Pressing primary shaft out of bearing (five-speed) (Sec 6)

Fig. 6.8 Primary shaft nut (3) (five-speed) (Sec 6)

Fig. 6.9 Pressing primary shaft from synchro-hub (five-speed) (Sec 6)

Fig. 6.10 5th gear primary shaft components (Sec 6)

7 Washer	10 Synchro-hub
8 Bush	11 Nut
9 5th gear	

Fig. 6.11 Primary shaft (five-speed) double taper bearing (Sec 6)

3 Bearing	5 Washer
4 Bush	6 Bearing

Fig. 6.12 Primary shaft (five-speed) single taper roller bearing (Sec 6)

6.2 Primary shaft bearing and circlip

6.6 Primary shaft nut (five-speed)

6.7 Primary 5th gear synchro sleeve

6.8 Removing 5th gear synchro-hub

6.9A 5th gear

6.9B 5th gear bush

6.9C 5th gear thrust washer

6.10 Primary shaft (five-speed)

2 Using a press or a suitable puller remove the bearing (four-speed) or bearing and 5th gear (five-speed) (photo).
3 Remove the spacer and 4th gear.
4 Mark the relationship of the hub to the sleeve of the 3rd/4th synchro unit and then remove the synchro unit.
5 Remove the key (7) and spacer (8), Fig. 6.17.
6 Take off 3rd gear (9), Fig. 6.18.
7 Take off the spacer (10).
8 Remove 2nd gear (11) and the spacer (14).
9 Mark the relationship of the hub to the sleeve of the 1st/2nd synchro unit and then take off the synchro unit (13).
10 Remove 1st gear (15).

7.2 Removing secondary shaft bearing with 5th gear

10 Press the shaft out of the bearings or draw off the bearings using a suitable puller. Remove the washer (photo).
11 When refitting the bearings, apply pressure to the centre track only.
12 The bearings at the opposite end of the shaft are of single roller type.
13 When refitting the synchro-hub use a new nut, tighten to the specified torque and stake the nut into the shaft groove to lock it.

Four and five-speed units
14 Never re-use a bearing which has been removed from a shaft.
15 Do not mix the components of one new bearing set with another and do not attempt to remove the new bearing grease.

7 Secondary shaft – overhaul

1 Secure the shaft in a vice fitted with jaw protectors and unscrew the nut.

Fig. 6.13 Secondary shaft (five-speed) (Sec 7)

1 Nut

Fig. 6.14 Removing secondary shaft 5th gear and bearing (Sec 7)

Fig. 6.15 Five-speed secondary shaft spacer (3) and 4th gear (4) (Sec 7)

Fig. 6.16 Five-speed secondary shaft synchro-hub (5) and sleeve (6) (Sec 7)

a   Alignment marks

Fig. 6.17 Five-speed secondary shaft key (7) and spacer (8) (Sec 7)

7.12 Fitting 1st gear to the secondary shaft

7.13 Fitting 1st/2nd synchro-hub to the secondary shaft

7.14 Fitting first spacer to the secondary shaft

Fig. 6.18 Five-speed secondary shaft components (Sec 7)

9 3rd gear	13 Synchro sleeve
10 Spacer	14 Spacer
11 2nd gear	15 1st gear
12 Synchro-hub	b Alignment marks

Reassembly

11 As work progresses, dip each component in clean engine oil.

12 To the shaft fit 1st gear (photo).

13 Fit the 1st/2nd synchro-hub (photo).

14 Fit the spacer and align its splines so that the key can be fitted (photo).

15 Fit the 1st/2nd synchro sleeve so that its mark made at dismantling aligns with the one on the hub. The lines on the spacer pins are towards 1st gear (photos).

16 Fit 2nd gear (photo).

17 Fit the spacer and align the splines so that the key can be fitted (photo).

18 Fit 3rd gear (photo).

19 Fit the spacer, once more aligning the splines so that the key can be fitted (photo).

7.15A Fitting 1st/2nd synchro sleeve to the secondary shaft

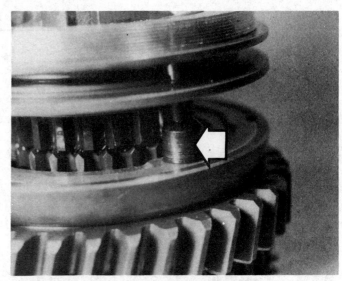

7.15B Lines on synchro spacer pins (arrowed)

7.16 Fitting 2nd gear to the secondary shaft

7.17 Fitting second spacer to the secondary shaft

7.18 Fitting 3rd gear to secondary shaft

7.19 Fitting third spacer to the secondary shaft

20 Push the key into the widest shaft groove so that the chamfered edge on the key is at the bottom of the groove. Push the key until it is flush with the spacer (photo).
21 Fit the 3rd/4th synchro-hub (photo).
22 Fit the 3rd/4th synchro sleeve so that its mark made at dismantling aligns with the one on the hub. The line on the spacer pin must be towards 3rd gear (photo).
23 Fit 4th gear (photo).
24 Fit the spacer (photo).
25 Press the bearing (four-speed) or the bearing and 5th gear (five-speed) onto the shaft (photos).
26 Engage a new circlip in the bearing outer track groove.
27 Screw on a new shaft nut to the specified torque and stake the nut into the groove in the shaft (photo).

8 Selector mechanism and reverse idler – dismantling and reassembly

1 Unscrew and remove the three threaded detent plugs and extract the coil springs and balls. If the plugs are very tight, tap their end-face hard using a rod and hammer.

Four-speed unit
2 Drive out the reverse fork roll pin.

Five-speed unit
3 Knock out the roll pin and unscrew the bolt and remove the reverse fork ball lock plate. Extract the two balls (4), Fig. 6.20. Move the position of the selector shaft slightly to release the second ball.

7.20 Pushing key into shaft groove

7.21 3rd/4th synchro-hub on the secondary shaft

7.22 Fitting 3rd/4th synchro sleeve to the secondary shaft

7.23 Fitting 4th gear to the secondary shaft

7.24 Fitting 4th gear spacer

7.25A Fitting secondary shaft bearing

7.25B Fitting 5th gear to the secondary shaft

7.27 Secondary shaft nut

Fig. 6.19 Driving out reverse fork roll pin (four-speed) (Sec 8)

Fig. 6.21 Interlock disc (5) (five-speed) (Sec 8)

Fig. 6.20 Detent ball retaining plate (3) and detent balls (4)
(Sec 8)

Fig. 6.22 Driving out 3rd/4th selector fork roll pin (Sec 8)

4   Slide the 5th/reverse selector shaft so that the dog contracts the
housing web then drive out the roll pin which secures the dog.

All units
5   Withdraw the reverse selector shaft and retrieve the interlock disc
(5), Fig. 6.21.
6   Drive out the roll pin which secures the 3rd/4th fork to the selector
shaft. Remove the fork from the shaft.
7   Drive out the roll pin which secures the fork to the 1st/2nd selector
shaft.

Five-speed unit
8   Drive out the roll pin which secures the dog to the 1st/2nd selector
shaft. Before doing this, slide the shaft so that the dog is in contact with
the housing web.

All units
9   Withdraw the 1st/2nd selector shaft.
10 Withdraw the 3rd/4th selector shaft.
11 Remove the 1st/2nd and reverse selector forks.
12 Drive out the reverse idler shaft roll pin (1), Fig. 6.25.

Fig. 6.23 Selector components (Sec 8)

1	1st/2nd selector shaft	3	1st/2nd selector fork
2	3rd/4th selector shaft	4	Reverse fork

Fig. 6.24 Removing 1st/2nd selector dog roll pin (Sec 8)

a   Casing web

Fig. 6.26 Selector lever (4) and pivot bolt (Sec 8)

Fig. 6.25 Reverse idler components (Sec 8)

1   Roll pin   *3   Stop*
2   Idler shaft

Fig. 6.27 Selector finger (6) and roll pins (5) (Sec 8)

Fig. 6.28 Compressing selector finger coil spring to remove cup (7) (Sec 8)

13 Remove reverse idler shaft (2) the stop (3) and reverse idler gear.
14 Remove the pivot bolt and withdraw the selector shaft lever (4), Fig. 6.26.
15 Drive out the dual roll pins (5) at the selector finger (6) and remove the finger, Fig. 6.27.
16 Compress the coil spring using an open-ended spanner or forked tool and remove the cups (7), Fig. 6.28.
17 Remove the remote control rod (8) and extract the oil seal (9), Fig. 6.29.

Reassembly
18 Lubricate all components with clean engine oil as work proceeds. Renew all roll pins and the remote control rod O-ring.
19 Fit the O-ring into its recess in the remote control rod housing.
20 Fit the remote control rod, together with spacer, spring and stop.

Fig. 6.29 Remote control rod (8) and casing oil seal (9) (Sec 8)

Fig. 6.31 Alignment of selector finger and lever bellcrank (Sec 8)

Fig. 6.32 Gearchange rod bellcrank pivot arrangement (Sec 8)

Fig. 6.30 Selector identification (Sec 8)

1	1st/2nd selector shaft	6	Reverse (4-speed)
2	1st/2nd selector fork		Reverse/5th (5-speed)
3	1st/2nd selector dog		selector shaft
4	3rd/4th selector shaft	7	Reverse selector fork
5	3rd/4th selector fork	8	5th gear selector shaft
		9	5th/reverse selector dog

21 Compress the coil spring and fit the half cups.
22 Fit the selector finger, check for correct alignment and drive in the dual roll pins.
23 Using the pivot bolt, fit the gearchange rod lever. Tighten the pivot bolt to the specified torque.
24 Fit reverse idler gear, the stop and the idler shaft. Drive in the shaft roll pin (photos).
25 Place reverse fork in position and then fit the 1st/2nd selector shaft with its fork. The shaft will pass through the reverse fork cut-out (photos).

8.24A Reverse idler gear stop and shaft

8.24B Reverse idler shaft roll pin

8.25A 1st/2nd selector shaft with reverse fork viewed from oil pick-up screen side

8.25B 1st/2nd selector shaft with reverse fork viewed from inner side

Four-speed unit
26 Pin the fork to the 1st/2nd selector shaft.

Five-speed unit
27 Pin the dog to the 1st/2nd selector shaft (photo).

8.27 1st/2nd selector shaft dog and roll pin

All units
28 Fit the 3rd/4th selector shaft with its fork and drive in the securing pin.

Five-speed unit
29 Secure the fork to the 1st/2nd selector shaft by driving in the roll pin.

All units
30 Insert the reverse interlock disc so that it engages positively in the slots in the selector shafts (photo).
31 Slide the reverse selector shaft without disturbing the interlock disc.

Four-speed unit
32 Secure the reverse fork to the selector shaft with a roll pin (photo).

Five-speed unit
33 Fit the 5th/reverse dog to its selector shaft and secure it with a roll pin (photos).
34 Place one detent ball in the reverse fork then fit the plate with the second ball (photos).
35 Tighten the plate fixing bolt to the specified torque.

All units
36 Fit the three detent balls and their springs. Apply thread locking fluid to clean threads of the detent plugs and tighten the plugs to the specified torque (photos). Do not apply too much fluid or it will run down and cause the balls to seize.

9 Final drive/differential – dismantling and reassembly

1 Unscrew the fixing bolts and remove the crownwheel from the differential case.
2 Remove the pinion shaft, pinion gears with friction washers and side gears with thrust washers.
3 Clean all components and examine for worn or chipped gearteeth. Renew components as necessary.
4 Commence reassembly by fitting the differential side gears and thrust washers. The grooved side of the washer must be towards the gear.

8.30 Interlock disc

8.32 Reverse fork roll pin (four-speed)

8.33A 5th/reverse selector dog roll pin

8.33B Selector shaft locations

8.34A Fitting first ball to reverse fork

8.34B Reverse fork second ball

8.34C Reverse fork lockplate

8.36A Using a pencil magnet to locate detent ball

8.36B Detent spring and plug

8.36C Location of remaining two detent springs and plugs

8.36D Allen key used to tighten detent plug

Fig. 6.33 Exploded view of final drive/differential (Sec 9)

5   Fit the friction washers, pinion gears and push the pinion shaft into position.

6   Locate the crownwheel with the differential case, insert the connecting bolts and tighten to the specified torque. Make sure that the pinion shaft is retained by two of the crownwheel bolts.

10 Transmission – reassembly

1   Renew all gaskets and oil seals, also the shaft nuts. As reassembly proceeds, apply clean engine oil to all components.

2   Check that the housing half casing positioning dowels are in place.

3   Make sure that new bearing shells are in their recesses in the casings. If the original shells are being used, check that they are returned to their original locations and their recesses and the shell backs are perfectly clean and free from grit.

4   The selector mechanism will already have been fitted, as described in Section 8.

5   Fit the final drive/differential, together with the thrust washers, into the selector shaft half-casing. Make sure that the copper side of the thrust washer is towards the crownwheel and the tabs offset upwards (photo).

6   Fit the secondary shaft geartrain into the half-casing, making sure that the selector forks engage in the synchro sleeve grooves and the bearing circlip fits into its casing groove.

10.5 Differential thrust washer with tabs offset

7 Fit the primary shaft geartrain, remembering that on four-speed units the shaft must be fitted with bearing outer tracks and thrust washer. On five-speed units, the 5th/reverse synchro assembly must be positioned on the shaft with the longer spacer pins towards the end of the shaft (photo).

8 Make sure that the casing locating dowels are in position and then apply jointing compound to the mating face of the half casings (photo).

9 Fit the casings together, making sure that the selector finger engages in the selector shaft dog cut-outs.

10 Use new lock washers and screw in the connecting bolts finger tight. Note the location of the various bolt sizes and lengths, Fig. 6.34.

11 On four-speed transmissions, the primary shaft bearing preload must now be adjusted. Screw in the bearing ring nut finger tight and then tighten the casing internal bolts accessible through the sump plate aperture and upper casing.

12 Engage any gear and turn the nut on the end of the secondary shaft to settle the bearings.

13 Tighten the ring nut to 20 Nm (15 lbf ft) then loosen it and retighten to 9 Nm (7 lbf ft).

14 Finally stake the nut into the shaft groove. In order to be able to turn the ring nut, make up an adaptor (to engage in the nut cut-outs) to which a torque wrench can be connected.

10.7 Geartrains and final drive (five-speed)

10.8 Applying jointing compound to casing flanges

Fig. 6.34 Transmission casing connecting bolt locations (Sec 10)

1	M10 x 1.50 x 75	7	M10 x 1.50 x 90
2	M8 x 1.25 x 55	8	M10 x 1.50 x 65
3	M8 x 1.25 x 55	9	M8 x 1.25 x 55
4	M8 x 1.25 x 55	10	M7 x 1.00 x 30
5	M7 x 1.00 x 75	a	Dowel protrusion.
6	M7 x 1.00 x 30		Measurement in mm

All units

15 Refer to Fig. 6.34 and tighten the bolts in the following order.

Stage 1	Torque
Bolts 2, 3, 4, 9	9 Nm (7 lbf ft)
Bolts 5, 6, 10	12 Nm (9 lbf ft)
Bolts 1, 7, 8	20 Nm (15 lbf ft)
Stage 2	
Bolts 2, 3, 4, 9	17 Nm (13 lbf ft)
Bolts 1, 7, 8	45 Nm (33 lbf ft)

10.17 Sump cover bolt with reinforcement washer

10.18 Oil drain plug showing magnet

10.21 Driveshaft oil seal at transmission

16 Fit the oil pick-up filter, tightening the bolts to the specified torque.
17 Refit the sump cover plate with a new gasket. Tighten the bolts to the specified torque. Fit the protective plate (photo).
18 Fit and tighten the drain plug (photo).
19 Refit the speedometer drive pinion with a new O-ring.
20 Screw in the reverse lamp switch.
21 If new driveshaft oil seals have not already been fitted drive them squarely into position now and fill their lips with grease (photo).

Fig. 6.35 Ring nut adaptor tool (Sec 10)

11 Differential/driveshaft oil seals – renewal

1 The differential oil seals can be removed and refitted with the engine/transmission unit in position in the car, but the driveshafts will obviously have to be removed. This operation is covered in Chapter 7.
2 With the driveshafts withdrawn, the old oil seals can be extracted from the differential housing using a suitable screwdriver.
3 Clean out the seating before fitting a new seal. Lubricate the seal to assist assembly and drift carefully into position, with the lip facing inwards. Fill the seal lips with grease.
4 Always take care not to damage the oil seals when removing or refitting the driveshafts.

PART C: BE 1/5 GEARBOX

12 Transmission – removal and refitting

1 The BE 1 gearbox can be removed independently of the engine using the following procedure.
2 Disconnect the bonnet stay from the right-hand suspension tower and use suitable U-brackets in the bonnet hinge holes to hold the bonnet in a vertical position.
3 Remove the starter, as described in Chapter 12, but it is not necessary to disconnect the wiring as the unit may be placed to one side.
4 Remove the airflow sensor and associated hoses, as described in Chapter 3.
5 Remove the battery, as described in Chapter 12.
6 Disconnect the clutch cable and remove the pushrod and intermediate lever, as described in Chapter 5.

Fig. 6.36 Right-hand driveshaft intermediate bearing bracket and right-hand rear engine mounting link (Sec 12)

1 Link
2 Intermediate bearing nuts
3 Intermediate bearing bolts with special heads

7 Jack up the car and support on axle stands. Apply the handbrake.
8 Drain the transmission oil by removing the gearbox and final drive drain plugs (photo). Clean and refit the plugs on completion.
9 Unscrew and remove both front clamp bolts securing the hub carriers to the bottom of the front suspension struts.
10 Loosen the two nuts retaining the right-hand driveshaft intermediate bearing in the bracket bolted to the rear of the cylinder block, then turn the bolts so that their heads move through 90°.
11 Unbolt the right-hand rear engine mounting link from the subframe, loosen the front bolt, and let the link hang free.
12 Disconnect all three gearchange control rods (photos).
13 Turn the steering to full right-hand lock then pull the left-hand lower suspension arm down from the hub carrier and unbolt the balljoint guard plate.
14 Pull the hub carrier outwards, and at the same time withdraw the inner end of the driveshaft from the final drive unit. Refer to Chapter 7 and fit a suitable tool to the differential side gear in order to prevent it from falling into the final drive housing.

12.8 Final drive drain plug (arrowed)

12.12A Gearchange lower control rod

12.12B Gearchange upper control rods (arrowed)

15 Withdraw the right-hand driveshaft from the final drive unit using the procedure described in paragraphs 13 and 14 with the steering on full left-hand lock.

16 Disconnect the wiring from the reverse lamp switch and tie it to one side.

17 Disconnect the speedometer cable, as described in Chapter 12.

18 Using a hoist, take the weight of the engine then unscrew and remove the top nut from the left-hand engine mounting.

19 Unbolt and remove the battery tray.

20 Lower the engine until the timing cover touches the body at the same time pulling the unit forwards to prevent the final drive housing fouling the subframe.

21 Temporarily reconnect the right-hand rear engine mounting link to the subframe.

22 Support the gearbox with a trolley jack then remove the clutch housing-to-engine mounting bolts and remove the cover plate.

23 Withdraw the gearbox from the engine until the input shaft is clear of the clutch, then lower it through the engine compartment and remove from under the car.

24 Refitting is a reversal of removal, but note the following points:

(a) *It is recommended that the driveshaft oil seals in the final drive housing are renewed, as described in Chapter 7, Section 3*

(b) *Tighten all nuts and bolts to the specified torque*

(c) *Refill the transmission with the correct quantity of oil (photo).*

(d) *Adjust the clutch cable, with reference to Chapter 5*

(c) *Check the operation of the gearchange linkage and adjust it if necessary*

12.24 Filling the transmission with oil

13 Gearchange linkage – adjustment

1 Place the gear lever in neutral, then move it gently to the left until the commencement of resistance is felt.

2 Position a ruler against the gear knob with the zero marking aligned with the 1/2 mark on the knob.

3 Push the gear lever as far as possible to the left without moving the ruler and note the distance travelled by the knob. Repeat the operation two or three times. The desired travel is 36 to 40 mm.

4 If adjustment is necessary, unclip the gaiter from the surround and pull it up the gear lever.

5 If fitted, remove and discard the O-ring from the bottom of the gear lever.

6 Extract the spring clip and lift the plastic cam off its splines (photo), then reposition the cam on the splines to give the correct lever movement described in paragraphs 1 to 3. Refit the spring clip on completion.

13.6 Gear lever cam and stop

14.2 Removing the gearbox end cover

H14033

Fig. 6.37 Gearchange linkage adjustment (Sec 13)

6   Engagement rod Y = 284 mm   5   Selection rod X = 122 mm

7   If the correct adjustment cannot be achieved due to the cam's being at its minimum or maximum position, the selection rod (Fig. 6.37) should be lengthened by 6.0 mm (0.24 in) to provide extra movement or shortened by 6.0 mm (0.24 in) to provide less movement. The normal initial length of the selection rod is given in Fig. 6.37. Adjust the cam position again after altering the selection rod length.
8   Check that the length of the engagement rod is as given in Fig. 6.37 and adjust if necessary.
9   Apply a little grease to the gear lever stop, and refit the gear lever gaiter.

14 Transmission – dismantling into major assemblies

1   With the unit removed from the car, clean all exterior surfaces and wipe dry.
2   Remove the eight bolts and washers which secure the end cover. Remove the cover (photo).

3   Make alignment marks between the 5th gear synchro-hub and its sliding sleeve.
4   Engage 5th gear, then drive out the roll pin which secures 5th gear selector fork to the selector rod (photo).
5   Hold 5th gear selector fork in the engaged position and return the gear selector to neutral so that the selector rod moves through the fork.
6   Engage any other gear to lock up the shafts, then unscrew and remove the 28 mm nut from the end of the input shaft. If the nut is staked in position it may be necessary to relieve the staking (photo).
7   Remove 5th gear synchro-hub, sliding sleeve and selector fork from the input shaft. Be prepared for the ejection of the detent ball from the selector fork.
8   Refit the 5th gear sliding sleeve and hub and engage 5th gear again. Relieve the staking from the output shaft nut and remove the nut (photo). Remove the sliding sleeve and hub again.
9   Remove from the input shaft the 5th gear, its bush and the spacer.
10   Remove the two bolts and washers which secure the output shaft rear bearing.
11   Remove the circlip from the output shaft rear bearing by prising up

14.4 5th gear selector fork showing roll pin (arrowed)

14.6 Unscrewing the input shaft nut

14.8 Unscrewing the output shaft nut

14.12 Selector rod lockplate bolt

its ends. The circlip should be renewed anyway, so do not be afraid of breaking it. Raise the output shaft if the circlip is jammed in its groove.
12 Extract its securing bolt and remove the selector rod lockplate (photo).
13 Remove the bolt which retains the reverse idler gear spindle.
14 Remove the thirteen bolts and washers which secure the end casing to the main casing. Withdraw the end casing: it is located by dowels, and may need striking with a wooden or plastic mallet to free it. Do not use a metal hammer, nor lever in between the joint faces. Note the location of the clutch cable bracket.
15 Remove the selector arm and spring from the gear selector shaft. Remove the circlip and washer, push the shaft in and recover the O-ring (photo).
16 Drive out the roll pins which secure the selector finger and the interlock bracket to the selector shaft.

17 Inspect the cover which protects the end of the selector shaft. If it is tapered, proceed to the next paragraph. If it is cylindrical, use pliers or a self-gripping wrench to extract it, then press the gear selector shaft towards the cover so that the circlip and washer can be extracted from the end of the shaft (photos). These components are not fitted to earlier models; there are associated changes in the shaft itself, the main casing and 5th gear selector fork.
18 Pull the selector shaft out of the gearbox. From inside the gearbox recover, as they are freed from the shaft, the selector finger, the inlerlock bracket, the spring and its cup washers. Notice which way round the washers are fitted.
19 Screw the reverse idler spindle retaining bolt back into the spindle and use it as a lever to extract the spindle. Remove the reverse idler gear itself (photo).
20 Remove the swarf-collecting magnet from the casing (photo).

14.15 Gear selector shaft is secured by a circlip

14.17A Cylindrical cover must be removed ...

14.17B ... to extract the circlip

14.19 Removing the reverse idler spindle

14.20 The swarf-collecting magnet

21 Carefully lift out the two geartrains with their shafts, the selector forks and the selector rods.

22 Remove the spring support bracket from inside the main casing.

23 If not already removed, drive out the selector shaft end cover, using a drift of diameter no greater than 14 mm.

24 Extract the lubrication jet, using a wire hook.

25 Unscrew and remove the reversing lamp switch.

26 Remove the nut and washer which secure the reverse selector fork spindle. Remove the spindle and the selector fork. Recover the detent plunger and spring (photos).

27 Unscrew and remove the breather from the main casing (photo).

28 Turning to the clutch housing, remove the clutch release bearing (if not already done). Pull off the release fork.

29 Unbolt and remove the release bearing guide tube.

30 From behind the tube remove the preload shim and the outer track of the input shaft front bearing.

31 To remove the final drive unit, first unbolt and remove the speedometer pinion and its adaptor (photo).

32 Unbolt and remove the extension housing (photo). Recover the speedometer driving gear and the bearing preload shim (photo).

14.27 Removing the breather

14.26A Reverse selector fork

14.31 Removing the speedometer pinion

14.26B Reverse detent plunger and spring

14.32A Removing the final drive extension housing

14.32B Removing the speedometer driving gear

16.1A Input shaft bearing ...

33 Unbolt the final drive half housing. Remove the half housing and final drive unit. Note the location of the gearchange pivot bracket.
34 Identify the final drive bearing outer tracks: if they are to be re-used they must be refitted on the same sides.
35 Remove the selector lever from the main casing. It is retained by a circlip and a washer.
36 If it is wished to remove the clutch release lever balljoint, do so with a slide hammer having a suitable claw. (A new gearbox will not necessarily be fitted with a balljoint).
37 The gearbox is now dismantled into its major assemblies.

15 Transmission – examination and renovation

1   Clean all components and examine them thoroughly for wear and damage.
2   Circlips, roll pins, gaskets, oil seals and locking devices should all be renewed as a matter of course. Prise out the old oil seal from the clutch release bearing guide tube, but do not fit the new seal until so instructed during reassembly. Renew the input and output shaft nuts.
3   If new input shaft or differential bearings are to be fitted, a selection of preload shims will be required. Read through the relevant procedures before starting work.

16.1B ... 4th gear ...

16 Input shaft – dismantling and reassembly

1   Remove the 3rd and 4th gear components from the input shaft by supporting the assembly under the 3rd gear and pressing or driving the shaft through. Protect the end of the shaft. Once the rear bearing is free, the other components can be removed from the shaft in order: 4th gear and its bush, 3rd/4th synchro sleeve and hub and 3rd gear (photos).
2   Mark the synchro sleeve and hub relative to each other and to show which side faces 4th gear.
3   Remove the front bearing from the shaft, preferably with a press or a bearing puller. As a last resort it may be possible to support the bearing and drive the shaft through: be sure to protect the end of the shaft if this is done.
4   Once the input shaft bearings have been removed, they must be renewed. Press the rear bearing outer track from the end casing and press in the new track, making sure it enters squarely.
5   Before commencing reassembly, make sure that the input shaft is free from burrs and wear marks. Lubricate all parts as they are fitted.
6   Fit a new front bearing to the shaft, using a suitable tube to press or drive it home.

16.1C ... 4th gear bush ...

16.1D ... 3rd/4th synchro sleeve ...

16.1G Input shaft with all components removed except the front bearing

16.1E ... synchro-hub ...

7   Fit 3rd gear, 3rd/4th synchro-hub and sleeve, 4th gear and its bush. Take care not to get 3rd and 4th gears mixed up, they are similar in appearance (4th gear has more teeth). If the original synchro components are being refitted, observe the mating marks made during dismantling.
8   Fit a new rear bearing to the shaft, again using a piece of tube.
9   The input shaft is now reassembled.

17 Output shaft – dismantling and reassembly

1   Remove 5th gear and the rear bearing from the output shaft. Use a puller or bearing extractor if they are a tight fit on the shaft (photo).
2   Remove 3rd/4th gear assembly, 2nd gear and its bush (photos).
3   Make alignment marks between the 1st/2nd synchro-hub and sleeve, then remove them from the shaft (photos).
4   Remove 1st gear and the half washers (early models) or needle thrust bearing and circlip (later models) (photos).

16.1F ... and 3rd gear

17.1 Output shaft rear bearing

17.2A 3rd/4th gear assembly ...

17.2B ... 2nd gear ...

17.2C ... and 2nd gear bush

17.3A 1st/2nd synchro sleeve ...

17.3B ... and hub

17.4A Remove 1st gear ...

17.4B ... the needle thrust bearing ...

17.4C ... and the bearing circlip

Fig. 6.38 Detail of early type output shaft (Sec 17)

1   1st/2nd synchro   3   Half washers
2   1st driven gear

5   Press or drive the shaft out of the pinion end bearing, protecting the end of the shaft.
6   Before commencing reassembly, make sure that the shaft is free from burrs or wear marks. Lubricate all parts as they are fitted.
7   Fit the pinion end bearing to the shaft, using a piece of tube to drive or press it home. On later models, fit a new circlip.
8   Fit the half washers above the bearing, using a smear of grease to hold them in position. On later models, fit the needle thrust bearing instead.
9   Refit 1st gear, taking care not to dislodge the half washers (when fitted).
10 Refit the 1st/2nd synchro unit, observing the mating marks made when dismantling. The chamfer on the external teeth must face towards 1st gear.
11 Fit 2nd gear and its bush.
12 Fit the 3rd/4th gear assembly, making sure it is the right way round.
13 Fit the rear bearing, with the circlip groove nearest the tail of the shaft.
14 Fit the 5th gear with its boss towards the bearing.

15 Fit a new nut to the output shaft but do not tighten it yet. Assembly of the output shaft is now complete.

18 Selector mechanism – dismantling and reassembly

1   One of the unusual features of this gearbox is that the detent springs and balls are located in the forks (photo). If a spring is weak, the whole fork must be renewed. (This does not apply to 5th gear fork).
2   Rotate the 1st/2nd and 3rd/4th selector rod to disengage the detent slots from the balls, then remove the rod from the forks.

18.1 Gear selector fork showing captive detent ball and spring (arrowed)

18.7 Selector forks and rods in neutral

Fig. 6.39 Selector forks and rods (Sec 18)

1   3rd/4th fork   4   1st/2nd fork
2   1st/2nd and 3rd/4th rod   5   5th rod
3   Locking slot

3   Remove the 5th gear selector rod from the 1st/2nd fork.
4   Examine the forks and rods for wear and damage and renew as necessary.
5   Commence reassembly by inserting 5th gear selector rod into the 1st/2nd fork.
6   Offer the 3rd/4th fork to the 1st/2nd fork so that their holes and selector fingers align.
7   Insert the 1st/2nd and 3rd/4th selector rod, positioning the locking slot as shown (Fig. 6.40). Bring all the selector finger slots into line to position the selectors in neutral (photo).

Fig. 6.40 Correct position of locking slot (arrowed) with forks and rods assembled (Sec 18)

Fig. 6.41 Differential components (Sec 19)

1	Crownwheel	3	Roll pin	5	Differential gear
2	Side gear	4	Washer		

19 Differential – dismantling and reassembly

1   Unbolt the crownwheel from the differential housing.
2   Remove the side gears by pushing them round inside the housing until they can be removed (photo).
3   Drive out the roll pins which secure the differential gear spindle.
4   Remove the spindle, the differential gears and their washers (photo).
5   Use a press or bearing extractor to remove the bearings.
6   Examine all parts for wear and damage, and renew as necessary. Lubricate all parts as they are assembled.
7   Fit the bearings, using a piece of tube to press or drive them home.

19.4 Removing the differential spindle, gears and washers

19.2 Removing a differential side gear

8   Fit the spindle with the differential gears and washers. Secure the spindle with new roll pins, which should be driven in until they are centrally located in their holes (photo).
9   Fit the side gears, one at a time, and work them into their proper positions. Retain them in this position using tool 80317 M or equivalent (see Section 12, paragraph 14), inserted from the crownwheel side (photo).
10 Fit the crownwheel with its chamfer towards the differential housing. Secure with the bolts, tightening them in diagonal sequence to the specified torque.

19.8 Roll pin correctly located

20.2 Differential unit in position – note locating dowel

19.9 Side gear retaining tool in position

20.6A Measure from the joint face to the bearing outer track ...

20 Transmission – reassembly

1   Commence reassembly by fitting the selector lever into the main casing. Make sure that the locating dowel is in position in the final drive housing mating face.
2   Apply jointing compound to the mating face, then fit the differential assembly with its bearing tracks (photo).
3   Fit the final drive half housing and the extension housing, but only tighten their securing bolts finger tight at this stage.
4   Fit a new oil seal, lips well greased, to the other side of the final drive housing from the extension.
5   Remove the extension housing, fit a preload shim 2.2 mm thick to the bearing outer track and refit the extension housing (without its O-ring). Rotate the crownwheel while tightening the extension housing bolts until the crownwheel *just* starts to drag. This operation seats the bearings.
6   Remove the extension housing and the preload shim. With an accurate depth gauge, measure the distance from the final drive housing joint face to the bearing outer track. Call this dimension A.

20.6B ... and measure the spigot protrusion

Similarly measure the protrusion of the spigot on the extension housing above the joint face. Call this dimension B (photos).
7   The thickness S of preload shim required is determined by the formula:

$$S = (A - B) + 0.10 \text{ mm}$$

The extra 0.10 mm is the preload factor for the bearings. Shims are available in thicknesses of 1.1 to 2.2 mm in steps of 0.1 mm.
8   Tighten the final drive half housing securing bolts to the specified torque.
9   Fit the preload shim just determined, the speedometer driving gear and the extension housing with a new O-ring. Tighten the securing bolts to the specified torque (photo). Make sure that the crownwheel is still free to rotate.
10 Fit and secure the speedometer pinion and its adaptor.
11 Fit a new oil seal, lips well greased, into the extension housing.
12 Fit a new gear selector shaft oil seal in the main casing.
13 From the clutch housing side, fit the clutch release bearing guide tube. Do not use a gasket under the guide tube flange, and only tighten the bolts finger tight. Invert the casing and fit a preload spacer (any size) and the input shaft bearing outer track (photos).
14 Fit the gear selector shaft spring bracket and tighten its securing bolts to the specified torque. If removed, fit the two locating dowels in the main casing mating face.
15 Fit and tighten the breather.
16 Refit the lubrication jet (photo).

20.13B ... and front bearing outer track

20.9 Fitting the preload shim

20.16 Fitting the lubrication jet

20.13A Input shaft preload shim ...

17 Fit the reverse detent spring and plunger. Depress the plunger and fit the reverse selector fork and its spindle. Tighten the spindle securing nut to the specified torque.
18 Fit the reversing lamp switch using a new copper washer. Tighten it to the specified torque (photo).
19 Assemble the geartrains and the selector forks and rods. Offer the whole assembly to the gearcase (photo).
20 Fit the reverse idler spindle and gear, with the chamfer towards the rear of the gearbox. Make sure the pin in the shaft is correctly located.
21 Refit the swarf-collecting magnet.
22 Insert the spring and washers into the bracket (photo).
23 Enter the selector shaft into the casing, passing it through the compressed spring and washers inside the casing (photo). Also engage the shaft wth the selector finger and the interlock bracket. It may be helpful to keep the finger and the bracket together with a short length of rod (maximum diameter 14 mm) which can be withdrawn as the selector shaft enters.
24 Make sure that the flat on the shaft and the roll pin hole are correctly orientated (Fig. 6.42). Secure the selector finger and the interlock bracket with two new roll pins (photo). The slots in the roll pins should be 180° away from each other and in line with the longitudinal axis of the shaft.

152

20.18 The reversing lamp switch

20.19 Fitting the geartrains and selector mechanism

20.22 Spring and washers in the bracket

20.23 Fitting the selector shaft

Fig. 6.42 Selector shaft fitting details (Sec 20)

3   Flat on shaft
4   Selector finger and interlock bracket
5   Cover (early type)

20.24 Selector finger/interlock bracket roll pins

25 On later models, fit the washer and a new circlip to the cover end of the shaft.

26 On all models, refit the selector shaft cover if it was removed.

27 To the lever end of the selector shaft fit a new O-ring, a washer and a new circlip.

28 Apply jointing compound to the main casing/end casing mating face. Fit the end casing, making sure that the input and output shafts and the selector rod pass through their respective holes. Fit the thirteen securing bolts and tighten them progressively to the specified torque; remember to fit the clutch cable bracket (photo).

29 Fit the reverse idler spindle bolt, using a new washer. Tighten the bolt to the specified torque.

30 Fit the drain plugs, using new washers, and tighten them to the specified torque.

31 Fit the selector rod lockplate. Secure it with its bolt and washer, tightening the bolt to the specified torque.

32 Fit the output shaft bearing circlip, making sure it is properly located in the groove.

33 Fit the output shaft rear bearing retaining washers and bolts. Tighten the bolts to the specified torque.

34 Fit the spacer (shoulder towards the bearing), 5th gear bush and 5th gear to the input shaft. Also fit the sliding sleeve and hub, but not the selector fork (photos).

35 Lock up the geartrains by engaging 5th gear with the sliding sleeve and any other gear with the selector shaft. Fit the output shaft nut and tighten it to the specified torque, then lock it by staking its skirt into the groove.

36 Remove the 5th gear sliding sleeve and hub, then refit them with the selector fork. If the original components are being refitted, observe the mating marks made when dismantling. As the fork is being lowered into position, insert the detent ball into its hole. Alternatively, extract the roll pin and insert the detent ball and spring from the other end (photos).

37 Engage two gears again, then fit the input shaft nut and tighten it to the specified torque. Lock the nut by staking.

38 Secure 5th gear selector fork to its rod with a new roll pin.

39 Coat the mating faces with jointing compound, then refit the rear cover. Use thread locking compound on the securing bolts and tighten them to the specified torque.

40 Turn the clutch housing and remove the release bearing guide tube. If a new release lever balljoint is to be fitted, do so now: put thread locking compound on its splines and drive it in.

41 Refit the clutch release bearing guide tube with a preload spacer 2.4 thick and without a gasket. Insert the retaining bolts and tighten them progressively, at the same time rotating the input shaft. Stop tightening when the shaft *just* starts to drag: the bearings are then correctly seated.

42 Remove the guide tube and the shim. Using a depth gauge, accurately measure the distance from the bearing outer track to the joint face on the casing. Call this dimension C. Similarly measure the protrusion of the spigot on the guide tube flange above the joint face. Call this dimension D (photos).

43 The thickness T of the shim required is given by the formula:

$$T = (C - D) + 0.03 \text{ mm}$$

The extra 0.03 mm is to provide the required bearing endfloat, and allows for the thickness of the gasket which will be fitted. Shims are available in thicknesses from 0.7 mm to 2.4 mm in steps of 0.1 mm.

44 Fit a new oil seal, lips well greased, to the guide tube.

45 Fit the preload shim (of calculated thickness), a new gasket and the guide tube. Secure with the bolts and tighten them to the specified torque (photo).

46 Refit the clutch release fork and release bearing (see Chapter 5).

47 If not already done, refit the gearchange levers, making sure that they are in the correct position. Also refit the gearchange pivot bracket (photos).

48 Reassembly of the transmission is now complete. Do not refill it with oil until the driveshafts have been engaged.

20.28 Clutch cable bracket is secured by two of the casing bolts

20.34A 5th gear spacer ...

20.34B ... 5th gear bush ...

20.34C ... and input shaft 5th gear

20.36A Insert the detent ball and spring ...

20.36B ... and secure with the roll pin

20.42A Measure the distance from the joint face to the bearing outer track

20.42B Measure the spigot protrusion

20.45 Input shaft preload shim

20.47A Remember to fit the spring under the gearchange lever

20.47B Fitting the gearchange pivot bracket – note spring washers

PART D: FAULT DIAGNOSIS

21 Fault diagnosis – transmission

Symptom	Reason(s)
Weak or ineffective synchromesh	Synchromesh units worn, or damaged
Jumps out of gear	Gearchange mechanism worn Synchromesh units badly worn Selector fork badly worn
Excessive noise	Incorrect grade of oil or oil level too low Gearteeth excessively worn or damaged Intermediate gear thrust washers worn allowing excessive end play Worn bearings
Difficulty in engaging gears	Clutch pedal adjustment incorrect Worn selector components Worn synchromesh units

Chapter 7 Driveshafts

For modifications, and information applicable to later models, see Supplement at end of manual

Contents

Specifications

Type .... Open, with constant velocity joint at each end; solid or tubular, according to model

Driveshaft CV joint lubricant type .... Special lubricant supplied in repair kit

Torque wrench settings

	Nm	lbf ft
Hub carrier to strut clamp bolt	58	43
Hub nut:		
Non-GTI models	250	185
GTI models	260	192
Front suspension lower balljoint (GTI models)	35	26
Intermediate bearing bolt	18	13

1 General description

Drive to the front wheels is transmitted from the final drive unit to the front hubs by two driveshafts. The driveshafts incorporate inner and outer joints to accommodate suspension and steering angular movement.

The inner ends of the driveshafts are splined to the final drive/differential side gears, and the outer ends are splined to the front hubs.

2 Routine maintenance

Carry out the following procedures at the intervals given in Routine Maintenance at the beginning of the manual.
1 Jack up the front of the car and support on axle stands. Apply the handbrake.
2 Thoroughly examine the rubber bellows at each end of the driveshafts for splitting, damage and grease leakage (photo). If evident renew the bellows.
3 On GTI models, check the right-hand driveshaft intermediate housing for excessive wear by attempting to move the driveshaft up and down. Also turn the right-hand wheel and listen for excessive

2.2 Driveshaft outboard joint and bellows

noise which would indicate pitted tracks or balls. Renew the bearing if necessary.

4 If the driveshaft joints are excessively noisy, perhaps more noticeable when turning corners, renew the driveshaft or obtain an exchange unit.

---

3 Driveshaft (non-GTI models) – removal and refitting

1 Place a container beneath the engine and transmission unit and drain the oil. Clean the drain plug then refit and tighten it.

2 It is now necessary to prevent the front suspension coil spring expanding in subsequent operations. Peugeot garages use two special cables inserted through the holes at the top of the front suspension tower and engaged with further holes in the bottom coil spring seat. If available use these, otherwise fit coil spring compressors. **Do not** attempt to use any makeshift tool as considerable damage could occur if the spring breaks free. To fit either type of tool it will be necessary to turn the front wheel to full lock in alternate directions.

3 Loosen, but do not remove, the three top strut mounting nuts. This will allow the strut to be moved sideways later.

4 Fully apply the handbrake then, where possible, remove the front wheel centre trim and loosen the hub nut. On models without a centre trim the hub nut must be loosened after removing the front wheel. **Do not** apply the footbrake when loosening the nut as damage can occur to the brake disc retaining screws.

5 Jack up the front of the car and support on axle stands. Remove the wheel.

6 If the hub nut has yet to be loosened, use two wheel bolts and a length of bar to hold the hub.

7 Unscrew the clamp bolt securing the hub carrier to the bottom of the strut.

8 Release the front brake flexible and rigid pipes from the body bracket by pulling out the retaining plate (see Chapter 8).

9 Drive a suitable wedge into the slot in the hub carrier and slide the carrier from the bottom of the strut. If available, use the special Peugeot

Fig. 7.2 Method of expanding the hub carrier to release the strut (Sec 3)

A Special tool inserted   *B Tool turned through 90°*

Fig. 7.1 Method of retaining front coil spring using Peugeot cables (Sec 3)

A Cables fitted to strut
B Side view of cables located in bottom coil spring seat
C Strut top mounting with cables in position

Fig. 7.3 Disconnecting the driveshaft from the hub (Sec 3)

tool which consists of a cranked rod inserted in the slot and turned through 90°.

10 Move the top of the hub carrier outwards and at the same time withdraw the outer end of the driveshaft from the hub.

11 Withdraw the inner end of the driveshaft from the gearbox.

12 With the driveshaft removed, the opportunity should be taken to renew the oil seal in the gearbox. To do this, prise out the old seal and wipe clean the recess. Fill the space between the new oil seal lips with grease then use a suitable block of wood to tap it into the casing. When fully fitted it should be slightly recessed.

13 Refitting is a reversal of removal, but make sure that the hub carrier is located fully onto the strut by using a trolley jack. Renew all self-locking nuts and tighten the nuts and bolts to the specified torque. After tightening the hub nut lock it by staking the shoulder into the two grooves on the end of the driveshaft.

H145824

Fig. 7.4 Driveshaft fitted to non-GTI models (Sec 3)

1   Tulip
2   Inner joint kit

3   Driveshaft assembly
4   Outer joint kit

5   Hub nut and washer

4   Driveshaft (GTI models) – removal and refitting

1   Place a container beneath the gearbox and final drive casing then remove the two drain plugs and drain the oil. Clean the drain plugs then refit and tighten them.

2   Fully apply the handbrake then, where possible, remove the front wheel centre trim and loosen the hub nut. On models without a centre trim the hub nut must be loosened after removing the front wheel. **Do not** apply the footbrake when loosening the nut as damage can occur to the brake disc retaining screws.

3   Jack up the front of the car and support on axle stands. Remove the wheel.

4   If the hub nut has yet to be loosened use two wheel bolts and a length of bar to hold the hub.

5   Unscrew the clamp bolt securing the front suspension lower balljoint to the bottom of the hub carrier then pull the lower suspension arms down from the carrier.

6   Recover the balljoint guard plate.

Left-hand driveshaft

7   Turn the front wheels to full right-hand lock, and remove the hub nut.

8   Pull the hub carrier outwards and at the same time withdraw the outer end of the driveshaft from the hub.

9   Withdraw the inner end of the driveshaft from the final drive unit.

10   Note that the design of the differential unit is such that if both driveshafts are removed the differential side gears will fall down into the final drive housing. It is therefore important to retain the side gears using Peugeot tool 80317 (M and N), or alternatively re-insert the inner end of one driveshaft before removing the other. Another possibility is to improvise using a length of wooden dowel 1 inch in diameter, ground down slightly at one end to enter the splines in the side gear.

11   Note also that the weight of the car **must not** be taken by the front wheels with the driveshaft(s) removed otherwise damage may occur to the hub bearings.

Right-hand driveshaft

12   Loosen the two nuts retaining the intermediate bearing in the bracket bolted to the rear of the cylinder block, then turn the bolts so that their heads move through 90°.

13   Turn the front wheels to full left-hand lock, and remove the hub nut.

14   Pull the hub carrier outwards and at the same time withdraw the outer end of the driveshaft from the hub.

15   Withdraw the inner end of the driveshaft from the final drive unit and guide it through the intermediate bearing bracket.

16   Note the cautions given in paragraphs 10 and 11.

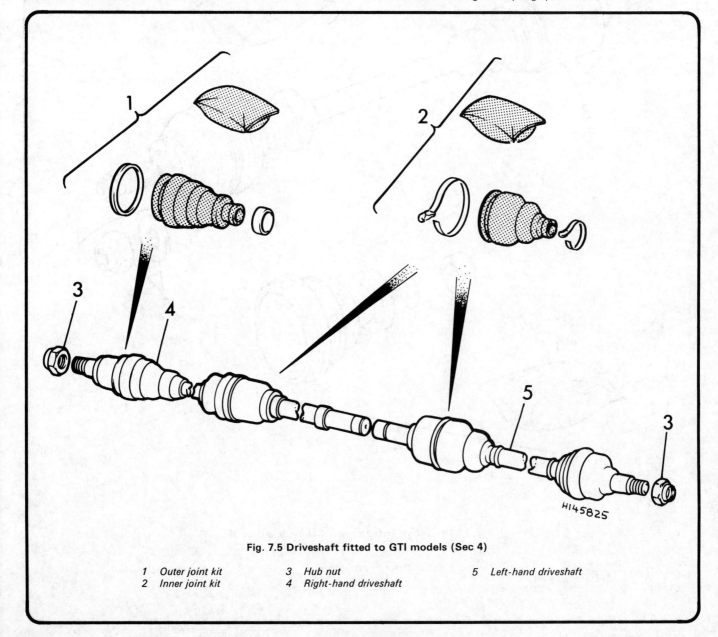

H145825

Fig. 7.5 Driveshaft fitted to GTI models (Sec 4)

1 Outer joint kit	3 Hub nut	5 Left-hand driveshaft
2 Inner joint kit	4 Right-hand driveshaft	

Both driveshafts

17 With the driveshafts removed, the opportunity should be taken to renew the oil seal in the final drive housing. To do this, prise out the old seal and wipe clean the recess. Fill the space between the new oil seal lips with grease then use a suitable block of wood to tap it into the housing. The right-hand oil seal should be flush with the housing, but the left-hand oil seal recessed. Fit the special protector to the right-hand oil seal.

18 Refitting is a reversal of removal, but tighten all nuts and bolts to the specified torque. When refitting the right-hand driveshaft make sure that the lugs on the intermediate bearing bolt heads are located over the bearing outer track, and after tightening the nuts remove the special protector from the oil seal. After tightening the hub nut lock it by staking the shoulder into the two grooves on the end of the driveshaft. Refill the gearbox with oil.

Fig. 7.8 Special oil seal protector for use when renewing the final drive housing right-hand oil seal on GTI models (Sec 4)

5 Driveshaft joint bellows – renewal

It is not practicable for the home mechanic to renew the driveshaft joint bellows on GTI models as special tools are required, therefore on these models the driveshaft should be removed and taken to a Peugeot garage. This Section describes the procedure for non-GTI models.

Inboard joint

1 With the driveshaft removed from the car, prise back the lip of the cover and then tap the cover off to expose the tulip yoke.
2 Remove the tulip yoke, spring and thrust cup.
3 Wipe away as much of the original grease as possible.

Fig. 7.6 Disconnecting the front suspension lower balljoint on GTI models (Sec 4)

1   Clamp bolt

Fig. 7.7 Using the Peugeot tool to retain the differential side gears (Sec 4)

Fig. 7.9 Prising back driveshaft joint cover lip (Sec 5)

a   Oil seal rubbing surface

4 If retaining circlips are not fitted, wind adhesive tape around the spider bearings to retain their needle rollers.

5 If it is now possible, borrow or make up a guide tool similar to the one shown (Fig. 7.12). The defective bellows can be cut off and the new ones slid up the tool (well greased) so that they will expand sufficiently to ride over the joint and locate on the shaft.

6 Where such a tool cannot be obtained, proceed in the following way.

7 Mark the relative position of the spider to the shaft.

8 Remove the spider retaining circlip.

9 Either support the spider and press the shaft from it, or use a suitable puller to draw it from the shaft.

10 Remove the bellows/cover and the small rubber retaining ring.

11 Commence reassembly by smearing the inside of the cover with grease, fit the spacer to the new bellows which are supplied as a repair kit complete with grease sachet.

12 Insert the spacer/gaiter into the cover.

13 Slide the small rubber ring onto the shaft followed by the bellows/cover assembly.

Fig. 7.10 Tapping off driveshaft joint cover (Sec 5)

Fig. 7.11 Driveshaft inboard joint components (Sec 5)

2	Tulip	4	Spring
3	Thrust cap		

Fig. 7.13 Extracting spider circlip (Sec 5)

1	Shaft	6	Taped needle rollers
5	Needle roller cage		

H145878

Fig. 7.12 Suitable tool for fitting a new bellows (Sec 5)

Fig. 7.14 Pressing shaft out of spider (Sec 5)

14 Using a piece of tubing as a drift, align the marks made before dismantling and drive the spider onto the shaft. Note that the chamfered side of the spider should go onto the shaft first.

15 Fit a new spider retaining circlip.

16 Remove the bearing retaining tape.

17 Draw the cover over the spider and apply grease from the sachet to all components. Refit the tulip yoke with spring and thrust cap. Use a new O-ring seal.

18 Peen the rim of the cover evenly all around the yoke.

19 Engage the rubber retaining ring over the narrow end of the bellows.

20 Carefully insert a thin rod under the narrow end of the bellows and released trapped air.

21 Set the dimension as shown in the diagram by sliding the bellows or cover (Fig. 7.19).

Fig. 7.15 Driveshaft inboard joint (Sec 5)

1   Rubber ring   2   Bellows

Fig. 7.17 Driving spider onto shaft (Sec 5)

6   Chamfered side

Fig. 7.16 Driveshaft inboard joint cover (1), spacer (2) and bellows (3) (Sec 5)

Fig. 7.18 Assembling inboard joint (Sec 5)

2   Thrust cap   4   Tulip
3   Spring   5   O-ring

Fig. 7.19 Inboard joint bellows setting diagram (Sec 5)

1   Rod for air release   2   Protective tape

Measurement in mm

Outboard joint

22 If the guide tool mentioned in paragraph 5 is available, it is possible to cut the defective bellows from the shaft and fit the new bellows without dismantling the shaft. Where such a tool is not available, proceed in the following way.

23 With the driveshaft removed from the car and the inboard joint dismantled, as previously described, take off the spring clip which retains the larger diameter end of the bellows.

24 Prise off the rubber ring from the smaller diameter end of the bellows and slide the bellows down the shaft.

25 Wipe away as much grease as possible from the joint and discard the defective bellows.

26 Apply the grease supplied with the repair kit evenly between the bellows and joint.

27 Locate the new bellows, clip and rubber ring.

28 Insert a thin rod under the narrow end of the bellows to release any trapped air.

29 Refit the inboard joint, as previously described.

Fig. 7.20 Removing bellows clip from driveshaft outboard joint (Sec 5)

Fig. 7.21 Removing the outer bellows (Sec 5)

3   Rubber ring   5   Shaft
4   Bellows   6   Outboard joint

Fig. 7.22 Greasing the outboard joint (Sec 5)

6   Driveshaft intermediate housing (GTI models) – renewal

1   Remove the right-hand driveshaft, as described in Section 4.

2   Place the bearing and driveshaft in a vice with the inner track resting on the vice, then use a soft-faced mallet to drive out the driveshaft. Remove the end cover and oil seal from the driveshaft and intermediate bearing bracket. If the bearing has remained in the bracket when the driveshaft was removed use a metal tube on the inner track to drift it out.

3   Clean the bearing recess in the bracket.

4   Locate a new end cover on the driveshaft then use a metal tube on the inner track to drive the new bearing onto the special shoulder.

5   Press a new oil seal into the intermediate bearing bracket.

6   Refit the driveshaft, as described in Section 4.

Fig. 7.23 Driveshaft intermediate bearing components fitted to GTI models (Sec 6)

1 *Oil seal*
2 *Bracket/engine mounting*
3 *Bearing*
4 *End cover*
5 *Bolts*

H145829

---

7   Fault diagnosis – driveshafts

Symptom	Reason(s)
Knocking noise, particularly on full lock	Worn driveshaft joints
Metallic grating varying with roadspeed	Worn intermediate bearing on right-hand driveshaft

Chapter 8 Braking system

For modifications, and information applicable to later models, see Supplement at end of manual

Contents

Specifications

Type	Front disc brakes, rear drum brakes (self-adjusting). Servo assistance on all non-basic models. Rear brake compensator (inertia type on GTI). Cable-operated handbrake on rear wheels
Brake fluid type/specification	Hydraulic fluid to SAE J1703 or DOT 3 (Duckhams Universal Brake and Clutch Fluid)

Disc brakes
Disc diameter	247 mm
Disc thickness (new):	
Except GTI (non-ventilated)	10.0 mm
GTI (ventilated)	20.4 mm
Disc thickness (minimum after resurfacing):	
Except GTI (non-ventilated)	8.5 mm
GTI (ventilated)	18.9 mm
Disc run-out (maximum) measured 22.0 mm from rim	0.07 mm
Disc pad minimum lining thickness	2.0 mm

Drum brakes
Drum internal diameter (new)	180.0 mm
Drum internal diameter (maximum after resurfacing)	181.0 mm
Drum out-of-round (maximum)	0.10 mm
Shoe minimum lining thickness	1.0 mm

Vacuum servo unit
Type:	
Except GTI	Isovac 178 mm
GTI (RHD)	Isovac 178 mm
GTI (LHD)	Isovac 229 mm

Torque wrench settings
	Nm	lbf ft
Caliper mounting bolts:		
Girling	97	72
DBA Bendix	120	89
Rear backplate	37	27
Rear hub nut	215	159

1 General description

The braking system is of hydraulic type with discs on the front and drums on the rear. The handbrake is cable-operated on the rear wheels.

The hydraulic circuit is of two independent sections so that, in the event of the failure of one section, the remaining section is still functional. On non-GTI models the circuit is split diagonally, but on GTI models it is split front and rear.

A compensating valve (or valves) reduces the hydraulic pressure to the rear brakes under heavy applications of the brake pedal in order to prevent rear wheel lock-up.

A vacuum servo unit is fitted to all non-basic models.

Fig. 8.1 Braking system layout for non-GTI models (Sec 1)

Fig. 8.2 Braking system layout for GTI models (Sec 1)

2 Routine maintenance

Carry out the following procedures at the intervals given in Routine Maintenance.

1 Check that the brake fluid level is near the top of the reservoir located on the master cylinder (photo). A slight fall in level is normal as the front disc pads wear, but a considerable drop will need investigating. If necessary top up the level after removing the filler cap.

2 Examine the hydraulic circuit lines and hoses for damage and deterioration, and for any signs of leakage. Do not overtighten union nuts as this may distort the sealing faces.

3 Apply the handbrake and check that both rear wheels are locked.

4 To renew the hydraulic fluid, remove the filler cap from the reservoir and use a syringe to remove the fluid from both compartments. Fill the reservoir with new hydraulic fluid and proceed to bleed the system, as described in Section 12. Allow 5 or 6 depressions of the brake pedal to clear old fluid.

3.3A Pad sliding key clip – arrowed (DBA Bendix type)

2.1 Topping-up the brake fluid level

3.3B Disconnecting the pad wear wiring

3 Disc pads – inspection and renewal

1 Jack up the front of the car and support on axle stands. Apply the handbrake and remove the roadwheels.

2 If the friction material has worn down to 2.0 mm (0.079 in) (this is indicated if the groove in the pad has disappeared) then the pads must be renewed as an axle set. The removal and refitting operations will vary according to the type of caliper, but first reduce the fluid level in the reservoir.

DBA Bendix disc caliper

3 Remove the clip from the end of the upper sliding key (photo). Disconnect the pad wear wiring as necessary (photo).

4 Pull out the upper sliding key (photo).

5 Using a lever against the front suspension strut, push the cylinder towards the brake disc so that the outer pad can be withdrawn from the caliper (photo).

6 Push back the caliper and withdraw the inner pad (photo).

7 Clean away all dust and dirt from the caliper. **Do not** inhale the dust, as it may be injurious to health. Check for brake fluid leakage around the piston dust seal and, if evident, overhaul the caliper, as described later in the Chapter. Check the brake disc for wear and also check that the rubber bellows on the cylinder sliding rods are in good condition.

8 Clean the backs of the disc pads and apply a little anti-squeal brake grease. Also apply the grease to the lower pad locating lip of the caliper (photo).

3.4 Removing the pad sliding key (DBA Bendix type)

9 With the caliper pushed inwards, insert the inner pad then push the caliper outwards and insert the outer pad.
10 Check that the pads are correctly located on the caliper lip (photo) then tap in the upper sliding key to lock them. Fit the sliding key clip.

Girling disc caliper
11 Extract the spring clips and tap out the pad retaining pins. Disconnect the pad wear wiring as necessary.
12 Lever the cylinder outwards and withdraw the outer pad then push in the caliper and withdraw the inner pad.
13 Clean and check the caliper, as described in paragraph 7, then clean the backs of the disc pads and apply a little anti-squeal brake grease. Note that, as from early 1985, a special spring is fitted to the inner pads to prevent pad knock within the caliper. The spring (obtainable from a

3.5 Removing the outer pad

3.6 Removing the inner pad

3.10 The correct location of the anti-rattle clips on the disc pads (DBA Bendix type)

3.8 Applying anti-squeal brake grease to the pad locating lip on the caliper

Fig. 8.3 Girling disc caliper and pads – without disc (Sec 3)

Fig. 8.4 Method of fitting anti-knock spring to Girling inner disc pad (Sec 3)

1 Loop for rivet
2 Loop for lower retaining pin
3 Anti-knock spring

Peugeot parts store) may be fitted to earlier models by tapping the inner pad control rivet through the backing plate so that the clip may be located on both sides (Fig. 8.4).

14 With the caliper pushed inwards, insert the inner pad then push the caliper outwards and insert the outer pad.

15 Tap in the pad retaining pins and fit the spring clips.

16 Where fitted, hook the anti-knock spring on the lower pad retaining pin.

DBA Bendix and Girling disc calipers

17 Repeat the operations on the opposite disc caliper.

18 Apply the footbrake several times to position the pads against the discs.

19 Top up the master cylinder reservoir to its correct level.

20 Refit the roadwheels and lower the car to the ground.

4 Rear brake shoes – inspection and renewal

1 Jack up the rear of the car and support it on axle stands. Chock the front wheels and release the handbrake.

2 The lining thickness may be checked without removing the drums/hubs. Pull out the rubber plugs from the backplates by the handbrake cables and use a torch, if necessary, to check the lining thickness (photo). If it is at or near the specified minimum remove the drums and make a more thorough inspection.

3 Remove the rear roadwheels.

4 Tap off the grease cap, taking care not to damage its outer lip, then relieve the staking on the rear hub nut, using a suitable drift or chisel. Unscrew the nut and recover the washer (photos). Should the stub axle rotate within the trailing arm, hold it stationary with a suitable Allen key on the inner end (photo).

5 Withdraw the hub/drum from the stub axle. If difficulty is experienced, due to the shoes wearing grooves in the drum, insert a screwdriver through one of the wheel bolt holes and depress the handbrake lever on the rear brake shoe so that it slides back behind the shoe (photo). This will retract the shoes and allow the hub/drum to be removed.

6 Brush the dust and dirt from the shoes, backplate and drum. **Do not** inhale it, as it may be injurious to health.

4.2 Remove the rubber plug (arrowed) from the rear brake backplate and use a torch in the hole to check the lining thickness

7 It is now possible to inspect both shoe linings for wear. If either is worn down the specified minimum amount, renew them both.

8 Note the position of each shoe and the location of the return and steady springs (photo).

9 Unhook and remove the upper return spring (photo).

10 Remove the steady springs using pliers to depress the outer cups and turn them through 90° (photo). Remove the pins from the backplate.

11 Move the serrated automatic adjuster lever quadrant against spring tension (photo), move the lever forwards and release the strut from the top of the shoes (DBA Bendix type only).

4.4A Remove the grease cap ...

4.4B ... then unscrew the staked nut ...

4.4C ... and remove the washer

4.4D Inner end of rear stub axle (arrowed) which can be held with an Allen key

4.5A If the drum is difficult to remove, insert a screwdriver through a wheel bolt hole ...

4.5B ... and push the handbrake lever behind the shoe

4.8 Rear brake assembly

4.11 Automatic adjuster lever (arrowed) and bottom return spring location

4.9 Upper return spring location

12 Expand the shoes over the wheel cylinder then release them from the bottom anchor.

13 Unhook the lever return spring and the handbrake cable.

14 If necessary, position a rubber band over the wheel cylinder to prevent the pistons coming out. Should there be evidence of brake fluid leakage from the wheel cylinder, renew it or overhaul it, as described in Section 7.

15 Transfer the handbrake and automatic adjuster levers to the new shoes as required. Note that the levers and strut on each rear wheel are different, and that the leading and trailing shoes are fitted with different grade linings.

16 Place the shoes on the bench in their correct location and fit the lower return spring.

4.10 Shoe steady spring (arrowed)

Fig. 8.5 Diagram of DBA Bendix type rear brake (Sec 4)

Arrow indicates wheel rotation

Fig. 8.6 Diagram of Girling type rear brake (Sec 4)

Arrow indicates wheel rotation

4.24A Tighten the rear hub nut ...

4.24B ... then stake it to the stub axle

17 Apply brake grease sparingly to the metal contact points of the shoes, then position them on the backplate and reconnect the handbrake cable. Locate the shoe ends on the bottom anchor.

18 Engage the strut with the slots at the top of the shoes, making sure it is located correctly on the automatic adjuster lever. Engage the upper shoe ends on the wheel cylinder pistons.

19 Insert the steady spring pins in the backplate and through the shoe webs, then fit the springs and outer cups.

20 Fit the upper return spring.

21 Move the serrated automatic adjuster lever quadrant against the spring tension to set the shoes at their minimum diameter.

22 Check that the handbrake lever on the rear brake shoe is positioned with the lug on the edge of the shoe web and not behind the shoe.

23 Fit the hub/drum on the stub axle and retain with the washer and nut. Always renew the nut.

24 Tighten the nut to the specified torque then lock it by staking the nut flange into the groove on the stub axle (photos).

25 Tap the grease cap into the hub/drum.

26 Repeat all the operations on the opposite rear brake then refit the roadwheels and lower the car to the ground.

27 Apply the footbrake several times to set the shoes in their adjusted position.

28 Adjust the handbrake, as described in Section 14.

5 Disc caliper – removal, overhaul and refitting

1 Remove the disc pads, as described in Section 3.

2 Fit a brake hose clamp to the flexible hose connected to the caliper. Alternatively remove the brake fluid reservoir filler cap and tighten it down onto a piece of polythene sheeting to reduce the loss of fluid when disconnecting the hose.

3 Loosen the flexible hose union connection at the caliper.

4 Unscrew the two mounting bolts (photo), withdraw the caliper from the disc then unscrew the caliper from the flexible hose. Plug the hose to prevent loss of fluid.

5 Clean the exterior of the caliper.

5.4 Disc caliper mounting bolts (arrowed)

Fig. 8.7 Bendix type disc caliper components (Sec 5)

1	*Mounting bolt*	3	*Sliding key kit*	5	*Retaining plate*	7	*Repair kit with grease*
2	*Caliper assembly*	4	*Bleed screw*	6	*Sliding guide kit with grease*

6   On the Bendix type, unbolt the caliper frame from the cylinder.

7   Prise the dust cover and ring from the end of the piston.

8   Withdraw the piston from the cylinder. If necessary use air pressure from a foot pump in the fluid inlet to force the piston out.

9   Prise the seal from inside the cylinder, taking care not to damage the cylinder wall.

10 If required, dismantle the sliding guides. On the Bendix type unbolt the endplate from the guides and remove the rubber dust covers. Keep the guides identified for location.

11 Clean all the components using methylated spirit or clean brake fluid then examine them for wear and damage. Check the piston and cylinder surfaces for scoring, excessive wear and corrosion, and if evedent renew the complete caliper assembly. Similarly check the sliding guides. If the components are in good condition obtain a repair kit which will contain all the necessary rubber seals and other renewable items.

12 Dip the new seal in fresh brake fluid then locate it in the cylinder groove using the fingers only to manipulate it.

13 Dip the piston in brake fluid and insert it in the cylinder, twisting it as necessary to locate it in the seal.

Fig. 8.9 Removing a brake disc (Sec 6)

Fig. 8.8 Girling type disc caliper components (Sec 5)

1   Mounting bolt   4   Bleed screw
2   Caliper assembly   5   Repair kit
3   Pad retaining pin and spring

14 Fit the dust cover and ring over the end of the piston and cylinder.
15 Lubricate the sliding guides with the grease supplied and refit them, together with the new seals. On the Bendix type refit the endplate and tighten the bolts.
16 On the Bendix type, refit the caliper frame and tighten the bolts.
17 To refit the caliper, first screw it onto the flexible hose and locate it over the brake disc so that the hose is not twisted.
18 Clean the mounting bolt threads and apply locking fluid. Insert the mounting bolts and tighten them to the specified torque.
19 Tighten the flexible hose union on the caliper. Check that the hose is clear of the strut and surrounding components and, if necessary, loosen the rigid pipe union on the body bracket, reposition the hose and retighten the union.
20 Refit the disc pads, as described in Secion 3.
21 Remove the brake hose clamp or polythene sheeting and bleed the hydraulic system, as described in Section 12. On GTI models it is only necessary to bleed the front circuit.

6 Brake disc – inspection, removal and refitting

1   Remove the disc pads, as described in Section 3.
2   Using a dial gauge or feelers and a fixed block, check that the disc run-out is within the specified limit. Do not confuse wheel bearing endfloat with disc wear. Also check the condition of the disc for scoring. Light scoring is normal, but if excessive either renew the disc or have it ground to within the specified limit.
3   On certain models, it may be necessary to remove the brake caliper with reference to Section 5 in order to allow sufficient clearance to remove the disc. Note that there is no need to disconnect the flex-

6.4 Disc retaining screws (arrowed)

ble hose from the caliper. Support the caliper with wire or string, taking care not to strain the hose.
4   To remove the disc, unscrew the two cross-head screws (where fitted) and withdraw the disc, tilting it as necessary to clear the hub and caliper if the caliper is still fitted (photo).
5   Refitting is a reversal of removal, but make sure that the disc-to-hub mating surfaces are clean and that the securing screws are tightened fully. If the caliper has been removed, coat the caliper mounting bolt threads with locking fluid on refitting. Refer to Section 3 when refitting the disc pads.

7 Rear brake wheel cylinder – removal, overhaul and refitting

1   Jack up the rear of the car and support on axle stands. Chock the front wheels and remove the relevant rear wheel.
2   Remove the hub/drum, as described in Section 4.
3   Note the location of the brake shoe upper return spring then unhook and remove it.
4   Pull the handbrake lever on the rear shoe fully forwards so that the upper ends of the shoes are clear of the wheel cylinder. Wedge the lever in this position using a block of wood.
5   Fit a brake hose clamp to the flexible hose supplying the rear

Fig. 8.10 Cross-section of a rear wheel cylinder incorporating a compensator (Sec 7)

1 Ball valve	2 Piston	3 Spring	4 Tappets

Fig. 8.11 Exploded view of a rear wheel cylinder (Sec 7)

1	Cap	5	Seal
2	Bleed screw	6	Spring seat
3	Dust excluder	7	Spring
4	Piston	8	Body

reverse order; making sure that the lips of the seals face into the cylinder. When completed, wipe clean the outer surfaces of the dust excluders.

13 Clean the backplate and refit the wheel cylinder using a reversal of the removal procedure. Refer to Section 4 when refitting the hub/drum

14 Make sure that the brake hose clamp or polythene sheeting is removed then bleed the hydraulic system, as described in Section 12. On GTI models it is only necessary to bleed the rear circuit.

7.7 Rear wheel cylinder mounting bolts (arrowed)

brakes. Alternatively remove the brake fluid reservoir filler cap and tighten it down onto a piece of polythene sheeting to reduce the loss of fluid when disconnecting the wheel cylinder.

6 Unscrew the hydraulic pipe union nut from the rear of the wheel cylinder.

7 Unscrew the two mounting bolts and withdraw the wheel cylinder from the backplate (photo). Take care not to spill any brake fluid on the brake shoe linings.

8 Clean the exterior of the wheel cylinder. Note that on all non-GTI models with a diagonally split hydraulic circuit the rear wheel cylinders incorporate compensators which **must not** be dismantled.

9 Pull off the dust excluders.

10 Extract the pistons, seals and return spring; keeping each component identified for location.

11 Check the surfaces of the cylinder bore and pistons for scoring and corrosion and, if evident, renew the complete wheel cylinder. If the components are in good condition discard the seals and obtain a repair kit which will contain all the necessary renewable components.

12 Clean the pistons and cylinder with methylated spirit or clean brake fluid then dip each component in fresh brake fluid and reassemble in

8 Rear brake drum – inspection and renovation

1 Whenever the hub/brake drum is removed to check the linings, take the opportunity to inspect the interior of the drum.

2 If the drum is grooved, owing to failure to renew worn linings or after a very high mileage has been covered, then it may be possible to regrind it, provided the maximum internal diameter is not exceeded.

3 Even if only one drum is in need of grinding both drums must be reground to the same size in order to maintain even braking characteristics.

4 Judder or a springy pedal felt when the brakes are applied can be caused by a distorted (out-of-round) drum. Here again it may be possible to regrind the drums, otherwise a new drum will be required.

9 Master cylinder – removal, overhaul and refitting

1   Unscrew the filler cap from the brake fluid reservoir and draw out the fluid using a syringe.

2   Prise the reservoir from the master cylinder and remove the seals.

3   Unscrew the union nuts securing the rigid brake lines to the master cylinder and pull out the lines. Cap the pipe ends to prevent loss of fluid.

4   Unscrew the mounting nuts and withdraw the master cylinder from the bulkhead or servo unit, as applicable. Remove the gasket on non-servo models.

5   Clean the exterior of the master cylinder. It is not possible to overhaul the master cylinder fitted to non-servo models, therefore if it is known to be leaking or damaged the complete master cylinder must be renewed. On servo models proceed as follows.

6   Using circlip pliers, extract the circlip from the mouth of the cylinder.

7   Remove the primary and secondary piston components noting their locations. If necessary tap the cylinder on a block of wood.

8   Clean all the components in methylated spirit. Check the surfaces of the cylinder bore and pistons for scoring and corrosion, and if evident renew the complete master cylinder. If the components are in good condition remove and discard the seals and obtain a repair kit which will contain all the necessary renewable components.

9   Dip the new seals in fresh brake fluid and fit them to the pistons using the fingers only to manipulate them.

10   Reassemble the master cylinder in reverse order to dismantling and make sure that the circlip is fully engaged with the groove in the mouth of the cylinder.

11   On non-servo models check that the foot pedal pushrod protrudes from the bulkhead between 9.0 and 9.6 mm (0.355 and 0.378 in). If not, loosen the locknuts and adjust the position of the stop lamp switch inside the car on the pedal bracket.

12   Refitting is a reversal of removal, but fit a new gasket on non-servo models. Finally bleed the complete hydraulic system, as described in Section 12.

Fig. 8.12 Master cylinder components (Sec 9)

1 Body for non-servo models	3 Body for servo models	5 Secondary piston components
2 Gasket	4 Mounting nut	6 Primary piston components
		7 Servo unit

Fig. 8.13 Diagram of master cylinder fitted to non-servo models (Sec 9)

1 Stoplamp switch
a Clevis pin in upper hole
A = 197.0 mm (7.762 in)
B = 9.0 to 9.6 mm
(0.355 to 0.378 in)

Fig. 8.14 Diagram of master cylinder fitted to servo models (Sec 9)

a Clevis pin in lower hole
A = 184.0 mm (7.250 in)
B = 114.0 mm (4.492 in)
C = 3.5 mm (0.138 in)

Fig. 8.15 Operation of the inertia type rear brake compensator fitted to GTI models (Sec 10)

A Rest position	B Cut-off position
1 Steel ball	3 Ramp
2 Diffuser	4 Piston

Movement of the ball seals the piston drilling

10 Rear brake compensator (GTI models) – description, removal and refitting

1 On GTI models the brake hydraulic circuit is split front and rear, and an inertia type compensator is incorporated in the rear brake circuit to prevent rear wheel lock-up during hard braking. The compensator is located in the engine compartment on the lower left-hand side panel (photo), and incorporates a steel ball which stops fluid entry to the rear circuit at a preset deceleration.

2 To remove the compensator, first remove the brake fluid reservoir filler cap and tighten it down onto a piece of polythene sheeting in order to reduce the loss of fluid when disconnecting the hydraulic pipes.

3 Jack up the front of the car and support on axle stands. Apply the handbrake and remove the relevant front wheel.

4 Unscrew the union nuts and disconnect the rigid hydraulic lines from each end of the unit while holding the unit on the flats provided.

5 Unbolt the clamp and withdraw the compensator.

6 Refitting is a reversal of removal, but note that the nose of the unit must face forwards and be inclined upwards at an angle of 22° to the horizontal. Provided that the mounting bracket is undamaged, this angle will automatically be achieved. Finally bleed the rear hydraulic circuit, as described in Section 12.

11 Flexible and rigid hydraulic lines – inspection and renewal

1 Examine all the unions for signs of leaks. Then look at the flexible hoses for signs of fraying and chafing (as well as for leaks). This is only a preliminary inspection of the flexible hoses as exterior condition does not necessarily indicate interior condition which will be considered later.

2 The steel pipes must be examined equally carefully. They must be thoroughly cleaned and examined for signs of dents or other percussive damage, rust and corrosion. Rust and corrosion should be scraped off and, if the depth of pitting in the pipes is significant, they will need renewal. This is most likely in those areas underneath the

10.1 Rear brake compensator fitted to GTI models

chassis and along the rear suspension arms where the pipes are exposed to the full force of road and weather conditions.

3   Rigid pipe removal is usually quite straightforward. The unions at each end are undone and the pipe drawn out of the connection. The clips which may hold it to the car body are bent back and it is then removed. Underneath the car exposed unions can be particularly stubborn, defying the efforts of an open-ended spanner. As few people will have the special split ring spanner required, a self-grip wrench is the only answer. If the pipe is being renewed, new unions will be provided. If not then one will have to put up with the possibility of burring over the flats on the union and use a self-grip wrench for replacement also.

4   Flexible hoses are always fitted to a rigid support bracket where they join a rigid pipe, the bracket being fixed to the chassis or rear suspension arm (photos). The rigid pipe unions must first be removed from the flexible union, then the retaining plate must be pulled out and the flexible hose and fitting released from the bracket.

5   Depending upon the make of the particular caliper, the flexible hose may be connected simply by screwing it into its tapped hole or by using a hollow bolt with banjo end fitting. Use a new copper sealing washer on each side of the banjo union.

6   Once the flexible hose is removed examine the internal bore. If clear of fluid it should be possible to see through it. Any specks of rubber which come out, or signs of restriction in the bore, mean that the inner lining is breaking up and the hose must be renewed.

7   Rigid pipes which need replacement can usually be purchased at any local garage where they have the pipe, unions and special tools to make them up. They will need to know the pipe length required and the type of flare used at the ends of the pipe. These may be different at each end of the same pipe.

8   Installation of the pipes is a reversal of the removal procedure. The pipe profile must be pre-set before fitting. Any acute bends must be put in by the garage on a bending machine, otherwise there is the possibility of kinking them and restricting the fluid flow.

9   All hose and pipe threads and unions are to metric standards. Screw in new components by hand initially to ensure that the threads are compatible.

10   Remember that a metric hose end fitting seals at the tip of its threaded section and will leave a gap between the hexagon of the end fitting and the surface of the component. Do not attempt to overtighten the hose end fitting in order to eliminate the gap.

11   The hydraulic system must be bled on completion of hose or rigid pipe renewal.

12 Hydraulic system – draining and bleeding

1   If the hydraulic system is to be drained follow the procedure given in Section 2. If the master cylinder or connecting pipes have been removed, the complete hydraulic system must be bled, but if only a caliper or wheel cylinder has been removed then only that particular circuit need be bled.

2   If the complete system is being bled, the sequence of bleeding should be as follows:

Non-GTI models (ie diagonally split system)
RH rear wheel
LH front wheel
LH rear wheel
RH front wheel

GTI models (ie front and rear split system)
LH rear wheel and inertia compensator
RH rear wheel
LH front wheel
RH front wheel

3   Unless the pressure bleeding method is being used, do not forget to keep the fluid level in the master cylinder reservoir topped up to prevent air from being drawn into the system which would make any work done worthless. Before commencing operations, check that all system hoses and pipes are in good condition with unions tight and free from leaks.

4   Take great care not to allow hydraulic fluid to come into contact with the vehicle paintwork as it is an effective paint stripper. Wash off any spilled fluid immediately with cold water.

5   On models with a vacuum servo destroy the vacuum by giving several applications of the brake pedal in quick succession.

Bleeding – two man method

6   Gather together a clean jar and a length of rubber or plastic tubing which will be a tight fit on the brake bleed screws.

7   Engage the help of an assistant.

8   Push one end of the bleed tube onto the first bleed screw (photo) and immerse the other end in the jar which should contain enough hydraulic fluid to cover the end of the tube.

9   Open the bleed screw one half a turn and have your assistant depress the brake pedal fully then slowly release it. Tighten the bleed screw at the end of each pedal downstroke to obviate any chance of air or fluid being drawn back into the system.

10   Repeat this operation until clean hydraulic fluid, free from air bubbles, can be seen coming through into the jar.

11   On GTI models only it is now important to dislodge air trapped in the inertia compensator. To do this, open the bleed screw again and have your assistant fully depress and release the brake pedal rapidly 4 or 5 times, finally keeping the pedal depressed before tightening the bleed screw.

12   With the bleed screw tightened, remove the bleed tube and proceed to the next wheel.

Bleeding – using one-way valve kits

13   There are a number of one-man, one-way brake bleeding kits available from motor accessory shops. It is recommended that one of these kits is used wherever possible as it will greatly simpliy the bleeding operation and also reduce the risk of air or fluid being drawn back into the system, quite apart from being able to do the work without the help of an assistant. To use the kit, connect the tube to the bleed screw and open the screw one half a turn.

11.4A Front brake pipe bracket behind the suspension strut

11.4B Rear brake pipe bracket on the suspension arm

12.8 The bleed screw on the front disc caliper

14 Depress the brake pedal fully then slowly release it. The one-way valve in the kit will prevent expelled air from returning at the end of each pedal downstroke. Repeat the operation several times to be sure of ejecting all the air from the system. Some kits include a translucent container which can be positioned so that the air bubbles can actually be seen being ejected from the system.

15 Tighten the bleed screw, remove the tube and repeat the operations on the remaining brakes, on GTI models first carry out the procedure described in paragraph 11.

16 On completion, depress the brake pedal. If it still feels spongy, repeat the bleeding operations as air must still be trapped in the system.

Bleeding – using a pressure bleeding kit

17 These kits are available from motor accessory shops and are usually operated by air pressure from the spare tyre.

18 By connecting a pressurised container to the master cylinder fluid reservoir, bleeding is then carried out simply by opening each bleed screw in sequence and allowing the fluid to run out, rather like turning on a tap, until no air is visible in the expelled fluid.

19 By using this method, the large reserve of hydraulic fluid provides a safeguard against air being drawn into the master cylinder during bleeding which may occur if the fluid level in the reservoir is allowed to fall too low.

20 Pressure bleeding is particularly useful when bleeding the complete system at time of routine fluid renewal.

All methods

21 When bleeding is completed, check and top up the fluid level in the master cylinder reservoir.

22 Check the feel of the brake pedal. If it feels at all spongy, air must still be present in the system and the need for further bleeding is indicated. Failure to bleed satisfactorily after a reasonable repetition of the bleeding operations may be due to worn master cylinder seals.

23 Always discard brake fluid which has been bled from the system. It is almost certain to be contaminated with moisture, air and dirt, making it unsuitable for further use.

24 Clean fluid should always be stored in an airtight container as it absorbs moisture readily which lowers its boiling point and could affect braking performance under severe conditions.

13 Vacuum servo unit – description, testing, maintenance, removal and refitting

Description

1 The vacuum servo unit is fitted into the brake hydraulic circuit in series with the master cylinder to provide power assistance to the driver when the brake pedal is depressed.

2 The unit operates by vacuum obtained from the engine induction manifold and consists of, basically, a booster diaphragm and non-return valve.

3 The servo unit and the master cylinder are connected so that the servo piston rod acts as the master cylinder pushrod.

4 The driver's braking effort is transmitted from the brake pedal to the servo unit piston and its integral control system.

5 The forward chamber of the servo unit is held under vacuum at all times whilst the rear chamber is held under vacuum conditions only when the brake pedal is in the released position. When the pedal is depressed, the rear chamber opens to atmospheric pressure which causes the servo piston to move forward and so operate the master cylinder pushrod.

6 It is emphasised that a servo unit provides assistance only and, should a fault occur, the normal hydraulic braking system is unaffected except that the need for higher pedal pressure will be noticed.

Testing

7 With the engine switched off, depress the brake pedal several times. The distance by which the pedal moves should now alter over all applications.

8 Depress the brake pedal fully and hold it down then start the engine. The pedal should be felt to move downward slightly.

9 Hold the pedal depressed with the engine running, switch off the ignition and continue to hold the pedal depressed for 30 seconds during which period the pedal should neither rise nor drop.

10 Start the engine whilst the brake pedal is released, run it for a minute and switch off. Give several applications of the brake pedal. The pedal travel should decrease with each application.

11 Failure of the brake pedal to act in the way described will indicate a fault in the servo unit.

12 The servo unit should not be serviced or overhauled beyond the operations described in this Section and in the event of a fault developing, renew the servo complete.

13 Periodically check the condition of the vacuum hose and security of the clips.

14 Renew the hose if necessary.

15 If the servo hose right-angled non-return valve is loose in its sealing grommet, or if the grommet shows evidence of cracking or perishing, renew it. Apply some hydraulic fluid to the rubber to facilitate fitting.

Air filter – renewal

16 Although not a specified operation, the air filter through which the pushrod passes at the rear of the servo can become clogged after a high mileage. Disconnect the rod from the pedal, cut the filter diagonally having slipped the dust excluder off the rod. Fit the new filter.

Removal and refitting

17 Remove the master cylinder, as described in Section 9. Disconnect the servo vacuum hose.

18 Working inside the car, disconnect the pushrod from the brake pedal; noting that it is on the lower hole.

19 Unscrew the mounting nuts behind the pedal bracket then withdraw the servo unit into the engine compartment. Remove the gasket.

20 Before fitting a servo unit, check the pushrod dimensions shown in Fig. 8.16 and adjust where possible.

21 Refitting is a reversal of removal, but fit a new gasket and fully tighten the mounting nuts. Refer to Section 9 when refitting the master cylinder. Finally, with the brake pedal released, check that the clearance between the stop-lamp switch threaded shank and pedal is 3.5 mm (0.138 in). If necessary loosen the locknuts, adjust the switch and tighten the locknuts (photo).

13.21 Stoplamp switch (arrowed)

14 Handbrake – adjustment

1 The handbrake is normally kept adjusted by the action of the automatic adjusters on the rear brake shoes. However, in due course, the cables will stretch and will have to be adjusted in order to fully apply the handbrake.

2 To adjust, first place the handbrake lever onto the fifth notch.

3 Jack up the rear of the car and support on axle stands. Chock the front wheels.

Fig. 8.16 Cross-section of the vacuum servo unit showing pushrod adjustment dimensions (Sec 13)

1   Adjustment screw

A = 22.2 to 22.4 mm (0.875 to 0.883 in)   B = 86.5 to 89.5 mm (3.408 to 3.526 in)

4   Working inside the car, remove the screw and lift the cover from the handbrake lever (photo).
5   Turn the adjustment nut on the rear of the cable compensator so that both rear wheels are just binding on the brake shoes (photo).
6   Fully apply the handbrake lever and check that both rear wheels are locked.
7   Fit the cover over the handbrake lever and lower the car to the ground.
8   Over-adjustment will prevent the automatic adjusters operating correctly so make sure that the handbrake is fully applied after being pulled up between 5 and 8 notches, no fewer.

14.4 Removing the handbrake lever cover

15.4 Handbrake cable clip and bracket located on the rear suspension arm

16 Brake pedal – removal and refitting

1   Remove the lower facia panel from the steering column in order to gain access to the pedal bracket.
2   Remove the clevis pin and disconnect the pushrod from the brake pedal. Note that on models with a vacuum servo unit the pushrod is on the lower hole, whereas the upper hole is used for models without a servo unit (photo).

14.5 Handbrake adjustment and locking nuts (arrowed)

15 Handbrake cables – renewal

1   Remove the rear brake shoes, as described in Section 4.
2   Working inside the car, remove the screw and lift the cover from the handbrake lever.
3   Unhook the cable(s) from the compensator.
4   Release the cable(s) from the retaining clips, the floor, the fuel tank, and the rear brake backplate(s) and withdraw from under the car (photo).
5   Fit the new cable(s) using a reversal of the removal procedure with reference also to Section 4. Finally adjust the cable(s) as described in Section 14.

16.2 Pushrod-to-brake pedal clevis pin – arrowed (note location in lower hole for models with vacuum servo)

3   Unscrew the self-locking nut from the pivot bolt, pull out the bolt and lower the brake pedal. Note that on non-servo models a return spring is also fitted to the pedal.
4   Examine the pedal bushes for wear and renew them if necessary.
5   Refitting is a reversal of removal, but lightly grease the bushes and clevis pin and renew the self-locking nut.

Fig. 8.17 Brake pedal components fitted to non-servo models (Sec 16)

1 Bracket	8 Spacer
2 Stop-lamp	9 Bush
3 Plate	10 Pivot bolt
4 Nut	11 Pushrod
5 Bush	12 Retainer
6 Pedal	13 Clevis pin
7 Return spring	14 Pad

17 Handbrake warning light switch – removal and refitting

1   Move the front seats fully forward then remove the screw and lift the cover from the handbrake lever.
2   With the handbrake applied, remove the mounting screw, withdraw the switch and disconnect the wiring (photo).
3   Refitting is a reversal of removal.

18 Handbrake lever – removal and refitting

1   Move the front seats fully forward then remove the screw and lift the cover from the handbrake lever.

17.2 Handbrake warning light switch (arrowed)

2   Fully release the handbrake then unscrew the adjustment nut on the rear of the cable compensator until both cables can be unhooked.
3   Unbolt and remove the handbrake lever assembly from the floor (photo).
4   Refitting is a reversal of removal, but adjust the handbrake, as described in Section 14.

18.3 Handbrake lever mounting bolts (arrowed)

19 Fault diagnosis – braking system

Before diagnosing faults from the following chart, check that any braking irregularities are not caused by:
  (a) Uneven and incorrect tyre pressures
  (b) Incorrect mix of radial and crossply tyres
  (c) Wear in the steering mechanism
  (d) Misalignment of the chassis geometry

Symptom	Reason(s)
Pedal travels a long way before the brakes operate	Brake shoes set too far from the drums due to faulty self-adjusting mechanism
Stopping ability poor, even though pedal pressure is firm	Linings/pads and/or drums/disc badly worn or scored One or more wheel hydraulic cylinders or caliper pistons seized resulting in some brake shoes/pads not pressing against the drums/discs Brake linings/pads contaminated with oil Wrong type of linings/pads fitted (too hard) Brake shoes/pads wrongly assembled Faulty servo unit (where fitted)
Car veers to one side when the brakes are applied	Brake linings/pads on one side are contaminated with oil Hydraulic wheel cylinder/caliper on one side partially or fully seized A mixture of lining materials fitted between sides Unequal wear between sides caused by partially seized wheel cylinders/pistons
Pedal feels spongy	Air in the hydraulic system
Pedal feels springy when the brakes are applied	Brake linings/pads not bedded into the drums/discs (after fitting new ones) Master cylinder or brake backplate mounting bolts loose Out-of-round drums or discs with excessive run-out
Pedal travels right down with little or no resistance and brakes are virtually non-operative	Leak in hydraulic system resulting in lack of pressure for operating wheel cylinders/caliper pistons If no signs of leakage are apparent the master cylinder internals seals are failing to sustain pressure
Binding, juddering, overheating	One or a combination of causes given in the foregoing sections Handbrake over-adjusted Handbrake cable(s) seized
Lack of servo assistance	Vacuum hose leaking Non-return valve defective or leaking grommet Servo internal fault

Chapter 9 Suspension, hubs, wheels and tyres

For modifications, and information applicable to later models, see Supplement at end of manual

Contents

Specifications

Front suspension

Type	Independent, McPherson struts, coil springs, anti-roll bar
Coil spring free length:	
Models with engines XV8, XW7 and XY7	492.0 mm
Models with engine XY8	360.7 mm
Models with engine XU5J	335.0 mm
Hub bearings	Double row ball-bearings
Hub bearing lubricant type/specification	Multi-purpose lithium-based grease (Duckhams LB 10)

Rear suspension

Type	Independent, cross-tube with trailing arms, torsion bars, inclined shock absorbers, anti-roll bar
Ride height:	
Except GTI	420 to 434 mm
GTI	403 to 417 mm
Hub bearings	Taper roller (non-adjustable)

Roadwheels

Type:	
Non-GTI	Pressed steel
GTI	Light alloy
Size:	
Non-GTI	4.5 B (or J) 13 FH 4.35 or 5 B 13 FH 4.28
GTI	5.5 J 14 FH H 4.24

Tyres

Size:		
Non-GTI	135 SR 13, 145 SR 13 or 165/70 SR 13	
GTI	185/60 HR 14	
Pressures – bar (lbf/in²):	**Front**	**Rear**
135 SR 13	2.0 (29)	2.1 (30)
145 SR 13	1.9 (28)	2.1 (30)
165/70 SR 13	1.7 (25)	1.9 (28)
185/60 HR 14	2.0 (29)	2.0 (29)

Torque wrench settings
Front suspension

	Nm	lbf ft
Top mounting	12	9
Shock absorber piston rod:		
Self-locking	45	33
Crimped	70	52
Strut clamp bolt	58	43
Anti-roll bar clamp	35	26
Anti-roll bar end (non-GTI)	75	55
Bottom balljoint	35	26
Anti-roll bar guide bar	30	22
Lower suspension arm pivot bolt	35	26
Anti-roll bar end (GTI)	58	43
Lower suspension arm rear pivot bolt (GTI)	78	58

Rear suspension

	Nm	lbf ft
Shock absorber upper mounting	75	55
Shock absorber lower mounting	118	87
Anti-roll bar arm	35	26
Torsion bar plug	20	15
Suspension top mountings	45	33
Suspension front mounting pivot bolt	80	59

Roadwheels

	Nm	lbf ft
Roadwheel bolts (all wheel types)*	85	63

* On alloy wheels, oil the ends of the bolt threads over a maximum length of 10 mm before fitting

1 General description

The front suspension is of independent type; incorporating McPherson struts with coil springs and integral shock absorbers. On non-GTI models the lower suspension arm movement is controlled by the anti-roll bar, but on GTI models the arm has two inner pivot points and the anti-roll bar operates separately on the struts.

The rear suspension is also of independent type; incorporating a cross-tube with trailing arms set in each end and supported on needle or plain bearings. Torsion bars are fitted to the trailing arms and, on certain models, an anti-roll bar located inside the cross-tube stabilizes the car when cornering. The telescopic shock absorbers are inclined with their top mountings attached to the suspension side-members. A rubber cone bump stop is provided on each side for times of excessive movement of the trailing arms (photo).

2 Routine maintenance

Carry out the following procedures at the intervals given in Routine Maintenance at the beginning of the manual.
1 Check and adjust the tyre pressures and make sure that the caps are securely fitted to the valves.
2 Thoroughly examine the tyres for wear, damage and deterioration. If necessary, use a trolley jack to raise each wheel clear of the ground so that a complete check can be made.
3 Jack up each wheel in turn, then grip the top and bottom and attempt to rock the wheel. Any excessive play indicates wear in the hub bearings although, on the front wheels, check that the movement is not due to a worn lower suspension balljoint.

1.2 Rear suspension bump stop

4 Place the car on ramps or jack it up and support on axle stands, then check the front and rear shock absorbers for leakage of fluid. If evident, renew the shock absorber or strut as necessary. The efficiency of the shock absorbers can be checked as described later in this Chapter.

Fig. 9.1 Front suspension for non-GTI models (Sec 1)

Fig. 9.2 Front suspension for GTI models (Sec 1)

Fig. 9.3 Rear suspension for all models (Sec 1)

3.2 Anti-roll bar mounting in the lower suspension arm on non-GTI models

3.3 Anti-roll bar guide bar bolt (arrowed) on non-GTI models

3.4 Anti-roll bar mounting clamp bolts (arrowed)

3 Front anti-roll bar – removal and refitting

Non-GTI models

1 Remove the lower suspension arm from one side, as described in Section 5.
2 Unscrew the nut securing the remaining end of the anti-roll bar to the other suspension arm and recover the washer (photo).
3 Unbolt the guide bar from the subframe (photo).
4 Unscrew the mounting clamp bolts (photo) and withdraw the anti-roll bar over the subframe.
5 Examine the rubber bearings for damage and deterioration, and renew them if necessary. The bearings in the suspension arms can be prised or driven out.
6 Refitting is a reversal of removal, but delay fully tightening the clamp bolts until the full weight of the car is on the suspension. The guide bar bolts should also remained loosened until after the bearing clamp bolts have been tightened and its length should be suitably adjusted (see Fig. 9.4).

GTI models

7 Jack up the front of the car and support on axle stands. Apply the handbrake and remove both front roadwheels.
8 Unscrew the self-locking nuts from the bottom of the link arms (photo) and if necessary use a separator tool to release the joints.
9 Unscrew the bearing clamp bolts and withdraw the anti-roll bar over the subframe.
10 Unscrew the self-locking nuts from the tops of the link arms and

remove the arms from the suspension struts, again using a separator tool if required.
11 Examine the rubber bearings for damage and deterioration and renew them if necessary. Check the balljoints on the link arms for excessive wear, and the rubber boots for any damage. The balljoints cannot be renewed separately, so if any damage is evident the complete link arm must be renewed.
12 The left-hand side anti-roll bar bearing incorporates a location ring and therefore the bearings must always be fitted to their correct sides. The left-hand bearing is colour-coded in grey or red and the right-hand bearing in yellow or white.
13 Refitting is a reversal of removal, but delay fully tightening the mountings until the weight of the car is on the suspension.

4 Front suspension strut – removal, overhaul and refitting

1 Before raising the car it is recommended that a retaining tool is fitted to the coil spring to enable easier removal of the strut. Peugeot garages use two special cables inserted through the holes at the top of the front suspension tower and engaged with further holes in the bottom coil spring seat. If available use these, otherwise fit universal coil spring compressors. **Do not** attempt to use any makeshift tool, as considerable damage could occur if the spring breaks free. To fit either type of tool it will be necessary to turn the front wheel to full lock in alternate directions.
2 Loosen, but do not remove, the three top strut mounting nuts (photo).

Fig. 9.4 Cross-section of front suspension showing anti-roll bar guide dimension (Sec 3)

X = 330.0 mm (13.0 in)

H145843

3.8 Anti-roll bar link arm bottom joint on GTI models

4.4 Hub carrier-to-strut clamp bolt removal

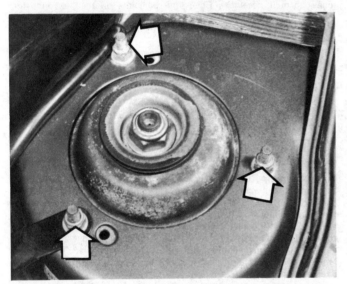

4.2 Front suspension top mounting nuts (arrowed)

refitting to the strut. If the spring is to be renewed, release the compressors very gently and evenly until they can be removed and fitted to the new spring.

13 If necessary, remove the gaiter and bump stop from the piston rod. Note the location of each component to ensure correct refitting.

14 Check the strut for signs of fluid seepage at the piston rod seal. Temporarily refit the upper mounting to the piston rod and, with the bottom of the strut gripped in a vice, fully extend and retract the piston rod. If the resistance is not firm and even in both directions, or if there are signs of leakage or damage, the strut must be renewed.

15 Refitting is a reversal of removal, but note that the bump stop must be fitted with the largest diameter uppermost. Renew the piston rod nut and tighten it to the specified torque. Make sure that the strut fully enters the hub carrier; if there is any doubt about this loosen the clamp bolts with the full weight of the car on the suspension and the strut will be forced fully home. Retighten the bolt to the specified torque.

3   Jack up the front of the car and support on axle stands. Apply the handbrake and remove the roadwheel on the relevant side.

4   Unscrew the clamp bolt securing the hub carrier to the bottom of the strut (photo).

5   On GTI models, unscrew the nut and disconnect the anti-roll bar link from the strut.

6   In order to prevent any damage to the driveshaft joints, fit a length of wire from the top of the hub carrier to the subframe.

7   Drive a suitable wedge into the slot on the hub carrier and slide the carrier from the bottom of the strut. If available, use the special Peugeot tool which consists of a cranked rod inserted in the slot and turned through 90° (see Chapter 7).

8   Support the strut then unscrew the top mounting nuts and withdraw it from under the wing. Recover the washers.

9   Clean away all external dirt from the strut and coil spring.

10 Fit spring compressors to the coil spring (if applicable) and tighten them evenly until the spring is released from the upper mounting. If applicable, remove the Peugeot cables.

11 Unscrew the piston rod nut, if necessary using a 7 mm Allen key to hold the rod stationary.

12 Remove the washer and upper mounting, followed by the coil spring. The spring may remain in the compressed state ready for

Fig. 9.5 Coil spring retaining cables fitted to the front suspension (Sec 4)

5.2 Front lower suspension arm inner pivot bolt (arrowed) on non-GTI models

Fig. 9.6 Front suspension strut components (Sec 4)

1	Top mounting nut	7	Cap
2	Piston rod nut	8	Stop
3	Washer	9	Coil spring
4	Spacer	10	Bump stop
5	Top mounting	11	Piston rod
6	Pad	12	Strut

5 Front lower suspension arm – removal, overhaul and refitting

1 Jack up the front of the car and support on axle stands. Apply the handbrake and remove the front roadwheel.
2 Unscrew and remove the inner pivot bolt(s), noting the fitting direction (photo).
3 On non-GTI models, unscrew the nut securing the anti-roll bar to the suspension arm and remove the washer.
4 Unscrew the clamp bolt securing the lower balljoint to the hub carrier, then drive a suitable wedge into the slot and release the lower suspension arm. Remove the balljoint protector where fitted.
5 On non-GTI models, lever down the anti-roll bar and withdraw the arm.
6 Check the inner pivot bushes for wear and deterioration. Check the lower balljoint on the outer end of the arm for excessive wear indicated by up and down movement of the ball in the socket. Check the arm for damage or deterioration. The bushes may be renewed using a simple puller consisting of a metal tube and washers, together with a long bolt and nut. It is not possible to renew the balljoint separately.
7 Refitting is a reversal of removal, but delay tightening the inner pivot bolt until the full weight of the car is on the suspension.

6 Front suspension hub carrier – removal and refitting

1 Refer to Chapter 7 and disconnect the outer end of the driveshaft

Fig. 9.7 Front lower suspension arm components on GTI models (Sec 5)

1	Nut	6	Bush
2	Washer	7	Nuts
3	Bush	8	Hub carrier
4	Suspension arm	9	Clamp bolt
5	Bolts		

from the hub. Note that it is not necessary to drain the oil from the engine/transmission unit.
2 Unbolt the brake disc caliper from the hub carrier and either place it on a stand or tie it to one side.
3 Remove the two screws and withdraw the brake disc.
4 Unscrew the nut and use a balljoint removal tool to separate the track rod arm from the steering arm.
5 On non-GTI models, unscrew the lower suspension balljoint clamp

bolt, then drive a suitable wedge into the slot and lift the hub carrier from the lower suspension arm.

6 On GTI models, unscrew the clamp bolt then drive a suitable wedge into the slot on the hub carrier and slide the carrier from the bottom of the strut. If available, use the special Peugeot tool described in Chapter 7 instead of the wedge.

7 Where applicable, unbolt the balljoint protector.

8 Refitting is a reversal of removal, but refer to Chapters 7 and 8 respectively when refitting the driveshaft and brake disc caliper.

7 Front hub and bearing – renewal

1 Remove the hub carrier, as described in Section 6. Note that the hub and bearing can be renewed with the hub carrier attached to the track rod and lower suspension arm (non-GTI models) or strut (GTI models).

2 Clean away all external dirt with a wire brush.

3 Using circlip pliers, extract the bearing retaining circlip from the inner side of the hub carrier.

Fig. 9.8 Using Peugeot tool 80613B to remove the front hub (Sec 7)

Fig. 9.9 Using Peugeot tool 80613B to refit the front hub (Sec 7)

4 The hub must now be pressed or driven from the bearing using force from the inner side of the hub carrier. If available, use Peugeot tool 80613 B which locates in the circlip groove, otherwise use a suitable soft metal drift. Note that the bearing becomes unsuitable for further use after removal of the hub.

5 Using a puller, remove the bearing inner track half from the hub and refit it to the outside of the bearing.

6 Press or drive the bearing from the hub carrier.

7 Clean the hub and bearing recess in the carrier. Do not attempt to remove the seals or plastic ring from the new bearing.

8 Smear a little grease on the bearing recess in the carrier.

9 Press (do not use hammer blows) the new bearing into the hub carrier using force on the outer track only, then refit the circlip in the groove.

10 Press the hub into the bearing inner tracks using the special Peugeot tool shown in Fig. 9.9 or a similar tool made from metal tubing, washers, a long bolt and nut. Note that the tube must locate on the inner track and there must be a space provided to receive the plastic ring which is pushed out by the hub.

11 Refit the hub carrier with reference to Section 6.

8 Rear anti-roll bar – removal and refitting

1 Jack up the rear of the car and support on axle stands. Chock the front wheels and remove the rear wheels.

2 Working on the right-hand side, unscrew the bolt securing the anti-roll bar lever and bracket to the trailing arm. Move the bracket down, leaving it still attached to the handbrake cable.

3 Unscrew the plug from the end of the anti-roll bar then insert a well oiled bolt into the lever and tighten it until the lever is forced off. If available use the bolt included in the Peugeot tool kit 70908.

4 Working on the left-hand side, unscrew the bolt securing the anti-roll bar lever and bracket to the trailing arm, then move the bracket down leaving it still attached to the handbrake cable.

5 Withdraw the anti-roll bar to the left.

6 Mount the anti-roll bar in a vice with the lever uppermost then remove the lever using the procedure described in paragraph 3.

7 Before refitting the anti-roll bar, clean the splines both on the bar and levers and coat them with Esso Norva 275 grease.

8 Mount the anti-roll bar in the vice with its left-hand end uppermost. Note that the left-hand end has an additional shoulder, as shown in Fig. 9.11.

9 Fit a new sealing ring to the left-hand lever. The left-hand lever has a single identification line on its inner face. Locate the ring with the curved end facing inwards and apply some Kluber Proba grease to its outer surface.

10 Slide the lever on the bar with the identification line aligned with the line on the bar shoulder.

11 Press the lever fully onto the splines using Peugeot tool 70908 or a suitable nut, bolt and washer. If the lever is particularly tight it is permissible to drive it on with a length of metal tube.

12 Remove the tool and fit a temporary bolt in the bar to ensure the lever does not move in subsequent work.

13 Where the lever incorporates a 2 mm recess, fit a new seal; otherwise apply some sealant to the lever shoulder.

14 Insert the anti-roll bar into the left-hand side of the suspension tube then position the handbrake lever bracket, insert the bolt and tighten it to the specified torque.

15 Fit a new sealing ring to the right-hand lever. The right-hand lever has three identification lines at 120° intervals on its inner face. Locate the ring with the curved end facing inwards and apply some Kluber Proba grease to its outer surface.

16 Slide the lever on the bar so that the bolt holes in the lever and trailing arm are aligned.

17 Locate a 1.0 mm (0.039 in) spacer between the lever and trailing arm, as shown in Fig. 9.12, then press on the lever using the method described in paragraph 11. If a metal tube is used, the left-hand lever must be suitably supported.

18 Remove the tool and spacer, then position the handbrake lever bracket, insert the bolt, and tighten it to the specified torque.

19 Remove the temporary bolt fitted in paragraph 12.

20 Apply sealing compound to the threads and collars of the end plugs and screw them into the levers.

21 Refit the rear wheels then lower the car to the ground.

Fig. 9.10 Cross-section of the
rear suspension
(Secs 8, 9 and 10)

1 Cross tube
2 Trailing arm
3 Left-hand torsion bar
4 Right-hand torsion bar
5 Housing
6 Anti-roll bar (if fitted)
All measurements in mm

Fig. 9.11 The shoulder at the left-hand end of the rear
anti-roll bar – arrowed (Sec 8)

9 Rear shock absorber – testing, removal and refitting

1 The efficiency of a rear shock absorber can be checked by depressing the rear corner of the car then releasing it quickly. If the body rises then stabilises, the shock absorber is good, but if there are several oscillations it should be renewed.
2 Position the rear of the car on ramps or alternatively jack it up and support it beneath the wheels. Apply the handbrake.
3 Unscrew the shock absorber bottom mounting nut and tap the bolt outwards until it clears the shock absorber (photo). If the bolt head fouls the handbrake cable bracket, loosen the bracket bolt on the side of the trailing arm and lift the bracket as required. Do not forget to tighten the bolt after refitting the shock absorber.

Fig. 9.12 Using feeler blades to check the rear anti-roll bar
end gap (Sec 8)

9.3 Rear shock absorber bottom mounting

4   Unscrew the upper mounting nut, remove the washer, and tap out the bolt.

5   Withdraw the shock absorber from under the car.

6   A more thorough check of the shock absorber may now be made by gripping the bottom mounting in a vice and attempting to extend and retract it. If the resistance is not firm and even in both directions, or if there are signs of leakage or damage, the shock absorber must be renewed.

7   Refitting is a reversal of removal, but renew the self-locking nuts. The nuts must be tightened when the distance between the mounting bolt centres is 288.0 mm (11.347 in). The Peugeot tool 80911 for this operation consists of a bar and adjustable bolt located beneath the lifting ramp and hooked on the suspension tube; however, loading the rear of the car by trial and error will produce the same result.

10 Rear torsion bar – removal and refitting

1   Jack up the rear of the car and support on axle stands under the body. Chock the front wheels and remove the rear wheels.

2   Remove the rear anti-roll bar, as described in Section 8 (where applicable).

3   Remove the shock absorber on the side being worked on, with reference to Section 9.

4   In order to retain the suspension ride height it is necessary to hold the trailing arm stationary with the torsion bar relaxed. Note that the arm itself must be slightly raised to eliminate the effect of its own weight. If available use Peugeot tool 70908 fitted in place of the shock absorber, otherwise firmly support the trailing arm and record the distance between the shock absorber mounting bolt centres.

5   Unscrew and remove the nut and washer from the torsion bar end fitted to the suspension tube.

6   Unscrew the bolt and remove the seal and thrust washer from the torsion bar end fitted to the trailing arm.

7   Using a centre punch, mark the torsion bar and trailing arm in relation to each other.

8   Support the trailing arm then extract the torsion bar using a slide hammer and adaptor screwed into the end of the bar. When removing the left-hand side torsion bar take care not to damage the hydraulic brake line.

9   Unscrew the shouldered stud from the end of the bar.

10 Note that the right and left-hand torsion bars are different – the right one is identified by one painted ring whereas the left one has two painted rings.

11 If the original torsion bar is being refitted and the ride height is correct, check that the dimension recorded in paragraph 4 is still correct. If the ride height is being adjusted refer to Section 11 and set

Fig. 9.13 Peugeot tool 70908 for use on a dummy rear shock absorber (Sec 10)

the dimension accordingly. If a new torsion bar is being fitted, set the dimension by raising or lowering the trailing arm to the following table:

Models with engines XV, XW and XY7 ....   340.0 mm
                                                (13.396 in)
Models with engine XY8 ....   336.0 mm
                                                (13.238 in)
Models with engine XU5J ....   330.5 mm
                                                (13.022 in)

12 Screw in the shouldered stud fully into the 22.5 mm (0.887 in) diameter end of the torsion bar.

13 Coat the torsion bar splines with Esso Norva 275 grease, then insert the small end through the arm and engage it with the splines on the suspension tube bracket. It will be necessary to try the bar in several positions if the original is not being refitted, and the bar will initially only enter by approximately 10.0 mm (0.4 in) as the splines at each end are not in the same plane. When the correct splines are engaged, drive the bar fully into position using the slide hammer and adaptor or a suitable drift.

14 Pack the recess in the arm with grease then fit the thrust washer, a new seal and the bolt. Tighten the bolt to the specified torque.

15 Using a feeler gauge, check that the gap between the trailing arm and suspension tube is 0.05 mm (0.002 in). If it is greater strike the outer surface of the arm with a wooden mallet.

16 Unscrew the shouldered stud at the opposite end of the bar until it just contacts the cup. Recheck the gap, as in paragraph 15, then fit the washer and nut and tighten the nut. To prevent the stud moving hold it with a screwdriver while tightening the nut.

17 Refit the shock absorber (Section 9) and anti-roll bar (Section 8).

18 Refit the rear wheels and lower the car to the ground.

11 Rear suspension ride height – adjustment

1   The rear suspension ride height must be checked with the car on a level surface with the correct tyre pressures and unladen, but with a full

Fig. 9.14 Rear suspension ride height measurement points – arrowed (Sec 11)

fuel tank. The height dimension is given in the Specifications and is taken from the points indicated in Fig. 9.14. The difference between the dimension on each side must not exceed 10.0 mm (0.4 in).

2 It is recommended that the rear of the car is bounced before taking a measurement, and that the average of three successive measurements be taken as the final reading.

3 Note that an adjustment on one side will slightly alter the ride height on the opposite side.

4 To adjust the ride height the torsion bar must be removed and repositioned after setting the trailing arm. A change in the dimension between the shock absorber mounting bolt centres of 2.0 mm (0.08 in) is equivalent to a change in ride height of 3.0 mm (0.12 in). Therefore it is essential to record the existing shock absorber and ride height dimensions before making an adjustment. The torsion bar removal and refitting procedure is given in Section 10.

12 Rear suspension assembly – removal and refitting

1 Remove the handbrake cables, with reference to Chapter 8.
2 Remove the complete exhaust system, with reference to Chapter 3.
3 Disconnect the flexible brake hoses from the rear suspension assembly, with reference to Chapter 8.
4 Unscrew the left-hand rear mounting nut, remove the exhaust bracket then temporarily refit the nut.
5 Unbolt and remove the front clamp and bracket (photo), but do not unscrew the seat belt anchorage.

12.5 Rear suspension cross-tube front clamp and seat belt anchorage

6 Adjust the position of the car on the stands so that the rear wheels are just touching the ground, then place additional stands beneath the suspension tube.
7 Working in the luggage compartment unscrew the front and rear mounting nuts.
8 Jack up the rear of the car and withdraw the assembly from under the car.
9 Refitting is a reversal of removal, but tighten all nuts and bolts to the specified torque. When tightening the front clamp make sure that the ring is centred in the seat belt anchorage bracket. Refer to Chapter 3 and 8 as required and finally bleed the brake hydraulic system.

13 Rear hub/drum – servicing

1 The removal and refitting of the rear hub/drum is described in Chapter 8, together with the inspection of the drum for wear.
2 It is not possible to obtain replacement hub bearings from Peugeot

although they do in fact supply a bearing retaining circlip separately (photo). If the bearings are worn excessively it will therefore be necessary to renew the complete hub/drum unless non-genuine bearings become available.

3 If the hub/drum oil seal is worn or damaged it can be renewed by prising it out with a screwdriver and pressing in the new one with a metal tube (photo). Clean and grease the seal contact surface on the trailing arm before refitting the hub/drum.

13.2 Rear hub bearing retaining circlip (arrowed)

13.3 Oil seal (arrowed) in the rear hub/drum

14 Rear suspension trailing arm and bearings – removal and refitting

1 Jack up the rear of the car and support on axle stands. Chock the front wheels and remove the rear wheels.
2 Remove the handbrake cable and brake shoes on the side being worked on, with reference to Chapter 8.
3 Remove the anti-roll bar, as described in Section 8 (where applicable).
4 Remove the torsion bar, as described in Section 10.

Fig. 9.15 Peugeot tool 70526 for removing the rear suspension trailing arm bearings (Sec 14)

5   Disconnect the hydraulic brake pipes from the wheel cylinder, with reference to Chapter 8.
6   Slide the trailing arm from the suspension tube.
7   Prise the oil seal from the end of the tube and remove the seal sleeve.
8   An extractor is required to remove both the inner and outer bearings and it is recommended that Peugeot tool 70526 is used. The tool comprises a rod and tilting washer which locates behind the bearing – the outer bearing is removed using a slide hammer attachment and the inner bearing is removed using a threaded rod, spacer and nut. If the inner bearing is very tight, a length of rod can be inserted from the opposite end of the tube to release it. Note that the inner bearing may be either of plain or needle roller type.
9   If necessary the shaft may be removed from the trailing arm using a press, but first note the fitted position of the shaft, as on some models it is recessed by 2.0 mm (0.08 in) from the outer surface, on others it is flush. Always refit the shaft in its original position.
10 To fit the bearings, first pack them with multi-purpose grease then use the special tool to pull or drive them into position. When fitting the needle bearings the side with the manufacturer's name on it must face towards the relevant open end of the tube.
11 Drive the seal sleeve into the end of the tube.
12 Locate the new seal over the trailing arm shaft, having first filled the spacers between the lips with grease.
13 Insert the trailing arm in the tube until the seal contacts the sleeve, then position a 0.05 mm (0.002 in) feeler gauge between the arm and tube and use a wooden mallet to drive the arm into position.
14 Refit the hydraulic brake pipe to the wheel cylinder and tighten the union.
15 Refit the torsion bar (Section 10) and anti-roll bar (Section 8) as applicable.
16 Refit the handbrake cable and brake shoes then bleed the brakes, as described in Chapter 8.
17 Refit the wheels and lower the car to the ground.

15 Rear suspension mountings and bushes – renewal

1   Remove the rear suspension assembly, as described in Section 12.
2   Unbolt the rear mountings from the side-members (photo).
3   Identify the front mounting brackets for position then unscrew the bolts and remove the brackets.
4   Saw off the ends of the front mounting bushes then drive them out with a metal bar.
5   Dip the new bushes in soapy water and press them into position

15.2 Rear suspension rear mounting and retaining nut (arrowed)

Fig. 9.16 The notch in the rear suspension mounting bushes (arrowed) must be fitted in the vertical plane (Sec 15)

using a long bolt, nut and spacers. Note that the notch in the flange must be in the vertical plane (ie facing up or down when fitted).
6 Refit the front mounting bracket, insert the bolts from the rear and tighten the nuts with the brackets horizontal.
7 Fit the new rear mountings with the studs towards the wheel side and tighten the nuts.
8 Refit the suspension assembly, with reference to Section 12.

16 Wheels and tyres – general care and maintenance

Wheels and tyres should give no problems in use provided that a close eye is kept on them with regard to excessive wear or damage. To this end, the following points should be noted.

Ensure that tyre pressures are checked regularly and maintained correctly. Checking should be carried out with the tyres cold and not immediately after the vehicle has been in use. If the pressures are checked with the tyres hot, an apparently high reading will be obtained owing to heat expansion. Under no circumstances should an attempt to made to reduce the pressures to the quoted cold reading in this instance, or effective underinflation will result.

Underinflation will cause overheating of the tyre owing to excessive flexing of the casing, and the tread will not sit correctly on the road surface. This will cause a consequent loss of adhesion and excessive wear, not to mention the danger of sudden tyre failure due to heat build-up.

Overinflation will cause rapid wear of the centre part of the tyre tread coupled with reduced adhesion, harsher ride, and the danger of shock damage occurring in the tyre casing.

Regularly check the tyres for damage in the form of cuts or bulges, especially in the sidewalls. Remove any nails or stones embedded in the tread before they penetrate the tyre to cause deflation. If removal of a nail *does* reveal that the tyre has been punctured, refit the nail so that its point of penetration is marked. Then immediately change the wheel and have the tyre repaired by a tyre dealer. Do *not* drive on a tyre in such a condition. If in any doubt as to the possible consequences of any damage found, consult your local tyre dealer for advice.
to the possible consequences of any damage found, consult your local tyre dealer for advice.

Periodically remove the wheels and clean any dirt or mud from the inside and outside surfaces. Examine the wheels rims for signs of rusting, corrosion or other damage. Light alloy wheels are easily damaged by 'kerbing' whilst parking, and similarly steel wheels may become dented or buckled. Renewal of the wheel is very often the only course of remedial action possible.

The balance of each wheel and tyre assembly should be maintained to avoid excessive wear, not only to the tyres but also to the steering and suspension components. Wheel imbalance is normally signified by vibration through the vehicle's bodyshell, although in many cases it is particularly noticeable through the steering wheel. Conversely, it should be noted that wear or damage in suspension or steering components may cause excessive tyre wear. Out-of-round or out-of-true tyres, damaged wheels and wheel bearing wear/maladjustment also fall into this category. Balancing will not usually cure vibration caused by such wear.

Wheel balancing may be carried out with the wheel either on or off the vehicle. If balanced on the vehicle, ensure that the wheel-to-hub relationship is marked in some way prior to subsequent wheel removal so that it may be refitted in its original position.

General tyre wear is influenced to a large degree by driving style – harsh braking and acceleration or fast cornering will all produce more rapid tyre wear. Interchanging of tyres may result in more even wear, but this should only be carried out where there is no mix of tyre types on the vehicle. However, it is worth bearing in mind that if this is completely effective, the added expense of replacing a complete set of tyres simultaneously is incurred, which may prove financially restrictive for many owners.

Front tyres may wear unevenly as a result of wheel misalignment. The front wheels should always be correctly aligned according to the settings specified by the vehicle manufacturer.

Legal restrictions apply to the mixing of tyre types on a vehicle. Basically this means that a vehicle must not have tyres of differing construction on the same axle. Although it is not recommended to mix tyre types between front axle and rear axle, the only legally permissible combination is crossply at the front and radial at the rear. When mixing radial ply tyres, textile braced radials must always go on the front axle, with steel braced radials at the rear. An obvious disadvantage of such mixing is the necessity to carry two spare tyres to avoid contravening the law in the event of a puncture.

In the UK, the Motor Vehicle Constructions and Use Regulations apply to many aspects of tyre fitting and usage. It is suggested that a copy of these regulations is obtained from your local police if in doubt as to the current legal requirements with regard to tyre condition, minimum tread depth, etc.

17 Fault diagnosis – suspension, hubs, wheels and tyres

Symptom	Reason(s)
Car pulls to one side	Worn front suspension lower balljoint Incorrect tyre pressures
Excessive pitching or rolling	Worn shock absorbers
Wheel wobble or vibration	Unbalanced wheels Damaged wheels Worn wheel bearings Worn shock absorbers
Excessive tyre wear	Incorrect tyre pressures Worn front suspension lower balljoint Unbalanced wheels

Chapter 10 Steering system

For modifications, and information applicable to later models, see Supplement at end of manual

Contents

Specifications

General

Type	Rack and pinion, steering column with universal joint
Steering wheels turns, lock to lock	3.8
Turning circle (between kerbs)	9.95 m (32.6 ft)
Steering rack lubricant type/specification	Lithium-based molybdenum disulphide grease (Duckhams LBM 10)

Front wheel alignment *

Toe-in:	
Non-GTI models	2.5 to 4.5 mm
GTI models	1.0 to 3.0 mm
Castor:	
Non-GTI models	1°15' to 2°15'
GTI models	1°20' to 2°20'
Camber:	
Non-GTI models	0° to 1°
GTI models	− 30° to 30'
Steering axis inclination:	
Non-GTI models	8°15' to 9°15'
GTI models	9° to 10°

* Refer to a Peugeot dealer for manufacturer's latest recommendations

Torque wrench settings

	Nm	lbf ft
Steering gear	35	26
Column-to-pinion clamp bolt	15	11
Track rod balljoint nut	35	26
Track rod inner joint	50	37
Steering wheel nut	30	22

Fig. 10.1 Cutaway diagram of the steering gear (Sec 1)

1 General description

The steering system is of rack and pinion type with side track rods connected to the hub carriers by balljoints. Further balljoints on the inner ends of the track rods are screwed into the rack.

The steering column incorporates a single universal joint at its lower end connected to an intermediate shaft which also incorporates a universal joint at its connection to the pinions on the steering gear. The steering column is angled to prevent direct movement into the passenger compartment in the event of a front end impact.

2 Routine maintenance

Carry out the following procedures at the intervals given in Routine Maintenance at the beginning of the manual.

1 Jack up the front of the car and support on axle stands. Apply the handbrake. Thoroughly examine the bellows at each end of the steering gear for splitting and deterioration, and renew if necessary.
2 Check the track rod ends for excessive wear by attempting to move them up and down. If there is more than the very slightest movement the track rod end should be renewed. Similarly check the track rod inner joints by gripping the track rod through the bellows and attempting to move them up and down. Track rod ends should also be renewed if the rubber boots are split or damaged.

3 Steering wheel – removal and refitting

1 Set the front wheels in the straight-ahead position.
2 Prise out the centre pad, then use a socket to unscrew the retaining nut (photo).
3 Mark the hub in relation to the inner column then pull off the steering wheel. If it is tight a rocking action may release it from the splines.

3.2 Steering wheel retaining nut

4 Refitting is a reversal of removal, but check that the steering wheel is correctly centred with the front wheels straight ahead. Tighten the nut while holding the steering wheel rim.

4 Steering column and lock – removal and refitting

1 Remove the steering wheel, as described in Section 3.
2 Remove the lower trim panel from under the steering column (photo).
3 Mark the column lower universal joint in relation to the intermediate shaft then unscrew and remove the clamp bolt (photo).
4 Remove the combination switches, as described in Chapter 12.
5 Disconnect the ignition switch wiring multi-plugs.
6 Unscrew the mounting nuts and bolts, disconnect the inner column from the intermediate shaft, and withdraw the steering column from the car. Where shear bolts are fitted they must be drilled to remove the heads, then unscrewed after removing the column.
7 If necessary, the intermediate shaft can be removed after prising out the grommet and unscrewing the bottom clamp bolt (photos).
8 To remove the steering lock, unscrew the retaining bolt then, with the ignition key aligned with the small arrow between the 'A' and 'M' positions, depress the plunger in the housing and withdraw the lock.
9 Refitting is a reversal of removal.

HI45854

Fig. 10.2 Steering column intermediate shaft components
(Sec 4)

1 Grommet	4 Bolt
2 Intermediate shaft	5 Steering gear
3 Nut	

4.2 Steering column lower trim panel screws (arrowed)

4.7B Steering column intermediate shaft (arrowed)

4.3 Steering column lower universal joint and clamp bolt (arrowed)

4.7A Removing the intermediate shaft grommet

Fig. 10.3 Steering column assembly (Sec 4)

1 Bolt
2 Steering lock and ignition switch
3 Steering column
4 Mounting nut
5 Clamp bolt and nut

5 Steering gear – removal and refitting

1 Jack up the front of the car and support on axle stands. Apply the handbrake and remove the front wheels.
2 Unscrew the track rod end nuts then use a separator tool to detach the track rod end balljoints from the hub carriers (photo).

5.2 Separating the track rod end from the hub carrier

Fig. 10.4 Steering gear mounting bolt locations – arrowed (Sec 5)

3 Mark the lower column in relation to the pinion on the steering gear.
4 Unscrew and remove the column-to-pinion clamp bolt.
5 Unscrew and remove the two mounting bolts and withdraw the steering gear from one side of the subframe.
6 Refitting is a reversal of removal, but tighten all nuts and bolts to the specified torque and check the front wheel alignment on completion.

6 Steering gear – overhaul

The steering gear has a very long life before any wear becomes evident; always provided that the bellows are kept in order to maintain adequate lubrication.

In view of the special tools and gauges required to overhaul the steering gear it is recommended that, when the need for this arises, the assembly should be changed for a new or factory reconditioned one rather than dismantle the worn unit.

7 Track rod end – removal and refitting

1 Jack up the front of the car and support on axle stands. Apply the handbrake and remove the relevant roadwheel.
2 Loosen the locknut on the track rod.
3 Unscrew the balljoint nut and use an extractor tool to separate the taper from the hub carrier.
4 Unscrew the track rod end from the track rod, noting the number of turns necessary to remove it.
5 Screw the new track rod end the same number of turns on the track rod.
6 Clean the taper surfaces then fit the balljoint to the hub carrier and tighten the nut to the specified torque. **Note:** *If difficulty is experienced in loosening or tightening a balljoint taper pin nut due to the taper pin turning in the eye, apply pressure with a jack or long lever to the balljoint socket to force the taper pin into its conical seat.*
7 Tighten the locknut on the track rod end.
8 Refit the roadwheel and lower the car to the ground.
9 Check and if necessary adjust the front wheel toe-in setting, as described in Section 10.

8 Steering rack bellows – renewal

1 Remove the relevant track rod end, as described in Section 7.
2 Release the clips from each end of the bellows then ease the bellows from the steering gear and pull it from the track rod.
3 Clean the track rod and bellows location on the steering gear. If necessary, add grease to the steering gear.
4 Slide the new bellows onto the track rod and steering gear, check that it is not twisted, then fit the clips.
5 Refit the track rod end with reference to Section 7.

9 Track rod – renewal

1 Remove the steering rack bellows, as described in Section 8.
2 Using open-ended spanners, hold the rack and loosen the track rod joint socket. Unscrew the socket and withdraw the track rod.

Fig. 10.5 Track rod components (Sec 9)

1 Bellows	4 Self-locking nut
2 Lock washer	5 Track rod end
3 Track rod	

3   Fit the new track rod using a reversal of the removal procedure, but fit a new lock washer and tighten the joint socket to the specified torque.

10 Steering angles and front wheel alignment

1   Accurate front wheel alignment is essential to provide good steering and roadholding characteristics and to ensure slow and even tyre wear. Before considering the steering angles, check that the tyres are correctly inflated, that the front wheels are not buckled, the hub bearings are not worn and that the steering linkage is in good order, without slackness or wear at the joints.
2   Wheel alignment consists of four factors:
Camber is the angle at which the roadwheels are set from the vertical when viewed from the front or rear of the vehicle. Positive camber is the angle (in degrees) that the wheels are tilted outwards at the top from the vertical.
Castor is the angle between the steering axis and a vertical line when viewed from each side of the vehicle. Positive castor is indicated when the steering axis is inclined towards the rear of the vehicle at its upper end.
Steering axis inclination is the angle when viewed from the front or rear of the vehicle between vertical and an imaginary line drawn between the upper and lower strut mountings.
   Camber, castor and steering axis inclination are set during production of the car and any deviation from specified tolerance must therefore be due to gross wear in the suspension mountings or collision damage.
Toe is the amount by which the distance between the front inside edges of the roadwheel rims differs from that between the rear inside edges. If the distance between the front edges is less than that at the rear, the wheels are said to toe-in. If the distance between the front inside edges is greater than that at the rear, the wheels toe-out.
3   To check the front wheel alignment, first make sure that the lengths of both track-rods are equal when the steering is in the straight-ahead position.
4   The length of each track rod should be as shown in Fig. 10.6 or very near this dimension. If it is necessary to check the dimension, release the bellows from the steering gear and double it back over the track rod. Refit the bellows after making the check.

5   Obtain a tracking gauge. These are available in various forms from accessory stores or one can be fabricated from a length of steel tubing suitably cranked to clear the sump and bellhousing and having a setscrew and locknut at one end.
6   With the gauge, measure the distance between the two wheel inner rims (at hub height) at the rear of the wheel. Push the vehicle forward to rotate the wheels through 180° (half a turn) and measure the distance between the wheel inner rims, again at hub height, at the front of the wheel. This last measurement should differ from the first by the appropriate toe-in according to specification (see Specifications Section).
7   Where the toe-in is found to be incorrect, release the track rod end locknuts and turn the track-rods equally. Only turn them a quarter of a turn at a time before rechecking the alignment, and release the bellows outer clips to prevent the bellows from twisting.
8   On completion tighten the track rod end locknuts, and refit the bellows clips.

Fig. 10.6 Track rod initial setting dimension (Sec 10)

a = 356.0 mm (14.03 in)

11 Fault diagnosis – steering system

Symptom	Reason(s)
Stiff action	Lack of rack lubrication
	Seized track rod end balljoint
	Seized track rod inner balljoint
Excessive movement at steering wheel	Worn track rod end balljoints
	Worn rack and pinion
Tyre squeal when cornering and excessive tyre wear	Incorrect wheel alignment

Chapter 11 Bodywork and fittings

For modifications, and information applicable to later models, see Supplement at end of manual

Contents

1 General description

The body shell is of one-piece design and safety cell construction, whereby the outer members yield progressively and in a controlled direction in the event of impact, giving maximum protection to the passenger compartment. The body panels are of lightweight high strength steel.

The front wings are bolted to the main body for ease of removal. The complete body is given an extensive anti-corrosion treatment during manufacture; including stone chip protection and wax injection. Peugeot guarantee the body against perforation as a result of corrosion for a period of six years provided the car is given periodic inspections by a Peugeot garage.

2 Maintenance – bodywork and underframe

1 The general condition of a vehicle's bodywork is the one thing that significantly affects its value. Maintenance is easy but needs to be regular. Neglect, particularly after minor damage, can lead quickly to further deterioration and costly repair bills. It is important also to keep watch on those parts of the vehicle not immediately visible, for instance the underside, inside all the wheel arches and the lower part of the engine compartment.

2 The basic maintenance routine for the bodywork is washing – preferably with a lot of water, from a hose. This will remove all the loose solids which may have stuck to the vehicle. It is important to flush these off in such a way as to prevent grit from scratching the finish. The wheel arches and underframe need washing in the same way to remove any accumulated mud which will retain moisture and tend to encourage rust. Paradoxically enough, the best time to clean the underframe and wheel arches is in wet weather when the mud is thoroughly wet and soft. In very wet weather the underframe is usually cleaned of large accumulations automatically and this is a good time for inspection.

3 Periodically, except on vehicles with a wax-based underbody protective coating, it is a good idea to have the whole of the underframe of the vehicle steam cleaned, engine compartment included, so that a thorough inspection can be carried out to see what minor repairs and renovations are necessary. Steam cleaning is available at many garages and is necessary for removal of the accumulation of oily grime which sometimes is allowed to become thick in certain areas. If steam cleaning facilities are not available, there are one or two excellent grease solvents available such as Holts Engine Cleaner or Holts Foambrite which can be brush applied. The dirt can then be simply hosed off. Note that these methods should not be used on vehicles with wax-based underbody protective coating or the coating will be removed. Such vehicles should be inspected annually, preferably just prior to winter, when the underbody should be washed down and any damage to the wax coating repaired using Holts Undershield. Ideally, a completely fresh coat should be applied. It would also be worth considering the use of such wax-based protection for injection into door panels, sills, box sections, etc, as an additional safeguard against rust damage where such protection is not provided by the vehicle manufacturer.

4 After washing paintwork, wipe off with a chamois leather to give an unspotted clear finish. A coat of clear protective wax polish, like the many excellent Turtle Wax polishes, will give added protection against chemical pollutants in the air. If the paintwork sheen has dulled or oxidised, use a cleaner/polisher combination such as Turtle Extra to restore the brilliance of the shine. This requires a little effort, but such dulling is usually caused because regular washing has been neglected. Care needs to be taken with metallic paintwork, as special non-abrasive cleaner/polisher is required to avoid damage to the finish. Always check that the door and ventilator opening drain holes and pipes are completely clear so that water can be drained out (photos). Bright work should be treated in the same way as paint work. Windscreens and windows can be kept clear of the smeary film which

Fig. 11.1 Peugeot 205 one-piece body shell (Sec 1)

often appears, by the use of a proprietary glass cleaner like Holts Mixra. Never use any form of wax or other body or chromium polish on glass.

3   Maintenance – upholstery and carpets

Mats and carpets should be brushed or vacuum cleaned regularly to keep them free of grit. If they are badly stained remove them from the vehicle for scrubbing or sponging and make quite sure they are dry before refitting. Seats and interior trim panels can be kept clean by wiping with a damp cloth and Turtle Wax Carisma. If they do become stained (which can be more apparent on light coloured upholstery) use a little liquid detergent and a soft nail brush to scour the grime out of the grain of the material. Do not forget to keep the headlining clean in the same way as the upholstery. When using liquid cleaners inside the vehicle do not over-wet the surfaces being cleaned. Excessive damp could get into the seams and padded interior causing stains, offensive odours or even rot. If the inside of the vehicle gets wet accidentally it is worthwhile taking some trouble to dry it out properly, particularly where carpets are involved. *Do not leave oil or electric heaters inside the vehicle for this purpose.*

4   Minor body damage – repair

The colour bodywork repair photographic sequences between pages 32 and 33 illustrate the operations detailed in the following sub-sections. **Note:** *For more detailed information about bodywork repair, the Haynes Publishing Group publish a book by Lindsay Porter called The Car Bodywork Repair Manual. This incorporates information on such aspects as rust treatment, painting and glass fibre repairs, as well as details on more ambitious repairs involving welding and panel beating.*

Repair of minor scratches in bodywork

If the scratch is very superficial, and does not penetrate to the metal of the bodywork, repair is very simple. Lightly rub the area of the scratch with a paintwork renovator like Turtle Wax New Color Back, or a very fine cutting paste like Holts Body + Plus Rubbing Compound, to remove loose paint from the scratch and to clear the surrounding bodywork of wax polish. Rinse the area with clean water.

Apply touch-up paint, such as Holts Dupli-Color Color Touch or a paint film like Holts Autofilm, to the scratch using a fine paint brush; continue to apply fine layers of paint until the surface of the paint in the scratch is level with the surrounding paintwork. Allow the new paint at least two weeks to harden; then blend it into the surrounding paintwork by rubbing the scratch area with a paintwork renovator or a very fine cutting paste, such as Holts Body + Plus Rubbing Compound or Turtle Wax New Color Back. Finally, apply wax polish from one of the Turtle Wax range of wax polishes.

Where the scratch has penetrated right through to the metal of the

2.4A Checking a sill drain hole for blockage

2.4B Checking a door drain hole for blockage

bodywork, causing the metal to rust, a different repair technique is required. Remove any loose rust from the bottom of the scratch with a penknife, then apply rust inhibiting paint, such as Turtle Wax Rust Master, to prevent the formation of rust in the future. Using a rubber or nylon applicator fill the scratch with bodystopper paste like Holts Body + Plus Knifing Putty. If required, this paste can be mixed with cellulose thinners, such as Holts Body + Plus Cellulose Thinners, to provide a very thin paste which is ideal for filling narrow scratches. Before the stopper-paste in the scratch hardens, wrap a piece of smooth cotton rag around the top of a finger. Dip the finger in cellulose thinners, such as Holts Body + Plus Cellulose Thinners, and then quickly sweep it across the surface of the stopper-paste in the scratch; this will ensure that the surface of the stopper-paste is slightly hollowed. The scratch can now be painted over as described earlier in this Section.

Repair of dents in bodywork

When deep denting of the vehicle's bodywork has taken place, the first task is to pull the dent out, until the affected bodywork almost attains its original shape. There is little point in trying to restore the original shape completely, as the metal in the damaged area will have stretched on impact and cannot be reshaped fully to its original contour. It is better to bring the level of the dent up to a point which is about ⅛ in (3 mm) below the level of the surrounding bodywork. In cases where the dent is very shallow anyway, it is not worth trying to pull it out at all. If the underside of the dent is accessible, it can be hammered out gently from behind, using a mallet with a wooden or plastic head. Whilst doing this, hold a suitable block of wood firmly against the outside of the panel to absorb the impact from the hammer blows and thus prevent a large area of the bodywork from being 'belled-out'.

Should the dent be in a section of the bodywork which has a double skin or some other factor making it inaccessible from behind, a different technique is called for. Drill several small holes through the metal inside the area – particularly in the deeper section. Then screw long self-tapping screws into the holes just sufficiently for them to gain a good purchase in the metal. Now the dent can be pulled out by pulling on the protruding heads of the screws with a pair of pliers.

The next stage of the repair is the removal of the paint from the damaged area, and from an inch or so of the surrounding 'sound' bodywork. This is accomplished most easily by using a wire brush or abrasive pad on a power drill, although it can be done just as effectively by hand using sheets of abrasive paper. To complete the preparation for filling, score the surface of the bare metal with a screwdriver or the tang of a file, or alternatively, drill small holes in the affected area. This will provide a really good 'key' for the filler paste.

To complete the repair see the Section on filling and re-spraying.

Repair of rust holes or gashes in bodywork

Remove all paint from the affected area and from an inch or so of the surrounding 'sound' bodywork, using an abrasive pad or a wire brush on a power drill. If these are not available a few sheets of abrasive paper will do the job just as effectively. With the paint removed you will be able to gauge the severity of the corrosion and therefore decide whether to renew the whole panel (if this is possible) or to repair the affected area. New body panels are not as expensive as most people think and it is often quicker and more satisfactory to fit a new panel than to attempt to repair large areas of corrosion.

Remove all fittings from the affected area except those which will act as a guide to the original shape of the damaged bodywork (eg headlamp shells etc). Then, using tin snips or a hacksaw blade, remove all loose metal and any other metal badly affected by corrosion. Hammer the edges of the hole inwards in order to create a slight depression for the filler paste.

Wire brush the affected area to remove the powdery rust from the surface of the remaining metal. Paint the affected area with rust inhibiting paint like Turtle Wax Rust Master; if the back of the rusted area is accessible treat this also.

Before filling can take place it will be necessary to block the hole in some way. This can be achieved by the use of aluminium or plastic mesh, or aluminium tape.

Aluminium or plastic mesh or glass fibre matting, such as the Holts Body + Plus Glass Fibre Matting, is probably the best material to use for a large hole. Cut a piece to the approximate size and shape of the hole to be filled, then position it in the hole so that its edges are below the level of the surrounding bodywork. It can be retained in position by several blobs of filler paste around its periphery.

Aluminium tape should be used for small or very narrow holes. Pull a piece off the roll and trim it to the approximate size and shape required, then pull off the backing paper (if used) and stick the tape over the hole; it can be overlapped if the thickness of one piece is insufficient. Burnish down the edges of the tape with the handle of a screwdriver or similar, to ensure that the tape is securely attached to the metal underneath.

Bodywork repairs – filling and re-spraying

Before using this Section, see the Sections on dent, deep scratch, rust holes and gash repairs.

Many types of bodyfiller are available, but generally speaking those proprietary kits which contain a tin of filler paste and a tube of resin hardener are best for this type of repair, like Holts Body + Plus or Holts No Mix which can be used directly from the tube. A wide, flexible plastic or nylon applicator will be found invaluable for imparting a smooth and well contoured finish to the surface of the filler.

Mix up a little filler on a clean piece of card or board – measure the hardener carefully (follow the maker's instructions on the pack) otherwise the filler will set too rapidly or too slowly. Alternatively, Holts No Mix can be used straight from the tube without mixing, but daylight is required to cure it. Using the applicator apply the filler paste to the prepared area; draw the applicator across the surface of the filler to achieve the correct contour and to level the filler surface. As soon as a contour that approximates to the correct one is achieved, stop working the paste – if you carry on too long the paste will become sticky and begin to 'pick up' on the applicator. Continue to add thin layers of filler paste at twenty-minute intervals until the level of the filler is just proud of the surrounding bodywork.

Once the filler has hardened, excess can be removed using a metal plane or file. From then on, progressively finer grades of abrasive paper should be used, starting with a 40 grade production paper and finishing with 400 grade wet-and-dry paper. Always wrap the abrasive paper around a flat rubber, cork, or wooden block – otherwise the surface of the filler will not be completely flat. During the smoothing of the filler surface the wet-and-dry paper should be periodically rinsed in water. This will ensure that a very smooth finish is imparted to the filler at the final stage.

At this stage the 'dent' should be surrounded by a ring of bare metal, which in turn should be encircled by the finely 'feathered' edge of the good paintwork. Rinse the repair area with clean water, until all of the dust produced by the rubbing-down operation has gone.

Spray the whole repair area with a light coat of primer, either Holts Body + Plus Grey or Red Oxide Primer – this will show up any imperfections in the surface of the filler. Repair these imperfections with fresh filler paste or bodystopper, and once more smooth the surface with abrasive paper. If bodystopper is used, it can be mixed with cellulose thinners to form a really thin paste which is ideal for filling small holes. Repeat this spray and repair procedure until you are satisfied that the surface of the filler, and the feathered edge of the paintwork are perfect. Clean the repair area with clean water and allow to dry fully.

The repair area is now ready for final spraying. Paint spraying must be carried out in a warm, dry, windless and dust free atmosphere. This condition can be created artificially if you have access to a large indoor working area, but if you are forced to work in the open, you will have to pick your day very carefully. If you are working indoors, dousing the floor in the work area with water will help to settle the dust which would otherwise be in the atmosphere. If the repair area is confined to one body panel, mask off the surrounding panels; this will help to minimise the effects of a slight mis-match in paint colours. Bodywork fittings (eg chrome strips, door handles etc) will also need to be masked off. Use genuine masking tape and several thicknesses of newspaper for the masking operations.

Before commencing to spray, agitate the aerosol can thoroughly, then spray a test area (an old tin, or similar) until the technique is mastered. Cover the repair area with a thick coat of primer; the thickness should be built up using several thin layers of paint rather than one thick one. Using 400 grade wet-and-dry paper, rub down the surface of the primer until it is really smooth. While doing this, the work area should be thoroughly doused with water, and the wet-and-dry paper periodically rinsed in water. Allow to dry before spraying on more paint.

Spray on the top coat using Holts Dupli-Color Autospray, again building up the thickness by using several thin layers of paint. Start spraying in the centre of the repair area and then work outwards, with a side-to-side motion, until the whole repair area and about 2 inches of the surrounding original paintwork is covered. Remove all masking material 10 to 15 minutes after spraying on the final coat of paint.

Allow the new paint at least two weeks to harden, then, using a paintwork renovator or a very fine cutting paste such as Turtle Wax New Color Back or Holts Body + Plus Rubbing Compound, blend the edges of the paint into the existing paintwork. Finally, apply wax polish.

5 Major body damage – repair

The construction of the body is such that great care must be taken when making cuts, or when renewing major members, to preserve the basic safety characteristics of the structure. In addition, the heating of certain areas is not advisable.

In view of the specialised knowledge necessary for this work, and the alignment jigs and special tools frequently required, the owner is advised to consult a specialist body repairer or Peugeot dealer.

6 Bonnet – removal and refitting

1   Open the bonnet and support with the stay.
2   Using a pencil, mark the position of the hinges on the bonnet (photo).

6.3 Braided lead fitted to the bonnet

6.2 Bonnet hinge

7.2A Top view of the bonnet lock

3   Unbolt the braided lead and disconnect the windscreen washer tubing (photo).
4   While an assistant supports the bonnet, unscrew the nut and remove the bottom of the stay from the right-hand suspension tower.
5   Place some cloth beneath the rear corners of the bonnet, unscrew the hinge bolts and withdraw it from the car.
6   Refitting is a reversal of removal, but check that the bonnet is central within its aperture and flush with the front wings. If necessary loosen the hinge bolts and move it within the elongated holes to reposition it, then adjust the bonnet lock and striker, as described in Section 7.

7 Bonnet lock and remote control cable – removal, refitting and adjustment

1   Remove the front grille, as described in Section 8.
2   Unbolt the lock from the crossmember and disconnect the control cable (photos).

7.2B Bottom view of the bonnet lock

7.3A Removing the bonnet release lever screws (facia panel in position)

7.3B View of the bonnet release lever (facia panel removed)

7.5 Bonnet striker and safety spring

8.2A Remove the screws ...

8.2B ... and lift the front grille from the outer ...

8.2C ... and inner mounting holes

3 Working inside the car, remove the cross-head screws from the cable release lever located below the left-hand end of the facia (photos).
4 Unclip the cable and withdraw it from inside the car.
5 If necessary the bonnet striker may be unscrewed from the bonnet and the safety spring unclipped (photo).
6 Refitting is a reversal of removal, but check that the striker enters the lock centrally and holds the front of the bonnet level with the front wings. If necessary loosen the lock bolts and move the lock within the elongated holes. Adjust the bonnet height by screwing the striker pin in or out. Adjust the rubber buffers to support the front corners of the bonnet.

8 Front grille – removal and refitting

1 Open the bonnet and support with the stay.
2 Remove the screws from the top of the grille then lift it upwards from the lower mounting holes (photos).
3 Refitting is a reversal of removal.

9 Front wing – removal and refitting

1 Remove the front indicator lamp, as described in Chapter 12. Support the bonnet in its open position.
2 Remove the front bumper, as described in Section 10.
3 Unscrew the mounting bolts located on the top flange, rear flange and inner rear lower edge of the wheel arch (photo). Access to the rear flange is gained by opening the front door.
4 Prise the wing from the mastic bead and remove it from the car.

5 Refitting is a reversal of removal, but apply mastic to the inner surface of the flanges. If a new wing is being fitted, paint the inside surfaces and apply an anti-corrosion sealant.

9.3 A front wing mounting bolt

10 Bumpers – removal and refitting

Front

1   The bumper is removed complete with the front spoiler.
2   Working under the vehicle, unscrew the two front bumper mounting nuts at the brackets.
3   On non-GTI models, unscrew the side mounting nuts beneath the front wheel arches and withdraw the bumper from the car, together with the side mounting rubbers (photo).
4   On GTI models, disconnect the battery negative lead, and disconnect the wiring from the front driving lamps.
5   Remove the clip securing the front wing trim to the bumper.
6   Unscrew the bolts securing the driving lamp brackets to the body, loosen the side bumper mounting nuts beneath the front wheel arches, and withdraw the bumper from the car.
7   The brackets may be removed separately if required.
8   Refitting is a reversal of removal.

Rear

9   Unscrew the rear, side and bottom mounting nuts and withdraw the bumper rearwards. On certain models, additional fixing clips must also be released and a lower moulding removed before the bumper can be withdrawn.
10 The brackets may be removed separately if required.
11 Refitting is a reversal of removal.

10.3 Front bumper side mounting nut (arrowed)

Fig. 11.2 Front bumper components (Sec 10)

1   Side mounting (non-GTI)
2   Side mounting (GTI)
3   Side bracket (non-GTI)
4   Bracket
5   Side bracket (GTI)
6   Seal clip
7   Seal
8   Bumper
9   Moulding
10 Mounting plate
11 Headlight washer bracket

H145860

Fig. 11.3 Rear bumper components (Sec 10)

1 Moulding	4 Side mounting and nut	7 Mounting bolt	9 Bracket nut and washers
2 Mounting plates	5 Rubber buffer	8 Nuts	10 Bracket
3 Bumper	6 Bracket		

11 Door – removal and refitting

1 The door hinges are welded to the body pillar and bolted to the door (photo).
2 Remove the plastic caps from the hinge pivot pins.
3 Drive out the roll pin from the door check strap.
4 Where applicable, remove the trim panel (Section 12) and disconnect the loudspeaker wiring from the door.
5 Support the door in the fully open position by placing blocks, or a jack and a pad of rag, under its lower edge.
6 Drive out the hinge pivot pins and remove the door.
7 Refit by reversing the removal operations.
8 Where necessary, the striker on the body pillar may be adjusted to ensure correct closure of the door (photo).

11.1 Door hinge

12.1 Removing the armrest

11.8 Front door striker

12.2 Removing the side pocket

12 Door trim panel – removal and refitting

Front doors

1 Remove the two screws and withdraw the armrest (photo).
2 Remove the screws and withdraw the side pocket (photo).
3 Fully close the window and note the position of the window regulator handle, then pull the handle from the spindle (photo).
4 Prise out the interior door handle surround (photo).
5 Using a wide-bladed screwdriver, or similar tool, prise the trim panel from the door – working progressively from the bottom upwards and inserting the screwdriver adjacent to each clip.
6 Refitting is a reversal of removal, but first make sure that the clips are correctly located in the panel.

Rear doors

7 The procedure is as given for the front doors, but there are slight trim differences.

Models with electric windows

8 The procedure is basically the same as given previously, but there will be no regulator handle to remove. Be sure to disconnect the battery before releasing the motor switch wiring.

12.3 Removing the window regulator handle

12.4 Removing the interior door handle surround

13.2B The window regulator lifting arms and window glass channel

13 Door – dismantling and reassembly

1   Remove the trim panel, as described in Section 12.

Window regulator
2   To remove the window regulator, unscrew the mounting nuts, slide the two lifting arms from the channels, and withdraw the regulator through the access aperture (photos). Support the glass during this operation.

Door lock
3   To remove the door lock and inner remote handle, disconnect the link rods as necessary and, unscrew the Torx screws retaining the lock (photos).

Exterior handle
4   To remove the exterior handle, disconnect the link rod and unscrew the bolts. The private lock is removed by disconnecting the link rod and pulling out the retaining clip (photo).

13.3A Door lock and mounting screws

13.2A Window regulator mounting nuts (arrowed)

13.3B Door inner remote handle

13.4 View of the private lock from inside the door

13.6B ... and remove the exterior mirror mounting screws

Door glass

5   To remove the door glass, first remove the window regulator then unbolt the glass side channels, tilt the glass and withdraw it upwards.

Exterior mirror

6   To remove the exterior mirror, prise off the inner cover and use an Allen key to remove the mounting screws (photos).

General reassembly

7   Reassembly of the door is a reversal of the dismantling procedure. However, when refitting the door glass, adjust the position of the side channels so that the glass moves smoothly without excessive play.

14 Tailgate – removal and refitting

1   Open the tailgate and have an assistant support it.
2   Disconnect the struts from the body by prising out the plastic clips and pulling off the sockets (photos).
3   Disconnect the wiring for the heated rear window and tailgate wiper motor. Also disconnect the washer tube.

14.2A Prise out the plastic clips ...

13.6A Remove the inner cover ...

14.2B ... and disconnect the tailgate struts

14.4 Tailgate mounting nuts behind the headlining

4   Prise the blanking plates from the rear of the headlining, then unscrew the mounting nuts and lift the tailgate from the car (photo).
5   Refitting is a reversal of removal, but before fully tightening the mounting nuts check that the tailgate is positioned centrally in the body aperture and make any adjustments to the lock and striker, as described in Section 15.

15 Tailgate lock – removal and refitting

1   Open the tailgate and prise off the trim panel using a wide-bladed screwdriver (photo).
2   Unbolt the latch and disconnect the operating rod.
3   Slide out the spring clip and withdraw the lock barrel and escutcheon (photo).
4   Refitting is a reversal of removal. Check that the latch engages the striker correctly and, if necessary, adjust the striker position within the elongated bolt holes. Adjust the rubber stops so that the tailgate is supported firmly at the corners when shut (photo).

16 Windscreen and tailgate glass – general

Both the windscreen and tailgate glass are bonded in position and therefore it is recommended that a professional fitter is employed in the event of breakage. Special equipment and adhesive are required for removal of the old glass and fitting of the new, which may not be readily available to the home mechanic.

17 Rear quarter glass (GTI models) – removal and refitting

1   Open the quarter window and remove the screw securing the glass to the latch. Remove the special nut from the glass.
2   Open the window further then support it and remove the screws securing the glass to the front hinges. Remove the special nuts.
3   Refitting is a reversal of removal.

18 Seats – removal and refitting

Front
1   Move the seat fully forward and remove the rear inner mounting bolts (photo).
2   Remove the remaining mounting bolts from under the car and from the brackets, then remove the seat from the car (photo).
3   Refitting is a reversal of removal.

Rear
4   Fold the cushion forwards and unbolt it from the hinges (photo).
5   Fold the backrest down, unscrew the nuts from the outer pivot bracket(s) (photo) and withdraw the backrest from the inner pivot (where applicable).
6   Refitting is a reversal of removal.

19 Grab handles – removal and refitting

1   Prise up the cover plates for access to the screws (photo).
2   Remove the screws and the grab handles.
3   Refitting is a reversal of removal.

20 Sunroof – general

1   The sunroof fitted to some models incorporates an outer glass and inner cover. The control handle operates lock latches located at the rear of the sunroof. The handle also operates a vacuum seal system which holds and seals the sunroof in any desired position (photo).
2   The vacuum seal is operated by engine vacuum. With the handle shut, the vacuum valve is closed and the seal exerts pressure under the periphery of the glass. When the handle is opened, the vacuum valve opens and causes the seal to collapse, enabling the glass to be moved.
3   Refer to the Supplement for details of sunroof glass removal and refitting.

15.1 Tailgate trim panel clip

15.3 Tailgate lock and lock barrel

15.4 Tailgate rubber stop

18.1 Front seat rear inner mounting bolts

18.2 The front seat rear outer mounting on a GTI model

18.4 Rear seat cushion hinge

18.5 Rear seat backrest outer pivot bracket

19.1 Grab handle mounting screw location

20.1 Sunroof handle in open position

Fig. 11.4 Sunroof components (Sec 20)

1   Cover and slide
2   Glass channel
3   Glass
4   Support
5   Latch

6   Rear stop
7   Support
8   Rear seal
9   Glass seal
10 Water drain pipes

11 Vacuum seal
12 Slide
13 Frame
14 Handle
15 Console

16 Control cable
17 Vacuum pipe
18 Front seal
19 Stop

20 Support
21 Swivel
22 Latch
23 Control rod

Fig. 11.5 Cross-sections of the sunroof components (Sec 20)

1 Handle	3 Swivel	5 Latch	7 Vacuum valve
2 Plunger	4 Cable	6 Vacuum seal	8 Cam

21 Glovebox – removal and refitting

1 Open the glovebox.
2 Remove the pivot retainers from under the facia, disconnect the pivots from the hinge plates and withdraw the glovebox.
3 If necessary the striker can be unbolted and removed.
4 Refitting is a reversal of removal.

22 Facia panel – removal and refitting

1 Remove the steering wheel (Chapter 10) and instrument panel (Chapter 12).
2 Remove the screws and withdraw the steering column lower shroud.
3 Remove the ashtray (photo).
4 Prise out the central air vents (photo).
5 Prise out the digital clock which is retained by plastic barbs (photo).

22.5 Digital clock and retaining barbs (arrowed)

22.3 Removing the ashtray

6 Using a hooked instrument, withdraw the rear of the oddments recess (photo).
7 Remove the radio, as described in Chapter 12, or prise out the blank (as required).
8 Remove the gear lever surround and centre console, noting that the console is held at the top by plastic clips (photo).
9 Remove the screw from inside the ashtray recess (photo).
10 Unscrew the facia bottom mounting bolts including the one on the bonnet release handle (photo).
11 With the glovebox open, remove the mounting screw located near the glovebox lamp (photo).
12 Remove the central lower panels (photo).
13 With the bonnet open, remove the plastic grille and unscrew the front facia mounting nuts (photo).
14 Withdraw the facia panel at the same time disconnecting the relevant switches and cigar lighter. Reconnect the switch wiring immediately to ensure correct refitting.
15 Refitting is a reversal of removal.

22.4 Removing the central air vents

22.6 Removing the rear of the oddments tray

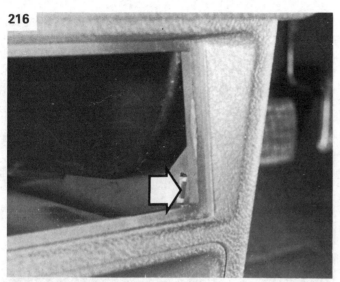

22.8 Centre console upper clip (arrowed)

22.9 Facia mounting screw located in the ashtray recess (arrowed)

22.10 A facia bottom mounting bolt

22.11 Removing a facia mounting screw

22.12 Facia central lower panels and bracket

22.13 Facia front mounting nut

23 Heater assembly – removal, dismantling and refitting

Note: *This procedure is only necessary if the complete heater assembly is to be removed. The heater blower motor can be removed independently by reaching up behind the glovebox and extracting the three securing screws from the base of the unit (see photos 23.7A and 23.7B). Disconnect the wiring plug after lowering the unit.*

1   Remove the facia panel, as described in Section 22.
2   Disconnect the lower air vents (photo).
3   Note the position of the wiring loom and switches then remove the clips and withdraw the wiring to the left (photo). Lower the fuse board with reference to Chapter 12, Section 11.
4   Drain the cooling system, with reference to Chapter 2, and disconnect the heater hoses located on the bulkhead in the engine compartment.
5   Unscrew the five heater assembly mounting nuts and withdraw it from the car (photos).
6   To remove the matrix, disconnect the pipe clip and unscrew the mounting screws then slide the matrix from the casing. If necessary the pipes can be removed by unscrewing the flange screws (photo). Use water from a hose to clean both the inside and outside of accumulated debris.
7   To remove the heater blower, unscrew the mounting screws and lift the unit from the casing (photos).
8   If necessary remove the heater control panel and cable (photos).
9   Refitting is a reversal of removal, but fill the cooling system with reference to Chapter 2.

23.5A Heater lower mounting bracket

23.2 Disconnecting the lower air vents

23.5B Left-hand heater mounting

23.3 Wiring loom with facia removed

23.5C Upper heater mounting

23.6A Heater matrix mounting screws (arrowed)

23.6B Removing the heater matrix

23.6C Heater matrix pipes and flanges

23.7A Remove the mounting screws ...

23.7B ... and lift out the heater blower unit

23.8A Heater control panel

23.8B Heater air inlet control levers

23.8C Heater fresh air control levers and cable

23.8D Heater temperature control levers

Chapter 12 Electrical system

For modifications, and information applicable to later models, see Supplement at end of manual

Contents

Specifications

System type .... 12 volt negative earth, battery, alternator, and pre-engaged starter motor

Battery

XV8 and XW7 engines	150 amp; 25 amp/hour
XY7 and XY8 engines	175 amp; 29 amp/hour
XU5J engine	175 amp; 29 amp/hour or 200 amp; 33 amp/hour

Alternator

Rating	750 watt
Drivebelt tension:	
XV8, XW7, XY7 and XY8 engines	Deflection: 12.5 mm
XU5J engine:	
Without tensioner	Deflection: approx 6.0 mm
Using Krikit tensioner	60 kg/span (new belt) or 40 kg/span (used belt)

Wiper blades .... Champion X4503

Wiper arms .... Champion CCA6

Starter motor

Type	Pre-engaged
Minimum brush length	12.7 mm
Starter drive pinion-to-stop clearance with solenoid energised	1.5 mm

Fuses

No	Circuit protected	Rating (amp)
1	Reverse lamp, cooling fan relay, tachometer (GTI)	10
2	Accessories, indicators, fuel gauge, warning lights, heater blower motor	25
3	Ignition switch, wash/wipe system, stop-lamps, tachometer (non-GTI option), radio, heated rear window, electric window relay (option), clock illumination (GTI)	25

No	Circuit protected	Rating (amp)
4	Central door locking (option)	10
5	Cooling fan	25
6	Hazard warning switch	10
7	Spare	–
8	Cigarette lighter, clock, interior lamps, glovebox illumination, radio	20
9	Electric front windows	25
10	Heated rear window, horns	20
11	Rear foglamp	5
12	Side/tail lamps/warning light, instrument panel illumination, number plate lamps	5
13	(In-line) fuel pump (GTI)	25

Bulbs

	Wattage
Headlamps:	
Non-GTI	45/40
GTI	H4 (55)
Front parking lamps	5
Direction indicator lamps	21
Front driving lamp (GTI)	H3 (55)
Tail/stop-lamps	5/21
Reverse lamp	21
Rear foglamps	21
Interior lamp	5

Torque wrench settings

	Nm	lbf ft
Alternator mounting bolt (non-GTI)	45	33
Alternator adjuster link bolt (non-GTI)	17	13
Starter motor mounting bolts (non-GTI)	12	9
Alternator pivot bolt (GTI)	39	29
Alternator strap bolt (GTI)	20	15
Starter motor bolts (GTI)	34	25

1 General description

The electrical system is of the 12 volt negative earth type and the major components consist of a battery, of which the negative terminal is earthed, an alternator which is belt-driven from the crankshaft pulley, and a starter motor.

The battery supplies a steady amount of current for the ignition, lighting and other electrical circuits and provides a reserve of electricity when the current consumed by the electrical equipment exceeds that being produced by the alternator.

The alternator is controlled by a regulator which ensures a high output if the battery is in a low state of charge or the demand from the electrical equipment is high, and a low output if the battery is fully charged and there is little demand for the electrical equipment.

When fitting electrical accessories it is important, if they contain silicone diodes or transistors, that they are connected correctly, otherwise serious damage may result to the components concerned. Items such as radios, tape recorders, electronic ignition systems, electronic tachometer, automatic dipping etc, should all be checked for correct polarity.

It is important that both battery leads are always disconnected if the battery is to be boost charged; also, if body repairs are to be carried out using electric arc welding equipment, the alternator must be disconnected, otherwise serious damage can be caused to the more delicate instruments. Whenever the battery has to be disconnected it must always be reconnected with the negative terminal earthed.

2 Routine maintenance

Carry out the following procedures at the intervals given in Routine Maintenance at the beginning of the manual

1 Remove the battery cell covers and check the electrolyte level, as described in Section 3. Top up if necessary. Note that topping-up is not usually necessary for the standard low maintenance battery used under normal conditions.

2 Check and, if necessary, adjust the alternator drivebelt, as follows. Firmly depress the drivebelt midway between the pulleys (water pump and alternator on non-GTI models) and check that it deflects by the amount given in the Specifications (photo). If not, loosen the pivot

and adjustment bolts, reposition the alternator then retighten the bolts. On non-GTI models lever the alternator, but on GTI models turn the special adjustment screw as required (photo).

3 Battery – maintenance and inspection

1 The battery fitted as original equipment is of low maintenance type; however, on some models, it incorporates the standard cell covers for checking the electrolyte level (photo). Under normal conditions it is not necessary to check the level, but if the battery is subject to severe conditions such as taxi work or extreme temperatures, the level should be checked every 10 000 miles (15 000 km).

2 When topping-up is required use only distilled water and cover the battery plates to a depth of 10.0 mm (0.40 in).

3 Acid should never be required if the battery has been correctly filled from new, unless spillage has occurred.

4 Inspect the battery terminals and mounting tray for corrosion. This is the white fluffy deposit which grows at these areas. If evident, clean it away and neutralise it with ammonia or baking soda. Apply petroleum jelly to the terminals and paint the battery tray with a suitable anti-corrosion preparation.

5 Keep the top surface of the battery casing dry.

6 An indication of the state of charge of a battery can be obtained by checking the electrolyte in each cell using a hydrometer. The specific gravity of the electrolyte for fully charged and fully discharged conditions at the electrolyte temperature indicated, is listed below.

Fully discharged	Electrolyte temperature	Fully charged
1.098	38°C (100°F)	1.268
1.102	32°C (90°F)	1.272
1.106	27°C (80°F)	1.276
1.110	21°C (70°F)	1.280
1.114	16°C (60°F)	1.284
1.118	10°C (50°F)	1.288
1.122	4°C (40°F)	1.292
1.126	–1.5°C (30°F)	1.296

7 There should be very little variation in the readings between the different cells, but if a difference is found in excess of 0.025 then it will probably be due to an internal fault indicating impending battery

2.2A Checking the alternator drivebelt tension

2.2B Adjusting the alternator drivebelt tension on GTI models

3.1 Checking the battery electrolyte level

failure. This assumes that electrolyte has not been spilled at some time and the deficiency made up with water only.

8 If electrolyte is accidentally spilled at any time, mop up and neutralise the spillage at once. Electrolyte attacks and corrodes metal rapidly; it will also burn holes in clothing and skin. Leave the addition of acid to a battery cell to your dealer or service station as the mixing of acid with distilled water can be dangerous.

9 Never smoke or allow naked lights near the battery; the hydrogen gas which it gives off is explosive.

10 With normal motoring, the battery should be kept in a good state of charge by the alternator and never need charging from a mains charger.

11 However, if the daily mileage is low, with much use of starter and electrical accessories, it is possible for the battery to become discharged owing to the fact that the alternator is not in use long enough to replace the current consumed.

12 Also, as the battery ages, it may not be able to hold its charge and some supplementary charging may be needed. Before connecting the charger, disconnect the battery leads, negative lead first or, better still, remove the battery from the vehicle.

13 Specially rapid 'boost' charges which are claimed to restore the power of the battery in 1 to 2 hours are most dangerous as they can cause serious damage to the battery plates through overheating.

14 While charging the battery note that the temperature of the electrolyte should never exceed 38°C (100°F).

15 When charging a low maintenance battery **do not** remove the cell covers; however, on other types of battery, the cell covers should be removed.

4 Battery – removal and refitting

1 The battery is located in the front left-hand corner of the engine compartment.

2 Disconnect the battery leads, negative lead first. On non-GTI models the negative lead has a wing type terminal nut which, if unscrewed two or three turns, will isolate the battery without the need for complete removal. This is a useful facility when undertaking routine electrical jobs on the car.

3 Release the battery clamp and lift the battery carefully from the engine compartment.

4 Refitting is a reversal of removal, but smear the terminals with petroleum jelly on completion.

5 Alternator – general description and maintenance

1 All models covered by this manual are fitted with alternators. The alternator generates alternating current (AC) which is rectified by diodes into direct current (DC) which is the current needed for charging the battery.

2 The main advantage of the alternator lies in its ability to provide a high charge at low revolutions. Driving slowly in heavy traffic with a dynamo invariably means no charge is reaching the battery. In similar conditions, even with the heater, wiper, lights and perhaps radio switched on, the alternator will ensure a charge reaches the battery.

3 The alternator is of the rotating field ventilated design and comprises principally a laminated stator, on which is wound the output winding, a rotor carrying the field winding and a diode rectifier.

4 The rotor is belt-driven from the engine through a pulley keyed to the rotor shaft. A fan adjacent to the pulley draws air through the unit. Rotation is clockwise when viewed from the drive end.

5 The voltage regulator is mounted externally on the rear cover of the alternator.

6 The equipment has been designed for the minimum amount of maintenance in service, the only items subject to wear being the brushes and bearings.

7 Brushes should be examined after about 80 000 miles (120 000 km) and renewed if necessary. The bearings are pre-packed with grease for life, and should not require further attention.

8 Regularly check the drivebelt tension, as described in Section 2.

6 Alternator – removal and refitting

1 Disconnect the battery negative lead.

2 Loosen the pivot and adjustment bolts, swivel the alternator towards the engine then remove the drivebelt.

3 On non-GTI models, move the air cleaner to one side (Chapter 2).

4 Disconnect the wiring from the alternator (photo).

5 Unscrew the pivot and adjustment bolts and lift the alternator from the engine. On GTI models note that the alternator front bracket is slotted to allow the pivot bolt to remain in the bracket on the engine.

6 Refitting is a reversal of removal, but tension the drivebelt, as described in Section 2.

6.4 The alternator wiring connections

7 Alternator – brush renewal

1 Remove the alternator (Section 6) then remove the rear shield (where fitted).

2 Remove the regulator/brush holder mounting screws and withdraw the assembly. Disconnect the regulator lead, where necessary.

3 With the brush holder removed, check the condition of the slip rings. If they are blackened, clean them with a fuel-moistened rag. If they are deeply scored or grooved then it will probably indicate that the alternator is coming to the end of its life.

4 Unsolder the old brushes and solder in the new ones. Have this done professionally if you lack skill in soldering.

5 Refit the regulator/brush holder and tighten the mounting screws. Reconnect the regulator lead, where necessary.

6 Refit the rear shield (where fitted) then refit the alternator, with reference to Section 6.

8 Starter motor – description and testing

1 The starter motor is mounted on the front of the engine and is of the pre-engaged type, where the drive pinion is brought into mesh with the starter ring gear on the flywheel before the main current is applied.

2 When the starter switch is operated, current flows from the battery to the solenoid which is mounted on the top of the starter motor body. The plunger in the solenoid moves inwards, so causing a centrally pivoted lever to push the drive pinion into mesh with the starter ring gear. When the solenoid plunger reaches the end of its travel, it closes an internal contact and full starting current flows to the starter field coils. The armature is then able to rotate the crankshaft, so starting the engine.

3 A special freewheel clutch is fitted to the starter drive pinion so that as soon as the engine fires and starts to operate on its own it does not drive the starter motor.

4 When the starter switch is released, the solenoid is de-energised

Fig. 12.1 Exploded diagram of the Bosch alternator (Sec 7)

1 Pulley	5 Rotor	9 Brush end housing
2 Fan	6 Bearing	10 Brush holder/regulator
3 Drive end housing	7 Stator	11 Condenser
4 Bearing	8 Diode plate	

Fig. 12.2 Exploded diagram of the Paris-Rhône alternator (Sec 7)

1 Pulley
2 Fan
3 Drive end housing
4 Stator

5 Rotor
6 Bearing
7 Brush end housing

8 Brush holder/regulator
9 Diode plate
10 Cover

and a spring moves the plunger back to its rest position. This operates the pivoted lever to withdraw the drive pinion from engagement with the starter ring.

5 If the starter motor fails to turn the engine when the switch is operated there are four possible reasons why:

(a) *The battery is discharged or faulty*
(b) *The electrical connections between switch, solenoid, battery and starter motor are somewhere failing to pass the necessary current from the battery, through the starter to earth*
(c) *The solenoid has an internal fault*
(d) *The starter motor is electrically defective*

6 To check the battery, switch on the headlights. If they go dim after a few seconds the battery is discharged. If the lamp glows brightly, next operate the ignition/starter switch and see what happens to the lights. If they do dim it is indicative that power is reaching the starter motor but failing to turn it. If the starter should turn very slowly go on to the next check.

7 If, when the ignition/starter switch is operated, the lights stay bright then the power is not reaching the starter motor. Check all connections from the battery to solenoid for cleanliness and tightness. With a good battery fitted this is the most usual cause of starter motor problems. Check that the earth cable between the engine and body is

also intact and cleanly connected. This can sometimes be overlooked when the engine is taken out.

8 If no results have yet been achieved turn off the headlights, otherwise the battery will soon be discharged. It may be possible that a clicking noise was heard each time the ignition/starter switch was operated. This is the solenoid switch operating but it does not necessarily follow that the main contact is closing properly. (If no clicking has been heard from the solenoid it is certainly defective.) The solenoid contact can be checked by putting a voltmeter or bulb between the main cable connection on the starter side of the solenoid and earth. When the switch is operated there should be a reading or a lighted bulb. If not, the switch has a fault.

9 Starter motor – removal and refitting

1 Disconnect the battery negative lead.
2 On non-GTI models, remove the air cleaner. On GTI models, remove the inlet manifold, with reference to Chapter 3.
3 Disconnect the wiring from the solenoid (photo).
4 Unscrew the bolts securing the brush end bracket to the engine (photo).
5 Unscrew the mounting bolts at the flywheel end (photo).

9.3 Starter motor solenoid wiring

9.4 Starter motor brush end bracket (non-GTI models)

9.5 Removing starter motor mounting bolts (non-GTI models)

6 Withdraw the starter motor from the engine (photo).
7 Refitting is a reversal of removal, but first insert all mounting bolts finger tight, then tighten the flywheel end bolts followed by the brush end bolts.

10 Starter motor – overhaul

1 The starter motor may be of Paris-Rhône, Bosch or Ducellier make. The following paragraphs describe the overhaul of a Paris-Rhône starter motor, but overhaul of the other makes is similar if reference is made to Figs. 12.3 to 12.6.

2 With the starter removed from the car, disconnect the solenoid leads (photo), then unscrew the nuts and remove the brush end bracket (photo).
3 Unscrew the three nuts and remove the solenoid (photos).
4 Prise the plastic cap from the endplate (photo).
5 Unscrew the two tie-rod nuts.
6 Mark the set position of the head of the engagement lever pivot pin. The pin is of eccentric type and its rotation and final setting control the end stop clearance.
7 Tap out the pivot pin (photo).
8 Withdraw the drive end housing complete with tie-bolts. Note the internal shaft shim (photos).
9 Lift off the engagement fork (photo).

9.6 Removing the starter motor (non-GTI models)

10.2A Starter field coil-to-solenoid lead

10.2B Removing brush end bracket

10.3A Starter solenoid nuts

10.3B Withdrawing starter solenoid

10.4 Removing cap from starter endplate

10.7 Starter engagement lever pivot pin

10.8 Removing starter drive end housing

10.9 Starter engagement fork

98.8
89.1
100.9
93.5
102.4
104.5

Fig. 12.3 Exploded diagram of the Bosch starter motor on non-GTI models (Sec 10)

1 Cover	3 Field coils	5 Fork	7 Drive pinion assembly
2 Brush holder plate	4 Armature	6 Solenoid	8 Drive end housing

Fig. 12.4 Exploded diagram of the Bosch starter motor on GTI models (Sec 10)

1 Yoke	3 Cover	5 Drive end housing	7 Fork
2 Brush holder plate	4 Solenoid	6 Drive pinion assembly	8 Armature

H145865

Fig. 12.5 Exploded diagram of the Ducellier starter motor (Sec 10)

1	Solenoid	3	Drive end and housing	5 Armature	7 Bearing assembly
2	Fork	4	Drive pinion assembly	6 Field coils	8 Cover

H14586

Fig. 12.6 Exploded diagram of the Paris-Rhône starter motor (Sec 10)

1	Solenoid	3 Drive end housing	5 Drive pinion assembly	7 Brush holder plate
2	Fork	4 Armature	6 Brush end housing	8 Field coils

10 Depress and then unscrew the armature endplate bolt. Note the wave and plain washers (photo).
11 Remove the endplate, noting that located under it are a wave washer, two plain washers and a fibre washer (photo).
12 Withdraw the armature, noting the shim, wave washer, shim and

fibre washer (in that order) located against the commutator end face (photo).
13 If the brushes are worn down they can be renewed (photo). The brush lead from the field coil must be cut and the new one soldered on. Take care not to allow heat to damage the field coils nor to allow solder to run down the lead or their flexibility will be ruined.

10.10 Starter armature endplate bolt

10.11 Removing starter endplate

10.12 Starter armature

10.13 Starter motor brushes

10.18 Starter drive jump ring

10.19 Drawing jump ring cover sleeve over jump ring

14 Undercut the separators of the commutator using an old hacksaw blade to a depth of about 0.5 to 0.8 mm (0.02 to 0.03 in). The commutator may be further surface cleaned using a strip of very fine glass paper. Do not use emery cloth for this purpose as the carborundum particles will become embedded in the copper surfaces.

15 Testing of the armature is best left to an auto-electrician, but if an ohmmeter is available it can be done by placing one probe on the armature shaft and the other on each of the commutator segments in turn. If there is a reading indicated at any time during the test, then the armature is defective and must be renewed.

16 The field coil can also be tested using an ohmmeter. Connect one probe to the field coil positive terminal and the other to the positive brush holder. If there is no indication of a reading then the field coil circuit has a break in it.

17 Connect one lead of the meter to the field coil positive lead and the other one to the yoke. If there is a low resistance then the field coil is earthed due to a breakdown in the insulation. If this proves to be the case the field coils must be renewed. As field coil replacement requires special tools and equipment it is a job that should be entrusted to your auto-electrician. In fact it will probably prove more economical and beneficial to exchange the starter motor for a reconditioned unit.

18 If the starter drive is faulty, it can be removed if the sleeve is tapped up the shaft, using a piece of tubing, to expose the jump ring. Remove the jump ring and starter drive (photo).

19 Once the starter drive has been refitted with its jump ring, draw the covering sleeve over it using a small puller of claw type (photo).

20 Reassembly is a reversal of dismantling, but observe the following points.

21 Apply high melting-point grease to the armature shaft bearings.

22 Note the locating pip on the yoke which aligns with the notch in the rim of the endplate (photo).

23 If the setting of the engagement lever pivot pin was not marked at dismantling, energise the starter solenoid and check that the clearance between the end face of the pinion shaft and the stop button within the drive end housing is 1.5 mm (0.059 in). If not, withdraw the eccentric type pivot pin from the engagement lever and rotate it a few splines then recheck the clearance.

10.22 Yoke/endplate alignment 'pip' and notch (arrowed)

11 Fuses and relays

1   The fuse board is located above the glovebox on the left-hand side of the facia. Access to it is gained by opening the glovebox then depressing the spring clip and lowering the fuse board.
2   Blade type fuses are used and symbols by the fuses denote the circuit protected (photo).
3   On GTI models an in-line fuse for the fuel pump is located near the rear of the fuse board. The fuse board also incorporates a connector which can be adjusted to supply the radio with negative or positive current according to the polarity of the radio fitted.
4   Should a fuse blow, replace it only with one of identical rating and if the new one blows again immediately, trace and rectify the cause; usually due to a bare wire touching the bodywork due to the insulation having chafed.
5   The fuse board is retained at the rear by two plastic ball and socket joints which can be snapped apart to remove the assembly (photo).
6   Relays are incorporated in most circuits and are mounted on the fuse board or within the engine compartment. Refer to the wiring diagram key for a list of relays.

12 Direction indicator/hazard warning flasher unit – general

1   The unit is located on the fuse board and controls both the direction indicator and hazard warning functions.

11.2 Removing a fuse

A

B

Fig. 12.7 Early (A) and later (B) fuse/relay boards (Sec 11)

For further information, use in conjunction with wiring diagrams/keys at the end of the Supplement

11.5 Fuse board ball and socket (arrowed)

6   Make sure that the lamp casing or bulb earth connection is making a good contact.

13 Steering column combination switches – removal and refitting

1   Disconnect the battery negative lead.
2   Remove the steering wheel and column shrouds, with reference to Chapter 10 (photo).
3   Disconnect the wiring harness plug.
4   Remove the relevant screws and withdraw the switch from the column platform (photo).
5   Refitting is a reversal of removal.

14 Facia-mounted switches – removal and refitting

1   Carefully prise out the switch against the tension of the plastic retaining tabs (photos).
2   Disconnect the wiring or multi-plug, noting the fitted location, and remove the switch.
3   Refitting is a reversal of removal.

15 Courtesy lamp switch – removal and refitting

1   The switch is secured to the door pillar by a self-tapping screw. Extract the screw and withdraw the switch and leads (photo).
2   If the leads are disconnected, tape them to the pillar to prevent them from slipping inside the pillar cavity.
3   It is recommended that the metal contacts of the switch are smeared with petroleum jelly as a precaution against corrosion.
4   Refit by reversing the removal operation.

2   In the event of either system not operating, or one lamp flashing very quickly, carry out the following checks before renewing the flasher unit itself.
3   Inspect the circuit fuse and renew it if it is blown.
4   Check the condition of all wiring and the security of the connections.
5   Check the lamp which is malfunctioning for a broken bulb.

13.2 Removing the steering column shrouds

13.4 Combination switch screws (arrowed)

14.1A Instrument illumination rheostat

14.1B Heated rear window switch and cigar lighter removed from facia

15.1 Removing a courtesy lamp switch

16 Glovebox illumination switch – removal and refitting

1   Disconnect the battery negative lead.
2   Open the glovebox then reach up and release the switch from the inside of the facia (photo).
3   Disconnect the wiring.
4   Refitting is a reversal of removal.

17 Instrument panel – removal and refitting

1   Disconnect the battery negative lead.
2   On non-GTI models, using an Allen key, unscrew the two upper retaining screws at each end of the panel surround (photo).
3   On GTI models, remove the plastic tray from the top of the panel surround by pushing it towards the windscreen to release the secur-

ing clips. Unscrew the now-exposed panel surround securing screw.
4   Unscrew the two lower surround retaining screws located either side of the steering column shroud (photo).
5   Withdraw the surround from the facia.
6   Pull out the instrument panel while depressing the lower spring supports, then disconnect the multi-plugs and speedometer cable (photos).
7   If necessary, the individual components can be removed for repair or renewal – with reference to Figs. 12.8 and 12.9 (photos).
8   Refitting is a reversal of removal.

18 Speedometer cable – renewal

1   Disconnect the speedometer cable from the transmission by removing the retaining bolt or rubber plug (photo).

16.2 Glovebox illumination switch

17.2 Removing the instrument panel upper ...

17.4 ... and lower retaining screws

17.6A Instrument panel spring support

17.6B Instrument panel right-hand upper multi-plug

17.6C Instrument panel left-hand upper multi-plugs

17.7A View of instrument panel face

17.7B View of instrument panel rear

18.1 Removing the speedometer cable from the transmission (non-GTI models)

Fig. 12.8 Exploded diagram of non-GTI instrument panel (Sec 17)

Fig. 12.9 Exploded diagram of GTI instrument panel (Sec 17)

2   Remove the instrument panel, as described in Section 17.
3   Prise the rubber grommet from the bulkhead beneath the facia (photos).
4   Remove the retaining clips, where fitted, and withdraw the speedometer cable.
5   Refitting is a reversal of removal.

18.3A Speedometer cable end with instrument panel removed

18.3B Speedometer cable grommet on the bulkhead

19 Bulbs (exterior) – renewal

Headlamps
1   Where fitted, remove the cover from the rear of the headlamp.
2   Pull the connector from the bulb (photo).
3   Remove the rubber cover, noting that the water drain hole is at the bottom (photo).
4   Release the spring clips and withdraw the bulb (photos).
5   Fit the new bulb with the locating tab uppermost. **Do not** touch the glass as this can shorten the bulb's life. If necessary, clean with methylated spirit before fitting.

19.2 Pull off the connector ...

19.3 ... remove the rubber cover ...

19.4A ... release the spring clips ...

19.4B ... and withdraw the headlamp bulb

19.7 Remove the front direction indicator lamp bulbholder ...

Front parking lamps
6   Pull the bulbholder from the rear of the headlamp then depress and twist the bulb to remove it (photo).

Front direction indicator lamps
7   Turn the bulbholder anti-clockwise and withdraw it from the rear of the lamp (photo).
8   Depress and twist the bulb to remove it (photo).

Front driving lamps (GTI models)
9   Remove the two lens surround retaining screws and withdraw the surround, lens and reflector (photos).
10 Release the spring clips and place the lens assembly to one side (photo).
11 Detach the bulb feed wire at the connector.

Rear lamp cluster
12 Remove the lens upper retaining screws then tilt the lens back and release it from the lower tabs (photos).
13 Depress and twist the bulb to remove it (photo).

19.8 ... and extract the bulb

19.6 Removing the front parking lamp bulbholder

19.9A Remove the screws from the front driving lamp ...

19.9B ... withdraw the reflector assembly ...

19.10 ... and remove the bulb

19.12A Remove the rear lamp cluster screws ...

19.12B ... and release the lens from the tabs

19.13 Removing a rear lamp cluster bulb

19.14 Remove the rear foglamp lens ...

Rear foglamp

14 Remove the screws and withdraw the lens (photo).
15 Depress and twist the bulb to remove it (photo).

Rear number plate lamp

16 Twist off the lens (photo).
17 Depress and twist the bulb to remove it (photo).

All bulbs

18 Refitting is a reversal of removal.

20 Bulbs (interior) – renewal

Interior lamp

1 Prise the lamp from the console (photo).
2 Extract the festoon type bulb (photo).

Map reading lamp

3 Prise the lamp from the console and extract the festoon type bulb (photo).

19.17 ... and extract the bulb

19.15 ... and extract the bulb

20.1 Prise out the interior lamp ...

19.16 Remove the rear number plate lamp lens ...

20.2 ... for access to the bulb

20.3 Removing the map reading lamp

Instrument panel lamps

4   Remove the instrument panel, as described in Section 17.
5   Two types of bulb are fitted. Pull out the square type bulbholder and remove the wedge type holder (photo). Twist the round type bulbholder through 90° to remove it, but on this type the bulb cannot be separated from the holder (photo).

Glovebox lamp

6   Remove the switch, with reference to Section 16.
7   Depress and twist the bulb to remove it.

Digital clock illumination lamp

8   Prise the clock from the facia.
9   Twist the bulbholder from the rear of the clock (photo).

Heater control panel illumination lamps

10 Remove the facia centre air vents, with reference to Chapter 11.
11 Pull the bulbholder from the rear of the panel and extract the bulb (photo).

All bulbs

12 Refitting is a reversal of removal.

21 Headlamp – removal and refitting

1   Remove the headlamp and front parking lamp bulbs, as described in Section 19.
2   Remove the radiator front grille (Chapter 11)
3   Release the spring clips from the pivot pins on each side of the headlamp (photo).
4   Press the load level adjustment arm from the lever ball (photo).
5   Withdraw the headlamp
6   Refitting is a reversal of removal.

22 Headlamp – beam adjustment

1   It is recommended that the adjustment of the headlamp beams is left to a service station having suitable equipment.

20.5A Removing square type instrument panel bulbholder

20.5B Removing round type instrument panel bulbholder

20.9 Removing digital clock illumination lamp bulb

20.11 Heater control panel illumination lamp bulb (arrowed)

21.3 Releasing the headlamp spring clips

21.4 Disconnecting the headlamp load level adjustment arm

23.3A Remove the mounting screw ...

2   Each headlamp incorporates a manual adjustment to compensate for different loads (photo). If this fails to provide the correct beam, emergency adjustment is possible by turning the screw in the top of the manual adjustment for vertical movement and the knob at the rear of the headlamp for horizontal movement.
3   Holts Amber Lamp is useful for temporarily changing the headlight colour to conform with the normal usage on Continental Europe.

23.3B ... and withdraw the front direction indicator lamp

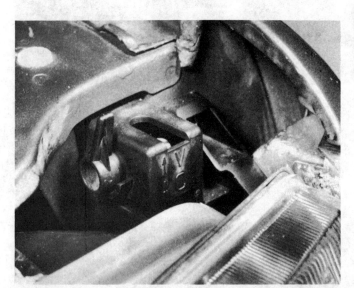

22.2 Headlamp manual adjustment lever

23 Front direction indicator lamp – removal and refitting

1   Remove the headlamp, as described in Section 21.
2   Remove the indicator bulb (Section 19).
3   Remove the screw securing the lamp to the headlamp adjustment assembly and withdraw the lamps (photos).
4   Refitting is a reversal of removal.

24 Windscreen wiper blades and arms – removal and refitting

1   Whenever the wiper blades fail to clean the screen, the blades or their rubber inserts should be renewed.
2   To remove a blade, pull the arm from the glass, swivel the blade, pinch the two sides of the U-shaped plastic block together and slide the assembly out of the hook of the arm (photo).
3   When refitting, note the pivot pin in the blade is offset to allow the blade to swivel fully against the glass. Make sure, therefore, that the blade is fitted the right way round so the the 'pip' on the plastic block locates in the cut-out in the hook of the wiper arm.
4   Before removing a wiper arm, stick some masking tape along the edge of the blade so that its position on the glass can be restored when the arm is being refitted to its spindle splines.
5   Flip up the plastic cover, unscrew the nut and pull the arm from the spindle (photo).
6   Refitting is a reversal of removal.

24.2 Wiper blade attachment

24.5A Unscrew the nut ...

24.5B ... and remove the wiper arm

25 Windscreen wiper motor and linkage – removal and refitting

1 Remove the wiper blades and arms, as described in Section 24.
2 Disconnect the battery negative lead.
3 Open the bonnet then remove the air intake grille by removing the screws and easing the grille from the windscreen weatherstrip (photo).
4 Unscrew the nuts from the wiper spindle bodies (photo).
5 Disconnect the wiper motor multi-plug (photo).
6 Unscrew the mounting bolt and disengage the wiper motor from the upper location pins.
7 The motor can be separated from the linkage by removing the nut securing the crank to the spindle.

8 Refitting is a reversal of removal, but use a screwdriver to lift the weatherstrip as the grille is inserted (photo).

26 Tailgate wiper motor – removal and refitting

1 Remove the wiper arm and blade, as described for the windscreen in Section 24.
2 Remove the tailgate trim, with reference to Chapter 11.
3 Disconnect the battery negative lead.
4 Disconnect the wiring and the relay multi-plug (photos).
5 Unscrew the spindle nut and remove the spacer and washer.
6 Unscrew the mounting bolts and withdraw the motor assembly, noting the location of the washers and earth wires (photo).

25.3 Removing the air intake grille screws

25.4 Wiper spindle body

25.5 Windscreen wiper motor and multi-plug

25.8 Inserting the intake grille beneath the weatherstrip

26.4A Tailgate wiper motor wiring connection

26.4B Tailgate wiper motor relay

26.6 Tailgate wiper motor and mounting bolts

27.1A Upper view of washer fluid reservoir

7   The relay can be removed by removing the mounting screw.
8   Refitting is a reversal of removal.

27 Washer system – general

1   The washer fluid reservoir is located in the left-hand front corner of the engine compartment with the bulk of the unit below the wheel arch (photos). The reservoir supplies both the windscreen and tailgate jets. On some models a headlight washer system is installed with the reservoir in the right-hand front corner of the engine compartment.
2   The washer jets are adjustable by inserting a pin into their nozzles and moving them to give an acceptable pattern on the glass.
3   The use of a good quality screen wash product is recommended. In winter add some methylated spirit to the fluid to prevent freezing. **Never** use cooling system anti-freeze as it will damage the paintwork.

28 Tailgate heated window – general

1   Take great care not to scratch the heater elements with carelessly stacked luggage or rings on the fingers.

2   Avoid sticking labels over the elements, and clean the glass interior surface with warm water and a little detergent, wiping in the same direction as the elements run.
3   Should an element be scratched, so that the current is interrupted, it can be repaired using one of the silver paint products now available for the purpose.

29 Electrically-operated front windows – general

1   Operation of the front door windows on some models is by electric motors controlled by two switches on the driver's door and a single switch on the passenger door.
2   Access to the motors is gained by dismantling the doors, as described in Chapter 11.

27.1B Lower view of washer fluid reservoir

H145870

Fig. 12.10 Window regulator with electric motor (Sec 29)

30 Central door locking system – general

1   On models fitted with the central door locking system it is possible to lock all doors, including the tailgate, simply by locking the driver's door.
2   The system uses electric actuators to move the door lock mechanisms. The actuators can be removed by dismantling the doors, as described in Chapter 11.

Fig. 12.11 Electric actuators fitted on models with central door locking (Sec 30)

31 Horn – removal and refitting

1   Remove the relevant headlamp, as described in Section 21.
2   Disconnect the battery negative lead.
3   Unscrew the mounting nut, remove the horn and disconnect the wiring (photo).
4   Refitting is a reversal of removal.

32 Radio – general

1   A standard radio aperture is provided in the centre console.
2   To remove the radio, pull off the control knobs and unscrew the mounting nuts. The surround can then be withdrawn and the radio removed after disconnecting the aerial and wiring (photo).
3   An in-line fuse is normally fitted to the feed wire behind the radio.
4   Loudspeakers are fitted in the doors and/or rear quarter panels (see next Section).

33 Mobile radio equipment – interference-free installation

Aerials – selection and fitting

The choice of aerials is now very wide. It should be realised that the quality has a profound effect on radio performance, and a poor, inefficient aerial can make suppression difficult.

31.3 Horn and mounting nut

32.2 Removing the radio

A wing-mounted aerial is regarded as probably the most efficient for signal collection, but a roof aerial is usually better for suppression purposes because it is away from most interference fields. Variants which are not fitted with a roof aerial as standard are still equipped with the relevant aerial wiring, and also have the roof cut to accept the Peugeot fitment. Therefore it is obviously worthwhile to approach your dealer for the parts which will bolt straight on. Stick-on wire aerials are available for attachment to the inside of the windscreen, but are not always free from the interference field of the engine and some accessories.

Motorised automatic aerials rise when the equipment is switched on and retract at switch-off. They require more fitting space and supply leads, and can be a source of trouble.

There is no merit in choosing a very long aerial as, for example, the type about three metres in length which hooks or clips on to the rear of the car, since part of this aerial will inevitably be located in an interference field. For VHF/FM radios the best length of aerial is about one metre. Active aerials have a transistor amplifier mounted at the base and this serves to boost the received signal. The aerial rod is sometimes rather shorter than normal passive types.

A large loss of signal can occur in the aerial feeder cable, especially over the Very High Frequency (VHF) bands. The design of feeder cable is invariably in the co-axial form, ie a centre conductor surrounded by a flexible copper braid forming the outer (earth) conductor. Between the inner and outer conductors is an insulator material which can be in solid or stranded form. Apart from insulation, its purpose is to maintain the correct spacing and concentricity. Loss of signal occurs in this insulator, the loss usually being greater in a poor quality cable. The quality of cable used is reflected in the price of the aerial with the attached feeder cable.

The capacitance of the feeder should be within the range 65 to 75 picofarads (pF) approximately (95 to 100 pF for Japanese and American equipment), otherwise the adjustment of the car radio aerial trimmer may not be possible. An extension cable is necessary for a long run between aerial and receiver. If this adds capacitance in excess of the above limits, a connector containing a series capacitor will be required, or an extension which is labelled as 'capacity-compensated'.

Fitting an alternative to the roof aerial will normally involve making a ⅞ in (22 mm) diameter hole in the bodywork, but read the instructions that come with the aerial kit. Once the hole position has been selected, use a centre punch to guide the drill. Use sticky masking tape around the area for this helps with marking out and drill location, and gives protection to the paintwork should the drill slip. Three methods of making the hole are in use:

(a) Use a hole saw in the electric drill. This is, in effect, a circular hacksaw blade wrapped round a former with a centre pilot drill.
(b) Use a tank cutter which also has cutting teeth, but is made to shear the metal by tightening with an Allen key.
(c) The hard way of drilling out the circle is using a small drill, say ⅛ in (3 mm), so that the holes overlap. The centre metal drops out and the hole is finished with round and half-round files.

Whichever method is used, the burr is removed from the body metal and paint removed from the underside. The aerial is fitted tightly ensuring that the earth fixing, usually a serrated washer, ring or clamp, is making a solid connection. *This earth connection is important in reducing interference.* Cover any bare metal with primer paint and topcoat, and follow by underseal if desired.

Aerial feeder cable routing should avoid the engine compartment and areas where stress might occur, eg under the carpet where feet will be located.

Fig. 12.12 Drilling the bodywork for aerial mounting (Sec 33)

Loudspeakers

Speakers should be matched to the output stage of the equipment, particularly as regards the recommended impedance. Power transistors used for driving speakers are sensitive to the loading placed on them.

Models which do not have speakers already fitted are partially prepared to accept them behind the ready-fitted grilles in the front doors and rear quarter panels. Some models have the speaker electrical leads in position, but others do not and will require the installation of suitable cable. If it is necessary to drill holes for speaker cables fit grommets in the holes to stop chafing.

Before choosing loudspeakers, check that they will fit and not obstruct the glass or winder mechanism. Do not omit a waterproofing cover, usually supplied with door speakers. If the speaker has to be fixed to metal, use self-tapping screws.

On some models it will be necessary to remove the grille from the door trim and cut a suitable hole in the trim and waterproofing sheet so

Fig. 12.13 Speaker connections must be correctly made as shown (Sec 33)

as not to obstruct the speakers. Removal of the rear quarter panel trim is straightforward; once again it may be necessary to cut suitable apertures.

When connecting up speakers, ensure the polarity is correct.

Unit installation

Many vehicles have a dash panel aperture to take a radio/audio unit, a recognised international standard being 189.5 mm x 60 mm. Alternatively a console may be a feature of the car interior design and this, mounted below the dashboard, gives more room. If neither facility is available a unit may be mounted on the underside of the parcel shelf; these are frequently non-metallic and an earth wire from the case to a good earth point is necessary. A three-sided cover in the form of a cradle is obtainable from car radio dealers and this gives a professional appearance to the installation; in this case choose a position where the controls can be reached by a driver with his seat belt on.

Installation of the radio/audio unit is basically the same in all cases, and consists of offering it into the aperture after removal of the knobs (*not* push buttons) and the trim plate. In some cases a special mounting plate is required to which the unit is attached. It is worthwhile supporting the rear end in cases where sag or strain may occur, and it is usually possible to use a length of perforated metal strip attached between the unit and a good support point nearby. In general it is recommended that tape equipment should be installed at or nearly horizontal.

Connections to the aerial socket are simply by the standard plug terminating the aerial downlead or its extension cable. Speakers for a stereo system must be matched and correctly connected, as outlined previously.

Note: *While all work is carried out on the power side, it is wise to disconnect the battery earth lead.* Before connection is made to the vehicle electrical system, check that the polarity of the unit is correct. Most vehicles use a negative earth system, but radio/audio units often have a reversible plug to convert the set to either + or – earth. *Incorrect connection may cause serious damage.*

The power lead is often permanently connected inside the unit and terminates with one half of an in-line fuse carrier. The other half is fitted with a suitable fuse (3 or 5 amperes) and a wire which should go to a power point in the electrical system. This may be the accessory terminal on the ignition switch, giving the advantage of power feed with ignition or with the ignition key at the 'accessory' position. Power to the unit stops when the ignition key is removed. Alternatively, the lead may be taken to a live point at the fusebox with the consequence of having to remember to switch off at the unit before leaving the vehicle.

Before switching on for initial test, be sure that the speaker connections have been made, for running without load can damage the output transistors. Switch on next and tune through the bands to ensure that all sections are working, and check the tape unit if applicable. The aerial trimmer should be adjusted to give the strongest reception on a weak signal in the medium wave band, at say 200 metres.

Fig. 12.14 Mounting component details for radio/cassette unit (Sec 33)

Fig. 12.15 Voltage stabiliser interference suppression (Sec 33)

Interference

In general, when electric current changes abruptly, unwanted electrical noise is produced. The motor vehicle is filled with electrical devices which change electric current rapidly, the most obvious being the contact breaker.

When the spark plugs operate, the sudden pulse of spark current causes the associated wiring to radiate. Since early radio transmitters used sparks as a basis of operation, it is not surprising that the car radio will pick up ignition spark noise unless steps are taken to reduce it to acceptable levels.

Interference reaches the car radio in two ways:

(a) by conduction through the wiring.
(b) by radiation to the receiving aerial.

Initial checks presuppose that the bonnet is down and fastened, the radio unit has a good earth connection *(not* through the aerial download outer), no fluorescent tubes are working near the car, the aerial trimmer has been adjusted, and the vehicle is in a position to receive radio signals, ie not in a metal-clad building.

Switch on the radio and tune it to the middle of the medium wave (MW) band off-station with the volume (gain) control set fairly high. Switch on the ignition (but do not start the engine) and wait to see if irregular clicks or hash noise occurs. Tapping the facia panel may also produce the effects. If so, this will be due to the voltage stabiliser, which is an on-off thermal switch to control instrument voltage. It is located usually on the back of the instrument panel, often attached to the speedometer. Correction is by attachment of a capacitor and, if still troublesome, chokes in the supply wires.

Switch on the engine and listen for interference on the MW band. Depending on the type of interference, the indications are as follows.

A harsh crackle that drops out abruptly at low engine speed or when the headlights are switched on is probably due to a voltage regulator.

A whine varying with engine speed is due to the dynamo or alternator. Try temporarily taking off the fan belt – if the noise goes this is confirmation.

Regular ticking or crackle that varies in rate with the engine speed is due to the ignition system. With this trouble in particular and others in general, check to see if the noise is entering the receiver from the wiring or by radiation. To do this, pull out the aerial plug, (preferably shorting

out the input socket or connecting a 62 pF capacitor across it). If the noise disappears it is coming in through the aerial and is *radiation noise.* If the noise persists it is reaching the receiver through the wiring and is said to be *line-borne.*

Interference from wipers, washers, heater blowers, turn-indicators, stop lamps, etc is usually taken to the receiver by wiring, and simple treatment using capacitors and possibly chokes will solve the problem. Switch on each one in turn (wet the screen first for running wipers!) and listen for possible interference with the aerial plug in place and again when removed.

Electric petrol pumps are now finding application again and give rise to an irregular clicking, often giving a burst of clicks when the ignition is on but the engine has not yet been started. It is also possible to receive whining or crackling from the pump.

Note that if most of the vehicle accessories are found to be creating interference all together, the probability is that poor aerial earthing is to blame.

Component terminal markings

Throughout the following sub-sections reference will be found to various terminal markings. These will vary depending on the manufacturer of the relevant component. If terminal markings differ from those mentioned, reference should be made to the following table, where the most commonly encountered variations are listed.

Alternator	Alternator terminal (thick lead)	Exciting winding terminal
DIN/Bosch	B+	DF
Delco Remy	+	EXC
Ducellier	+	EXC
Ford (US)	+	DF
Lucas	+	F
Marelli	+ B	F

Ignition coil	Ignition switch terminal	Contact breaker terminal
DIN/Bosch	15	1
Delco Remy	+	–
Ducellier	BAT	RUP
Ford (US)	B/+	CB/–
Lucas	SW/+	–
Marelli	BAT/+ B	D

Voltage regulator	Voltage input terminal	Exciting winding terminal
DIN/Bosch	B+/D+	DF
Delco Remy	BAT/+	EXC
Ducellier	BOB/BAT	EXC
Ford (US)	BAT	DF
Lucas	+/A	F
Marelli		F

Suppression methods – ignition

Suppressed HT cables are supplied as original equipment by manufacturers and will meet regulations as far as interference to neighbouring equipment is concerned. It is illegal to remove such suppression unless an alternative is provided, and this may take the form of resistive spark plug caps in conjunction with plain copper HT cable. For VHF purposes, these and 'in-line' resistors may not be effective, and resistive HT cable is preferred. Check that suppressed cables are actually fitted by observing cable identity lettering, or measuring with an ohmmeter – the value of each plug lead should be 5000 to 10 000 ohms.

A 1 microfarad capacitor connected from the LT supply side of the ignition coil to a good nearby earth point will complete basic ignition interference treatment. *NEVER fit a capacitor to the coil terminal to the contact breaker – the result would be burnt out points in a short time.*

If ignition noise persists despite the treatment above, the following sequence should be followed:

(a) Check the earthing of the ignition coil; remove paint from fixing clamp.
(b) If this does not work, lift the bonnet. Should there be no change in interference level, this may indicate that the bonnet is not electrically connected to the car body. Use a proprietary braided strap across a bonnet hinge ensuring a first class electrical connection. If, however, lifting the bonnet increases the interference, then fit resistive HT cables of a higher ohms-per-metre value.
(c) If all these measures fail, it is probable that re-radiation from metallic components is taking place. Using a braided strap between metallic points, go round the vehicle systematically – try the following: engine to body, exhaust system to body, front suspension to engine and to body, steering column to body (especially French and Italian cars), gear lever to engine and to body (again especially French and Italian cars), Bowden cable to body, metal parcel shelf to body. When an offending component is located it should be bonded with the strap permanently.
(d) As a next step, the fitting of distributor suppressors to each lead at the distributor end may help.
(e) Beyond this point is involved the possible screening of the distributor and fitting resistive spark plugs, but such advanced treatment is not usually required for vehicles with entertainment equipment.

Electronic ignition systems have built-in suppression components, but this does not relieve the need for using suppressed HT leads. In some cases it is permitted to connect a capacitor on the low tension supply side of the ignition coil, but not in every case. Makers' instructions should be followed carefully, otherwise damage to the ignition semiconductors may result.

Suppression methods – generators

For older vehicles with dynamos a 1 microfarad capacitor from the D (larger) terminal to earth will usually cure dynamo whine. Alternators

Fig. 12.16 Braided earth strap between bonnet and body (Sec 33)

should be fitted with a 3 microfarad capacitor from the B+ main output terminal (thick cable) to earth. Additional suppression may be obtained by the use of a filter in the supply line to the radio receiver.

It is most important that:

(a) Capacitors are never connected to the field terminals of either a dynamo or alternator.
(b) Alternators must not be run without connection to the battery.

Suppression methods – voltage regulators

Voltage regulators used with DC dynamos should be suppressed by connecting a 1 microfarad capacitor from the control box D terminal to earth.

Alternator regulators come in three types:

(a) Vibrating contact regulators separate from the alternator. Used extensively on continental vehicles.
(b) Electronic regulators separate from the alternator.
(c) Electronic regulators built-in to the alternator.

In case (a) interference may be generated on the AM and FM (VHF) bands. For some cars a replacement suppressed regulator is available. Filter boxes may be used with non-suppressed regulators. But if not available, then for AM equipment a 2 microfarad or 3 microfarad capacitor may be mounted at the voltage terminal marked D+ or B+ of the regulator. FM bands may be treated by a feed-through capacitor of 2 or 3 microfarad.

Electronic voltage regulators are not always troublesome, but where

Fig. 12.17 Line-borne interference suppression (Sec 33)

1000μF 16 VOLT ELECTROLYTIC CAPACITOR   Choke   12 VOLTS +

Fig. 12.18 Typical filter box for vibrating contact voltage regulator (alternator equipment) (Sec 33)

Fig. 12.19 Suppression of AM interference by vibrating contact voltage regulator (alternator equipment) (Sec 33)

Fig. 12.20 Suppression of FM interference by vibrating contact voltage regulator (alternator equipment) (Sec 33)

necessary, a 1 microfarad capacitor from the regulator + terminal will help.

Integral electronic voltage regulators do not normally generate much interference, but when encountered this is in combination with alternator noise. A 1 microfarad or 2 microfarad capacitor from the warning lamp (IND) terminal to earth for Lucas ACR alternators and Femsa, Delco and Bosch equivalents should cure the problem.

Fig. 12.21 Electronic voltage regulator suppression (Sec 33)

Fig. 12.22 Suppression of interference from electronic voltage regulator when integral with alternator (Sec 33)

Suppression methods – other equipment

Wiper motors – Connect the wiper body to earth with a bonding strap. For all motors use a 7 ampere choke assembly inserted in the leads to the motor.

Heater motors – Fit 7 ampere line chokes in both leads, assisted if necessary by a 1 microfarad capacitor to earth from both leads. ·

Electronic tachometer – The tachometer is a possible source of ignition noise – check by disconnecting at the ignition coil CB terminal. It usually feeds from ignition coil LT pulses at the contact breaker terminal. A 3 ampere line choke should be fitted in the tachometer lead at the coil CB terminal.

Horn – A capacitor and choke combination is effective if the horn is directly connected to the 12 volt supply. The use of a relay is an alternative remedy, as this will reduce the length of the interference-carrying leads.

Fig. 12.23 Wiper motor suppression (Sec 33)

Fig. 12.24 Use of relay to reduce horn interference (Sec 33)

Electrostatic noise – Characteristics are erratic crackling at the receiver, with disappearance of symptoms in wet weather. Often shocks may be given when touching bodywork. Part of the problem is the build-up of static electricity in non-driven wheels and the acquisition of charge on the body shell. It is possible to fit spring-loaded contacts at the wheels to give good conduction between the rotary wheel parts and the vehicle frame. Changing a tyre sometimes helps – because of tyres' varying resistances. In difficult cases a trailing flex which touches the ground will cure the problem. If this is not acceptable it is worth trying conductive paint on the tyre walls.

Fig. 12.25 Use of spring contacts at wheels (Sec 33)

Fuel pump – Suppression requires a 1 microfarad capacitor between the supply wire to the pump and a nearby earth point. If this is insufficient a 7 ampere line choke connected in the supply wire near the pump is required.

Fluorescent tubes – Vehicles used for camping/caravanning frequently have fluorescent tube lighting. These tubes require a relatively high voltage for operation and this is provided by an inverter (a form of oscillator) which steps up the vehicle supply voltage. This can give rise to serious interference to radio reception, and the tubes themselves can contribute to this interference by the pulsating nature of the lamp discharge. In such situations it is important to mount the aerial as far away from a fluorescent tube as possible. The interference problem may be alleviated by screening the tube with fine wire turns spaced an inch (25 mm) apart and earthed to the chassis. Suitable chokes should be fitted in both supply wires close to the inverter.

Radio/cassette case breakthrough
Magnetic radiation from dashboard wiring may be sufficiently intense to break through the metal case of the radio/cassette player. Often this is due to a particular cable routed too close and shows up as

ignition interference on AM and cassette play and/or alternator whine on cassette play.

The first point to check is that the clips and/or screws are fixing all parts of the radio/cassette case together properly. Assuming good earthing of the case, see if it is possible to re-route the offending cable – the chances of this are not good, however, in most cars.

Next release the radio/cassette player and locate it in different positions with temporary leads. If a point of low interference is found, then if possible fix the equipment in that area. This also confirms that local radiation is causing the trouble. If re-location is not feasible, fit the radio/cassette player back in the original position.

Alternator interference on cassette play is now caused by radiation from the main charging cable which goes from the battery to the output terminal of the alternator, usually via the + terminal of the starter motor relay. In some vehicles this cable is routed under the dashboard, so the solution is to provide a direct cable route. Detach the original cable from the alternator output terminal and make up a new cable of at least 6 mm² cross-sectional area to go from alternator to battery with the shortest possible route. *Remember – do not run the engine with the alternator disconnected from the battery.*

Ignition breakthrough on AM and/or cassette play can be a difficult problem. It is worth wrapping earthed foil round the offending cable run near the equipment, or making up a deflector plate well screwed down to a good earth. Another possibility is the use of a suitable relay to switch on the ignition coil. The relay should be mounted close to the ignition coil; with this arrangement the ignition coil primary current is not taken into the dashboard area and does not flow through the ignition switch. A suitable diode should be used since it is possible that at ignition

Fig. 12.26 Use of ignition coil relay to suppress case breakthrough (Sec 33)

switch-off the output from the warning lamp alternator terminal could hold the relay on.

Connectors for suppression components

Capacitors are usually supplied with tags on the end of the lead, while the capacitor body has a flange with a slot or hole to fit under a nut or screw with washer.

Connections to feed wires are best achieved by self-stripping connectors. These connectors employ a blade which, when squeezed down by pliers, cuts through cable insulation and makes connection to the copper conductors beneath.

Chokes sometimes come with bullet snap-in connectors fitted to the wires, and also with just bare copper wire. With connectors, suitable female cable connectors may be purchased from an auto-accessory shop together with any extra connectors required for the cable ends after being cut for the choke insertion. For chokes with bare wires, similar connectors may be employed together with insulation sleeving as required.

VHF/FM broadcasts

Reception of VHF/FM in an automobile is more prone to problems than the medium and long wavebands. Medium/long wave transmitters are capable of covering considerable distances, but VHF transmitters are restricted to line of sight, meaning ranges of 10 to 50 miles, depending upon the terrain, the effects of buildings and the transmitter power.

Because of the limited range it is necessary to retune on a long journey, and it may be better for those habitually travelling long distances or living in areas of poor provision of transmitters to use an AM radio working on medium/long wavebands.

When conditions are poor, interference can arise, and some of the suppression devices described previously fall off in performance at very high frequencies unless specifically designed for the VHF band. Available suppression devices include reactive HT cable, resistive distributor caps, screened plug caps, screened leads and resistive spark plugs.

For VHF/FM receiver installation the following points should be particularly noted:

(a) Earthing of the receiver chassis and the aerial mounting is important. Use a separate earthing wire at the radio, and scrape paint away at the aerial mounting.

(b) If possible, use a good quality roof aerial to obtain maximum height and distance from interference generating devices on the vehicle.

(c) Use of a high quality aerial download is important, since losses in cheap cable can be significant.

(d) The polarisation of FM transmissions may be horizontal, vertical, circular or slanted. Because of this the optimum mounting angle is at 45° to the vehicle roof.

Citizens' Band radio (CB)

In the UK, CB transmitter/receivers work within the 27 MHz and 934 MHz bands, using the FM mode. At present interest is concentrated on 27 MHz where the design and manufacture of equipment is less difficult. Maximum transmitted power is 4 watts, and 40 channels spaced 10 kHz apart within the range 27.60125 to 27.99125 MHz are available.

Aerials are the key to effective transmission and reception. Regulations limit the aerial length to 1.65 metres including the loading coil and any associated circuitry, so tuning the aerial is necessary to obtain optimum results. The choice of a CB aerial is dependent on whether it is to be permanently installed or removable, and the performance will hinge on correct tuning and the location point on the vehicle. Common practice is to clip the aerial to the roof gutter or to employ wing mounting

where the aerial can be rapidly unscrewed. An alternative is to use the boot rim to render the aerial theftproof, but a popular solution is to use the 'magmount' – a type of mounting having a strong magnetic base clamping to the vehicle at any point, usually the roof.

Aerial location determines the signal distribution for both transmission and reception, but it is wise to choose a point away from the engine compartment to minimise interference from vehicle electrical equipment.

The aerial is subject to considerable wind and acceleration forces. Cheaper units will whip backwards and forwards and in so doing will alter the relationship with the metal surface of the vehicle with which it forms a ground plane aerial system. The radiation pattern will change correspondingly, giving rise to break-up of both incoming and outgoing signals.

Interference problems on the vehicle carrying CB equipment fall into two categories:

(a) Interference to nearby TV and radio receivers when transmitting.

(b) Interference to CB set reception due to electrical equipment on the vehicle.

Problems of break-through to TV and radio are not frequent, but can be difficult to solve. Mostly trouble is not detected or reported because the vehicle is moving and the symptoms rapidly disappear at the TV/radio receiver, but when the CB set is used as a base station any trouble with nearby receivers will soon result in a complaint.

It must not be assumed by the CB operator that his equipment is faultless, for much depends upon the design. Harmonics (that is, multiples) of 27 MHz may be transmitted unknowingly and these can fall into other user's bands. Where trouble of this nature occurs, low pass filters in the aerial or supply leads can help, and should be fitted in base station aerials as a matter of course. In stubborn cases it may be necessary to call for assistance from the licensing authority, or, if possible, to have the equipment checked by the manufacturers.

Interference received on the CB set from the vehicle equipment is, fortunately, not usually a severe problem. The precautions outlined previously for radio/cassette units apply, but there are some extra points worth noting.

It is common practice to use a slide-mount on CB equipment enabling the set to be easily removed for use as a base station, for example. Care must be taken that the slide mount fittings are properly earthed and that first class connection occurs between the set and slide-mount.

Vehicle manufacturers in the UK are required to provide suppression of electrical equipment to cover 40 to 250 MHz to protect TV and VHF radio bands. Such suppression appears to be adequately effective at 27 MHz, but suppression of individual items such as alternators, clocks, stabilisers, flashers, wiper motors, etc, may still be necessary. The suppression capacitors and chokes available from auto-electrical suppliers for entertainment receivers will usually give the required results with CB equipment.

Other vehicle radio transmitters

Besides CB radio already mentioned, a considerable increase in the use of transceivers (ie combined transmitter and receiver units) has taken place in the last decade. Previously this type of equipment was fitted mainly to military, fire, ambulance and police vehicles, but a large business radio and radio telephone usage has developed.

Generally the suppression techniques described previously will suffice, with only a few difficult cases arising. Suppression is carried out to satisfy the 'receive mode', but care must be taken to use heavy duty chokes in the equipment supply cables since the loading on 'transmit' is relatively high.

34 Fault diagnosis – electrical system

Symptom	Reason(s)
Starter fails to turn engine	Battery discharged
	Battery defective internally
	Battery terminal leads loose or earth lead not securely attached to body
	Loose or broken connections in starter motor circuit
	Starter motor switch or solenoid faulty
	Starter brushes badly worn, sticking, or brush wires loose
	Commutator dirty, worn or burnt
	Starter motor armature faulty
	Field coils earthed
Starter turns engine very slowly	Battery in discharged condition
	Starter brushes badly worn, sticking or brush wires loose
	Loose wires in starter motor circuit
Starter motor noisy or excessively rough engagement	Pinion or flywheel gearteeth broken or worn
	Starter motor retaining bolts loose
Battery will not hold charge for more than a few days	Battery defective internally
	Electrolyte level too low or electrolyte too weak due to leakage
	Plate separators no longer fully effective
	Battery plates severely sulphated
	Drivebelt slipping
	Battery terminal connections loose or corroded
	Alternator not charging
	Short in lighting circuit continual battery drain
	Regulator unit not working correctly
Ignition light fails to go out, battery runs flat in a few days	Drivebelt loose and slipping or broken
	Alternator brushes worn, sticking, broken or dirty
	Alternator brush springs worn or broken
	Internal fault in alternator
	Regulator faulty

Failure of individual electrical equipment to function correctly is dealt with alphabetically, item-by-item, under the headings below

Horn

Horn operates all the time	Horn push either earthed or stuck down
	Horn cable to horn push earthed
Horn fails to operate	Cable or cable connection loose, broken or disconnected
	Horn has an internal fault
	Blown fuse
Horn emits intermittent or unsatisfactory noise	Cable connections loose

Lights

Lights do not come on	If engine not running, battery discharged
	Wire connections loose, disconnected or broken
	Light switch shorting or otherwise faulty
Lights come on but fade out	If engine not running, battery discharged
	Wire connections loose
	Light switch shorting or otherwise faulty

Wipers

Wiper motor fails to work	Blown fuse
	Wire connections loose, disconnected or broken
	Brushes badly worn
	Armature worn or faulty
Wiper motor works very slowly and takes excessive current	Commutator dirty, greasy or burnt
	Armature bearings dirty or unaligned
	Armature badly worn or faulty
Wiper motor works slowly and takes little current	Brushes badly worn
	Commutator dirty, greasy or burnt
	Armature badly worn or faulty

Heater blower

Motor does not work	Faulty wiring
	Faulty switch
	Faulty motor

Chapter 13 Supplement:
Revisions and information on later models

Contents

1 Introduction

This Supplement contains information which has become available since 1985. It covers the Cabriolet and automatic transmission models introduced in April 1986, later 1.6 and 1.9 GTI models, the TU engines and MA gearboxes introduced in 1988, and the BE 3/5 gearbox introduced in 1989. Details of various modifications made to later models, and details of later optional equipment are also given. In order to use the Supplement to the best advantage, it is suggested that it is referred to before the main Chapters of the manual; this will ensure that any relevant information can be noted and incorporated within the procedures given in Chapters 1 to 12. Time and cost will therefore be saved, and the particular job will be completed correctly.

Project vehicles

The vehicles used in the preparation of this Supplement, and appearing in many of the photographic sequences, were a 1987 1.9 GTI, a 1988 XS, and a 1993 GR.

2   Specifications

These specifications below are revisions of, or supplementary to, those at the beginning of the preceding Chapters

XV, XW and XY engines
Valve clearances (cold)
Early 1987 on, from engine number:

XV8	28401
XW7	42460
XY7	877201
XY8	877001
Inlet	0.15 mm (0.006 in)
Exhaust	0.30 mm (0.012 in)

All XU engines, early 1987 on
Cylinder liners
Protrusion from block (without seal)

liners identified by notch on top edge rim	0.03 to 0.10 mm

Torque wrench settings

	Nm	lbf ft
Cylinder head bolts (Torx type):		
Stage 1	60	44
Slacken, then immediately tighten to Stage 2	20	15
Stage 3	Angle-tighten by a further 300°	
Camshaft sprocket bolt (M10)	40	30
Oil filter mounting stub	60	44
Camshaft drivebelt tensioner roller bolt	20	15

XU5JA (B6D engine)
As XU5J engine, except for the following:

General

Maximum power (DIN)	83 kW (113 bhp) at 6250 rpm
Maximum torque (DIN)	131 Nm (96.6 lbf ft) at 4000 rpm

Camshaft

Cam lift	11.5 mm

Valves

Head diameter:	
Inlet	41.6 mm
Exhaust	34.5 mm
Stem diameter	7.98 mm
Seat angle (inclusive)	90°
Valve clearances (cold):	
Inlet	0.15 to 0.25 mm (0.006 to 0.010 in)
Exhaust	0.35 to 0.45 mm (0.013 to 0.017 in)
Valve springs:	
Identification	Green marking
Valve timing:	
Nominal clearance	1.0 mm
Inlet opens	8° BTDC
Inlet closes	42° ABDC
Exhaust opens	40°30' BBDC
Exhaust closes	2°30' ATDC

XU5JA/K (B6E) engine
As XU5JA (B6D) engine, except for the following:

General

Compression ratio	9.25:1

XU51C (B1A/A engine)
As XU5J engine, except for the following:

General

Compression ratio	9.35:1
Maximum power (DIN)	58 kW (79 bhp) at 5600 rpm
Maximum torque (DIN)	135 Nm (99.6 lbf ft) at 2850 rpm

Valves

Stem diameter	7.30 mm
Seat angle (inclusive)	90°

Valves (continued)

Valve clearances (cold):

Inlet	0.15 to 0.25 mm (0.006 to 0.010 in)
Exhaust	0.35 to 0.45 mm (0.013 to 0.017 in)

Valve timing:

Nominal clearance	1.0 mm
Inlet opens	10°16' BTDC
Inlet closes	28°28' ABDC
Exhaust opens	41°20' BBDC
Exhaust closes	4°37' ATDC

XU51 C/K (B1F) engine
As XU51C (B1A/A) engine, except for the following:

General

Maximum torque (DIN)	135 Nm (99.6 lbf ft) at 3000 rpm

XU5M2/Z, XU5M3/Z and XU5M3/L (BDY) engines
As XU51C (B1A/A) engine, except for the following:

General

Compression ratio	8.95:1
Maximum power (DIN)	66 kW (89 bhp) at 6400 rpm
Maximum torque (DIN)	135 Nm (99.6 lbf ft) at 3000 rpm

XU9JA and XU9JA/K (D6B) engine
As XU5J engine, except for the following:

General

Displacement	1905 cc
Bore x stroke	83 x 88 mm
Compression ratio	9.6:1
Maximum power (DIN)	94 kW (128 bhp) at 6000 rpm
Maximum torque (DIN)	168 Nm (124 lbf ft) at 4750 rpm

Crankshaft

Crankpin diameter	49.68 to 50.0 mm

Valves

Head diameter:

Inlet	41.6 mm
Exhaust	34.5 mm
Stem diameter	7.98 mm
Seat angle (inclusive)	90°

Valve clearances (cold):

Inlet	0.15 to 0.25 mm (0.006 to 0.010 in)
Exhaust	0.35 to 0.45 mm (0.013 to 0.017 in)

Valve springs:

Identification	Green marking

Valve timing:

Nominal clearance	1.0 mm
Inlet opens	11°30' BTDC
Inlet closes	43° ABDC
Exhaust opens	46° BBDC
Exhaust closes	2° ATDC

Oil filter
Oil filter	Champion F104 (metric)

Torque wrench settings

	Nm	lbf ft
Sump spacer plate bolt	10	7
Oil cooler union nuts	20	15

XU9JA/Z and XU9JA/L (DKZ) engines
As XU9JA (D6B) engine, except for the following:

General

Compression ratio	9.2:1
Maximum power (DIN)	90 kW (122 bhp) at 6000 rpm
Maximum torque (DIN)	151 Nm (111 lbf ft) at 3000 rpm

XU9J1/Z and XU9J1/L (DFZ) engines
As XU9JA (D6B) engine, except for the following:

General

Compression ratio	8.4:1
Maximum power (DIN)	76 kW (102 bhp) at 6000 rpm
Maximum torque (DIN)	146 Nm (108 lbf ft) at 3000 rpm

TU engines

General

Type	Four-cylinder, in-line, overhead camshaft. All alloy with wet cylinder liners. Mounted transversely and inclined 6° to the front. Transmission mounted on left-hand end of engine
TU9 series	70.0 x 62.0 mm
TU1 series	72.0 x 69.0 mm
TU3 series	75.0 x 77.0 mm
Bore and stroke:	
TU9 series	70.0 x 62.0 mm
TU1 series	72.0 x 69.0 mm
TU3 series	75.0 x 77.0 mm
Compression ratio:	
TU9 series and TU1 series	9.4:1
TU3 series	9.3:1
Maximum power:	
TU9 series	33.5 kW (45 bhp) at 5200 rpm
TU1	41.0 kW (55 bhp) at 5800 rpm
TU1M	45.0 kW (60 bhp) at 6200 rpm
TU3	48.5 kW (65 bhp) at 5400 rpm
TU3A	52.2 kW (70 bhp) at 5600 rpm
TU3M and TU3FM	56.0 kW (75 bhp) at 6200 rpm
TU3S	63.4 kW (85 bhp) at 6400 rpm
Maximum torque:	
TU9 series	73.6 Nm (54.3 lbf ft) at 2400 rpm
TU1	89.3 Nm (65.9 lbf ft) at 3200 rpm
TU3	110.0 Nm (82.0 lbf ft) at 3000 rpm
TU3A	110.8 Nm (81.8 lbf ft) at 3400 rpm
TU3M and TU3FM	108.5 Nm (80.0 lbf ft) at 4000 rpm
TU3S	115.8 Nm (85.4 lbf ft) at 4000 rpm
Firing order	1-3-4-2 (No 1 at clutch end)

Cylinder block

Material	Aluminium alloy
Height:	
TU9 series and TU1 series	187.43 to 187.53 mm
TU3 series	206.93 to 207.03 mm

Crankshaft

Number of main bearings	Five
Main journal diameter	49.965 to 49.981 mm
Regrind undersize	0.30 mm
Crankpin diameter:	
TU 9 series	37.992 to 38.008 mm
TU1 series and TU3 series	44.975 to 44.991 mm
Regrind undersize	0.01 to 0.30 mm
Thrustwasher thicknesses	2.40, 2.50, 2.55 and 2.60 mm

Cylinder liners

Type	Wet, removable, cast iron, matched to piston
Protrusion from block (without seal)	0.03 to 0.10 mm
Protrusion difference between liners	0.05 mm
Liner-to-cylinder block seal	O-ring

Grades:	
Piston	**Liner**
A	One file mark
B	Two file marks
C	Three file marks

Pistons

Type	Aluminium alloy, with two compression rings and one oil control ring
Piston diameter (standard):	
TU9 series	69.960 to 69.990 mm, in three grades
TU1 series	71.960 to 71.990 mm, in three grades
TU3 series	74.960 to 74.990 mm, in three grades
Piston-to-liner clearance	0.03 to 0.05 mm

Connecting rods
Length (between centres):
  TU9 series .... 122.80 to 122.85 mm
  TU1 series .... 112.30 to 112.37 mm
  TU3 series .... 126.80 to 126.87 mm
Maximum weight difference on any engine 3g

Gudgeon pin
Fit .... Clearance in piston, interference in connecting rod

Cylinder head
Material .... Aluminium alloy
Maximum permissible distortion .... 0.05 mm
Height .... 111.12 to 111.28 mm

Camshaft
Drive .... Toothed belt
Actuation .... Rocker arms
Valve lift:
  TU9A .... 7.2 mm
  TU1 and TU3 series .... 8.2 mm

Valves
Head diameter:
  Inlet:
    TU9 series .... 34.8 mm
    TU1 series .... 36.8 mm
    TU3, TU3A, TU3M and TU3S .... 36.8 mm
    TU3FM .... 39.5 mm
  Exhaust:
    TU9 series .... 27.9 mm
    TU1 series .... 29.4 mm
    TU3, TU3A, TU3M and TU3S .... 29.4 mm
    TU3FM .... 31.4 mm
Stem diameter:
  Inlet .... 6.99 mm
  Exhaust .... 6.97 mm
Valve length:
  Inlet .... 110.76 mm
  Exhaust .... 110.60 mm
Seat angle (inclusive):
  Inlet .... 120°
  Exhaust .... 90°
Valve clearances (cold):
  Inlet .... 0.15 to 0.25 mm (0.006 to 0.010 in)
  Exhaust .... 0.35 to 0.45 mm (0.013 to 0.017 in)

Lubrication system
Oil pump type .... Gear type, chain-driven from crankshaft
Sump capacity:
  With filter .... 3.5 litres (6.2 pints)
  Without filter .... 3.2 litres (5.6 pints)
Oil filter type .... Champion F104 (metric)
Difference between minimum and maximum marks on dipstick .... 1.4 litres (2.5 pints)
Minimum oil pressure at 90°C (194°F):
  650 rpm .... 1.5 bars (21.8 lbf/in^2)
  4000 rpm .... 4.0 bars (58.0 lbf/in^2)
Oil pressure warning light operates at .... 0.8 bars (11.6 lbf/in^2)
Lubricant type/specification .... Multigrade engine oil viscosity SAE 10W/40 or 15W/40 (Duckhams QXR, Hypergrade, or 10W/40 motor oil)

Torque wrench settings

	Nm	lbf ft
Crankshaft pulley	100	74
Camshaft sprocket	80	59
Big-end bearing cap	37.5	28
Flywheel	67	49
Distributor/fuel pump housing	8	6
Camshaft thrust fork	15	11
Thermostat	8	6
Main bearing cap casting main bearing cap bolts (models with plain No 5 main bearing half-shell fitted to cylinder block – see text):*		
Stage 1	20	15
Stage 2	Angle-tighten by a further 45°	

Under-bonnet view of TU3S engine

1	Brake fluid reservoir filler cap	6	Air cleaner cover
2	Brake master cylinder	7	Fuel pump
3	Brake vacuum servo unit	8	Cooling system expansion bottle
4	Servo vacuum hose	9	Fuel filter
5	Cooling system bleed screw	10	Washer fluid reservoir

11	Battery	17	Engine oil filler cap
12	Air temperature control unit	18	Exhaust manifold hot air shroud
13	Auxiliary fusebox	19	Alternator
14	Radiator filler cap	20	Engine oil level dipstick
15	Ignition coil	21	Inlet manifold
16	Bonnet lock	22	Right-hand engine mounting

View of front underside of TU3S engine model

1 Gearbox (type MA)	7 Fuel supply pipe	12 Rear lower engine mounting	17 Alternator
2 Disc caliper	8 Hydraulic brake lines	13 Lower suspension arm	18 Engine sump drain plug
3 LH driveshaft	9 Intermediate exhaust pipe	14 RH driveshaft	19 Oil filter
4 Anti-roll bar	10 Gearchange rod	15 Front towing eye	20 Exhaust front downpipe
5 Track rod	11 Subframe	16 Bottom hose	21 Radiator
6 Guide bar			

Torque wrench settings (continued)

	Nm	lbf ft
Main bearing cap casting main bearing cap bolts (models with grooved No 5 main bearing half-shell fitted to cylinder block – see text):*		
Stage 1	20	15
Stage 2	Angle-tighten by a further 55°	
Stage 3	Loosen bolt fully	
Stage 4	20	15
Stage 5	Angle-tighten by a further 45°	
Oil pump	8	6
Sump	8	6
Main bearing cap casting to block	8	6
Water pump housing:		
8 mm bolts	30	22
6 mm bolts	50	37
Cylinder head bolts (all except TU3F engine):		
Stage 1	20	15
Stage 2	Angle-tighten by a further 240°	
Cylinder head bolts (TU3F engine):		
Stage 1	20	15
Stage 2	Angle-tighten by a further 120°	
Stage 3	Angle-tighten by a further 120°	
Timing belt tensioner	20	15
Timing cover	6	4
Valve cover	5	3.5
Dipstick tube	15	11
Oil pressure switch	28	21
Oil filter	15	11

*Note: *These figures do not apply to the main bearing cap bolts on the TU3F engine. Refer to a Peugeot dealer for advice when carrying out work on this engine – see text*

Cooling system

General

System capacity:	
XU5JA, XU5JA/K, XU9JA, XU9JA/K, XU9JA/Z and XU9JA/L engines	6.6 litres (11.6 pints)
XU51C, XU51C/K, XU5M2/Z, XU5M3/Z and XU5M3/L engines	6.7 litres (11.8 pints)
TU9 series and TU3 series engines	5.8 litres (10.2 pints)
TU1 series engines (except Van)	7.0 litres (12.3 pints)
TU1 series engines (Van)	5.8 litres (10.2 pints)
Pressure cap setting (all models from April 1987)	1 bar (14.5 lbf/in^2)
Warning lamp switch operating temperature (all models from April 1987)	110°C (230°F)
Electric cooling fan operating temperatures (all models from April 1987):	
Cut-in – 1st speed	97°C (207°F) or 88°C (190°F)*
Cut-in – 2nd speed (where applicable)	101°C (214°F)
Cut-out – 1st speed	92°C (198°F) or 79°C (174°F)*
Cut-out – 2nd speed (where applicable)	96°C (205°F)

Revised switch with lower operating temperature fitted to certain models

Thermostat

Start-to-open temperature:	
XU5 series and XU9 series engines	82°C (180°F)
TU9 series, TU3 series and TU1 series (Van) engines	88°C (190°F)
TU1 series (except Van) engines	83°C (205°F)
Fully-open temperature:	
XU5 series and XU9 series engines	93°C (199°F)
TU9 series, TU3 series and TU1 series (Van) engines	102°C (216°F)
TU1 series (except Van) engines	96°C (205°F)

Torque wrench settings (TU engine models)

	Nm	lbf ft
Water pump upper stud	16	12
Water pump lower bolt	8	6
Housing inlet elbow	8	6
Housing to block:		
8 mm bolts	30	22
10 mm bolts	50	37

Fuel and exhaust systems

Carburettors

Type:	
XY8 and XU51C engines	Fixed jet, downdraught
TU9 series TU1 series, TU3, TU3A and TU3A/K engines	Single barrel fixed jet, downdraught
TU3S and TU3S/K engines	Double barrel progressive, fixed jet downdraught

Carburettors (continued)

Application:

XY8 from early 1985	Weber 35 IBSH
XU51C	Weber 36 TLC
TU9 series engines	Solex 32 PBISA 16 or Weber 32 ISBH 16
TU1 series engines	Solex 32 PBISA 16, Weber 32 IBS 15 or Weber 32 ISBH 17
TU3 engine	Weber 34 TLP3
TU3A and TU3A/K engines	Solex 34 PBISA 17
TU3S and TU3S/K engine	Solex 32-34 Z2

Calibration and settings:

	XY8	XU51C
Venturi diameter	26 mm	28 mm
Main jet	130 ± 5	137/42
Air correction jet	165 ± 15	150 ± 10
Emulsion tube	F104	F80
Accelerator pump injector	45 ± 5	40
Needle valve	150	150
Idling fuel jet	45 ± 5	48 ± 1
Idling speed	975 ± 25 rpm	750 rpm
CO%	2.0 ± 0.5	1.5 ± 0.5
Float level	9.0 mm (0.35 in)	28.0 mm (1.102 in)
Choke opening	3.25 mm (0.128 in)	–

	TU9 series Weber	TU9 series Solex
Venturi diameter	25	25
Main jet	122	127.5 ± 2.5
Air correction jet	135	155 ± 10
Emulsion tube	F112	31
Enrichener drilling	30	
Idling fuel jet	45	47 ± 4
Idling air jet	150	135 ± 10
Accelerator pump injector	40	40 ± 5
Fuel inlet needle valve	1.5	1.6
Float setting	8.0 mm	–
Idling speed (rpm)	700	700
CO%	1.5	1.5 ± 0.5

	TU1 series Weber 32 IBS 15	TU1 series Weber 32 IBSH 17	TU1 series Solex
Venturi diameter	26	25	25
Main jet	140 ± 5	132	127.5 ± 2.5
Air correction jet	180 ± 15	165	175 ± 10
Emulsion tube	F102	F100 EM	
Enrichener drilling	50 ± 10	50	35 ± 5
Idling fuel jet	45 ± 5	45	46 ± 4
Idling air jet	–	170	165 ± 10
Accelerator pump injector	45 ± 10	40	40 ± 10
Fuel inlet needle valve	1.5	1.5	1.6
Float setting	8.0 mm	–	
Idling speed (rpm)	700	700	700
CO%	1.0	1.5 ± 0.5	1.5 ± 0.5

	TU3	TU3A and TU3A/K	TU3S and TU3S/K
Venturi diameter	26	26	24/27
Main jet	132 (127)*	132	117/130
Air correction jet	145	155	145/170 (155/175)*
Emulsion tube	F80 (F115)*	EC	27/AZ
Enrichener drilling	40	55	
Idling fuel jet	43 (45)*	44 ± 2	44/80 (44/100)*
Idling air jet	140 (130)*	140	190/150
Accelerator pump injector	40	40	35/35
Fuel inlet needle valve	1.5	1.6	1.8
Float setting	28.0 mm	28 mm	–
Idling speed (rpm)	700	750	750
CO%	1.5 ± 0.5	1.0	1.5 ± 0.5

*1988 models on

Fuel injection systems

Application:

XU5JA, XU5JA/K, XU9JA and XU9JA/K engines	Bosch LE2-Jetronic
XU9JA/Z and XU9JA/L engines	Bosch Motronic M1.3
XU9J1/Z and XU9J1/L engines	Bosch LU2- Jetronic
TU1M/Z, TU3M/Z and TU3FM/L engines	Bosch Mono-Jetronic A2.2
XU5M2/Z engine	MMFD Mono-point G5
TU1M/L, XU5M3/Z and XU5M3/L engines	MMFD Mono-point G6

Fuel injection systems (continued)

Idling speed (not adjustable on all systems):
Bosch LE2-Jetronic, LU2-Jetronic and Motronic M1.3 systems	900 ± 50 rpm
Bosch Mono-Jetronic A2.2, MMFD Mono-point G5 and MMFD Mono-point G6 systems	850 ± 50 rpm

CO%:
All systems except Bosch LE2- Jetronic..	Not adjustable
Bosch LE2-Jetronic system	1.0

Air cleaner element
Carburettor models (1988-on)..	Champion U401
Fuel injection models	Champion W175

Fuel filter
All fuel injection models	Champion L205

Ignition system

Ignition timing (vacuum hose disconnected)*
XU5J engine from VIN 5520364 (early 1986)	10° BTDC at 850 ± 50 rpm
XU51C and XU51C/K engines..	10° BTDC at 750 rpm
XU5JA and XU5JA/K engines	10° BTDC at 900 rpm
XU9JA and XU9JA/K engines	5° BTDC at 700 rpm
XU9JA/Z and XU9JA/L engines	Controlled by Motronic M1.3 system (not adjustable)
XU5M2/Z, XU5M3/2 and XU5M3/L engines	Controlled by MMFD system (not adjustable)
XU9J1/Z and XU9J1/L engines	10° BTDC at 900 rpm
TU series engines (except engines equipped with MMFD fuel injection)	8° BTDC at idling speed
TU series engines equipped with MMFD fuel injection	Controlled by MMFD system (not adjustable)

Refer to Section 8 or 9, as applicable, for details of adjustments required to operate engines on unleaded petrol.

Spark plugs
XV8, XW7 and XY7 engines...	Champion RS9YCC or S281YC*
XY8 and XU5J engines...	Champion S7YCC or S279YC*
XU51C engines (up to 1988)...	Champion S9YCC or S281YC*
XU51C engines (from 1988)	Champion RC9YCC or C9YCX*
XU5JA engines (up to 1988)...	Champion S7YCC or S279YC*
XU5JA (from 1988), XU5JA/K, XU9JA, XU9JA/K, XU9JA/Z and XU9JA/L engines	Champion RC7YCC or C7YCX*
TU9 series, TU1 series, TU3 and TU3A engines	Champion RC9YCC or C9YCX*
TU3S engines..	Champion RC7YCC or C7YCX*

Peugeot recommendation

Ignition leads
Carburettor models from 1988	Champion LS20

Clutch

Driven plate
Diameter:
XU series engines	200.0 mm
TU series engines	180.0 mm

Manual transmission

BE1/5 and BE3/5 gearboxes – general
Application..	XU5JA, XU5JA/K, XU9JA, XU9JA/K, XU9JA/Z, XU9JA/L, XU9J1/Z and XU9J1/L engines

Gear ratios:

1st:
XU5JA and XU5JA/K engines	3.251:1
XU9 engines	2.923:1
2nd..	1.850:1
3rd...	1.360:1
4th...	1.069:1
5th...	0.865:1
Reverse	3.333:1

Final drive:
XU5JA and XU5JKA/K engines	4.063:1
XU9 engines	3.689:1

BE 1/5 and BE3/5 gearboxes – lubrication
Oil capacity (drain and refill)	2.0 litres (3.5 pints)
Lubricant type/specification (from August 1987)...............................	Gear oil, viscosity SAE 75W/80 (Duckhams Hypoid PT 75W/80)

MA gearbox – general

Type	Four or five forward speeds (all synchromesh) and reverse
Application	TU series engines

Gear ratios – MA4:

1st	3.418:1
2nd	1.809:1
3rd	1.129:1
4th	0.814:1
Reverse	3.584:1

Final drive:

TU1 series engines	3.765:1
TU3 series engines	3.939:1
TU9 series engines	4.290:1

Gear ratios – MA5:

	TU1 series, TU3 and TU3A	TU3S, TU3M and TU3FM
1st	3.418:1	3.418:1
2nd	1.809:1	1.950:1
3rd	1.276:1	1.357:1
4th	0.975:1	1.054:1
5th	0.767:1	0.854:1
Reverse	3.584:1	3.584:1

Final drive:

TU1 series engines	3.939:1
TU3 series	3.765:1
TU3A and TU3A/K engines	4.062:1
TU3S and TU3S/K engines	4.286:1

MA gearbox – lubrication

Oil capacity (drain and refill)	2.0 litres (3.5 pints)
Lubrication type/specification	Gear oil, viscosity SAE 75W/80 (Duckhams Hypoid PT 75W/80)

MA gearbox – torque wrench settings

	Nm	lbf ft
Gearbox housing to clutch/final drive housing	18	13
Intermediate plate to clutch/final drive housing	50	37
Pressed-steel housing	18	13
Bearing half-rings	18	13
Output shaft nut (MA5)	140	103
Drain and filler plugs	25	19
Gearbox to engine	45	33

Automatic transmission

General

Make	ZF
Type	4 HP 14
Number of speeds	Four forward and one reverse
Application	XU51C, XU51C/K, XU5M2.Z, XU5M3/Z and XU5M3/L engines

Gear ratios:	Pre-1987	1987-on
1st	2.511:1	2.511:1
2nd	1.392:1	1.425:1
3rd	1.034:1	1.041:1
4th	0.769:1	0.769:1
Reverse	2.943:1	2.943:1
Final drive	3.824:1	3.824:1

Lubrication

Lubrication type/specification	Dexron type ATF (Duckhams Uni-Matic or D-Matic)

Lubricant capacity:

From dry	6.2 litres (10.9 pints)
Drain and refill	2.4 litres (4.25 pints)

Note: *Final drive uses transmission fluid although it is drained separately*

Torque wrench settings

	Nm	lbf ft
Inhibitor switch	41	30
Fluid cooler	50	37
Dipstick tube nut	45	33
Selector cable bracket	30	22
Torque converter to driveplate	35	26
Transmission to engine	45	33
LH mounting to transmission	35	26
LH mounting to body	18	13

Driveshafts

Torque wrench setting

	Nm	lbf ft
Hub nut (models with automatic transmission)	265	196

Braking system (1.9 GTI)

Type .... Ventilated front and solid rear servo-assisted disc brakes, rear brake
compensators, cable-operated handbrake on rear wheels

Disc brakes – general

	Front	Rear
Disc diameter	247 mm	247 mm
Disc thickness:		
New	20.4 mm	8.0 mm
Minimum (after resurfacing)	18.5 mm	7.0 mm
Disc run-out (maximum)...	0.07 mm	0.07 mm
Disc pad minimum lining thickness....................................	2.0 mm (0.079 in)	2.0 mm (0.079 in)

Torque wrench settings

	Nm	lbf ft
Front disc caliper	100	74
Rear disc caliper...	120	88
Caliper guide bolt	35	26

Suspension and roadwheels

Rear wheel alignment

Toe-in:

All models, except GTI, CTI, and Automatic – up to 1988	0.5 ± 1.0 mm (0.02 ± 0.04 in)
GTI, CTI and Automatic – up to 1988	1.0 ± 2.0 mm (0.04 ± 0.08 in)
All models – 1988-on..	1.0 ± 2.0 mm (0.04 ± 0.08 in)

Camber:

All models, except GTI, CTI, and Automatic – up to 1988	–0°30' ± 30'
GTI, CTI, and Automatic – up to 1988	–0°50' ± 30'
All models – 1988-on..	–0°50' ± 30'

Roadwheels

Type:

CTI	Light alloy
1.9 GTI	Pressed-steel or light alloy

Size:

CTI	5.5J 14 FH H4.24
1.9 GTI	6.6J 15 CH 4.19

Tyres

Size:

CTI	185/60 HR 14
1.9 GTI	185/55 VR 15

Pressures – bars (lbf/in²):

	Front	Rear
145 SR 13 (Van)	1.9 (28)	2.3 (33) unladen, 2.6 (38) laden
165/70 SR 13 (Automatic)..	2.0 (29)	2.1 (30)
185/60 HR 14 (CTI)...	2.0 (29)	2.1 (30)
185/55 VR 15 (1.9 GTI)...	2.0 (29)	2.0 (29)

Torque wrench setting

	Nm	lbf ft
Front suspension bottom balljoint (models with automatic transmission)	45	33

Steering system

General

Turning circle (between kerbs):

CTI	10.30 m (33 ft 9 in)
1.9 GTI	11.20 m (36 ft 9 in)

Front wheel alignment

Toe-in:

All models, except GTI and CTI – up to 1988	3.0 ± 1.0 mm (0.12 ± 0.04 in)
1.6 GTI – up to 1988..	2.0 ± 1.0 mm (0.08 ± 0.04 in)
1.9 GTI – up to 1988..	2.5 ± 1.0 mm (0.09 ± 0.04 in)
Automatic – up to 1988...	3.5 ± 1.0 mm (0.13 ± 0.04 in)
All models from 1988	1.0 ± 0.5 mm (0.04 ± 0.02 in)

Camber:

All models, except GTI and CTI – up to 1988	0°30' ± 30'
1.6 GTI – up to 1988..	0° ± 30'
1.9 GTI – up to 1988..	0°10' ± 30'
CTI – up to 1988..	0°15' ± 30'
All models from 1988	0° ± 30'

Castor:

All models up to 1988, except GTI, CTI and Automatic......................	1°45' ± 30'
1.6 GTI – up to 1988..	1°50' ± 30'
1.9 GTI – up to 1988..	2°00' ± 30'
CTI up to 1988	1°35' ± 30'
Automatic – up to 1988...	1°50' ± 30'
All models from 1988, except GTI and CTI	3°00' ± 30'
1.6 GTI and CTI from 1988	3°15' ± 30'
1.9 GTI from 1988..	2°50' ± 30'

Front wheel alignment (continued)

Steering axis inclination:

All models, except GTI and CTI up to 1988..................................	8°45' ± 30'
1.6 and 1.9 GTI – up to 1988	9°30' ± 30'
CTI up to 1988	9°20' ± 30'
All models from 1988, except GTI and CTI	9°45' ± 30'
1.6 GTI and CTI from 1988	10°55' ± 30'
1.9 GTI from 1988	10°00' ± 30'

Power steering system

Power steering fluid type .... Dexron II type ATF (Duckhams Uni-Matic or D-Matic)

Torque wrench settings

	Nm	lbf ft
Power steering fluid pipe unions..	23	17
Power steering gear securing nuts	36	26

Electrical system

Battery type

XU series engines..	29 amp hour or 33 amp hour
TU series engines	25 amp hour or 29 amp hour

Alternator

Drivebelt tension – XU series and TU series engines .... As for XU5J engine (see Chapter 12 Specifications)

Fuses (1986 to 1988 GTI and CTI)

No	Circuit protected	Rating (amp)
1	Reversing lamps, tachometer..	10
2	Direction indicators, heater blower motor, oil pressure gauge, oil temperature gauge, heated seats, fuel gauge, coolant temperature gauge, low battery charge warning, oil pressure warning, brake system warning, coolant temperature warning, low coolant level warning...	25
3	Windscreen wiper/washer, stop-lights, headlamp washer, radio, accessories..	25
4	Spare..	–
5	Hazard warning	10
6	Spare..	–
7	Cigarette lighter, clock, interior lights, boot lamp, central door locking, radio	25
8	Horns	25
9	Electrically-operated windows	20
10	Rear foglamp	5
11	Tail lamp (RH), number plate light...................................	5
12	Tail lamp (LH)	5
13	Instrument panel illumination, side lights.......................	5
14	Fuel pump...	15

Fuses (1988 to 1989 models, except GTI and CTI)

No	Circuit protected	Rating (amp)
1	Reversing lamps	10
2	Direction indicators, heater blower motor, ignition warning light	25
3	Fuel gauge, stop-lamps, front and rear wash/wipe, tachometer, headlamp wash, radio, storage tray light, warning lights (coolant temperature, oil pressure, coolant level, handbrake, choke)...	25
4	Spare..	–
5	Hazard warning	10
6	Spare..	–
7	Cigarette lighter, clock, interior lights, boot lamp, central door locking, radio	25
8	Horns, heated rear window	25
9	Electrically-operated windows	20
10	Rear foglamp	5
11	Tail lamps, number plate light	5
12	Spare..	–
13	Instrument panel illumination, side lights.......................	5
14	Fuel pump...	15

Fuses (1988 to 1989 GTI and CTI)

No	Circuit protected	Rating (amp)
1	Reversing lamps, tachometer	10
2	Direction indicators, heater blower motor, oil pressure gauge, oil temperature gauge, heated seats, fuel gauge, coolant temperature gauge, low battery charge warning, oil pressure warning, brake system warning, coolant temperature warning, low coolant level warning	25
3	Front and rear wash/wipe, stop-lights, headlamp washer, radio, accessories, storage tray light, map reading lamp	25
4	Spare...	–
5	Hazard warning	10
6	Spare...	–
7	Cigarette lighter, clock, interior lights, boot lamp, central door locking, radio	20
8	Horns, heated rear window..	25
9	Electrically-operated windows	20
10	Rear foglamp	5
11	Tail lamp, number plate light	5
12	Spare...	5
13	Instrument panel illumination, side lights	5
14	Fuel pump	15

Fuses (1989 to 1991 models)

No	Circuit protected	Rating (amp)
1	Reversing lamps, tachometer, fuel gauge, warning lamps (low battery charge, coolant temperature, oil pressure, low coolant level, brake system, choke)	10
2	Direction indicators, gauges (fuel, oil temperature, coolant temperature, oil pressure), heater blower motor, warning lamps (low battery charge, coolant temperature, oil pressure, low coolant level, brake system, choke)	25
3	Map reading lamp, stop-lamps, windscreen and tailgate wash/wipe, tachometer, radio, glovebox lamp, electric windows, heated rear window	25
4	Driving lamps..	15
5	Hazard warning lamps	10
6	Spare...	–
7	Cigarette lighter, clock, interior lamps, luggage compartment lamp, central locking, radio, power feed to towbar	25
8	Horn, heated rear window..	25
9	Electric windows	20
10	Rear fog lamp	5
11	Tail lamps, number plate lamps......................................	5
12	Spare...	–
13	Instrument panel illumination, side lamps	5
14	Electric fuel pump..	15

Fuses (1991-on models)

No	Circuit protected	Rating (amp)
1	Reversing lamps, tachometer, fuel gauge, warning lamps (low battery charge, coolant temperature, oil pressure, low coolant level, brake system, choke).........	10
2	Direction indicators, gauges (fuel, oil temperature, coolant temperature, oil pressure), heater blower motor, warning lamps (low battery charge, coolant temperature, oil pressure, low coolant level, brake system, choke, ABS)..	25
3	Map reading lamp, stop-lamps, windscreen and tailgate wash/wipe, tachometer, radio, glovebox lamp, heated rear window	25
4	Driving lamps..	15
5	Hazard warning lamps	10
6	Not used..	–
7	Clock, interior lamps, luggage compartment lamp, central locking, radio, power feed to towbar.....................	25
8	Horn, heated rear window, cigarette lighter....................	30
9	Electric windows	20
10	Rear fog lamps	5
11	Tail lamps	5
12	Not used..	–
13	Instrument panel illumination, side lamps	5
14	Electric fuel pump..	15

Fuses in engine compartment

No	Circuit protected	Rating (amp)
	ABS	30
	Power supply to ABS electronic control unit...................	15
	Cooling fan...	30
	Oxygen sensor	10

Bulbs

		Wattage
Number plate lamps		5

3 Routine maintenance

As from 1988 model year, the manual gearboxes types MA and BE 1 are filled with a special gearbox oil which does not require draining at the previously stated intervals. However, it is necessary to carry out an oil level check every 36 000 miles (60 000 km) and, should topping-up be required, it is important to use only the specified type of oil as given in 'Recommended lubricants and fluids'.

Models fitted with XU9J1/L engine and automatic transmission (in the UK, the 205 'Gentry' model) have a smaller engine oil filter fitted. On these models, it is therefore necessary to change the oil filter every 6000 miles (10 000 km) – ie at every oil change.

4 XV, XW and XY engines

Main bearing shells – modifications

1 As from early 1986, the locating tabs of the main bearing shells on XV, XW and XY engines are offset, as shown in Fig. 13.1 It is not possible to fit the earlier type of main bearing shell to later models with this modification.

Cylinder head – modifications

2 As from early 1986 on XV, XW and XY engines, the two cylinder head-to-block locating dowels are reduced in diameter from 16.0 mm to 14.0 mm. A new cylinder head gasket with reduced-diameter holes is also fitted.

3 From the same date, three additional locating dowels are fitted to the rocker shaft pedestals, and the bolt holes in the camshaft cover are increased in diameter.

4 If necessary, it is possible to mate the cylinder head to a non-compatible block by using stepped locating dowels, together with the later-type head gasket.

Valve clearances – adjustment

5 As from January 1987, XV, XW and XY engines are fitted with bi-metal rockers consisting of an aluminium arm and steel pad. This modification has resulted in revised valve clearances, as given in the Specifications. Note also that the valve timing is revised.

5 XU engines

XU5JA engine – description

1 As from February 1986, GTI models may be fitted with the XU5JA engine. The CTI model had been fitted with this engine since its introduction in April 1986. This engine is an uprated version of the XU5J engine described in Chapter 1, and the main differences are described in the following paragraphs.

← FRONT

Fig. 13.1 Main bearing shell tab offset – 1986-on XV, XW and XY engines (Sec 4)

2 The recommended plain and grooved bearing arrangement for the XU5JA engine is as follows (Chapter 1, Section 36):

Bearing No.	1	2	3	4	5
Top (block)	G	G	G	G	G
Bottom(cap)	G	P	P	P	P

3 The XU5JA engine is also fitted with improved liners, connecting rods and valve springs. Larger valves are fitted, together with modified combustion chambers and inlet/exhaust ports. A modified camshaft is fitted, with a lift of 11.5 mm.

4 Unless otherwise stated in this Supplement, all procedures are as described in Chapter 1 for the XU5J engine.

XU51C engine – description

5 The XU51C engine is fitted to automatic transmission models. It is identical to the XU5J engine described in Chapter 1, but it is fitted with a carburettor instead of fuel injection equipment. All procedures are basically as given in Chapter 1, but references to the fuel injection components should be ignored, and where necessary carburettor removal and refitting substituted.

XU9JA and XU9JA/K engines – description

6 The XU9JA and XU9JA/K engines are fitted to the 1.9 GTI, and the general construction is identical to that of the XU5JA as fitted to the 1.6 GTI and 1.6 CTI.

7 Apart from the differences given in the Specifications, the main changes concern the camshaft, sump, pistons, and the addition of an oil cooler. The camshaft endfloat is controlled by machined shoulders on the No 1 bearing instead of a thrust plate. The height of the sump is reduced to accommodate a spacer plate, which acts as a stiffener. The pistons have special dished crowns. The oil cooler is mounted in front of the radiator on the right-hand side.

Dimensions in mm

Fig. 13.2 Stepped locating dowels available for matching the cylinder head to the block on XV, XW and XY engines (Sec 4)

Fig. 13.3 The 25 mm cylinder head bolt spacer is identified by a groove (arrowed) – XU engines (Sec 5)

Fig. 13.4 Torx type cylinder head bolt – XU engines (Sec 5)

8   Work procedures are as for the XU5JA engine, except for the differences described in paragraphs 7, and elsewhere in this Section.

XU9JA/Z and XU9JA/L engines – description

9   The XU9JA/Z engine was fitted to 1.9 GTI models from 1991, and was replaced by the XU9JA/L engine in 1993. The engines operate in conjunction with a catalytic converter, to reduce harmful exhaust gas emissions.

10   Apart from the differences given in the Specifications, this engine is identical to the XU9JA engine described previously in this Section, but a Motronic M1.3 integrated fuel injection system is used, to provide the fine degree of engine control necessary for operation with a catalytic converter.

11   All procedures are basically as described for the XU9JA engine, noting that details of the Motronic fuel injection system components are given in Section 9D of this Chapter.

XU5M engine – description

12   The XU5M engine was introduced in 1992, and is fitted to auto-matic models. The engine is similar to the XU5J engine described in Chapter 1, noting the following points:

(a)   *The engine is fitted with MMFD single-point fuel injection, and a catalytic converter, as described in Section 9F of this Chapter.*

(b)   *All procedures are basically as described in Chapter 1 for the XU5J engine, but refer to later paragraphs of this Section for details of modifications applicable to all XU engines.*

XU9J1 engine – description

13   The XU9J1 engine was introduced in 1992, and is fitted to CTI and 'Gentry' models.

14   The engine is similar to the XU9JA engine described previously in this Section, noting the following differences:

(a)   *The engine is fitted with Bosch LU2-Jetronic fuel injection, and a catalytic converter, as described in Section 9C of this Chapter.*

(b)   *All procedures are basically as described in Chapter 1 for the XU5J engine, but refer to later paragraphs of this Section for details of modifications applicable to all XU engines.*

Engine (automatic transmission models) – removal and refitting

15   Due to the additional weight involved, it is recommended that the automatic transmission is removed independently, as described in Section 15 of this Supplement, before removing the engine. Refer to Chapter 1, Section 28 for the removal of the engine, and Section 38 for refitting.

Right-hand engine (XU engines) – modification

16   As from March 1987 (chassis number 5737675), the adjustment shims have been deleted from the right-hand engine mounting, and the rubber buffers are increased in thickness by 5.5 mm. On vehicles with this modification, the adjustment procedure given in Chapter 1, Section 38 is not applicable.

17   To prevent scuffing noises from the buffers, it is recommended that the inner surfaces which contact the engine bracket are lubricated with rubber grease.

Cylinder head bolts and cylinder liners (XU engines) – modifications

18   As from early 1987, the cylinder head bolts are of No 55 Torx type, and 8 mm thick washers are fitted instead of the previous 3 mm thick washers fitted to the hexagon head bolts. The spacer fitted to the bolt at the timing belt end is now 25 mm thick, (previously 23 mm), and is identified by a groove around its perimeter.

19   A Torx bit will be required to loosen and tighten the head bolts, and this should be obtained from an auto accessory store or tool suppliers.

20   At the same time, the cylinder liners were reduced in height by 0.05 mm, and consequently the protrusion dimensions are reduced by the same amount, as given in the Specifications. A modified cylinder head gasket was also fitted, so it is important to quote the engine number accurately when obtaining a new one.

21   The tightening procedure for the Torx cylinder head bolts is different, as given in the Specifications, and this method must never be used on hexagonal cylinder head bolts. It is **not** necessary to retighten the bolts after initial running.

22   When fitting the Torx cylinder head bolts, apply a little molybde-num disulphide grease to their heads, and to the contact surface of their heads.

Camshaft sprocket bolt (XU engines) – modification

23   From early 1987, the camshaft sprocket bolt was reduced in size from M12 to M10, and the revised torque wrench setting given in the Specifications should be used for the smaller bolt.

Oil pump (XU engines) – modifications

24   From approximately April 1987, the oil pump has been modified.

25   The L-shaped spacer between the pump and the cylinder block is no longer fitted, and the locating dowel which fits in the cylinder block has been deleted.

26   The revised pump is slightly increased in height to compensate for the thickness of the spacer.

27   The revised pump can be fitted to earlier models, provided that the spacer and the locating dowel are removed, and three washers (avail-able from Peugeot dealers) are fitted under the oil pump securing bolts.

Piston rings (XU engines) – modifications

28   Various types of piston rings may be fitted in production, and from approximately July 1988, the lower compression ring has been modi-fied with a hook profile on its lower edge.

29   For all piston ring types, the top compression and oil control rings can be fitted either way up, but the lower compression ring must be fitted with the "TOP" or "TOPC" mark uppermost. When fitting a three-piece oil control ring, the expander ring gap should be positioned in line with the centre of the piston gudgeon pin, and the scraper ring gaps should be positioned 20.0 to 30.0 mm from the expander ring gap.

30   Various types of oil control ring may be fitted, including a one-piece "Uflex" type ring which has no ring gap, and is of a larger diameter than the piston. When fitting a "Uflex" type oil control ring, the following procedure must be observed.

31   Fit the compression rings, noting that the lower ring must be fitted with the "TOP" or "TOPC" mark uppermost, and position the ring gaps at 120° to each other.

32   Oil the piston and the rings.

33   With the piston horizontal, position the oil control ring in its piston groove, then holding the piston in this position, fit a piston ring compres-sor tool and tighten it, ensuring that the oil control ring compresses in its groove.

34   Place the relevant liner on the bench, then position the piston on the liner.

35   Push the piston into the liner to engage the first two rings only.

36   *Before* engaging the oil control ring with the liner, ensure that the ring compressor is seated firmly against the liner.

Fig. 13.5 Oil cooler removal – 1.9 GTI (Sec 5)

1	Front crossmember	3	Stone guard
2	Air inlet hose	4	Cowling retaining bolt

Fig. 13.6 Oil cooler removal – 1.9 GTI (Sec 5)

1	Cowling clip	3	Oil cooler mounting nuts
2	Oil cooler connection stubs		

37   Continue to slide the piston into the liner, ensuring that the ring compressor stays in firm contact with the liner.
38   Push the piston fully into the liner, then withdraw the ring compressor,

Oil cooler (1.9 GTI) – removal and refitting

39   Remove the radiator grille and front bumper as described in Chapter 11 and Section 21 of this Chapter.
40   Unbolt the engine compartment front crossmember, and position it to one side, leaving the bonnet release cable still attached.
41   Remove the air inlet hose (photo).
42   Remove the stone guard from the front cowling (photos).
43   Unscrew the retaining bolts, then release the clips and move the front cowling forwards for access to the oil cooler (photos).
44   Place rags or a container beneath the oil cooler to collect any spilled oil. Unscrew the union nuts while holding the connection stubs stationary (photo). Plug the stubs, or tie them to one side.
45   Unscrew the nuts, release the oil cooler from the front cowling, and remove it from the car (photos).
46   Refitting is a reversal of removal, but tighten the union nuts carefully to the specified torque while holding the connection stubs stationary.

Cylinder block-mounted oil cooler (XU engines) – removal and refitting

47   Certain models may be fitted with an oil cooler mounted between the cylinder block and the oil filter.
48   To prevent the oil cooler from being unscrewed as the oil filter is removed, on later models, a retaining lug is provided on the cylinder block, which engages with a fork on the oil cooler – see Fig. 13.8.

Fig. 13.7 Removing the oil cooler (1) – 1.9 GTI (Sec 5)

5.41 Air inlet hose (arrowed) – 1.9 GTI

5.42A Stone guard outer clips (arrowed) ...

5.42B ... and inner clips (arrowed) - 1.9 GTI

Fig. 13.8 Cylinder block-mounted oil cooler – later XU engines (Sec 5)

| 1 | Mounting fork | 2 | Cylinder block lug –
aluminium cylinder block | 3 | Cylinder block lug –
cast-iron cylinder block | 4 | Oil filter mounting stud |

5.43A Radiator clip on the front cowling –
1.9 GTI

5.43B Separating the radiator and front
cowling – 1.9 GTI

5.44 Oil cooler union nut – 1.9 GTI

5.45A Oil cooler mounting nuts (arrowed) –
1.9 GTI

5.45B Oil cooler pipe bracket nut (arrowed) –
1.9 GTI

Fig. 13.9 Spacer plate (1) fitted to the sump on 1.9 GTI models (Sec 5)

49 To remove the oil cooler, first remove the oil filter.
50 Disconnect the coolant hoses from the filter. Be prepared for coolant spillage, and plug the open ends of the hoses to prevent dirt ingress and further coolant loss.
51 Unscrew the oil filter mounting stub, then withdraw the oil cooler from the engine.
52 Refitting is a reversal of removal, bearing in mind the following points.
53 When refitting the oil cooler, where applicable, ensure that the fork on the cooler engages with the lug on the cylinder block.
54 Before refitting the oil filter mounting stub, thoroughly clean the threads, and coat them with suitable thread-locking compound.
55 Tighten the mounting stub to the specified torque.
56 On completion, check and if necessary top-up the coolant level.

Sump spacer plate (1.9 GTI) – removal and refitting

57 Remove the sump and gasket.
58 Unscrew the two bolts from the diagonally-opposite corners, and remove the spacer plate from the cylinder block. If it is stuck, use a thin knife to cut into the jointing compound.
59 Thoroughly clean the surfaces of the block, spacer plate and sump.
60 Apply silicone jointing compound to the upper mating surface of the spacer plate, position the plate on the block, then insert and tighten the two bolts to the specified torque.
61 Refit the sump together with a new gasket. Insert and tighten the bolts to the specified torque.

Cylinder liner/piston identification markings (XU engines) – modifications

62 On later engines, the cylinder liner grades are identified by letters stamped on the top face of the liners, which should correspond to the relevant identification letters stamped on the piston crowns.

| EARLIER ASSEMBLY | LATER ASSEMBLY |

Fig. 13.10 Modified engine components – XU engines with eccentric roller camshaft drivebelt tensioner mechanism (Sec 5)

1 Right-hand engine mounting   2 Camshaft drivebelt   3 Tensioner roller   4 Tensioner roller nut

Fig. 13.11 Modified engine components – XU engines with eccentric roller camshaft drivebelt tensioner mechanism (Sec 5)

5   Water pump   6   Oil seal carrier plate

Fig. 13.12 Modified engine components – XU engines with eccentric roller camshaft drivebelt tensioner mechanism (Sec 5)

7   Intermediate camshaft drivebelt cover   8   Bottom camshaft drivebelt cover   9   Rear camshaft drivebelt cover

Camshaft drivebelt and tensioner assembly (XU engines) – modifications

63   In late 1992, the spring belt tensioner mechanism was superseded by an eccentric roller tensioner mechanism.

64   To accommodate the revised components, a number of the surrounding engine components have been modified as follows, and are shown in the accompanying illustrations.

> Tensioner assembly
> Camshaft drivebelt
> Front crankshaft oil seal carrier plate
> Water pump
> Right-hand engine mounting
> Cylinder block
> Camshaft drivebelt covers

65   Note that the modified camshaft drivebelt has 114 teeth and orange markings. The drivebelt used with the spring belt tensioner mechanism has 113 teeth and white markings. If the drivebelt is to be renewed, ensure that the correct type of replacement drivebelt is obtained.

Camshaft drivebelt (XU engines with eccentric roller tensioner mechanism) – removal and refitting

Note: *Peugeot specify the use of special tool (SEEM C.TRONIC type 105 or 105.5 belt tension measuring equipment) to correctly set the belt tension. If this equipment cannot be obtained, an approximate setting can be achieved using the method described below. If the method described here is used, the tension must be checked using the special equipment at the earliest opportunity. Do not drive the vehicle over large distances, or use high engine speeds until the belt tension is known to be correct. Refer to a Peugeot dealer for advice.*

66   Proceed as described in Chapter 1, Section 25, paragraphs 1 to 8, noting that the crankshaft pulley timing dowel must be of 10 mm diameter, stepped down to 8 mm at one end to engage with the smaller hole in the timing recess.

67   With the camshaft drivebelt covers removed, slacken the tensioner roller bolt to relieve the belt tension, then withdraw the belt, noting the direction of fitting and the markings.

68   Commence refitting by slipping the belt over the camshaft sprocket, followed by the crankshaft sprocket, the water pump sprocket, and finally over the tensioner roller. Observe the arrows on the belt indicating the direction of rotation, and the timing lines which align with corresponding marks on the crankshaft and camshaft sprockets.

69   With the camshaft timing dowel fitted, rotate the tensioner roller anti-clockwise by hand as far as possible to take up any slack in the belt, then tighten the tensioner roller bolt sufficiently to hold the roller in position. If the special belt tension measuring equipment is available, it should be fitted to the tensioned run of the belt, and the tensioner roller should be moved to give a reading of 30 ± 2 units. Tighten the roller bolt to the specified torque, taking care not to move the roller as the bolt is tightened.

70   Check that the crankshaft and camshaft are still positioned correctly by temporarily refitting the crankshaft pulley and re-inserting the timing dowel.

71   Remove the timing dowels, temporarily refit the crankshaft pulley, and turn the crankshaft through two full turns in the normal direction of rotation. Check that both timing dowels can still be inserted. If not, remove the drivebelt and start again. **Never** turn the crankshaft backwards during this procedure.

72   If all is well, remove the dowels, and turn the crankshaft through two further turns in the normal direction of rotation.

73   Refit the camshaft timing dowel, and check that the belt can just be twisted through 90° (using moderate pressure from the forefinger and thumb) at the midpoint of the longest belt run between the camshaft and crankshaft sprockets. If in doubt about this setting, it is better to err on the tight side until the tension can be checked by a Peugeot dealer; if the belt is too slack, it may jump on the sprockets, which could cause serious engine damage. If the special belt tension measuring equipment is available, it should be refitted to the tensioned run of the belt. The reading should now be between 42 and 46 units.

74   If the tension is not as specified, repeat the tensioning operation.

75   Refit the belt covers and the crankshaft pulley. Apply threadlocking compound to the crankshaft pulley bolt threads, and tighten the bolt to the specified torque.

76   On completion, refit all disturbed components, and tension the alternator drivebelt, as described in Chapter 12, Section 2.

Fig. 13.13 Electronic oil level sensor wiring diagram (Sec 5)

A Electronic control unit	M Earth
B Sensor	+ AA Accessory supply
C Warning lamp	+ AC Ignition supply
D Oil pressure switch	

Electronic oil level sensor – description

77   Some 1985 models have an oil level sensor fitted to the engine sump, together with a warning lamp on the instrument panel. The system was only fitted on the 1985 model year, and has been deleted from later models.

78   The sensor incorporates a high-resistance wire, which varies in conductivity depending on whether it is immersed in or above the oil. An electronic control unit mounted under the right-hand side of the facia monitors the conductivity, and operates the warning lamp when necessary.

79   It should be noted that the system only functions accurately if the car is on a level surface. When the ignition is initially switched on, the warning lamp should light for two seconds. If the oil level is correct, the lamp will then go out, but if it starts to flash the oil level is low.

80   To prevent the system functioning unnecessarily after the engine has started, the control unit is earthed through the oil pressure switch. The level check is made before starting the engine. Some early models are not earthed through the oil pressure switch and on these, the warning lamp may flash if for instance the engine is temporarily stalled and the oil has not returned to the sump. It is possible to modify the existing wiring; however this work is best entrusted to a Peugeot dealer.

Crankcase ventilation hoses – maintenance

81   Periodically, and particularly at high mileages, the crankcase ventilation hoses should be removed and cleaned. Check the interior of the hoses for collapsed linings or other restrictions.

82   Blockage of a crankcase ventilation hose can cause the engine oil filler cap to blow off, or the oil separators to fill with oil.

Crankcase ventilation hoses – maintenance

83   Periodically, and particularly at high mileages, the crankcase ventilation hoses should be removed and cleaned. Check the interior of the hoses for collapsed linings or other restrictions.

84   Blockage of a crankcase ventilation hose can cause the engine oil filler cap to blow off, or the oil separators to fill with oil.

Camshaft bearing cap lubrication pipe

85   As from 1988, the pipe has been modified, and incorporates an O-ring in a groove adjacent to the plastic adaptors. Only the new design of pipe is available as a replacement, and it may be fitted to eliminate tappet noise (resonance).

6   TU engines

Engine – general description

1   The TU engine is a development of the XU5J engine described in Chapter 1. The most significant difference is that the TU engine is inclined forward by 6°, with the exhaust manifold mounted on the front of the cylinder head, and the inlet manifold and carburettor mounted on the rear. Refer to the later paragraphs of this Section for details of modifications applicable to TU engines.

Operations possible without removing the engine from the car

2   The following components can be removed and refitted with the engine in the car:

> (a)   Cylinder dead
> (b)   Timing belt and camshaft
> (c)   Sump and oil pump
> (d)   Clutch and flywheel (after removal of transmission).

3   Since the sump and cylinder head can be removed *in situ*, it is

Fig. 13.14 Cutaway view of TU engine (Sec 6)

Fig. 13.15 Diagrammatic view of TU engine lubrication system (Sec 6)

6.6A Battery clamp bolt (arrowed)

6.6B Removing the battery tray bracket

6.9 Engine oil drain plug

6.14 Lower rear engine mounting yoke (arrowed)

possible to renew the pistons, liners and big-end bearings without removing the engine. However, this work is not recommended, since it can be performed more easily with the engine on the bench.

Engine – removal and refitting

4   The engine and transmission assembly is removed by lifting upwards from the engine compartment. The transmission is separated from the engine on the bench.

5   Remove the bonnet (Chapter 11) or alternatively disconnect the bonnet stay, fully raise the bonnet, and retain by inserting two suitable U-bolts in the special holes in the hinges.

6   Remove the battery (Chapter 12) and unbolt the tray bracket (photos).

7   Jack up the front of the car, and support on axle stands. Alternatively, position the front of the car on ramps or over an inspection pit.

8   Drain the cooling system (Section 7).

9   Drain the engine oil (photo) and gearbox oil.

10   Disconnect the choke and accelerator cables, and unbolt the bracket.

11   Remove the air cleaner (Section 8 or 9A).

12   Disconnect the fuel supply hose from the fuel pump.

13   Remove the radiator (Section 7).

14   Unscrew the two bolts from the lower rear engine mounting, and remove the yoke (photo).

15   Remove both driveshafts by referring to Chapter 7, and Section 16 of this Chapter.

16   Unbolt the exhaust front pipe from the exhaust manifold, and remove the metal gasket.

17   Unbolt the front pipe bracket from the gearbox, unbolt the flange from the rear exhaust system, and remove the front pipe.

18   Pull out the rubber cotter, and disconnect the speedometer cable from the gearbox (photo).

19   Disconnect the gearchange control rods (photo).

20   Unbolt the right-hand driveshaft bearing bracket from the cylinder block.

21   Disconnect the clutch cable (Chapter 5).

22   Disconnect the heater hoses and bottom hose from the engine (photo).

23   Unscrew the nut and remove the earth cable from the gearbox (photo).

24   Disconnect the brake servo vacuum hose.

25   Note the location of the engine wiring harness, then disconnect it from the various components (photos). Also unscrew the nut and disconnect the pink battery lead from the fusebox.

26   Connect a hoist to the two engine lifting eyes, and support the weight of the engine and gearbox.

27   Unscrew the left-hand mounting nuts, including the nut on the centre stud, and remove the mounting (photo).

28   Unscrew the right-hand mounting centre nut. If necessary, unscrew the nuts and remove the bracket completely (photo).

29   Lower the engine and gearbox so that the left-hand mounting stud clears the mounting bracket, turn the assembly so that it is positioned diagonally in the engine compartment, then slowly lift the assembly while guiding it clear of the components in the engine compartment (photo).

30   When clear of the front panel, move it forwards and lower to the ground.

31   Refitting is a reversal of removal, but note the following additional points:

(a)   Use a plastic protector (see Section 16) when refitting the right-hand driveshaft
(b)   Adjust the clutch cable with reference to Chapter 5
(c)   Adjust the choke and accelerator cables with reference to Chapter 3
(d)   Fill the engine and gearbox with oil
(e)   Fill the cooling system as described in Section 7
(f)   Tension the alternator drivebelt with reference to Chapter 12.

Engine – separation from transmission

32   Unbolt and remove the starter motor, together with the air cleaner bracket (photos).

33   Unscrew and remove the gearbox-to-engine bolts (photo).

34   Support the engine, and lift the gearbox away from it. Recover any loose dowels.

Engine dismantling – general

35   Refer to Chapter 1, Section 10.

Engine – complete dismantling

36   Disconnect the HT leads from the spark plugs, unbolt the lead support (photo), disconnect the HT lead from the coil, and remove the distributor cap.

37   Remove the spark plugs.

38   Disconnect the vacuum hose between the distributor and carburettor.

39   Disconnect the hoses between the fuel pump and carburettor, and between the water pump and thermostat housing (photo).

40   Unscrew the nuts and remove the inlet manifold, complete with carburettor, from the studs on the cylinder head (photo). Note that there is no gasket.

6.18 Disconnecting the speedometer cable (arrowed)

6.19 Gearchange control rods (arrowed) – engine removed for clarity

6.22 Bottom hose connection to water pump housing

6.23 Earth cable attachment at gearbox (arrowed)

6.25A Starter motor wiring

6.25B Carburettor stop solenoid wiring connector

6.25C Wiring harness clip on cylinder block

6.25D Wiring harness clip on timing cover

6.25E Water temperature sender (arrowed) and wiring

6.27 Left-hand engine mounting

6.28 Right-hand engine mounting bracket

6.29 Removing the engine and gearbox

6.32A Unscrew the bolts ...

6.32B ... and remove the starter motor

6.33 Gearbox-to-engine bolt (arrowed)

6.36 Unbolting the HT lead support

6.39 Hose from water pump to thermostat housing (arrowed)

6.40 Removing the inlet manifold complete with the carburettor

6.42A Alternator pivot(A), adjustment (B) and tension (C) bolts

6.42B Removing the alternator pivot bolt

6.43 Unbolting the crankshaft pulley

6.44A TDC connector on the coil (arrowed)

6.44B Coil location over the distributor

6.49 Removing the thermostat housing

6.50 Distributor mounting flange

6.51A TDC sensor wiring clip (arrowed) ...

6.51B ... and mounting bolt (arrowed)

6.52 Timing plate (arrowed)

6.53 Removing the oil filter

6.54 Oil pressure switch

6.55 Unscrewing the dipstick holder mounting bolt

6.57A Remove the spacers (arrowed) ...

6.57B ... and the baffle plate

6.58A Unscrew the bolts ...

6.58B ... and remove the upper timing cover ...

6.58C ... intermediate cover ...

6.58D ... and lower cover

6.59 Camshaft sprocket set to TDC

6.60 Bolt (arrowed) inserted through cylinder block rear flange into the flywheel TDC hole

6.61 Loosening the timing belt tensioner roller nut

6.65 Lifting off the rocker arm assembly

6.66 Lifting the cylinder head from the block

6.69 Removing the clutch pressure plate and friction disc

6.71A Unscrew the crankshaft pulley bolt ...

6.71B ... and remove the hub/sprocket ...

6.71C ... and oil seal flange

6.72 Prising out the crankshaft front oil seal

41   Unbolt and remove the fuel pump, and remove the gasket.

42   Loosen the alternator pivot and adjustment bolts, then unscrew the tension bolt, and slip the drivebelt from the pulleys. Remove the pivot and adjustment bolts, and remove the alternator (photos).

43   Unbolt the pulley from the front of the crankshaft (photo).

44   Unbolt and remove the coil, after unclipping the TDC connector (photos).

45   Unbolt the exhaust manifold hot air shroud.

46   Unscrew the brass nuts, remove the washers, and remove the exhaust manifold from the studs on the cylinder head. Remove the gaskets.

47   Remove the distributor with reference to Chapter 4.

48   Remove the thermostat with reference to Section 7.

49   Unbolt the thermostat housing from the cylinder head (photo).

50   Unbolt the distributor mounting flange from the cylinder head (photo).

51   Unbolt the TDC sensor from the flywheel end of the cylinder block, and unclip the lead from the timing plate (photos).

52   Unbolt the timing plate (photo).

53   Unscrew and remove the oil filter, using a removal strap tool if necessary (photo).

54   Unscrew and remove the oil pressure switch (photo).

55   Unscrew the mounting bolt, and pull the engine oil dipstick holder from the main bearing cap casting. Remove the dipstick from the holder (photo).

56   Unscrew the nuts and remove the valve cover. Remove the rubber gasket from the cover.

57   Remove the two spacers and baffle plate from the studs (photo).

58   Unbolt the upper timing cover, followed by the intermediate cover and lower cover (photos).

59   Turn the engine clockwise, using a socket on the crankshaft pulley bolt, until the small hole in the camshaft sprocket is aligned with the corresponding hole in the cylinder head. Insert the shank of a close-fitting twist drill (eg a 10 mm drill) into the holes (photo).

60   Align the TDC holes in the flywheel and cylinder block rear flange, and insert a further twist drill or long bolt, diameter 6 mm approx (photo).

61   Loosen the timing belt tensioner roller nut (photo), turn the tensioner clockwise using a suitable square drive extension in the special hole, then re-tighten the nut.

62   Mark the normal direction of rotation on the timing belt, then remove it from the camshaft, water pump, and crankshaft sprockets.

Fig. 13.16 Using two angled metal rods to free the cylinder head from the block – TU engine (Sec 6)

63   Unscrew the tensioner nut, and remove the tensioner roller.
64   Progressively loosen the cylinder head bolts, using the reverse sequence to that shown in Fig. 13.17, then remove all the bolts.
65   Lift off the rocker arm assembly (photo).
66   Rock the cylinder head to free it from the block, then lift it from the location dowels (photo). Two angled metal rods, shown in Fig. 13.16, may be used for this purpose.
67   Remove the cylinder head gasket from the block.
68   Fit the liner clamps (see Chapter 1, Section 24) if it is not proposed to remove the pistons and liners.
69   Progressively loosen the clutch pressure plate bolts, and remove the pressure plate and friction disc from the flywheel (photo).

70   Unbolt the water pump housing from the side of the block, and prise out the O-ring.
71   Have an assistant hold the flywheel stationary with a wide-bladed screwdriver inserted between the starter ring gear teeth, then unscrew the crankshaft pulley bolt and remove the hub/sprocket and oil seal flange (photos).
72   Using a screwdriver, prise the front oil seal from the block and main bearing casting (photo).
73   Hold the flywheel stationary as described in paragraph 71, and unscrew the flywheel bolts. Lift the flywheel from the dowel on the crankshaft rear flange.
74   Prise out the crankshaft rear oil seal using a screwdriver.
75   Invert the engine, and support on blocks of wood.
76   Unscrew the nuts and bolts securing the sump to the main bearing casting, and remove the sump by carefully prising it free of the jointing compound (photos).
77   Unbolt the oil pump, and tilt it to release the drive sprocket from the chain (photo).
78   Support the block on its flywheel end.
79   Mark the liners for position, starting with No 1 (at the flywheel end). Similarly mark the big-end bearing caps.
80   Temporarily refit the crankshaft pulley bolt, and turn the crankshaft so that Nos 1 and 4 pistons (No 1 at flywheel end) are at bottom dead centre (BDC).
81   Unscrew the nuts, and remove the big-end bearing caps (photo). Remove the lower big-end shells, keeping them identified for position.
82   Remove the clamps and withdraw the liners, complete with pistons, from the block (photo).
83   Remove the liner bottom O-rings (photo).
84   Repeat the procedure for Nos 2 and 3 pistons and liners.
85   Invert the engine again, and unscrew the bolts securing the main bearing cap casting to the block (photos).
86   Progressively unscrew the main bearing bolts, and lift the main bearing cap casting from the block. Gently tap it with a wooden or soft-headed mallet to release it. Prise out the main bearing shells, keeping them identified for location.
87   Remove the oil pump sprocket and chain from the crankshaft (photo).
88   Lift the crankshaft from the block, and remove the main bearing shells, keeping them identified for location. Also remove the endfloat rings from No 2 main bearing location (photos).

6.76A Unscrew the nuts and bolts ...

6.76B ... and remove the sump

6.77 Unscrewing an oil pump securing bolt

6.81 Removing a big-end bearing cap

6.82 Removing a liner and piston assembly

6.83 Liner bottom O-ring (arrowed)

6.85A Unscrew the main bearing cap casting front bolts ...

6.85B ... and side bolts (arrowed)

6.87 Removing the oil pump sprocket and chain

6.88A Removing a main bearing shell ...

6.88B ... and endfloat ring

6.89 Removing the camshaft sprocket – note location peg and cut-out (arrowed)

6.90 Camshaft thrust fork (arrowed)

6.91A Prise out the oil seal ...

6.91B ... and withdraw the camshaft

Cylinder head – dismantling, decarbonising and reassembly

89   Remove the twistdrill from the camshaft sprocket, then hold the sprocket stationary using an oil filter strap wrench or tool as shown in photo 6.96. Unscrew the bolt and remove the sprocket (photo).
90   Unbolt and remove the camshaft thrust fork (photo).
91   Prise out the oil seal, and carefully withdraw the camshaft from the cylinder head (photos).
92   Remove the valves and springs, clean and check the cylinder head, and refit the valves and springs with reference to Chapter 1, Section 32 (photos).
93   Oil the camshaft bearings, and insert the camshaft into the cylinder head.
94   Refit the camshaft thrust fork and tighten the bolt.
95   Dip the new oil seal in oil, and press it into the cylinder head until flush, using a metal tube or large socket and hammer.
96   Refit the camshaft sprocket so that the location peg enters the cut-out. Insert and tighten the bolt while holding the sprocket stationary using either method described in paragraph 89 (photo).

Engine components – examination and renovation (general)

97   Refer to Chapter 1, Section 13.

Examination and renovation of dismantled components

98   Refer to Chapter 1, Section 34, but note that there is no camshaft lubrication manifold, as the camshaft runs in an oil bath. Also note that although the timing belt should be renewed when the engine is over-hauled or if it is contaminated with oil, there is no specified replacement mileage. When handling the timing belt, do not bend it, as this may damage the internal fibres.

Engine reassembly – general

99   Refer to Chapter 1, Sections 16 and 17.

Engine – complete reassembly

Note: *For important details of modified pistons and connecting rods fitted to TU9 engines, and modified main bearing shells fitted to all TU engines refer to the later paragraphs of this Section.*

100   With the block upside-down on the bench, press the main bearing upper shells into position. Note that the grooved bearings are fitted to positions No 2 and 4.
101   Smear a little grease on the endfloat rings, and locate them each side of No 2 bearings with their grooves facing outwards.
102   Oil the bearings, and lower the crankshaft into position (photo).

6.92A Compress the valve spring and remove the collets ...

6.92B ... retainer ...

6.92C ... spring ...

6.92D ... spring seat ...

6.92E ... and valve

6.92F Valve components removed from the cylinder head

6.96 Using a home-made tool to hold the camshaft sprocket while tightening the bolt

6.102 Oiling the main bearing shells

6.106A Apply jointing compound to the mating faces ...

6.106B ... then lower the main bearing cap casting into position

6.107A Torque-tighten the main bearing bolts. ...

6.107B ... then angle-tighten a further 45°

6.113 Using a hammer handle to push the piston into the liner

6.116 Tightening a big-end bearing cap nut

6.122 Crankshaft rear oil seal located over crankshaft

6.123 Using the flywheel and four bolts to fit the crankshaft rear oil seal

6.124A Apply locking fluid to the flywheel bolts ...

6.124B ... and tighten to the specified torque

103   Check that the crankshaft endfloat is as given in the Specifications, using a feeler blade between an endfloat ring and the crankshaft web. The rings are available in four thicknesses.
104   Fit the oil pump sprocket and chain to the front of the crankshaft, locating the sprocket on the Woodruff key.
105   Press the main bearing lower shells into position in the main bearing cap casting, noting that the grooved bearings are fitted to positions No 2 and 4.
106   Apply jointing compound to the mating face, then lower the main bearing cap casting into position over the crankshaft. At the same time, feed the oil pump chain through the aperture (photos).
107   Insert the main bearing bolts key, then tighten them evenly to the initial torque wrench setting. Angle-tighten the bolts further by the specified angle (photos).
108   Refit the bolts securing the main bearing cap casting to the block, and tighten them to the specified torque.
109   Support the block on its flywheel end.
110   Check that the lower big-end bearing shells are fitted to the big-end caps, and the upper shells to the connecting rods.
111   Oil the liner bores and piston rings.
112   Position the piston ring end gaps at 120° from each other, so that neither is in line with another.
113   Fit a piston ring compressor to each piston in turn, and push the pistons in their respective liners using a hammer handle (photo). Make sure that the arrows on the piston crowns face the front (timing belt end) of the liners.
114   Fit the bottom O-rings to the liners, taking care not to twist them.
115   Check that the crankshaft rotates freely, then position Nos 1 and 4 crankpins at bottom dead centre (BDC). Oil the crankpins.
116   Insert No 1 liner/piston into the block, and guide the connecting rod big-end onto the crankpin. Refit the big-end bearing cap, and tighten the nuts evenly to the specified torque (photo).
117   Check that the crankshaft rotates freely, whilst holding the liner in position with a clamp. Temporarily refit the crankshaft pulley bolt to turn the crankshaft.

118   Repeat the procedure to fit the remaining pistons and liners.
119   Support the block upside-down on the bench.
120   Check that the oil pump location pin is fitted to the main bearing casting, then refit the oil pump while tilting it to engage the drive sprocket with the chain. Insert and tighten the bolts.
121   Apply jointing compound to the mating faces of the sump and main bearing casting. Refit the sump, insert the bolts and tighten them to the specified torque.
122   Dip the new crankshaft rear oil seal in oil, and locate it over the rear of the crankshaft (photo).
123   Peugeot dealer use their special tool (0132 U) to fit the oil seal, however it may be fitted by using the flywheel. Temporarily locate the flywheel on the crankshaft using four bolts, then tighten the bolts evenly until the flywheel contacts the rear flange (photo). Remove the flywheel, and use a metal tube or block of wood to drive the oil seal fully into position.
124   Apply locking fluid to the threads of the flywheel bolts, locate the flywheel on the crankshaft dowel, then insert the bolts and tighten them to the specified torque while holding the flywheel as described in paragraph 71 (photos).
125   Support the engine upright on the bench.
126   Dip the crankshaft front oil seal in oil, locate it over the front of the crankshaft, and drive it in flush with the front of the block using a metal tube or socket. There is no seating, so take care not to drive it in too far.
127   Fit the oil seal flange, followed by the hub/sprocket. Insert the pulley bolt and spacer, and tighten the bolt to the specified torque while holding the flywheel stationary.
128   Refit the water pump housing together with a new O-ring, and tighten the bolts to the specified torque.
129   Locate the clutch friction disc and pressure plate on the flywheel with the dowels engaged. Insert the bolts finger-tight.
130   Centralise the friction disc, using a universal tool, or by making a wooden adaptor to the dimensions shown in Fig. 13.61 (photo).
131   Tighten the pressure plate bolts evenly to the specified torque (photo).

6.130 Using a universal clutch centralising tool

6.131 Tightening the pressure plate bolts

6.135 Camshaft sprocket held at TDC

6.138 Tighten the cylinder head bolts to the specified torque ...

6.139 ... then angle-tighten further

6.142 Timing belt tensioner roller nut (arrowed)

132   Clean the cylinder head and block joint faces thoroughly. Also clean the cylinder head bolt holes.
133   Locate the new cylinder head gasket on the block dowels, with the manufacturer's name uppermost.
134   Align the TDC holes in the flywheel and block rear flange, insert a twist drill or long bolt.
135   Align the small hole in the camshaft sprocket with the hole in the cylinder head, and insert a twist drill or bolt (photo).
136   Lower the cylinder head onto the block so that it engages the two dowels.
137   Refit the rocker arm assembly.
138   Lubricate the cylinder head bolt threads and heads with molybdenum disulphide grease. Insert them and tighten to the initial torque using the sequence given in Fig. 13.17 (photo).
139   Using the same sequence, angle-tighten the bolts by the specified angle (photo).
140   Refit the timing belt tensioner roller, turn it clockwise, and tighten the nut.
141   Engage the timing belt with the crankshaft sprocket then, keeping it taut, feed in onto the camshaft sprocket, around the tensioner pulley, and onto the water pump sprocket.
142   Loosen the nut and turn the tensioner roller anti-clockwise by hand. Tighten the nut (photo).
143   Peugeot dealers use the special tool shown in Fig. 13.18 to

Fig. 13.17 Cylinder head bolt tightening sequence – TU engine (Sec 6)

Fig. 13.18 Using Peugeot tool 0132X to tension the timing belt (Sec 6)

6.143A Home-made tool and spring balance for tensioning timing belt

6.143B Using home-made tool and spring balance to tension timing belt

6.145 Timing covers refitted

tension the timing belt. A similar tool may be fabricated using an 8.0 cm long arm and a 1.5 kg weight or a spring balance (photos). The torque applied to the roller will approximate 12 kgf cm (10.5 lbf in). Pre-tension the timing belt with the tool and tighten the nut, then remove the timing pins and rotate the crankshaft through two complete turns. Loosen the nut and allow the roller to re-position itself. Tighten the nut.

144 If the special tool is not available, an approximate setting may be achieved by turning the roller hub anti- clockwise, until it is just possible to turn the timing belt through 90° by finger and thumb midway between the crankshaft and camshaft sprockets. The square in the roller hub should then be directly below the adjustment nut, and the deflection of the belt in the midway position should be approximately 6.0 mm (0.24 in). If using this method, the tension should be re-checked by a Peugeot dealer at the earliest opportunity.

145 Refit the lower, intermediate, and upper timing covers, and tighten the bolts (photo).

146 Adjust the valve clearances as described in paragraphs 176 to 185.

147 Refit the baffle plate with its edges pointing downwards, followed by the two spacers.

148 Fit the rubber gasket to the valve cover, locate the cover in position, and tighten the nuts.

149 Apply a little sealant to the end of the engine oil dipstick holder, and insert it in the main bearing cap casting. Insert and tighten the mounting bolt.

150 Insert and tighten the oil pressure switch.

151 Smear a little oil on the sealing ring, and tighten the oil filter into position by hand only.

152 Refit the timing plate and tighten the bolts.

153 Refit the TDC sensor and tighten the bolt. Fix the lead in the plastic clip on the timing plate. Note that the main body of the TDC

sensor should be 1.0 mm from the flywheel.

154 Apply jointing compound to the distributor mounting flange, then refit it to the cylinder head, and tighten the bolts.

155 Apply jointing compound to the thermostat housing, then refit it to the cylinder head, and tighten the bolts.

156 Refit the thermostat with reference to Section 7.

157 Refit the distributor with reference to Chapter 4.

158 Refit the exhaust manifold, together with new gaskets. Refit the nuts and washers, and tighten the nuts.

159 Refit the exhaust manifold hot air shroud, and tighten the bolts.

160 Locate the coil and bracket over the distributor, and tighten the bolts.

161 Position the pulley on the front of the crankshaft. Insert and tighten the bolts.

162 Refit the alternator, and insert the pivot and adjustment bolts. Slip the drivebelt onto the pulleys, and tighten the tension bolt until the deflection of the belt midway between the pulleys is approximately 6.0 mm (0.24 in) under firm thumb pressure. Tighten the pivot and adjustment bolts (photos).

163 Refit the fuel pump together with a new gasket, and tighten the bolts.

164 Thoroughly clean the mating faces of the inlet manifold and cylinder head, and apply jointing compound.

165 Refit the inlet manifold complete with carburettor, and tighten the nuts.

166 Reconnect the hose between the fuel pump and carburettor, and tighten the clips.

167 Reconnect the vacuum hose between the distributor and carburettor.

168 Refit and tighten the spark plugs.

169 Refit the HT leads and distributor cap.

6.162A Alternator pivot bolt (arrowed)

6.162B Alternator adjustment (A) and tension (B) bolts

Engine – reconnection to transmission

170   Check that the clutch release bearing is correctly fitted to the release fork. To prevent being disconnected while fitting the gearbox to the engine, tie the external release arm in the released position.
171   Lubricate the input shaft splines, clutch release bearing sleeve and fork fingers with molybdenum disulphide grease.
172   Refit any location dowels removed, then offer the gearbox to the engine, so that the input shaft enters the clutch friction disc and engages the splines.
173   Push the gearbox fully onto the engine location dowels.
174   Insert and tighten the gearbox-to-engine bolts, noting that the hose bracket with the two cable ties locates on the top right-hand bolt (viewed from gearbox end).
175   Refit the starter motor, together with the air cleaner bracket, and tighten the bolts.

Valve clearances – checking and adjustment (engine cold)

176   Disconnect the crankcase ventilation hose from the valve cover.
177   Unscrew the nuts and remove the valve cover.
178   Remove the two spacers and baffle plate from the studs.
179   Prepare to rotate the crankshaft, either by jacking up one front wheel and turning the wheel with 4th or 5th gear engaged, or by using a spanner on the crankshaft pulley bolt Rotation will be easier if the spark plugs are first removed.
180   Rotate the crankshaft until No 1 exhaust valve (flywheel end) is fully open. No 3 inlet valve and No 4 exhaust valve clearances may now be checked and adjusted. The inlet valve for each cylinder is to the rear, with the exhaust valve to the front.
181   Insert a feeler blade of the correct thickness between the rocker arm and valve stem. It should be a firm sliding fit if the clearance is correct. If adjustment is necessary, loosen the adjuster nut with a ring spanner, turn the adjuster as required with a screwdriver, then retighten the nut (photo).
182   Adjust the valve clearances in the following sequence:

Valve fully open	Adjust valve
No 1 Exhaust	No 3 inlet and No 4 Exhaust
No 3 Exhaust	No 4 Inlet and No 2 Exhaust
No 4 Exhaust	No 2 Inlet and No 1 Exhaust
No 2 Exhaust	No 1 inlet and No 3 Exhaust

183   When all the valve clearances have been adjusted, refit the baffle plate with its edges pointing downwards, followed by the two spacers.
184   Check that the rubber gasket is re-usable, then refit the valve cover and tighten the nuts.
185   Reconnect the crankcase ventilation hose.

Engine – initial start-up after overhaul

186   Refer to Chapter 1, Section 22, paragraphs 1 to 5.
187   The cylinder head bolts **do not** require re-tightening on the TU engine, and the timing belt does not require re-tensioning.
188   If new bearings and/or pistons have been fitted, treat the engine as new, and run it in at reduced speeds. Also change the engine oil at 1000 miles (1500 km).

6.181 Adjusting a valve clearance

Engine (TU9) – fitment of modified pistons

189   From the beginning of January 1988 (Engine No 155776), the TU9 engine was fitted with modified pistons, which can be identified by flanges on both sides, perpendicular to the piston centre-line.

Engine (TU9) – fitment of modified connecting rods

190   From July 1988 (Engine No 270010) modified connecting rods with drilled big-ends to improve piston lubrication have been fitted to TU9 engines. When fitting the piston/connecting rod assemblies, it is essential to ensure that the big-end drilling is positioned on the left-hand side of the engine when viewed from the timing belt end – Fig. 13.19. The modified connecting rods may be supplied as spares for fitment to earlier engines.

Engines (TU) – fitment of modified main bearing shells

191   It is possible that some engines may be fitted with modified main bearing shells, incorporating a grooved No 5 main bearing half-shell fitted to the cylinder block.
192   When reassembling an engine fitted with the modified bearing shells, the following procedure must be observed.
193   Fit the special grooved bearing shell to the No 5 bearing location in the cylinder block.
194   Fit the remaining bearing shells to the cylinder block, noting that the grooved bearing shells should be fitted to the No 2 and 4 bearing locations.
195   Proceed as described in paragraphs 101 to 105 inclusive.
196   Apply a thin coat of jointing compound to the mating faces, then without the centring dowels in place, lower the main bearing cap casting into position over the crankshaft. At the same time, feed the oil pump chain through the aperture.

Section AA

Assembly of the drilled connecting rod in the block

ESSENTIAL DIRECTION OF THE HOLE IN RELATION TO THE TIMING GEAR

TIMING GEAR END

Fig. 13.19 Correct orientation of modified connecting rod – TU9 engine (Sec 6)

Fig. 13.20 Engine number and code location (1) – TU3F engine (Sec 6)

197   Insert the main bearing bolts dry, then tighten them evenly to the Stage 1 torque wrench setting (see Specifications).
198   Angle-tighten the bolts to the Stage 2 torque wrench setting.
199   Refit the bolts securing the main bearing cap casting to the cylinder block, and tighten them to the specified torque.
200   Working on each bearing cap in turn, starting with No 3, loosen the bearing cap bolts, and then tighten them to the Stage 4 and then Stage 5 torque wrench settings.
201   Refit the centring dowels, and continue engine reassembly as described previously in this Section.

Timing belt (TU engines) – modifications
202   Later TU series engines are fitted with a modified timing belt, with improved resistance to oil contamination and high temperatures. The later type of belt can be identified by the 'HSN' marking on the rear of the belt.
203   If work is being carried out on the engine which involves removal of the timing belt, a later 'HSN' type belt should be fitted.

TU3F engine – general description
204   The TU3F engine is a development of the TU3 engine described previously in this Section, the main differences being that the TU3F engine has a cast-iron cylinder block without cylinder liners, and conventional main bearing caps are fitted in place of the main bearing cap casting.
205   Note that the engine code (KDY) for the cast-iron version of the engine is the same as that for the aluminium version. It is therefore important to quote the engine type number in addition to the engine code when obtaining spare parts.

TU3F engine – removal and refitting
206   The procedure is similar to that described previously in this Section for TU engines, bearing in mind the following points.
   (a)   The engine is fitted with Mono-Jetronic A2.2 single-point fuel injection in place of a carburettor. Details of the fuel injection system components are given in Section 9E of this Chapter.
   (b)   Ignore the references to the choke cable.
   (c)   The fuel injection system uses an electric fuel pump; therefore, ignore all references to the engine-mounted mechanical pump.
   (d)   An oxygen sensor is fitted to the exhaust downpipe; the wiring should be disconnected before disconnecting the downpipe.
   (e)   Make a careful note of all vacuum hose and wiring connections, to aid correct refitting.

TU3F engine – complete dismantling
207   The procedure is similar to that described previously in this Section for TU engines, bearing in mind the following points.
   (a)   The engine is fitted with Mono-Jetronic A2.2 single-point fuel injection in place of a carburettor. Details of the fuel injection system components are given in Section 9E of this Chapter.
   (b)   The fuel injection system uses an electric fuel pump; therefore, ignore all references to the engine-mounted mechanical pump.
   (c)   Ignore the references to the main bearing cap casting. The crankshaft main bearings are located in conventional bearing caps, and the sump and gasket are attached directly to the cylinder block.
   (d)   Ignore the references to cylinder liners. The pistons run in bores directly in the cylinder block.
   (e)   Ignore the references to removal of the water pump housing. The water pump housing is an integral part of the cylinder block.
   (f)   The crankshaft oil seals are located in carriers bolted to the front and rear of the cylinder block, which must be removed before the crankshaft can be removed.

Fig. 13.21 Cylinder block – TU3F engine (Sec 6)

1   Water pump housing   2   Crankshaft front oil seal carrier plate

4 Front oil seal carrier plate
5 Front oil seal
6 Rear oil seal
7 Rear oil seal carrier plate

Fig. 13.22 Crankshaft and associated components – TU3F engine (Sec 6)

TU3F engine – examination and renovation of dismantled components
208   The procedure is as described previously in this Section for TU engines, but ignore all references to cylinder liners.

TU3F engine – complete reassembly
209   The procedure is as described previously in this Section for TU engines, bearing in mind the following points.

(a) Ignore the references to the main bearing cap casting. The crankshaft main bearings are located in conventional bearing caps, and the sump and gasket are attached directly to the cylinder block.

(b) **Note:** At the time of writing, no information was available regarding recommended torque wrench settings for the main bearing cap bolts on the TU3F engine. Consult a Peugeot dealer for advice.

(c) Ignore the references to cylinder liners. The pistons run in bores directly in the cylinder block.

(d) Refit the oil seal carriers before refitting the crankshaft oil seals.

(e) Ignore the references to removal of the water pump housing. The water pump housing is an integral part of the cylinder block.

(f) Refer to the Specifications for details of the cylinder head bolt tightening stages.

(g) Ignore the references to the fuel pump.

(h) Ensure that all vacuum hoses and wiring are correctly and securely reconnected, as noted before removal.

7   Cooling system

Cooling system (XV, XW and XY engines) – purging of air
1   Air locks in the cooling system can cause fluctuations of the coolant level, and intermittent illumination of the system warning light when the level appears to be correct. Where this occurs, it is recommended that the following procedure is carried out.
2   With the engine cold, remove the expansion bottle cap, then tie the bottle as high as possible, as shown in Chapter 2.

3   Remove the filler plug from the top left-hand side of the radiator. Fill the radiator until it overflows, then refit and tighten the filler plug.
4   Carefully open the two bleed screws (Chapter 2, Section 3), and slowly pour water into the expansion bottle until air no longer emerges from them. Tighten the bleed screws.
5   Fill the expansion bottle to 30 mm above the maximum level.
6   Start the engine, leaving the cap off the bottle, and run it at 2000 rpm for one minute. During this time, squeeze the top and bottom radiator hoses several times to cause any trapped air to rise.
7   Slacken, and then retighten the bleed screws, to allow any air which has risen to escape.
8   Repeat paragraphs 6 and 7.
9   Refit the expansion bottle cap, and then start the engine and run at 2000 rpm until the cooling fan cuts in. Allow the engine to idle until the fan stops. Stop the engine, and squeeze the top and bottom hoses as described in paragraph 6.
10   Repeat paragraph 7.
11   Allow the engine to cool for at least 15 minutes.
12   Check that the coolant is at the maximum level on the expansion bottle. If it has risen to within 30.0 mm of the top of the bottle, there is still some air trapped in the system.
13   When satisfied that no further bleeding is necessary, refit the expansion bottle in its correct position, and allow the engine to cool for 2 hours. Top-up the coolant to the maximum level if necessary.
14   Note that the bleed screws should not be opened with the expansion bottle in its normal position, otherwise air may be drawn into the system. As bleeding depressurises the system, the engine should always be allowed to cool for at least one hour before normal use.

Cooling system (XU51C engine) – description
15   The XU51C is fitted to automatic transmission models. The transmission incorporates a fluid cooler, which is connected to the cooling system by a hose from the cylinder head outlet, and a further hose to the heater matrix inlet. Because of this additional circuit, the system capacity is increased (see Specifications).

Cooling system (TU engine) – description
16   The cooling system on the TU engine is similar to the system on GTi models, described in Chapter 2.

7.17 Radiator filler cap – TU engine

7.23A Loosening the thermostat housing bleed screw (arrowed)

7.23B Air bleed screw on heater hose – TU engine

7.32 Topping-up the expansion bottle – TU engine

7.33A Disconnecting the low coolant level sensor wiring – TU engine

7.33B Cooling fan relay (arrowed) – TU engine

7.33C Radiator thermo-switch (arrowed) – TU engine

7.33D Removing the radiator – TU engine

Cooling system (TU engine) – draining, flushing and refilling

17   With the engine cold, unscrew the filler caps from the expansion bottle and radiator (photo).
18   Place a suitable container beneath the left-hand side of the radiator, then unscrew the drain plug and drain the coolant.
19   Drain the cylinder block be removing the plug located on the front left-hand side of the block.
20   To flush the radiator, disconnect the top and bottom hoses, and insert a garden hose in the top inlet. Flush with cold water until there are no traces of sediment.
21   With the system clean, refit the hoses and tighten the drain plugs.
22   Release the rubber ring, and tie the expansion bottle to the bonnet as high as possible.
23   Loosen the bleed screws on the thermostat housing and heater hose (photos).
24   Fill the radiator with coolant. Tighten the thermostat housing bleed screw when the water flows free of air bubbles.
25   Fill the radiator to overflowing, then refit and tighten the radiator filler cap.
26   Fill the expansion bottle to the maximum level mark, then tighten

the heater hose bleed screw when the water flows free of air bubbles.
27   Add more coolant to the expansion bottle until the level is about 30.0 mm above the maximum mark. Refit and tighten the filler cap.
28   Start the engine, and run it at 1500 rpm until the electric cooling fan starts.
29   Let the engine idle, then when the cooling fan stops, unscrew the expansion bottle filler cap (using a thick cloth as a precaution against scalding).
30   Slowly loosen the radiator filler cap until coolant flows, then retighten it. Similarly purge any air from the bleed screws on the thermostat housing and heater hose.
31   Top-up the expansion bottle to 30.0 mm above the maximum mark, and refit the filler cap. The high level is necessary at this stage because the coolant is hot.
32   Refit the expansion bottle in its normal position, and secure with the rubber ring. Top-up when cold (photo).

Radiator (TU engine) – removal and refitting

33   The procedure is as described in Chapter 2, Section 6. However, additionally, the cooling fan relay must be removed from the clip on the top of the radiator (photos).

7.43A Coolant bypass hose connection to water pump housing (arrowed) – TU engine

7.43B Water pump housing and bolts (arrowed) – TU engine

7.44A Removing the water pump from the housing – TU engine

7.44B Water pump O-ring (arrowed) – TU engine

7.47 Water pump security bolts (arrowed) – TU3F engine

Water pump (TU engines, except TU3F) – removal and refitting

34   Drain the cooling system as previously described.

35   Unbolt and remove the upper and intermediate timing covers, leaving the lower cover in position.

36   Turn the engine clockwise using a socket on the crankshaft pulley bolt until the small hole in the camshaft sprocket is aligned with the corresponding hole in the cylinder head. Insert a close-fitting twist drill (diameter 10 mm) or bolt into the holes.

37   Align the TDC holes in the flywheel and cylinder block rear flange, and insert a further twist drill or long bolt, diameter 6 mm approx.

38   Loosen the timing belt tensioner roller nut, turn the tensioner clockwise using a screwdriver or square drive in the special hole, then re-tighten the nut.

39   Release the timing belt from the water pump sprocket.

40   Unscrew the nut from the right-hand engine mounting.

41   Using a trolley jack and block of wood, lift the right-hand side of the engine as far as possible.

42   Unscrew the nuts and remove the engine mounting bracket from the water pump housing.

43   Disconnect the hoses from the housing, then unbolt the housing from the block. Remove the O-ring seal (photos).

44   Unbolt the water pump from the housing, and remove the O-ring (photos). If necessary, similarly remove the inlet elbow.

45   Refitting is a reversal of removal, but note the following points:

(a)   Renew the O-rings

(b)   Make sure that the housing-to-block location dowels are in position

(c)   Tighten all nuts and bolts to the specified torque

(d)   Refit and tension the timing belt with reference to Section 5, paragraphs 141 to 144

Water pump (TU3F engines) – removal and refitting

46   Drain the cooling system as described previously in this Section. Remove the timing belt, with reference to paragraphs 35 to 39 of this Section.

47   Unscrew the two securing bolts, and withdraw the water pump from the cylinder block (photo). Recover the O-ring.

48   Refitting is a reversal of removal, bearing in mind the following points.

(a)   Use a new O-ring when refitting the pump.

(b)   Refit and tension the timing belt, as described in paragraphs 141 to 144 of Section 5 in this Chapter.

(c)   Refill the cooling system as described previously in this Section.

Cooling fan thermo-switch – testing

49   With the thermo-switch removed, connect an ohmmeter between the terminals.

50   Suspend the thermo-switch in a container of water which is being heated. Check the temperature of the water with a thermometer. With the unit cold, there should be no continuity, but when the cut-in temperature range is reached, the internal contacts should close and the ohmmeter should register nil resistance.

51   Allow the water to cool, and check that the switch cuts out within the specified temperature range.

Cooling fan thermo-switch (TU engines) – modifications

52   Certain models with TU engines may be fitted with a revised cooling fan thermo-switch which has a lower operating temperature. Refer to the Specifications for details

Thermostat (TU engine) – removal, testing and refitting

53   The procedure is as given in Chapter 2, Section 5, but note the different housing on the TU engine.

CONRAD 'click-on' radiator hose connections (early TU3FM engines) – general information, removal and refitting

54   Some models fitted with the TU3FM engine may also be fitted with pre-production 'click-on' radiator hose connections. These fittings were only fitted to a limited number of vehicles, and have now been discontinued in favour of the original hose clips.

55   The hose end fitting is retained by a large circlip, which must be extracted before pulling the hose out.

56   When refitting, first fit the circlip into the radiator fitting, placing the flat part in position first, and bringing the ends into position one at a time.

57   Ensure that the O-ring is in good condition, and securely located in the hose end fitting. It should not be necessary to lubricate the O-ring to fit it, but if any form of lubrication is used, the radiator **must** be refilled with fresh coolant, to avoid contamination.

58   Align the hose end fitting with the three lugs in the radiator connection, push firmly into place, and check that the hose is secure by pulling back on it. When the cooling system has been refilled, run the engine up to operating temperature, and check carefully for leaks.

59   Note that the 'click-on' fittings have been discontinued from production, and only the circlip and the O-ring are available as spares.

8   Fuel and exhaust systems – carburettor engines

Weber 35 IBSH carburettor – description
1   From early 1985, some XY8 (1360 cc) engines may be fitted with Weber 35 IBSH carburettors instead of the Solex type. The Weber carburettors are of single-barrel downdraught type, and two linked units are fitted to the XY8 engine. The choke is manually operated, but a vacuum-controlled opening device is fitted.

Weber 35 IBSH carburettors – idle speed and mixture adjustment
2   The procedure is as described in Chapter 3 for the Solex 35 PBISA 8 carburettors, but refer to Fig. 13.23.

Weber 35 IBSH carburettor – overhaul
3   The dismantling and reassembly procedure is straightforward, but refer to Fig. 13.24. Carry out the adjustments given in the following paragraphs during reassembly.

Float level
4   Hold the cover vertical with the float arm touching, but not depressing, the spring-tensioned ball on the needle valve.

5   Using vernier calipers, measure the dimension between the float and the fitted gasket (Fig. 13.25). If it is not 9.0 mm, bend the tongue on the arm as necessary.

Throttle normal idling position
6   This adjustment is made after overhauling the carburettors, and is necessary to enable the engine to be started and to prevent the throttle valve sticking in the closed position. The idle speed screw must be adjusted to set the throttle valve 6° open, though a special angle gauge is necessary to measure the movement of the valve. If unavailable, the setting can be made by inserting a piece of card which has been cut to the correct angle.

Fast idle setting
7   With the choke fully closed, the throttle valve should be open by 14°. Use a piece of card as described in paragraph 6 if an angle gauge is not available, and where necessary adjust the fast idle screw on the throttle lever.

Choke opening setting
8   This adjustment can be made with the carburettor removed using a vacuum pump, or with the carburettor fitted and the engine running.
9   Turn the choke lever so that the choke is fully closed.
10   With the engine running or vacuum applied, check that the gap between the lower edge of the choke valve and the barrel is 3.25 mm. Use a twist drill to make the check, and if adjustment is necessary, turn the screw located in the end of the vacuum capsule.

Weber 36 TLC carburettor – description
11   The Weber 36 TLC carburettor is fitted to the XU51C (1580 cc) engine on automatic transmission models. It is of single-barrel downdraught type, incorporating an automatic choke, and a temperature-controlled air cleaner is fitted.

Weber 36 TLC carburettor – idle speed and mixture adjustment
12   Where fitted, remove the tamperproof cap from the mixture screw (Fig. 13.28).
13   Select the Park (P) position with the transmission selector lever, then run the engine to normal operating temperature. Do not remove the air cleaner.
14   Connect a tachometer to the engine.

Fig. 13.23 Adjustment screw locations on the Weber 35 IBSH carburettors (Sec 8)

1 Mixture screw (control carburettor)	3 Combined idle speed screw	5 Vacuum pipe
2 Mixture screw (controlled carburettor)	4 Vacuum pipe	6 Throttle synchroniser adjustment screw

A and B Vacuum connections

1 Choke valve
2 Fuel filter
3 Cover
4 Choke pull-off capsule
5 Accelerator pump jet
6 Idle jet
7 Needle valve
8 Emulsion tube
9 Main jet
10 Float
11 Low vacuum enrichment device
12 Main body
13 Accelerator pump
14 Throttle valve housing

H1934

Fig. 13.24 Exploded view of the Weber 35 IBSH carburettor (Sec 8)

Fig. 13.25 Checking the float level dimension 'X' on the Weber 35 IBSH carburettor (Sec 8)

  1   Gasket   a   Adjustment tongue

Fig. 13.27 Checking the choke opening setting on the Weber 35 IBSH carburettor (Sec 8)

  2   Choke valve adjustment screw

Fig. 13.26 Fast idle adjustment on the Weber 35 IBSH carburettor using an angle gauge (Sec 8)

  1   Fast idle screw

Fig. 13.28 Mixture screw location (2) on the Weber 36 TLC carburettor (Sec 8)

Without an exhaust gas analyser
15   With the engine idling, adjust the idle speed screw (Fig. 13.29) so that the engine speed is 950 rpm.
16   Adjust the mixture screw (Fig. 13.28) to obtain the highest engine speed.
17   Repeat the procedure given in paragraphs 15 and 16 until the highest engine speed is 950 rpm.
18   Screw in the **mixture** screw until the engine idling speed is 900 rpm.

With an exhaust gas analyser
19   With the engine idling, adjust the idle speed screw (Fig. 13.29) until the engine speed is 900 rpm.
20   Adjust the mixture screw (Fig. 13.28) to obtain a CO reading of $1.0 \pm 0.5\%$.
21   Repeat the procedure given in paragraphs 19 and 20 as necessary.

Fig. 13.29 Idle speed adjustment screw (1) on the Weber 36 TLC carburettor (Sec 8)

Fig. 13.30 Upper view of the Weber 36 TLC carburettor (Sec 8)

1   Air correction jet   3   Emulsion tube
2   Idling jet

Fig. 13.31 Weber 36 TLC carburettor with cover removed (Sec 8)

1   Type number   2   Accelerator pump injector

Fig. 13.32 Inverted cover of the Weber 36 TLC carburettor (Sec 8)

1   Float   3   Secondary venturi
2   Main jet   4   Needle valve

Fig. 13.33 Float level setting on the Weber 36 TLC carburettor (Sec 8)

1   Gasket   x = 28.0 mm

Weber 36 TLC carburettor – overhaul

22   The procedure is straightforward, but refer to Figs. 13.30 to 13.32 for the positions of the various jets.

23   To check the float level, hold the cover vertically with the gasket in place. Check that the dimension shown in Fig. 13.33 is as specified, and if necessary bend the tongue on the float arm to correct it.

24   To adjust the cold start device choke opening after starting (COAS), Peugeot tool No 0.145G is essential The engine must be hot and idling (the cooling fan should have cut in and out at least twice), the air cleaner hose and the cold start device cover must be removed, and the transmission selector lever should be in the Park (P) position.

25   Refer to Fig. 13.35, and fit the tool as shown, then slacken the locknut (1) and turn the screw (4) to bring the end of the cam (5) just into contact with the peg (6).

Fig. 13.34 Peugeot tool 0145G (Sec 8)

Fig. 13.35 COAS adjustment on the Weber 36 TLC carburettor
(Sec 8)

1	Locknut	4	Adjusting screw
2	Hole	5	Cam
3	Roller	6	Peg on tool

Fig. 13.36 COAS adjusting screw (1) on the Weber 36 TLC
carburettor (Sec 8)

Fig. 13.37 COAS adjustment on the Weber 36 TLC carburettor
(Sec 8)

1   Hose

26   Using a 9.5 mm twist drill, check that the choke flap has opened by
9.5 mm – if not, adjust by means of the screw (1) in Fig. 13.36., if the
choke flap setting cannot be obtained by means of the screw (1), adjust
the lever as described in paragraph 10 until the twist drill will just pass.
27   Disconnect and plug the hose (1) shown in Fig. 13.37, and using
a 5.5 mm twist drill, check that the choke flap has opened by 5.5 mm – if
not, loosen screw (1) in Fig. 13.38 then hold the roller (1) in Fig. 13.39
against the top of the cam, and adjust the lever (2) until the drill will just
pass. Tighten the screw and reconnect the hose on completion.
28   To adjust the positive throttle opening (PTO), with the COAS
adjusted as described previously, press the roller to open the choke flap
and check that the engine speed is 2000 rpm with the cooling fan
stopped. If necessary, adjust the screw (2) in Fig. 13.40, to obtain the
specified speed.
29   To adjust the choke cam, Peugeot tool No 0.145G must again be
used. Fit the tool as shown in Fig. 13.41, loosen the locknut (6), and

Fig. 13.38 COAS adjustment on the Weber 36 TLC carburettor
(Sec 8)

1   Screw

Fig. 13.39 COAS adjustment on the Weber 36 TLC carburettor (Sec 8)

1 Roller   2 Lever

adjust the screw (3) until the cam (4) contacts peg (5). Tighten the locknut on completion.
30   With the adjustments completed, stop the engine and refit the cold start device cover and the air cleaner hose.

Fig. 13.40 PTO adjustment on the Weber 36 TLC carburettor (Sec 8)

1 Roller   2 Adjusting screw

Fuel pump (automatic models) – description

31   On automatic models manufactured from November 1986, an electric fuel pump submerged in the fuel tank is fitted instead of the previous mechanical type. A filter is incorporated in the pump. The two relays which supply the pump are located on the side of the heater. One relay incorporates a safety feature, in that its primary windings are short-circuited to earth via the engine oil pressure switch. When the engine is stationary, this relay will not operate the fuel pump, but as soon as the engine is running it will supply current to the pump. The other relay operates in conjunction with the starter motor to operate the fuel pump for starting.

Fig. 13.41 Choke cam adjustment on the Weber 36 TLC carburettor (Sec 8)

1	*Hole*	*4*	*Cam*
2	*Roller*	*5*	*Peg on tool*
3	*Adjusting screw*	*6*	*Locknut*

Fig. 13.42 Fuel pump fitted to later automatic models (Sec 8)

1	*Electric fuel pump*	*3*	*Fuel filter*
2	*Cover*		

8.32 Loosening the air cleaner ducting screw – TU engine

8.33A Disconnect the crankshaft ventilation hoses from the valve cover ...

8.33B ... and the inlet manifold – TU engine

8.34A Release the spring clips ...

8.34B ... and remove the air cleaner element – TU engine

8.35 Fuel pump inlet hose (arrowed) – TU engine

8.36 Disconnecting the hose from the vacuum motor – TU engine

8.37A Disconnecting the inlet ...

8.37B ... and warm air hoses – TU engine

Air cleaner and element (TU engine) – removal and refitting

32   Loosen the screw and release the air cleaner ducting from the carburettor (photo).
33   Disconnect the crankcase ventilation hose (photos) from the valve cover and inlet manifold.
34   Release the spring clips, and lift the element and ducting from the body (photos).
35   Disconnect the fuel pump inlet hose, and release it from the clip on the ducting (photo).
36   Disconnect the hose from the vacuum motor (photo).
37   Disconnect the inlet and warm air hoses (photos).
38   Remove the special clip (photo), then lift the air cleaner and ducting from the mounting on the starter motor.
39   Refitting is a reversal of removal.

Fuel pump (TU engine) – removal and refitting

40   Remove the air cleaner body as previously described.
41   Disconnect the inlet and outlet hoses (photo).
42   Unscrew the bolts and remove the fuel pump and gasket (photos).
43   Refitting is a reversal of removal.

Carburettors (TU engine) – description

44   A number of different Weber and Solex carburettors are fitted to the TU series engines, and their specific applications are given in the Specifications at the beginning of this Supplement.
45   The adjustment and overhaul procedures are as given for similar carburettors in Chapter 3, unless described specifically in the following paragraphs.

Weber 32 IBSH 16 and 34 TLP 3 carburettors – idling adjustments

46   With the engine hot and idling, adjust the idle speed screw to obtain 750 rpm.
47   Adjust the mixture screw to obtain the specified CO reading or, if an exhaust gas analyser is not available, adjust the mixture screw to obtain the highest engine speed, then screw it in to lower the speed by 50 rpm.
48   Adjust the idling speed screw to obtain 700 rpm.

8.38 Special clip securing air cleaner ducting to ignition coil bracket – TU engine

Fig. 13.43 Idling speed screw location (1) on the Weber 32 IBSH carburettor (Sec 8)

Fig. 13.44 Idling mixture screw location (2) on the Weber 32 IBSH carburettor (Sec 8)

Weber 32 IBSH 16 and 34 TLP 3 carburettors – fast idle setting

49 With the carburettor removed, invert it then pull the choke lever fully on.
50 Using a twist drill, check that the gap between the throttle valve and barrel is 0.8 mm. If not, turn the adjustment screw (Fig. 13.45).

Solex 32 PBISA 16 carburettor – idling adjustments

51 Refer to Chapter 3, Section 10, but adjust the idling speed to 700 rpm.

Solex 32 PBISA 16 carburettor – choke opening after starting adjustment

52 Close the choke lap, then fully operate the pneumatic opener either manually or by vacuum.
53 Using a twist drill, check that the gap between the choke flap and barrel is 3.0 mm. If not, turn the adjusting screw in the end of the opener.

Solex 32 PBISA 16 carburettor – fast idle setting

54 The procedure is as described in paragraphs 49 and 50, although the adjustment screw is different.

Solex 32-34 Z2 carburettor cover – removal and refitting

55 Remove the air cleaner as previously described.
56 Disconnect the fuel inlet hose (photo).
57 Disconnect the choke inner cable from the choke lever (photo).
58 Remove the screws, and lift the cover from the main body (photos).
59 If necessary, extract the pivot pin and remove the float, needle valve, and gasket (photo).
60 Clean the main body (photo), then refit the cover using a reversal of the removal procedure. Renew the gasket if necessary.

Solex 32-34 Z2 carburettor – idling adjustments

61 Proceed as described in Chapter 3, Section 10, but adjust the idling speed to 750 rpm. The adjustment screw locations are shown in Fig. 13.46.

8.41 Disconnecting the fuel pump inlet hose – TU engine

8.42A Unbolt the fuel pump ...

8.42B ... and recover the gasket – TU engine

Fig. 13.45 Fast idle adjustment on the Weber 32 IBSH carburettor (Sec 8)

1   Choke lever fully on   a = 0.8 mm
2   Adjustment screw

Fig. 13.46 Idling speed (1) and mixture (2) adjustment screws – Solex 32-34 Z2 carburettor (Sec 8)

Carburettor modifications – TU9 and TU1 engines

62   Certain models may have a throttle damper assembly fitted, to the carburettor to prevent engine stalling during gearchanges.
63   The assembly is mounted on a modified throttle cable support bracket, and the components are shown in Fig. 13.47.
64   The assembly should not require any adjustment, but if the throttle is held open by the damper excessively during gearchanges, adjustment can be made by loosening the locknut (6) in Fig. 13.47, and altering the position of the damper (3) in the bracket (2) as necessary. Tighten the locknut on completion of adjustment.

Fuel vapour separator – TU9 and TU1 engines

65   Certain models may be fitted with a fuel vapour separator, which purges vapour from the carburettor fuel supply, thus improving hot starting.
66   The vapour separator is located in the fuel supply line between the fuel tank and the carburettor, and is mounted on a bracket attached to the battery tray.
67   A fuel return line from the vapour separator to the fuel tank is fitted under the car, next to the fuel supply line from the fuel tank.
68   When removing the fuel tank, both the fuel supply and return hoses must be disconnected from the pipes on the tank.

Inlet manifold (TU engine) – removal and refitting

69   Remove the air cleaner and carburettor.

8.56 Disconnecting the carburettor fuel inlet hose – Solex 32-34 Z2

8.57 Choke inner cable (arrowed) – Solex 32-34 Z2

8.58A Remove the screws ...

8.58B ... and lift off the cover – Solex 32-34 Z2

8.59 Carburettor cover with gasket in place – Solex 32-34 Z2

8.60 Carburettor main body with cover removed – Solex 32-34 Z2

Fig. 13.47 Carburettor throttle damper – TU9 and TU1 engines (Sec 8)

1	Bracket	4	Cam
2	Bracket	5	Steady bar
3	Damper	6	Locknut

70   Disconnect the brake servo vacuum hose (photo).
71   Drain the cooling system, then disconnect the hose from the bottom of the inlet manifold.
72   Unscrew the nuts and withdraw the inlet manifold from the studs on the cylinder head (photo). There is no gasket.
73   When refitting, thoroughly clean the mating surfaces, and apply a thin coat of jointing compound.
74   Refitting is a reversal of removal.

Exhaust manifold (TU engine) – removal and refitting
75   Disconnect the hot air hose from the exhaust manifold shroud.
76   Unbolt the shroud from the exhaust manifold (photo).
77   Unscrew the nuts securing the front downpipe to the exhaust manifold, and remove the metal gasket.
78   Unscrew the nuts, and withdraw the exhaust manifold from the studs on the cylinder head. Remove the gaskets (photos).

Exhaust system (TU engine) – general
79   The exhaust system is in three sections; the front downpipe, intermediate pipe and silencer, and tail pipe and silencer.
80   A ball-and-socket type joint is provided between the front and intermediate pipes, to allow for engine movement (photo).
81   The front pipe is supported by a bracket attached to the gearbox (photo). However, the rest of the exhaust system is supported by conventional rubber mountings.

Exhaust system (XY and XW engines) – general
82   On later XY8, XY7 and XW7 engines, the exhaust front downpipe is of 'siamesed' type instead of twin-pipe type, and is attached to the manifold by a single spherical joint.
83   On automatic transmission models, the front exhaust pipe incorporates a special silencer.

Unleaded fuel
84   Only the following models may be operated on unleaded fuel, and where applicable, the ignition timing **must** be retarded as shown with reference to Chapter 4:

Engine	Code	Retard ignition by:
XY7 from engine		
No 598051	150D	3°
TU9	C1A	None
TU9/K	C1A	None
TU9A	C1A	None
TU1	H1A	None
TU1/K	H1A	None
TU3	K1A	4°
TU3A	K1G	4°
TU3A/K	K1G	4°
TU3S	K2A	4°
TU3S/K	K2A	None
TU3.2/K	K2D	None
XU51C/K	B1F	None

8.70 Disconnecting the brake servo vacuum hose – TU engine

8.72 Unscrewing an inlet manifold nut – TU engine

8.76 Unbolting the exhaust manifold shroud – TU engine

8.78A Unscrew the nuts ...

8.78B ... and withdraw the exhaust manifold ...

8.78C ... and gaskets – TU engine

8.80 Ball-and-socket joint between exhaust front and intermediate pipes – TU engine

8.81 Exhaust front pipe support bracket – TU engine

9　Fuel and exhaust systems – fuel injection engines

PART A: GENERAL

Unleaded fuel

1　With the exception of the XU9JA engine (fitted to 1.9 GTI models without a catalytic converter), all engines can be operated on 95 RON unleaded petrol. The XU9JA engine should **not** be operated on 95 RON unleaded petrol.

2　No adjustments to the ignition timing are necessary in order to operate engines on 95 RON unleaded petrol, with the exception of the XU5J and XU5JA engines, which must both have the ignition timing retarded by 2° Refer to Chapter 4 for details of ignition timing adjustment.

3　**Do not** operate an engine equipped with a catalytic converter on leaded petrol. If a catalytic converter is fitted, unleaded petrol **must** be used at all times.

Engine	Code	Retard ignition by:
TU1M/Z	HDZ	None (95 or 97/98 RON unleaded)
TU1M/L	HDZ	None (95 or 97/98 RON unleaded)
TU3M/Z	KDY	None (95 or 97/98 RON unleaded)
TU3FM/L	KDY	None (95 or 97/98 RON unleaded)
XU5J	180A	2° (95 or 97/98 RON unleaded)
XU5JA	B6D	2° (95 or 97/98 RON unleaded)
XU5JA/K	B6E	None (95 or 97/98 RON unleaded)
XU5M3/Z	BDY	None (95 or 97/98 RON unleaded)
XU5M3/L	BDY	None (95 or 97/98 RON unleaded)
XU9JA/K	D6B	95 RON fuel cannot be used. Use only 97/98 RON (leaded or unleaded) fuel - no adjustment is then required
XU9JA/Z	DKZ	None (95 or 97/98 RON unleaded)
XU9JA/L	DKZ	None (95 or 97/98 RON unleaded)
XU9J1/Z	DFZ	None (95 or 97/98 RON unleaded)
XU9J1/L	DFZ	None (95 or 97/98 RON unleaded)

4　In the UK, the nearest equivalent to 95 RON unleaded fuel is 'Premium'-grade unleaded petrol. The nearest equivalent to 97/98 RON unleaded fuel is 'Super/Superplus'-grade unleaded petrol.

Fuel system – depressurising

Warning: *The following procedures will relieve the pressure in the fuel system – remember that fuel will still be present in the system components. Petrol is a highly-volatile substance, and adequate fire precautions must be taken whenever working on fuel system components.*

5　All of the fuel system components contain fuel, which will be under pressure when the engine is running and/or while the ignition is switched on.

6　The pressure will still be present for some time after the ignition has been switched off, and the pressure must be relieved before any of the fuel system components can be worked on.

7　To depressurise the system, remove either the fuel pump fuse or the fuel pump relay, and start the engine. Allow the engine to idle until it stops. Turn the engine over on the starter once or twice to ensure that all pressure is released, then switch off the ignition. Always disconnect the battery negative lead before carrying out work on the fuel system.

8　Do not forget to refit the fuse or relay, as applicable, when work is complete.

Air cleaner – removal, refitting and element renewal

9　Although there are significant differences in the appearance of the air cleaner components fitted to later fuel injection-engined models, air cleaner element renewal and air cleaner removal and refitting are essentially as described in the relevant Sections of Chapter 3. Note that procedures may be complicated by the presence of additional pipes, hoses, etc. (photos).

10　The air cleaner assembly fitted to fuel injection TU engines is similar to that described for carburettor models in Section 8 of this Supplement.

11　On some types of air cleaner, the end (or top) cover is retained by a number of spring clips. Ensure that the cover is correctly seated, to

9A.9A Removing the air cleaner ducting from top of throttle body and air cleaner – TU fuel injection engine

9A.9B Removing the air cleaner housing fastener – TU fuel injection engine

9A.9C Unclipping fuel hoses from top of air cleaner housing – TU fuel injection engine

9A.9D Disconnecting hot air hose from exhaust manifold shroud – TU fuel injection engine

9A.9E Removing the air cleaner housing – TU fuel injection engine

prevent air leaks, before fastening the clips on reassembly (photos).

12   If any hoses or pipes are disturbed during servicing work, ensure that they are reconnected securely and free from kinks.

Fuel pump – removal and refitting

13   Refer to Chapter 3, Section 24. If more than one fuel hose is connected to the pump housing, ensure that each hose is marked before disconnection to ensure correct refitting.

14   Although it should be possible to remove the pump after removing the cover under the rear seats, as described in Chapter 3, in some cases, the hole in the floor may not be aligned with the pump, in which case the fuel tank may need to be lowered for access (refer to Chapter 3, Section 8 for details).

Electronic control unit (ECU) – removal and refitting

15   Disconnect the battery negative lead.

16   The ECU is located behind the facia, to the right of the steering column.

17   For improved access, remove the driver's side lower facia panel. The panel is secured by four screws, and a single bolt (photos).

18   Remove the nuts securing the ECU bracket to the facia, then lower the assembly. Withdraw the ECU from the bracket (photos).

19   Release the securing clip, or remove the securing screws, as applicable, and disconnect the wiring plug (photo).

20   Refitting is a reversal of removal, but ensure that the wiring plug is securely reconnected, and where applicable, ensure that the ECU locates correctly in the bracket.

9A.11A When refitting the air cleaner element and cover ...

9A.11B ... arrows on cover and casing should be aligned – TU fuel injection engine

9A.17A Driver's side lower facia panel securing bolt (arrowed)

9A.17B Removing the driver's side lower facia panel

9A.18A ECU bracket securing nut (arrowed)

9A.18B Removing the ECU from its bracket. Note securing lug (arrowed)

9A.19 Disconnecting the ECU wiring plug

9A.24 Catalytic converter (arrowed) – TU3F engine model

Fuel injection system fuses and relays – general

21 The relays are generally mounted on the left-hand side of the engine compartment bulkhead. The relays may be mounted on individual brackets, or on later models, in a plastic box.

22 Most of the fuses are located in the main fusebox inside the car, although on certain models, additional fuses may be located in a small fusebox mounted at the front left-hand corner of the engine compartment.

23 The number and type of fuses and relays fitted will depend on the type of fuel injection system fitted.

Exhaust system and catalytic converter – general

24 The catalytic converter is an integral part of the exhaust system, although the system configuration and the type of fittings and clamps used varies depending on model (photo).

25 Removal and refitting of all components is essentially as described in Chapter 3, Sections 16 and 30, but where applicable, ensure that the oxygen sensor wiring plug is disconnected before removing the downpipe.

PART B: LE2-JETRONIC SYSTEM (XU5J, XU5JA AND XU9JA ENGINES)

Idle speed and mixture (XU5JA and XU9JA engines) – adjustment

1 The procedure is as given in Chapter 3, Section 21, with the following amendments:

(a)   In paragraph 3 adjust the idling speed to 600 rpm
(b)   In paragraph 5 unscrew the air screw to set the idling speed to 900 rpm
(c)   In paragraph 6 check that the CO reading is 1%

Throttle switch (XU5JA and XU9JA engines) – checking and adjustment

2 The procedure is as given in Chapter 3, Section 22, with the following amendment:

The feeler blade described in paragraph 5 is not used. Fig. 3.13 therefore only applies to the 0.70 mm (0.028 in) feeler blade described in paragraph 8. The procedure given in paragraphs 6 and 7 is still applicable.

Tachometric relay (XU5JA and XU9JA engines) – revised location

3 From chassis no 7 900 001, the tachometric relay has been relocated on the facia, near the injection control unit.

Fuel pump (XU5JA and XU9JA engines) – modifications

4 From chassis No 24 293 700, a new type of fuel pump has been fitted.

5 The previous type of fuel pump is no longer supplied, and if the fuel pump on an earlier model is being renewed, the later-type pump must be fitted.

6 A sealed wiring connector (available from a Peugeot dealer) must be fitted to the original fuel pump wiring harness, to enable connection to the later-type pump.

Component removal and refitting (LE2-Jetronic system)
Fuel injectors
Note: *Ensure that the working area is clean before removing the injectors, and ensure that no dirt is allowed to enter the system during the procedure. No attempt should be made to overhaul the injectors. If a fault or contamination is suspected, seek specialist advice.*

7 Depressurise the fuel system, as described in Part A of this Section.

8 Disconnect the battery negative lead.

9 Disconnect the wiring plugs from the fuel injectors, labelling them if necessary to ensure correct refitting.

10 Disconnect the vacuum hose from the top of the fuel pressure regulator.

11 Unscrew the four bolts securing the fuel rail to the inlet manifold (two upper bolts, and two bolts at the right-hand end of the rail), then carefully lift the rail, complete with pressure regulator and fuel injectors, from the inlet manifold, taking care not to strain any of the hoses or pipes.

12 To remove a fuel injector from the fuel rail, carefully remove the metal securing clip, then pull the injector from the rail. Be prepared for fuel spillage, and take adequate fire precautions.

13 Refitting is a reversal of removal, but fit new injector O-rings.

Fuel pressure regulator

Note: *Ensure that no dirt is allowed to enter the fuel system during this procedure.*

14 For improved access to the lower pressure regulator securing nut, proceed as described in paragraphs 10 and 11.

15 If not already done, disconnect the vacuum hose from the top of the pressure regulator.

16 Slacken the hose clip, and disconnect the fuel return hose from the bottom of the pressure regulator. Be prepared for fuel spillage, and take adequate fire precautions.

17 Unscrew the two bolts securing the pressure regulator to the fuel rail bracket assembly, whilst counterholding the nuts. Note that on some models, a hose bracket is secured by the upper bolt.

18 Pull the regulator from the end of the fuel rail, and recover the O-ring.

19 Refitting is a reversal of removal, but use a new O-ring when refitting the pressure regulator to the fuel rail, and where applicable, use new injector O-rings.

Coolant temperature sensor

20 Disconnect the battery negative lead.

21 Drain the cooling system as described in Chapter 2.

22 For improved access, remove the distributor cap, with reference to Chapter 4.

23 Release the securing clip and disconnect the wiring plug from the sensor.

24 Unscrew the sensor from the cylinder head.

25 Refitting is a reversal of removal, but refill the cooling system as described in Chapter 2.

Throttle position switch

26 Disconnect the battery negative lead.

27 Release the securing clip and disconnect the wiring plug from the switch.

28 Remove the two securing screws, then withdraw the switch from the throttle body.

29 Refitting is a reversal of removal, but on completion, adjust the switch as described in Chapter 3, Section 22.

Throttle body

30 Disconnect the battery negative lead.

31 Release the securing clip, and disconnect the wiring plug from the throttle position switch.

32 Loosen the securing clamp, and disconnect the air trunking from the front of the throttle body.

33 Disconnect the throttle cable, with reference to Chapter 3.

34 Disconnect the vacuum and/or breather hoses from the throttle body, noting their locations to ensure correct refitting.

35 Unscrew the three throttle body securing nuts, and recover the washers. Remove the throttle cable bracket from the top throttle body securing stud, noting its orientation.

36 Withdraw the throttle body from the inlet manifold.

37 Refitting is a reversal of removal, bearing in mind the following points.

 (a) Ensure that the vacuum and/or breather hoses are correctly reconnected, as noted before removal.
 (b) After refitting the throttle body, check the adjustment of the throttle cable, as described in Chapter 3.
 (c) On completion, if any work has been carried out on the throttle body, check the adjustment of the throttle switch, as described in Chapter 3, Section 22.

Fault diagnosis – LE2-Jetronic system

38 Should the engine cut out intermittently or be difficult to start when hot, check that the fuel pump fuse is correctly fitted in its holder, and that the terminals are clean.

39 Fouling of the injector nozzles can cause misfiring and stalling. Where this occurs on an engine which is in good mechanical condition and tuned correctly, the injectors can be cleaned by adding a special

cleaning fluid to the fuel tank. Suitable cleaning fluid can be obtained from Peugeot dealers, or products such as Holts Redex Injector Treatment can be found in motor accessory shops.

PART C: BOSCH LU2-JETRONIC SYSTEM (XU9J1/Z AND XU9J1/L ENGINES)

LU2-Jetronic fuel injection system – general description and precautions

1 The principle of operation of the LU2-Jetronic system is similar to that described for the LE2-Jetronic system described in Chapter 3, Section 17. The only significant difference is that the LU2-Jetronic system incorporates an oxygen sensor in the exhaust system: this enables the electronic control unit to carry out fine fuel mixture adjustment, to allow the use of a catalytic converter.

2 Refer to Chapter 3, Section 17 for precautions to be observed when working on the system components.

Throttle initial position (LU2-Jetronic system) – checking and adjustment

3 The throttle initial position is set in production, and will not normally require adjustment unless the throttle housing has been tampered with. Adjustment should be entrusted to a Peugeot dealer.

Idle speed and mixture (LU2-Jetronic system) – adjustment

4 Before attempting to adjust the idle speed, the following conditions must be met.

 (a) The spark plugs and air cleaner element must be in good condition.
 (b) The throttle initial position and the throttle switch must be correctly adjusted.
 (c) The engine must be at normal operating temperature, but the cooling fan must not be operating.

Fig. 13.48 Idle speed adjustment screw (7) on LU2-Jetronic fuel injection engine (Sec 9C)

Fig. 13.49 Throttle switch and terminal numbers – LU2-Jetronic fuel injection system (Sec 9C)

5   Connect a tachometer to the engine in accordance with the equipment manufacturer's instructions, then run the engine at idle speed.
6   Turn the idle speed adjustment screw (7) in Fig. 13.48, to obtain the specified idle speed (see Specifications).
7   The idle mixture is not adjustable, being automatically regulated by the electronic control unit according to signals provided by the oxygen sensor.
8   Stop the engine and disconnect the tachometer on completion.

Throttle switch (LU2-Jetronic system) – checking and adjustment
9   The throttle initial position must be correctly adjusted before attempting to adjust the throttle switch.
10   Slacken the throttle switch securing screws.
11   Turn the switch unit fully clockwise, then turn it slowly back until the idling contacts are heard to close.
12   Tighten the securing screws.
13   Pull the wiring from the switch, then connect an ohmmeter between terminals 2 and 18 in the switch – see Fig. 13.49. The ohmmeter should read zero.
14   Operate the throttle linkage, and the ohmmeter should read infinity.
15   If the readings are not correct, repeat the procedure described in paragraphs 10 to 14 inclusive.
16   Connect the ohmmeter between switch terminals 3 and 18. The ohmmeter should read infinity.
17   Fully open the throttle, and the ohmmeter should read zero.
18   If the specified readings cannot be obtained, renew the switch.
19   Reconnect the switch wiring plug on completion.

Air intake system (LU2-Jetronic system) – checking for leaks
20   Follow the procedure given in Chapter 3, Section 23.

Component removal and refitting (LU2-Jetronic system)
General
21   The removal and refitting of all components is as described in Chapter 3, and Part B of this Section for the LE2-Jetronic system. To remove the oxygen sensor, proceed as follows.

Oxygen sensor
22   The sensor is located in the exhaust downpipe. When handling the sensor, note that it is fragile; take care not to drop it, and do not allow it to contact fuel or silicone substances.
23   Start the engine and run it until it reaches normal operating temperature, then switch it off and disconnect the battery negative lead.
24   If access is required from below, jack up the front of the car and support it securely on axle stands.
25   Release the securing clips, and separate the two halves of the sensor wiring connector.

26   Using a suitable spanner, and wearing heavy gloves as protection against the hot exhaust system and sensor, unscrew the sensor and withdraw it from the exhaust downpipe.
27   Refitting is a reversal of removal, bearing in mind the following points.

(a)   Apply anti-seize compound to the threads of the sensor.
(b)   The sensor must be tightened securely; this will required the use of either a spanner, or a deep socket, slotted to allow for the sensor wiring.

Fuel injection system (LU2-Jetronic system) – complete test
28   Follow the procedure given in Chapter 3, Section 26 for the LE2-Jetronic system.

Fault diagnosis – LU2-Jetronic system
29   Refer to Chapter 3, Section 31, and Part B of this Section.

PART D: BOSCH MOTRONIC M1.3 SYSTEM (XU9JA/Z AND XU9JA/L ENGINES)

Motronic M1.3 fuel injection system – general description and precautions
1   The Bosch Motronic fuel injection system is used to provide the fine degree of engine control necessary for operation with a catalytic converter. The system is under the overall control of the Motronic M1.3 engine management system, which also controls the ignition timing.
2   The principle of operation of the system is similar to that described for the LE2-Jetronic system in Chapter 3, Section 17, noting the following differences.

(a)   A double-barrel throttle housing is used, with two throttle valves operate simultaneously.
(b)   An oxygen sensor is fitted to the exhaust system, which allows fine mixture adjustment, to enable the use of a catalytic converter.
(c)   A TDC sensor is used, to provide the electronic control unit with information on crankshaft speed and position.

3   Refer to Chapter 3, Section 17 for precautions to be observed when working on the system components.

Throttle initial position (Motronic M1.3 system) – checking and adjustment
4   The throttle initial position is set in production, and will not normally require adjustment unless the throttle housing has been tampered with. Adjustment requires the use of Peugeot special tools, and should be carried out by a suitable-equipped Peugeot dealer.

Idle speed and mixture (Motronic M1.3 system) – adjustment
5   Proceed as described for the LU2-Jetronic system in Part C of this Section.

Throttle switch (Motronic M1-3 system) – checking and adjustment
6   Proceed as described for the LU2-Jetronic system in Part C of this Section.

Air intake system (Motronic M1.3 system) – checking for leaks
7   Follow the procedure given in Chapter 3, Section 23, but check for leakage at the points arrowed in Fig. 13.50.

Component removal and refitting (Motronic M1.3 system)
8   Although some of the components differ in detail, removal and refitting is basically as described in Chapter 3, and Part B of this Section (LE2-Jetronic system).
9   Removal and refitting of the TDC sensor is as described in Chapter 4, Section 9.

Fig. 13.50 Areas (arrowed) for checking air intake leakage – Motronic M1.3 fuel injection system (left-hand-drive model shown) (Sec 9D)

1	Airflow sensor	5	Crankcase breather hoses
2	Cylinder head	6	Air intake hose
3	Air distribution manifold		

8	Throttle housing	10	Injectors
9	Fuel pressure regulator	11	Brake servo vacuum hose

10   For details of oxygen sensor removal and refitting, refer to paragraphs 22 to 27 of Part C of this Section.

Fuel injection system (Motronic M1.3) – complete test
11   Due to the need for specialist test equipment to carry out accurate fault diagnosis, any fault occurring with the Motronic system should be referred to a Peugeot dealer. Before doing this, however, make sure that the problem is not being caused by a disconnected or damaged hose or vacuum line, loose or disconnected wiring plug, or by some other simple fault which may be obvious under close visual inspection.

Fault diagnosis – Motronic M1.3 system
12   Refer to Part B of this Section, paragraphs 38 and 39.

PART E: BOSCH MONO-JETRONIC A2.2 SYSTEM (TU1M/Z, TU3M/Z AND TU3FM/L ENGINES)

Mono-Jetronic A2.2 system – general description and precautions
1   The Mono-Jetronic A2.2 system is a single-point fuel injection system, incorporating a catalytic converter in the exhaust system.
2   The fuel pump, located in the fuel tank, pumps the fuel through a filter to the single fuel injector. The electronic control unit, which is triggered by the ignition circuit, sends impulses to the injector, which sprays fuel upstream of the throttle valve. A constant fuel pressure is maintained by a fuel pressure regulator, which returns excess fuel to the fuel tank. The electronic control unit also receives information from

various sensors to determine engine temperature, speed and load, and the quality of air entering the engine. The sensors inform the electronic control unit (ECU) of throttle position, intake air temperature, coolant temperature, and exhaust gas oxygen content. Engine speed and crankshaft position information is provided by the distributor. All the information supplied to the ECU is computed and compared with pre-set values stored in the module memory, to determine the required period of injection. The injector operates four times per engine cycle, and the injector opening duration is varied to control the quantity of fuel delivered.

3   The ECU constantly varies the fuel mixture and engine idle speed to provide optimum engine efficiency under all operating conditions, and to reduce exhaust gas emissions. The mixture strength is accurately controlled to maintain it within the operating limits of the catalytic converter.

4   The following paragraphs describe procedures which can be carried out by the home mechanic. Work involving the use of special test equipment is not included.

5   Refer to Chapter 3, Section 17 for precautions to be observed when working on the system components.

Idle speed and mixture (Mono-Jetronic A2.2 system) – adjustment

6   The idle speed and mixture are not adjustable, being automatically regulated by the ECU according to the signals provided by the various sensors.

7   If a fault is suspected, check the following before assuming that there is a problem with the system:

Check that the spark plugs (Chapter 4) and air cleaner (Part A of this Section) are in good condition.
Check that the engine breather and vacuum hoses are undamaged and free from obstructions.
Check that there are no leaks in the air intake system.
Check the valve clearances (Section 6 of this Chapter).
Check the compression pressures (Chapter 1).
Check that the fuel filter has been renewed at the recommended intervals, and renew if necessary.
Check that the exhaust system is free from leaks.
Check that the throttle cable is correctly adjusted (Chapter 3).

8   If all the above checks reveal no faults, and a fault in the fuel injection system is still suspected, consult a Peugeot dealer, who will have access to the necessary specialist diagnostic equipment.

Throttle switch (Mono-Jetronic A2.2 system) – checking and adjustment

9   The throttle switch is accurately matched on the throttle valve during manufacture, and is not adjustable.

Fig. 13.51 Areas (arrowed) for checking air intake leakage – Mono-Jetronic A2.2 system (left-hand-drive model shown) (Sec 9E)

1   *Throttle body*   2   *Cylinder head*   5   *Crankcase breather hose*   7   *Air cleaner*

9E.12 Fuel filter location – Mono-Jetronic A2.2 system

10   **Note: *Do not*** attempt to adjust the throttle switch setting, or that of the stop screw on the throttle valve external linkage; if the accurately-matched relationship between these components is lost, the components must be replaced. At the time of writing, this means renewing the **entire** throttle body assembly.

Air intake system (Mono-Jetronic A2.2 system) – checking for leaks

11   Follow the procedure given in Chapter 3, Section 23, but check for leakage at the points arrowed in Fig. 13.51.

Component removal and refitting (Mono-Jetronic A2.2 system)

Note: For details of removal, refitting and servicing of components such as the air cleaner, throttle cable, fuel pump, fuel level transmitter, fuel tank, the ECU, and the manifolds and exhaust systems, refer to Chapter 3 and Part A of this Section.

Fuel filter

12   The filter is located at the rear right-hand corner of the engine compartment (photo).
13   Depressurise the fuel system (Part A of this Section), then disconnect the battery negative lead.
14   Place wads of rag around the filter, to catch any fuel released during the following procedure. Take adequate fire precautions.
15   Release the clamps, then disconnect the fuel hoses from the filter. Plug the open ends of the hoses, to prevent dirt ingress and further fuel leakage. Label the hoses so that they can be reconnected correctly.
16   Release the filter from its clamp and withdraw it.
17   Refitting is the reverse of the removal procedure, noting the following points:

(a)   Ensure that the filter is positioned with the arrow marked on the casing (indicating direction of fuel flow) pointing upwards, and

with the feed hose to the throttle body connected to the filter upper union.

(b)   If necessary, use new clamps to secure the hose connections.
(c)   Start the engine and check carefully for signs of fuel leakage from any of the disturbed components. Rectify any leaks without delay.
(d)   Dispose of the old filter safely – it will still contain traces of petrol and vapour, and should be handled accordingly.

Fuel pressure regulator

18   The fuel pressure regulator (consisting of a valve operated by a spring-loaded diaphragm and a metal cover) is secured by four screws to the top of the throttle body (photo). Although the unit can be dismantled for cleaning, if required (once the air intake trunking and the fuel injector wiring clip have been removed for access), it should not be disturbed unless absolutely necessary.
19   Note that the regulator assembly is only available as part of the complete throttle body assembly; no individual components can be renewed separately.
20   Always depressurise the fuel system (Part A of this Section) before disturbing any components. If the regulator cover is removed, note its orientation on the throttle body before removal, to ensure correct refitting.

Fuel injector

Note: If a faulty injector is suspected, before condemning the injector, it is worth trying the effect of one of the proprietary injector-cleaning treatments such as Holts Redex Injector Treatment. If this fails, the vehicle should be taken to a Peugeot dealer for testing using the appropriate specialist equipment.

21   Depressurise the fuel system (Part A of this Section).
22   Disconnect the battery negative lead.
23   Remove the air intake trunking from the top of the throttle body.
24   Remove the Torx screws securing the injector wiring connector to the top of the throttle body, then carefully lift off the connector (photos).
25   Withdraw the injector (photo). Recover and discard the injector sealing rings.
26   Refitting is the reverse of the removal procedure, noting the following points.

(a)   Always renew both sealing rings: apply a smear of grease to each ring, to ease injector refitting.
(b)   Ensure that the injector is refitted so that its connector pins align with the connector when the connector is correctly located on the top of the throttle body.
(c)   Before refitting the injector securing screw, apply a few drops of a suitable thread-locking compound to the threads.
(d)   On completion, switch on the ignition and check carefully for signs of fuel leaks; if any signs of leakage are detected, the problem must be rectified before the engine is started.

Intake air temperature sensor

27   The sensor is located in the fuel injector wiring connector, and is available only as part of the connector assembly. To remove the connector assembly, proceed as follows.
28   Remove the air trunking from the top of the throttle body, then unscrew the three securing nuts, and remove the sealing ring. Recover the O-ring (photos).

9E.18 Fuel injector wiring clip (A), and fuel pressure regulator securing screws (B) – Mono-Jetronic A2.2 system

9E.24A Remove the Torx screw ...

9E.24B ... and lift off the wiring connector – Mono-Jetronic A2.2 system

9E.25 Withdrawing the fuel injector –
Mono-Jetronic A2.2 system

9E.28A Remove the sealing ring ...

9E.28B ... and recover the O-ring –
Mono-Jetronic A2.2 system

9E.29A Separate the two halves of fuel
injector wiring connector ...

9E.29B ... then release wiring from clip –
Mono-Jetronic A2.2 system

29   Release the securing clips, separate the two halves of the fuel
injector wiring connector, then release the wiring from the clip on the
top of the throttle body (photos).
30   Remove the Torx screw securing the fuel injector wiring connector
to the top of the throttle body, then carefully lift off the connector
(photo).

Idle speed control motor
31   Disconnect the battery negative lead.
32   Release the securing clip, and disconnect the wiring plug from the
motor (photo).
33   Unscrew the securing screws, and withdraw the motor from the
throttle body assembly (photo).
34   Refitting is the reverse of the removal procedure. Note that the
motor will reset itself as soon as the engine is restarted.

Throttle switch
35   As noted previously, this component must not be disturbed, and is
available only as part of the complete throttle body assembly.

Throttle body
36   Depressurise the fuel system (Part A of this Section).
37   Remove the air intake trunking from the top of the throttle body.
38   Disconnect the battery negative lead.
39   Disconnect the throttle cable (Chapter 3).
40   Release the securing clips, and disconnect the wiring plugs from
the fuel injector, the idle speed control motor, and the throttle switch
(photos).
41   Disconnect the fuel hoses from the unions on the throttle body.
Plug the open ends of the hoses, to prevent dirt ingress and further fuel
loss. Take note of the connections, and label them to ensure correct
refitting. Be prepared for fuel spillage, and take suitable safety precautions.
42   Disconnect the vacuum hoses and pipes from the throttle body
unions (photo). Label the hoses and pipes so that they can be correctly
reconnected on refitting.
43   Remove the screws securing the throttle body to the inlet manifold, then withdraw the assembly (photo). Recover the gasket, and
discard it.

9E.30 Intake air temperature sensor
(arrowed) – Mono-Jetronic A2.2 system

9E.32 Disconnecting wiring plug from idle
speed control motor (arrowed) –
Mono-Jetronic A2.2 system

9E.33 Unscrewing an idle speed control
motor securing screw – Mono-Jetronic A2.2
system

Fig. 13.52 Idle speed control motor (1) and throttle switch (2) – **Mono-Jetronic A2.2 system (Sec 9E)**

9E.39A Disconnecting the wiring plug from the fuel injector ...

9E.39B ... and the throttle switch – Mono-Jetronic A2.2 system

9E.41 Vacuum hose connection to throttle body (arrowed) – Mono-Jetronic A2.2 system

9E.42 Throttle body securing screws (arrowed) – Mono-Jetronic A2.2 system

9E.44 Fuel flow direction markings on throttle body – Mono-Jetronic A2.2 system

9E.46 Disconnecting the wiring from the coolant temperature sensor – Mono-Jetronic A2.2 system

9E.48 Oxygen sensor location (arrowed) in exhaust downpipe – Mono-Jetronic A2.2 system

44   If desired, the throttle body upper and lower sections may be separated by removing the securing screws. Note that a new gasket must be fitted on reassembly. As noted previously, **do not** disturb the throttle switch. The fuel inlet and return unions may be unscrewed from the throttle body, and the vacuum hose unions may be detached, but note that new sealing rings must be fitted on reassembly.
45   Refitting is the reverse of the removal procedure, noting the following points.

   (a) *Renew all gaskets and seals, and use suitable thread-locking compound where applicable.*
   (b) *Check the throttle cable operation and adjustment (Chapter 3).*
   (c) *Ensure that all vacuum hoses and pipes are correctly reconnected, as noted before removal.*
   (d) *Ensure that the fuel hoses are correctly reconnected. The direction of fuel flow is indicated by arrows cast into the throttle body next to each union (photo).*
   (e) *On completion, switch on the ignition, and check for signs of fuel leaks from all disturbed unions. If any signs of leakage are detected, the problem must be rectified before the engine is started.*

Coolant temperature sensor
46   The sensor is screwed into the left-hand end of the cylinder head.
47   To remove the sensor, partially drain the cooling system, then disconnect the wiring from the sensor (photo), and unscrew and remove the sensor.
48   When refitting the switch, ensure that the seal is in good condition, and take care not to overtighten the switch.

Oxygen sensor
49   The procedure is as described in Part C (paragraphs 22 to 27) of this Section (photo).

Fuel injection system (Mono-Jetronic A2.2) – complete test
50   Refer to Part D of this Section, paragraph 11.

Fault diagnosis – Mono-Jetronic A2.2 system
51   Refer to Part B of this Section, paragraphs 38 and 39.

PART F: MMFD MONO-POINT SYSTEMS G5 (XU5M2/Z ENGINE) AND G6 (TU1M/L, XU5M3/Z AND XU5M3/L ENGINES)

MMFD Mono-point G5 and G6 systems – general description and precautions
1   The Mono-point G5 and G6 systems are single-point fuel injection

systems, incorporating a catalytic converter in the exhaust system. The only difference between the two systems is that the idle speed is controlled via a control valve on the G5 system, and via a control motor on the G6 system. The system is under the overall control of an electronic control unit (ECU), which also controls the ignition system.
2   The fuel pump, located in the fuel tank, pumps the fuel through a filter to the single fuel injector. The electronic control unit sends impulses to the injector, which sprays fuel upstream of the throttle valve. A constant fuel pressure is maintained by the fuel pressure regulator, which returns excess fuel to the fuel tank. The electronic control unit receives information from various sensors to determine engine temperature, speed and load, and the quantity of air entering the engine. The sensors inform the ECU of the throttle position, crankshaft speed/position, intake air temperature, coolant temperature, inlet manifold pressure, and exhaust gas oxygen content. All the information supplied to the ECU is computed and compared with pre-set values stored in the module memory, to determine the required period of injection.
3   The ECU constantly varies the fuel mixture, engine idle speed, and ignition timing, to provide optimum engine efficiency under all operating conditions, and to reduce exhaust gas emissions. The mixture strength is accurately controlled, to maintain it within the operating limits of the catalytic converter.
4   The following paragraphs describe procedures which can be carried out by the home mechanic. Work involving the use of special test equipment is not included.

Idle speed and mixture (MMFD Mono-point G5 and G6 systems) – adjustment
5   The idle speed and mixture are not adjustable, being automatically regulated by the ECU according to the signals provided by the various sensors. The idle speed is controlled by the idle speed control valve of the G5 system, or by the idle speed control motor on the G6 system.
6   If a fault is suspected, check the following before assuming that there is a problem with the system:

   Check that the spark plugs (Chapter 4) and air cleaner (Part A of this Section) are in good condition.
   Check that the engine breather and vacuum hoses are undamaged and free from obstructions.
   Check that there are no leaks in the air intake system.
   Check the valve clearances (Chapter 1, or Section 6 of this Chapter, as applicable).
   Check the compression pressures (Chapter 1).
   Check that the fuel filter has been renewed at the recommended intervals, and renew if necessary.
   Check that the exhaust system is free from leaks.
   Check that the throttle cable is correctly adjusted (Chapter 3).

7   If all the above checks reveal no faults, and a fault in the fuel injection system is still suspected, consult a Peugeot dealer, who will have access to the necessary specialist diagnostic equipment.

Throttle settings (MMFD Mono-point G5 and G6 systems) – general
Note: *Do not attempt to adjust the throttle switch setting, or that of the stop screw on the throttle valve external linkage.*
8   The throttle valve is set in production, and must **not** be disturbed. Remember that the valve opening at idle is a basic setting only, as the idle speed is controlled by the idle speed control valve (or motor, as applicable).
9   The throttle switch cannot be adjusted.

Air intake system (MMFD Mono-point G5 and G6 systems) – checking for leaks
10   Follow the procedure given in Chapter 3, Section 23, but refer to Fig. 13.51 for guidance as to the areas which require special attention.

Component removal and refitting (MMFD Mono-point G5 and G6 systems)
Note: *For details of removal, refitting and servicing of components such as the air cleaner, throttle cable, fuel pump, fuel level transmitter, fuel tank, the ECU, and the manifolds and exhaust systems, refer to Chapter and part A of this Section.*

Fuel filter
11   The procedure is as described in Part E of this Section, paragraphs 12 to 17.

9F.12 Fuel pressure regulator (A) and fuel injector wiring plug (B) – MMFD G6 system

9F.19 Fuel injector retaining plate securing screw (arrowed) – MMFD G6 system

Fuel pressure regulator

12   The fuel pressure regulator (consisting of a valve operated by a spring-loaded diaphragm and a metal cover) is secured by four screws to the top of the throttle body (photo). Although the unit can be dismantled for cleaning, if required (once the air intake trunking has been removed for access), it should not be disturbed unless absolutely necessary.

13   Note that the regulator assembly is available only as part of the complete throttle body assembly; no individual components can be renewed separately.

14   Always depressurise the fuel system (Part A of this Section) before disturbing any components. If the regulator is removed, note its orientation on the throttle body before removal, to ensure correct refitting.

Fuel injector

Note: *If a faulty injector is suspected, before condemning the injector, it is worth trying the effect of one of the proprietary injector-cleaning treatments, such as Holts Redex Injector Treatment. If this fails, the vehicle should be taken to a Peugeot dealer for testing using the appropriate specialist equipment. Note that (at the time of writing), the injector does not appear to be available separately from the throttle body upper section assembly.*

15   Depressurise the fuel system (Part A of this Section).

16   Disconnect the battery negative lead.

17   Remove the air intake trunking from the top of the throttle body.

18   Release the securing clip, and disconnect the injector wiring plug.

19   Remove the Torx screw securing the injector retainer plate to the top of the throttle body (photo), lift off the retainer, then withdraw the injector. Recover and discard the injector sealing rings (check to ensure that new sealing rings can be obtained before discarding the old ones).

20   Refitting is the reverse of the removal procedure, noting the following points.

(a)   *Always renew both sealing rings (see text); apply a smear of grease to each, to ease injector refitting.*

(b)   *Refit the injector so that it wiring termninals point towards the front of the vehicle, and locate the edge of the retainer securely in the groove at the top of the injector.*

(c)   *Before refitting the injector securing screw, apply a few drops of a suitable thread-locking compound to the threads.*

(d)   *On completion, switch on the ignition, and check carefully for signs of fuel leaks; if any signs of leakage are detected, the problem must be rectified before the engine is started.*

Throttle switch

21   Disconnect the battery negative lead.

22   Disconnect the wiring plug, and disconnect the wiring plug from the switch.

23   Remove the two securing screws and withdraw the switch.

24   Refitting is a reversal of removal, noting the following points.

(a)   *Before refitting the switch, ensure that the throttle valve is fully closed.*

(b)   *Ensure that the switch wiper engages correctly with the throttle shaft.*

Idle speed control valve (MMFD G5 system)

25   For improved access, remove the air cleaner trunking.

26   Disconnect the battery negative lead.

27   Release the securing clip, and disconnect the wiring plug from the valve.

28   Loosen the securing clamps, and disconnect the air hoses from the valve. Note the locations of the hoses to ensure correct refitting.

29   Remove the securing screws, and withdraw the valve.

30   Refitting is a reversal of removal, noting that the arrows cast on the valve unions indicate the direction of airflow through the valve. Ensure that the hoses are securely refitted, to prevent air leaks.

Idle speed control motor (MMFD G6 system)

Note: *At the time of writing, it was not clear whether the motor is available separately from the throttle body assembly. It is advisable to seek the advice of a Peugeot dealer before deciding on the course of action to be followed of the stepper motor is thought to be faulty.*

31   For improved access, remove the air intake trunking.

32   Disconnect the battery negative lead.

33   Release the securing clip, and disconnect the wiring plug from the motor.

34   Remove the two securing screws, then withdraw the motor. Recover and discard the sealing ring (check to ensure that a new sealing ring can be obtained before discarding the old one).

35   Refitting is a reversal of removal bearing in mind the following points.

(a)   *Always fit a new sealing ring (see note above), greasing it lightly to ease installation.*

(b)   *The control motor will be reset by the ECU as soon as the engine is restarted.*

(c)   *Apply suitable thread-locking compound to the securing screw threads before refitting.*

Intake air temperature sensor

36   The sensor is screwed into the top of the inlet manifold.

37   Disconnect the battery negative lead.

38   Release the securing clip, and disconnect the wiring plug from the sensor.

39   Unscrew the sensor and withdraw it.

40   Refitting is a reversal of removal.

Throttle body

41   Depressurize the fuel system (refer to Part A of this Section).

42   Disconnect the battery negative lead.

43   Remove the air intake trunking from the top of the throttle body.

44   Disconnect the throttle cable (see Chapter 3).

45   Release the securing clips, then disconnect the wiring plugs from the fuel injector (remove the rubber throttle body/trunking seals to release the wiring), throttle switch, and the idle speed control motor (MMFD G6 system only).

**Fig. 13.53 MMFD G6 fuel injection system throttle body assembly
(Sec 9F)**

1 *Fuel injector wiring connector*	3 *Idle speed control motor*
2 *Fuel pressure regulator*	4 *Throttle switch*

46   Disconnect the fuel hoses from the unions on the throttle body,
labelling the hoses to ensure correct refitting. Be prepared for fuel
spillage, and take adequate fire precautions. Plug the open ends of the
hoses, to prevent dirt ingress and further loss of fuel.
47   Disconnect the vacuum pipes and hoses from the throttle body
unions. Label the hoses so that they can be correctly reconnected.
48   Unscrew the studs securing the throttle body to the inlet manifold,
and withdraw the assembly. Recover and discard the gasket.
49   If desired, the two halves of the throttle body (upper and lower)
can be separated by removing the securing screws. Note that in this
case, a new gasket must be used on reassembly.
50   Refitting is a reversal of removal, bearing in mind the following
points.

(a)   *Renew all disturbed gaskets and seals, and use suitable thread-
locking compound where necessary.*
(b)   *Check the throttle cable operation and adjustment (Chapter 3).*
(c)   *Ensure that all vacuum hoses and pipes are correctly reconnected as noted before removal.*
(d)   *When reconnecting the manifold absolute pressure sensor hose,
ensure that it is routed so that it falls steadily from the sensor to
the throttle body. This is necessary to prevent any fuel droplets
from entering the sensor (no fuel vapour trap is fitted), allowing
them to drain into the throttle body instead.*
(e)   *Ensure that the fuel hoses are correctly reconnected, as noted
before removal.*
(f)   *On completion, switch on the ignition, and check carefully for
signs of fuel leakage from all disturbed unions. If any signs of
leakage are detected, the problem must be rectified before the
engine is started.*

Manifold absolute pressure sensor
51   Disconnect the battery negative lead.
52   Release the securing clip, and disconnect the wiring plug from the
idle speed control motor (G6 systems only).
53   Slacken the clamp (if fitted), and disconnect the vacuum hose from
the sensor.
54   Remove the securing screws and withdraw the sensor, complete
with bracket, from the body front panel (or wing panel, as applicable).
55   Refitting is a reversal of removal, but note the following. When
reconnecting the vacuum hose to the sensor, ensure that the hose is
routed so that it falls steadily from the sensor to the throttle body. This is
necessary to prevent any fuel droplets from entering the sensor (no fuel
vapour trap is fitted), allowing them to drain into the throttle body
instead.

**Fig. 13.54 Coolant temperature sensor location (1) – MMFD fuel
injection systems (Sec 9F)**

Coolant temperature sensor
56   The sensor is screwed into the coolant housing on the left-hand
end of the cylinder head (see Fig. 13.54). Removal and refitting are as
described in Chapter 2, Section 8.

Oxygen sensor
57   The procedure is as described in Part C of this Section, paragraphs 22 to 27.

*Fuel injection system (MMFD Mono-point G5 and G6
systems) – complete test*
58   Refer to Part D, of this Section, paragraph 11.

Fault diagnosis – MMFD mono-point G5 and G6 systems
59   Refer to Part B of this Section, paragraphs 38 and 39.

PART G: EMISSION CONTROL SYSTEMS

Emission control components – description
1   Various systems may be fitted to reduce the emission of unburned
hydrocarbons and harmful exhaust gases into the atmosphere. Basically, these systems can be divided as follows:

(a)   *Air intake heating system*
(b)   *Crankcase ventilation system*
(c)   *Electro-pneumatic ignition timing retarding system*
(d)   *Catalytic converter*
(e)   *Fuel vapour recirculation system*

2   The operation of the systems is described briefly in the following
paragraphs.

Air intake heating system
3   This system is fitted to all single-point fuel injection models, and
assists the vaporisation of the fuel, providing more complete combustion of the fuel/air mixture. This is achieved by controlling the temperature of the air entering the engine.
4   The air drawn through the air intake pipe from the engine compartment is mixed with hot air drawn from a shroud around the exhaust
manifold. The proportions of hot and cold air are controlled by the
position of a flap valve, which in turn is controlled by a wax thermostat
and a vacuum capsule (connected to the inlet manifold).

Crankcase ventilation system
5   This system is fitted to all models, and prevents the gases produced
in the crankcase from being released into the atmosphere, at the same
time preventing a build-up of pressure in the crankcase.

1   Air cleaner
2   Air ducting
3   Exhaust manifold hot air duct
4   Flap valve
5   Wax thermostat
a   Cold air
b   Hot air

Fig. 13.55 Typical air intake heating system (Sec 9G)

1   Oil filler cap with oil trap
2   Air filter
3   Throttle valve
4   Inlet manifold
5   Jet
6   Ventilation hose
7   Calibrated jet
8   Sump
9   Camshaft cover

Fig. 13.56 Typical crankcase ventilation systepm (Sec 9G)

9G.17 Disconnecting wiring plug from ignition timing retarding system solenoid valve

Fig. 13.57 Electro-pneumatic ignition timing retarding system (Sec 9G)

1   Coolant temperature sensor   3   Solenoid valve
2   Electronic control unit   4   Distributor vacuum capsule

6   Crankcase gases are drawn into the air intake tract, where they are mixed with clean air. The gases are then burnt with the fuel/air mixture in the engine, and expelled through the exhaust.

Electro-pneumatic ignition timing retarding system
7   This system is used on models fitted with the Mono-Jetronic A2.2 fuel injection system, and reduces the nitrous oxide (NOx) content in the exhaust gases. This is achieved by reducing the temperature at the end of the combustion by reducing the ignition advance at certain engine temperatures.
8   The engine temperature is measured by a coolant temperature sensor, and this information is transmitted to the electronic control unit, which controls the solenoid valve. Under certain engine temperature conditions, the solenoid valve cuts off the vacuum to the distributor vacuum capsule, therefore reducing the ignition advance.

Catalytic converter
9   Catalytic converters have been introduced progressively on all models in the range, to meet emissions regulations.

10   The catalytic converter is located in the exhaust system, and operates in conjunction with an exhaust gas oxygen sensor to reduce exhaust gas emissions. The catalytic converter effectively cleans the exhaust gases by speeding up their decomposition.
11   In order for a catalytic converter to operate effectively, the air/fuel mixture must be very accurately controlled, and this is achieved by measuring the oxygen content of the exhaust gas. The oxygen sensor transmits information on the exhaust gas oxygen content to the electronic control unit, which adjusts the air/fuel mixture strength accordingly.

Fuel vapour recirculation system
12   This system has been introduced progressively on all fuel injection models, and prevents fuel vapour from the fuel tank from being ejected into the atmosphere.
13   The fuel filler cap is sealed, and the fuel vapours from the tank pass into a carbon canister, via a calibrated orifice and a pipe. The fuel vapour is absorbed by the carbon filling in the canister.
14   When the engine is running, it draws a proportion of its intake air through the carbon canister, and this air picks up the fuel vapour contained in the carbon canister.
15   A solenoid valve mounted in the pipe between the canister and the inlet manifold prevents the system from operating when the engine is cold. The solenoid valve is controlled by the electronic control unit, on the basis of information received from the coolant temperature sensor.

Electro-pneumatic ignition timing retarding system components – removal and refitting
Solenoid valve
16   The valve is located on a bracket at the rear of the engine compartment. To remove the valve, proceed as follows.
17   Disconnect the battery negative lead, then disconnect the wiring plug from the valve (photo).
18   Note the orientation of the valve, then disconnect the hoses from the valve, and pull the valve from its bracket.
19   Refitting is a reversal of removal, ensuring that the valve is correctly orientated, as noted before removal.

Coolant temperature sensor
20   The sensor is located in the left-hand end of the cylinder head, below the engine coolant temperature sensor for the fuel injection system.
21   To remove the sensor, partially drain the cooling system, then disconnect the wiring from the sensor, and unscrew and remove the sensor.
22   When refitting the sensor, ensure that the seal is in good condition, and take care not to overtighten the switch.

Catalytic converter – removal and refitting
23   Refer to Part A of this Section.

9G.24 Fuel vapour recirculation system carbon canister (A) and solenoid valve (B)

9G.30A Unscrew the securing nut ...

9G.30B ... and withdraw the solenoid bracket – fuel vapour recirculation system

1 Fuel filler cap
2 Charcoal canister
3 Hose
4 Calibrated orifice
5 Hose
6 Solenoid valve
7 Coolant temperature sensor
10 Safety valve

Fig. 13.58 Fuel vapour recirculation system (Sec 9G)

Fuel vapour recirculation system components – removal and refitting

Carbon canister
24 The carbon canister is located at the rear left-hand corner of the engine compartment (photo).
25 To remove the canister, first disconnect the hoses, noting their locations to ensure correct refitting.
26 Unscrew the clamp bolt, and lift the canister from its clamp on the body panel.
27 Refitting is a reversal of removal, but ensure that the hoses are correctly reconnected, as noted before removal.

Solenoid valve
28 The solenoid valve is mounted on a bracket next to the carbon canister, at the rear left-hand corner of the engine compartment.
29 To remove the valve, first disconnect the battery negative lead.
30 Unbolt the bracket from the body panel, then disconnect the wiring plug (photos).
31 Disconnect the hoses from the valve, noting their locations to ensure correct refitting, then withdraw the valve.
32 Refitting is a reversal of removal, ensuring that the hoses are correctly reconnected, as noted before removal.

10 Ignition system

Ducellier distributor cap – modification
1 From mid-1986, Ducellier distributor caps are retained by two screws instead of spring clips (photo). On some 1124 cc engines, this modification applies from *early* 1986.

Ignition timing (XU5J, XU5JA and XU9JA engines) – checking and adjustment
2 From VIN 5520364 (early 1985), GTI models with the XU5J engine are fitted with a revised distributor. The ignition timing procedure is as described in Chapter 4, Section 7, except that the advance figure is as given in the Specifications at the beginning of this Chapter.

10.1 Later distributor caps are retained by screws

Fig. 13.59 Improved routing of the HT lead from the ignition coil (Sec 10)

10.8 Disconnecting the LT wiring (arrowed) from the coil – TU engine

3   The revised timing value is also shown on a label attached to the airflow sensor.

4   Later GTI (post February 1986) and CTI models, with the XU5JA and XU9JA engines also have revised ignition timing – see Specifications.

Fault diagnosis – ignition system

5   If the HT lead from the ignition coil is routed too close to the distributor LT wiring or electronic control unit, misfiring may result under certain conditions. Where this occurs, reposition the HT lead as shown in Fig. 13.59.

Ignition coil (TU engine) – removal and refitting

6   Remove the air cleaner inlet ducting.
7   Disconnect the HT cable from the coil.
8   Disconnect the LT wiring (photo).
9   Unhook the TDC connector from the coil bracket.
10   Unbolt the mounting bracket and remove the coil.
11   Refitting is a reversal of removal.

Distributor (TU engine) – removal and refitting

12   Remove the ignition coil as previously described.
13   Identify the HT leads for position, then disconnect them from the spark plugs (photo).
14   Unbolt the HT lead support from the cylinder head.
15   Pull back the plastic cover, then extract the screws and remove the distributor cap.
16   Disconnect the wiring at the connector (photo).
17   Pull the hose from the vacuum advance unit (photo).
18   Mark the distributor mounting flange in relation to the distributor/fuel pump housing (photo).
19   Unscrew the mounting nuts, remove the small plates, and withdraw the distributor (photo).

20   Check the condition of the O-ring on the mounting flange, and renew it if necessary.
21   Refitting is a reversal of removal, but turn the rotor arm as required to align the lugs with the offset slot in the camshaft. If the old distributor is being refitted, align the previously-made marks before tightening the mounting nuts. If fitting a new distributor, initially set the distributor in the middle of the slotted holes, or follow the procedure given in Chapter 4, Section 7, then finally adjust the ignition timing.

Ignition module (TU engine) – removal and refitting

22   The module is attached to the side of the distributor. First disconnect the wiring at the connector.
23   Remove the two screws and withdraw the module from the distributor, taking care not to bend the terminals (photo).
24   Do not wipe away the special heat-conductive grease, as this protects the semi-conductor components within the module. If necessary, obtain new grease from a Peugeot dealer.
25   Refitting is a reversal of removal, but make sure that the special grease is spread evenly over the mating surfaces.

Spark plugs (1988-on)

26   The spark plugs used on later models are of conventional type, using a sealing washer instead of the taper-seat type used previously.

Ignition system (XU9JA/Z engine) – description

27   On the XU9JA/Z engine, the ignition system is an integral part of the Motronic engine management system, which controls both the ignition and fuel injection systems.
28   The Motronic module receives information from a TDC sensor, an engine coolant temperature sensor, a throttle position switch, an airflow sensor, and an oxygen sensor.
29   The module provides outputs to control the fuel pump, fuel injectors, and ignition circuit. Using the inputs from the various sensors,

10.13 Disconnecting an HT lead from a spark plug – TU engine

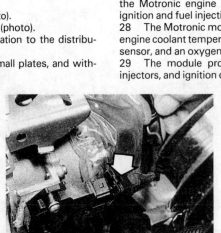

10.16 Disconnect the distributor wiring connector (arrowed) – TU engine

10.17 Distributor vacuum advance unit and hose – TU engine

10.18 Mark the distributor and housing, before ...

10.19 ... removing the distributor – TU engine

10.23 Removing the ignition module – TU engine

10.30 TDC sensor (arrowed)

the module computes the optimum ignition advance and fuel injector pulse duration to suit the prevailing engine conditions. This system gives very accurate control of the engine under all conditions, improving fuel consumption and driveability, and reducing exhaust gas emissions.

Ignition system components (XU9JA/Z engine) – removal and refitting

30 Although some of the components differ in detail, removal and refitting are basically as described in Chapter 4. Note that the TDC sensor acts as one of the system sensors, and is not solely for use with the diagnostic socket as described in Chapter 4, Section 9 (photo).

Ignition timing (XU9JA/Z engine) – checking and adjustment

31 No adjustment of the ignition timing is possible on the XU9JA/Z engine, as the adjustment is carried out automatically by the Motronic module. The ignition timing can be checked by a Peugeot dealer using specialist test equipment if a fault is suspected.

Fault diagnosis (XU9JA/Z engine) – ignition system

32 Specialist test equipment is required to carry out accurate fault diagnosis, and any fault occurring with the Motronic system should be referred to a Peugeot dealer. Before doing this however, a simple check of the spark plugs, HT leads, and distributor cap can be made as described in Chapter 4, Section 10.

Static ('distributorless') ignition system – general description

33 A static ignition system is used on models with MMFD G5 (XU5M2/Z engine) and G6 (TU1M/L, XU5M3/Z and XU5M3/L engines) engine management systems. The system is integrated with the fuel

Fig. 13.60 Static ignition system components (Sec 10)

1 Electronic control unit *4 TDC sensor*
3 Double coil

injection system, and is controlled by the MMFD electronic control unit. The control unit receives information from the various sensors described in Section 9, Part F, and using this information, the optimum ignition advance for the prevailing engine conditions is selected from a series of 'mapped' values stored in the module memory.

34 The single ignition module replaces the module, coil and distributor in a conventional system. The ignition module incorporates a double coil, with four high-tension outputs to the spark plugs, which dispenses with the requirement for a conventional distributor and rotor arm.

35 Each coil is controlled by the MMFD electronic control unit. Each time one of the coil primary circuits is switched, two sparks are provided, one to a cylinder on the compression stroke, and one to a cylinder on the exhaust stroke. The spark to the cylinder on the exhaust stroke is effectively a 'wasted spark', but has no detrimental effect on the performance of the engine.

10.38 Static ignition system module

19.70

Dimensions in mm

Fig. 13.61 Clutch centralising tool dimensions for the TU engine (Sec 11)

Ignition module (static ignition system) – removal and refitting
36   Disconnect the battery negative lead.
37   Where applicable, remove the air cleaner ducting for improved access.
38   Disconnect the HT leads from the module (photo). If necessary, take note of the lead connections to ensure correct refitting.
39   Release the securing clip, and disconnect the module wiring connector.
40   Unscrew the four securing screws, then withdraw the module from its bracket.
41   Refitting is a reversal of removal, ensuring that the HT leads are correctly reconnected.

Ignition timing (static ignition system) – checking and adjustment
42   No adjustment of ignition timing is possible with the static ignition system, as the adjustment is carried out automatically by the MMFD electronic control module. The system can be checked by a Peugeot dealer using specialist test equipment if a fault is suspected.

Fault diagnosis – static ignition system
43   Special test equipment is required to carry out accurate fault diagnosis, and any fault occurring with the MMFD system should be referred to a Peugeot dealer. Before doing this however, a simple check of the spark plugs and HT leads can be made as described in Chapter 4, Section 10 (ignore the references to the distributor cap).

---

11   Clutch

Clutch (all models) – removal and refitting
1   Whenever the clutch is removed, the clutch shaft splines, release bearing guide tube and the release fork ball-stud and fingers should be cleaned and lubricated with a molybdenum disulphide-based grease. This will prevent clutch judder or drag which would otherwise result in difficult engagement of gears. Do not, however, apply an excessive amount of grease, which could find its way onto the clutch driven plate linings or flywheel.

Transfer gears (with BH 3 gearbox) – modification
2   From December 1984, the transfer idler gear bearings are increased in diameter from 33.0 mm to 38.0 mm. The intermediate plate is also modified to accommodate the new bearings.
3   It is not possible to interchange components between the early and later types.

Clutch (TU engine) – refitting
4   When refitting the clutch, a centralising tool made to the dimen-

sions shown in Fig. 13.61 should be used to centralise the driven plate. The tool may be made out of wood.

Clutch release mechanism (models with MA or BE 3/5 gearbox) – overhaul
5   Remove the gearbox as described in Chapter 6 (or Section 14, as applicable).
6   Pull the clutch release bearing from the guide sleeve, then release the spring clips from the fork ends.
7   Using a suitable punch, drive out the roll-pin securing the release lever to the pivot shaft, then withdraw the release lever.
8   Prise the upper pivot shaft bush from the bellhousing.
9   Lift the lower end of the release lever pivot shaft from the lower bush in the bellhousing, then lower the pivot shaft into the bellhousing, and manipulate it as necessary to enable removal.
10   If desired, the lower pivot bush can be prised from the bellhousing.
11   Reassembly is a reversal of dismantling, but ensure that the pivot bushes are correctly located in the bellhousing.
12   Refit the gearbox as described in Chapter 6 (or Section 14, as applicable).

---

12   Manual transmission (BE1/5)

Gearchange linkage – modification
1   From mid-1985, the reverse gear stop is actuated by a cable on the gearbox, instead of an eccentric cam at the base of the gear lever. Reverse gear is still selected by lifting the sleeve on the gear lever.
2   When selecting reverse, the cable releases a detent from the selector rod, but for selection of all other gears, the detent prevents accidental engagement of reverse.
3   Where the cable is fitted, all references to the cam and stop in Part C of Chapter 6 may be ignored. The cable requires no adjustment.

Gear linkage – adjustment
4   Note that the adjustment procedure described in Chapter 6, Section 13 does not apply to later models. Although the linkage is adjustable as described for earlier models, no adjustment dimensions have been published.

Transmission – removal and refitting
5   On models fitted with the reverse stop cable described in paragraphs 1 to 3, it will be necessary to unscrew the nut and release the cable in addition to the procedure described in Part C of Chapter 6.

Differential – modifications
6   From early 1985, the differential side gears are positively located within the carrier, instead of being located only by insertion of the driveshafts. A location ring is now fitted as shown in Fig. 13.63, with corresponding cut-outs machined in the side gears and carrier. Shoul-

Fig. 13.62 Gearchange linkage showing the reverse gear stop cable fitted to the later BE 1/5 gearbox (Sec 12)

Fig. 13.63 Positive-location side gears on the later BE 1/5 differential (Sec 12)

Fig. 13.64 Shouldered thrustwasher fitted to the later BE 1/5 differential (Sec 12)

dered thrustwashers are now fitted over the location rings, instead of the earlier plain types (Fig. 13.64).

7   Due to these modifications, it is not possible to dismantle and reassemble the differential in the order described in Chapter 6, Section 19. When dismantling, the spindle and gears must be removed first before removal of the side gears. Reassemble the components in reverse order.

8   From early 1986, some units are fitted with a special differential extension housing which eliminates the need for bearing preload adjustment. The housing can be identified by measuring the length of the shoulder shown in Fig. 13.65. If the shoulder length is 10.0 mm, no preload shims must be fitted, but if it is 8.65 mm, the preload must be adjusted as described in Chapter 6, Section 20.

Fig. 13.65 Comparison of early (lower section) and later (upper section) BE 1/5 differential extension housing (Sec 12)

1   Bearing preload shim   x = 10 mm

9   When fitting the modified housing (ie without preload adjustment), the bolts should be tightened progressively while turning the differential unit to seat the bearings. The torque setting remains the same as for the earlier type.

Selector forks – modifications

10   From early 1986, the selector forks are modified to improve gear engagement, as shown in Fig. 13.66. The removal and refitting procedures remain the same as described in Part C of Chapter 6. Modified selection and engagement parts are used in conjunction with the forks. Some models may have a combination of the later selector and engagement parts with the earlier forks. If any parts are renewed, the new parts should be the same as that originally fitted; ie early and later parts are not interchangeable.

3rd/4th speed driven gears – modifications

11   To allow fitting of the modified selector forks described in paragraph 10, the diameter between the 3rd and 4th speed driven gears is reduced to 38 mm instead of 43 mm (Fig. 13.67). The later type of gears replace the earlier ones.

Transmission – draining and oil level checking

12   In early 1986, the gearbox drain plug was deleted. Draining of the gearbox from this date is through the final drive drain plug only ('b' in Fig. 6.3 in Chapter 6).

Fig. 13.66 Later-type selector forks on the BE 1/5 gearbox (Sec 12)

1 1st/2nd selector fork	*3 5th selector fork and rod*
2 3rd/4th selector fork	*4 Fixed selector rod*

Fig. 13.67 Later-type 3rd/4th speed driven gears from the BE 1/5 gearbox (Sec 12)

Fig. 13.68 Location of the level plug on the BE 1/5 gearbox from October 1986 (Sec 12)

Fig. 13.69 New position of reverse idler gear and 1st/2nd synchro unit on the BE 3/5 gearbox (Sec 13)

13   On later models with a cable-actuated reverse gear stop, the cable enters the top of the gearbox at the point where the breather was previously fitted. In order to fill the gearbox with oil, the reverse gear stop cable must be unscrewed from the adaptor on the gearbox casing.
14   From approximately October 1986, a gearbox/final drive level plug was fitted to the gearbox end cover (see Fig. 13.68). The plug is fitted with a copper washer, which should be cleaned and checked for condition before refitting. The oil level should reach the bottom of the level plug aperture.
15   From 1988 (chassis number 7 900 001 on), all models have a special gearbox oil which does not require changing at the routine maintenance intervals, and in addition, the oil level check intervals have been extended. It is important on these models to use only the specified oil for topping-up purposes.

13   Manual transmission (BE3/5)

Transmission – general description

1   The BE 3/5 gearbox is a refined development of the BE 1/5 gearbox, and was introduced to the Peugeot model range in 1989, to progressively replace its predecessor.
2   Most of the procedures described in Chapter 6 for the BE 1/5 gearbox are equally applicable to the BE 3/5 type, although many of the components have been modified as detailed in the following paragraphs.
3   When ordering spare parts, ensure that the correct new components are obtained, as many of the BE 1/5 and BE 3/5 gearbox components are not interchangeable.
4   BE 3/5 gearboxes can be identified by the revised gearchange pattern, with reverse positioned opposite 5th gear.

Transmission – draining and refilling

5   Note that the gearbox should be filled through the breather plug on the top of the gearbox casing (see 'c' in Fig. 6.3 in Chapter 6).
6   The BE 3/5 gearbox is filled with a special oil which does not require changing at the routine maintenance intervals, and in addition, the oil level check intervals are extended. It is important to use only the specified oil for topping-up purposes.

Reverse idler gear – modification

7   A modified reverse idler gear is fitted to the BE 3/5 gearbox, and the idler gear is repositioned on the reverse idler shaft – see Fig. 13.69.

Gear selector components – modifications

8   On the BE 3/5 gearbox, the gearchange pattern has been revised so that reverse is positioned opposite 5th gear.
9   The cable-operated reverse gear stop has been deleted, and a breather plug is fitted in its place.
10   Reverse gear is engaged by an additional selector finger on the selector shaft, which acts on the reverse selector fork.
11   All of the gear selector components have been modified in detail, but the dismantling and reassembly details given in Chapter 6 for the BE 1/5 gearbox components are still generally applicable.
12   Note that the gear selector shaft and selector finger assembly components are accurately matched, and no attempt should be made to dismantle the selector finger assembly, as no spares are available. If any of the components are worn or damaged, the complete selector shaft/finger assembly must be renewed as a unit.

Input shaft – modification

13   A modified input shaft is fitted to the BE 3/5 gearbox, to allow for the revised position of the reverse idler gear, but the overhaul procedure described in Chapter 6 remains unchanged.

Fig. 13.70 Gear selector shaft and selector finger assembly – BE 3/5 gearbox (Sec 13)

1 One-piece selector shaft/lever	4 Interlock key
2 Sleeve assembly with reverse finger	5 Cups
3 1st/2nd, 3rd/4th and 5th selector finger	6 Spring

1st/2nd gear synchro unit – modification

14   A modified 1st/2nd gear synchro unit is fitted to the BE 3/5 gearbox, which fits on the output shaft the opposite way round to that described for the BE 1/5 gearbox in Chapter 6; ie the synchro unit fits with the chamfer on the external teeth facing *away from* 1st gear. The remainder of the output shaft dismantling and reassembly procedure described in Chapter 6 remains unchanged.

14   Manual transmission (MA)

Transmission – general description

1   The MA gearbox is mounted on the left-hand side of the engine, and may be removed separately, leaving the engine in the car. It has either four or five forward gears depending on the model, all with synchromesh, and one reverse gear. All the synchromesh units are located on the output shaft, and the differential unit is located in the main gearbox casing.

Transmission – routine maintenance

2   There are no oil change requirements for the MA gearbox, but oil level checks should be carried out every 36 000 miles (60 000 km). Make sure that all topping-up is made using only the specified grade of oil.

Transmission – removal and refitting

3   Disconnect the bonnet stay from the right-hand suspension tower, and use suitable U-brackets in the bonnet hinge holes to hold the bonnet in a vertical position.
4   Remove the battery as described in Chapter 12.
5   Remove the air cleaner as described in Section 8 or 9 (Part A) of this Chapter.
6   Unscrew the nut, and detach the battery negative cable from the gearbox.
7   Disconnect the wiring from the reversing lamp switch.
8   Pull out the rubber cotter, and remove the speedometer cable from the gearbox.
9   Prise the two gearchange control rods from the gearbox levers. A small open-ended spanner may be used to good effect.
10   Disconnect the clutch cable, and position it to one side.
11   Release the heater hose from the clips.
12   Unbolt the starter motor and air cleaner bracket, and support them to one side. There is no need to disconnect the wiring.
13   Apply the handbrake, then jack up the front of the car and support on axle stands.
14   Unscrew the drain and filler plugs, and drain the gearbox oil into a suitable container (photos).

Fig. 13.71 Cutaway view of the MA 5-speed gearbox (Sec 14)

14.14A Gearbox drain plug (arrowed) – MA gearbox

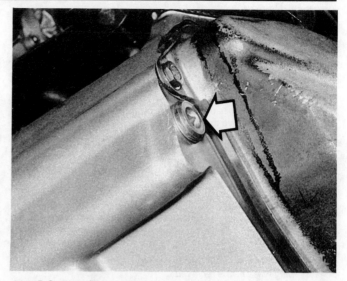

14.14B Gearbox filler plug (arrowed) – MA gearbox

MA.5

MA.4

Fig. 13.72 Cross-section of the MA gearbox (Sec 14)

1   Gearbox housing
2   Intermediate plate
3   Clutch and final drive housing
4   Clutch fork on shaft
5   Release bearing
6   Release bearing guide
7   Input shaft
8   Output shaft
9   1st speed driven gear
10 1st/2nd speed synchroniser (and reverse driven gear)
11 2nd speed driven gear
12 3rd speed driven gear
13 3rd/4th speed synchroniser
14 4th speed driven gear
15 5th speed drive gear
16 5th speed driven gear
17 5th speed synchroniser
18 Differential housing
19 Differential pinions
20 Differential gears
21 Speedometer drive worm
22 Speedometer drive pinion

Inset shows 4-speed gearbox

15   Remove both driveshafts with reference to Chapter 7 and Section 16 of this Chapter.
16   Unscrew and remove the lower rear bolt securing the gearbox to the engine, noting that the exhaust front pipe bracket is located on the bolt.
17   Support the left-hand side of the engine, using a hoist on the left-hand lifting eye, or a trolley jack and block of wood beneath the sump.
18   Unscrew the left-hand mounting nuts, including the nut on the centre stud, and remove the mounting.
19   Unbolt the battery tray.
20   Unscrew the nuts, and remove the left-hand mounting bracket from the gearbox.
21   Lower the engine until the exhaust front pipe contacts the front suspension crossmember.
22   Unscrew the remaining bolts securing the gearbox to the engine.
23   Support the gearbox with a trolley jack or suitable sling, then withdraw it from the engine until clear of the clutch, and lower it to the ground.
24   Refitting is a reversal of removal, but note the following points:

(a)   *It is recommended that the driveshaft oil seals and filler/drain plug washers are renewed.*

(b)   *Tighten all nuts and bolts to the specified torque.*
(c)   *Lubricate the input shaft splines, clutch release bearing sleeve and fork fingers with molybdenum disulphide grease.*
(d)   *Refill the gearbox with the correct grade and quantity of oil.*
(e)   *Adjust the clutch cable with reference to Chapter 5.*
(f)   *The gearbox control rods cannot be adjusted.*

Transmission – dismantling into major assemblies

25   With the unit removed from the car, clean all exterior surfaces and wipe dry.
26   Pull the clutch release bearing from the guide sleeve, and release the spring clips from the fork ends (photo).
27   Position the gearbox with the clutch end downwards.
28   Unbolt and remove the speedometer drive pinion (photos).
29   Unbolt the pressed-steel housing. Remove the rubber gasket (photos).

5-speed gearbox only

30   Drive the pin from the 5th speed selector fork.
31   Engage both reverse and 5th gears with reference to Fig. 13.73, then loosen the nut on the end of the output shaft. Return the gears to neutral.
32   Remove the nut and lockwasher (photos).

14.26 Removing the clutch release bearing – MA gearbox

14.28A Unscrew the bolt ...

14.28B ... and remove the speedometer drive pinion – MA gearbox

14.29A Unscrew the bolt

14.29B ... and remove the pressed-steel housing

14.32A Remove the 5th synchro nut ...

14.32B ... and lockwasher

14.33 Removing the 5th synchro unit and selector fork

14.34A Removing the 5th synchro ring ...

14.34B ... 5th speed driven gear ...

14.34C ... needle bearing ...

14.34D ... sleeve ...

14.34E ... and thrustwasher

14.35 Removing the special washer from the input shaft

14.36 Removing the 5th speed drive gear

Fig. 13.73 Sequence for selecting reverse and 5th gears – MA gearbox (Sec 14)

33   Remove the 5th synchro unit together with its selector fork, making sure that the sleeve remains central on the hub to avoid loss of the internal balls and springs (photo).

34   Remove from the output shaft the 5th synchro ring, followed by the 5th speed driven gear, needle bearing, sleeve, and thrustwasher (photos).

35   Extract the circlip from the end of the input shaft, followed by the special washer, noting that the convex side is uppermost (photo).

36   Using a suitable puller if necessary, pull the 5th speed drive gear from the splines on the input shaft (photo).

4 and 5-speed gearboxes

37   Unscrew the Torx screws and extract the half-rings from the grooves in the shaft bearings, noting their locations (photos).

38   Unscrew the bolts securing the gearbox housing to the clutch/final drive housing, noting the location of the bolts (photo).

39   Lift the gearbox housing from the clutch/final drive housing (photo), at the same time guiding the selector fork shafts through the housing. Do not prise the housings apart with a screwdriver; use a wooden or hide mallet to release them from the sealant.

40   Remove the plastic ring from the reverse idler gear shaft, then remove the shaft from the clutch/final drive housing and remove the idler gear (photos).

41   Press down on the reverse selector arm directly over the shaft, and at the same time extract the shaft from the intermediate plate. Remove the reverse selector arm (photos).

42   Lift the gate lever to the 1st/2nd position, and support with a block of wood.

43   Using a suitable pin punch, drive out the pin securing the selector finger to the selector shaft. Recover the pin, and return the gate lever to neutral.

44   Pull out the selector shaft, and remove the rubber boot from it (photo).

45   Prise out the neutral return spring, together with the two plastic cups (photo).

46   Lift the gate lever, and at the same time remove the interlocking key and selector finger (photos).

47   Tie the two selector fork shafts together as an aid to reassembly.

48   Using both hands, lift the input and output shafts, together with the selector fork shafts, directly from the clutch/final drive housing (photo). Separate the input shaft from the output shaft, and disengage the selector forks from the synchro units on the output shaft.

14.37A Unscrew the Torx screws ...

14.37B ... and extract the bearing half-rings

14.38 Unscrewing a gearbox housing bolt

14.39 Lifting the gearbox housing from the clutch/final drive housing

14.40A Removing the plastic ring ...

14.40B ... reverse idler gear shaft ...

14.40C ... and reverse idler gear

14.41A Removing the reverse selector shaft ...

14.41B ... and arm

14.44 Removing the selector shaft

14.45 Removing the neutral return spring and plastic cups

14.46A Interlocking key and selector finger assembly

14.46B Interlocking key and selector finger separated

14.48 Lifting input and output shafts with selector fork shafts from the clutch/final drive housing

14.49 Removing the intermediate plate

14.50A Removing the reverse locking plunger ...

14.50B ... and spring

14.51 Lifting out the differential unit

14.54 Removing the gate lever

14.56A Prising out the driveshaft oil seal ...

14.56B ... and input shaft oil seal

49   Unscrew the bolts and remove the intermediate plate from the clutch/final drive housing (photo). Adhesive is used on assembly, so some difficulty may be experienced, but do not lever directly on the mating faces.
50   Remove the reverse locking plunger and spring, using a magnet if available (photos).
51   Lift out the differential unit (photo).
52   The gearbox is now dismantled into its major assemblies.

Transmission – examination and renovation
53   Clean all components, and examine them thoroughly for wear and damage. Circlips, locking pins, gaskets and oil seals should all be renewed as a matter of course. Read through the reassembly sub-section, and obtain the necessary adhesive and sealants required.

Clutch/final drive housing – overhaul
54   Using a suitable punch, drive out the locking pin and remove the gate lever from the shaft (photo).

55   Withdraw the shaft, and prise the oil seal from the housing.
56   Prise out the driveshaft and input shaft oil seals (photos).
57   If necessary, drive out the location dowels.
58   If necessary, drive out the right-hand final drive bearing outer track, using a punch through the cut-outs provided (photo).
59   Unbolt the clutch release bearing guide sleeve (photo).
60   Clean all the components.
61   Commence reassembly by refitting the clutch release bearing guide sleeve, together with a new input shaft seal. Apply jointing compound to the threads, then insert and tighten the bolts. Smear a little oil on the seal.
62   Using a metal tube, drive the right-hand final drive bearing outer track fully into the housing.
63   Drive in the location dowels.
64   Oil the new driveshaft oil seal, and drive it into the housing using a block of wood.
65   Oil the new gate lever shaft oil seal, and drive it into the housing. Oil the shaft and refit it.

14.58 Right-hand final drive bearing outer track (arrowed)

14.59 Clutch release bearing guide sleeve (arrowed)

14.68 Left-hand final drive bearing outer track

14.73 Input shaft and bearings assembled

14.77A Removing the thrustwasher ...

14.77B ... 4th gear ...

14.77C ... 4th synchro ring ...

14.77D 3rd/4th synchro unit ...

14.77E ... and the 3rd synchro ring

66   Locate the gate lever on the shaft towards the final drive, align the holes, and drive in the new locking pin.

Gearbox housing – overhaul
67   Prise out the driveshaft oil seal.
68   If necessary, drive out the left-hand final drive bearing outer track using a punch through the cut-outs provided (photo).
69   Using a metal tube, drive the new outer track fully into the housing.
70   Oil the new driveshaft oil seal, and drive it into the housing using a block of wood.

Input shaft – dismantling and reassembly
71   On the 4-speed gearbox, extract the circlip with circlip pliers, and remove the washer.
72   On 4 and 5-speed gearboxes, pull the bearing from the 4th speed end of the input shaft using a suitable puller. Similarly pull the bearing from the 1st speed end. Note that the re-use of removed bearings is not recommended.
73   To reassemble, drive the bearing on the 1st speed end of the shaft using a length of metal tube on the inner track. Similarly drive the bearing on the 4th speed end, but note that the groove in the outer track must be towards the end of the shaft (photo).

74   Locate the washer over the end of the shaft on the 4-speed gearbox. Rest the circlip on the tapered end of the shaft, and use a socket to drive it into the groove. Check that the circlip is seated correctly by squeezing it with pliers.

Output shaft – dismantling and reassembly
75   On the 4-speed gearbox, extract the circlip with circlip pliers, and remove the washer.
76   On 4 and 5-speed gearboxes, pull the bearing from the shaft using a suitable puller if necessary.
77   Remove the thrustwasher, followed by 4th gear, the 4th synchro ring, the 3rd/4th synchro unit, and the 3rd synchro ring (photos). Keep the synchro unit sleeve central on the hub.
78   Tap out the C-clip using a screwdriver or a forked tool made with reference to Fig. 13.74 (photo).
79   Remove the 3rd gear, the C-clip, the 2nd gear, 2nd synchro ring, 1st/2nd synchro unit, 1st synchro ring, the C-clip, 1st gear, and the final C-clip (photos). Keep the synchro unit sleeve central on the hub.
80   Remove the final bearing using a suitable puller, or by supporting the bearing in a vice and driving the output shaft through it. Note that the re-use of removed bearings is not recommended.

14.78 Removing the C-clip

14.79A Remove the 3rd gear...

14.79B ... C-clip ...

14.79C ... 2nd gear ...

14.79D ... 2nd synchro ring ...

14.79E ... 1st/2nd synchro unit ...

14.79F ... 1st synchro ring ...

14.79G ... C-clip ...

14.79H ... 1st gear ...

14.79I ... and the final C-clip (arrowed)

14.82 Inserting a C-clip

14.88 Driving the bearing onto the input shaft

Fig. 13.74 Forked tool for removing C-clips (1) from the output shaft – MA gearbox (Sec 14)

81   To reassemble, drive the bearing onto the output shaft using a length of metal tube on the inner track. Do not support the shaft on the plastic lubrication disc.
82   Press the C-clip into its groove, followed by 1st gear and the next C-clip (photo).
83   Fit the 1st synchro ring, then lower the 1st/2nd synchro unit onto the splines with the selector groove downwards, at the same time aligning the projections on the 1st synchro ring with the rockers on the synchro unit.
84   Fit the 2nd synchro ring, aligning the projections as described in paragraph 83.
85   Fit the 2nd gear, the C-clip, 3rd gear, and the C-clip.
86   Fit the 3rd synchro ring, 3rd/4th synchro unit, and the 4th synchro ring as described in paragraph 83.
87   Fit the 4th gear and thrustwasher.
88   Locate the bearing on the shaft, with the groove towards the end of the shaft. Drive the bearing onto the shaft using a length of metal tube

on the inner track (photo). Do not support the shaft on the plastic lubrication disc.
89   On the 4-speed gearbox, locate the washer on the end of the shaft. Rest the circlip on the tapered end of the shaft, and use a socket to drive it into the groove. Check that the circlip is seated correctly by squeezing it with pliers.

Differential bearings – removal and refitting
90   Lever off the speedometer drive worm (photo).
91   Pull the bearings from both sides of the differential unit using a suitable puller. Identify them for location if they are to be re-used.
92   Drive the new bearings into position using a length of metal tube on their inner tracks.
93   Press the speedometer drive worm into position.

Selector fork shafts – dismantling and reassembly
94   Support the 3rd/4th selector fork shaft in a soft-jawed vice, then drive out the roll pin using a suitable punch. Slide off the selector fork, noting which way round it is fitted.
95   Similarly drive out the roll pin, and remove the 1st/2nd selector fork and the reverse control relay from the other shaft.
96   Reassembly is a reversal of dismantling, but use new roll pins.

Synchro units – dismantling and reassembly
97   Mark the hub and the outer sleeve in relation to each other, to ensure correct reassembly.
98   Wrap the unit in a cloth, then slide the sleeve from the hub. Recover the three balls, three springs, and three rockers.
99   To reassemble the units, first insert the hub in the sleeve. The rocker slots in the hub and sleeve must be in alignment.
100 Pull out the hub until the rockers, springs and balls can be inserted, then press in the balls and push the hub fully into the sleeve. A large worm drive clip, piston ring compressor, or three narrow strips of metal may be used to press in the balls.

Transmission – reassembly
101 With the clutch/final drive housing on the bench, lower the differential unit into position.
102 Insert the reverse locking spring and plunger.
103 Apply Loctite Autoform 549 adhesive to the contact area on the intermediate plate, then lower the plate onto the clutch/final drive housing, at the same time guiding the gate lever through the hole provided (photos).

1   1st/2nd selector fork
2   3rd/4th selector fork
3   5th selector fork (MA 5 gearbox)
4   Reverse selector arm
5   Reverse control relay
6   3rd/4th selector fork shaft
7   5th selector fork/reverse control relay shaft
a   Reverse selector arm-to-relay stud

Fig. 13.75 Selector fork shaft components – MA gearbox (Sec 14)

14.90 Speedometer drive worm (arrowed)

14.103A Applying adhesive to the intermediate plate

14.103B Guiding the gate lever through the intermediate plate

14.104A Apply locking fluid to the intermediate plate bolt threads ...

14.104B ... and tighten the bolts to the specified torque

14.105 Selector fork shaft assemblies tied together with a plastic strap

Fig. 13.76 Driving the roll pin from the reverse control relay – MA gearbox (Sec 14)

Fig. 13.77 Exploded view of a synchro unit – MA gearbox (Sec 14)

1	Sleeve	4	Spring
2	Hub	5	Rocker
3	Ball		

14.106 Shafts and selector forks assembled in the clutch/final drive housing

14.108A Neutral return spring and plastic cups (arrowed)

14.108B Neutral return spring showing gate lever (arrowed) engaged with interlocking key

14.109A Insert the locking pin ...

14.109B ... and drive it through the selector shaft

14.113 Applying jointing compound to the clutch/final drive housing

Fig. 13.78 Locating the selector finger in the interlocking key – MA gearbox (Sec 14)

104   Apply locking fluid to the intermediate plate bolt threads. Insert the bolts and progressively tighten them to the specified torque (photos). Clean the excess adhesive from the bearing locations.

105   Tie the two selector fork shaft assemblies together (photo).

106   Engage the selector forks in the synchro unit grooves, and mesh the input and output shaft assemblies together. Using both hands, lower the complete assembly into the clutch/final drive housing (photo).

107   Locate the selector finger within the interlocking key, then lift the gate lever and insert the key assembly in the clutch/final drive housing. Make sure that the selector finger engages the fork gates, and that the gate lever engages the outer plate of the interlocking key.

108   Engage the plastic cups with the neutral return spring, and insert them between the interlocking key and intermediate plate (photos).

109   Fit the rubber boot on the selector shaft. Insert the shaft through the intermediate plate, interlocking key and selector finger, align the holes and drive in the locking pin (photos).

110   Insert the reverse selector arm in the intermediate plate, press down on it to depress the plunger, and insert the shaft. Make sure that the stud on the arm enters the cut-out on the control relay.

111   Engage the reverse idler gear with the selector arm, with the projecting shoulder uppermost, and insert the shaft, cut- out end downwards. Turn the shaft until the cut-out drops in the recess.

112   Fit the plastic ring on the shaft.

113   Apply a thin, even, coat of a silicone-based jointing compound to the mating face of the clutch/final drive housing (photo).

114   Lower the gearbox housing onto the clutch/final drive housing, at the same time guiding the input and output shaft bearings and selector fork shafts through their holes.

115   Insert the bolts in their previously-noted locations, and tighten them evenly to the specified torque.

116   Fit the retaining half-rings in the bearing grooves with the chamfers uppermost, then insert and tighten the bolts.

5-speed gearbox only

117   Locate the 5th speed drive gear on the input shaft splines, support the opposite end of the shaft on a block of wood, and fully drive the gear on the splines using a metal tube.

118   Fit the washer on the input shaft, with its convex side uppermost.

14.119 Squeezing circlip into groove in input shaft

14.123 Tightening the 5th synchro nut

14.124 Driving in the 5th selector fork locking pin

119   Fit the circlip using a suitable socket and hammer. Check that it is fully entered in the groove by squeezing with pliers (photo).
120   Fit the thrustwasher to the output shaft (oil groove uppermost) followed by the sleeve, needle bearing, 5th speed driven gear and the 5th synchro ring.
121   Engage the selector fork with the 5th synchro unit, then lower them onto the output shaft and selector fork shafts. Make sure that the projections on the synchro ring are aligned with the rockers in the synchro unit.
122   Fit the special lockwasher and nut (finger-tight).
123   Engage both reverse and 5th speed gears with reference to Fig. 13.73. Tighten the nut to the specified torque, then return the gears to neutral (photo).
124   Align the holes in the 5th speed selector fork and shaft, and drive in the locking pin (photo).

4 and 5-speed gearboxes
125   Fit the dry rubber gasket to the pressed-steel housing. Locate the housing on the gearbox housing, insert the bolts and tighten them to the specified torque.
126   Refit the speedometer drive pinion. Insert and tighten the bolt.
127   Apply a little grease to the guide sleeve, then refit the clutch release bearing and engage the spring clips with the fork ends.

Reverse selector components – modifications
128   From May 1988, the reverse selector components have been modified.

129   The later components can be identified from the modifications shown in Fig. 13.79.
130   The early components are no longer available, and are not interchangeable with the later components. If any of the relevant components are renewed on a gearbox fitted with the early components, the other associated components must also be renewed as a set.
131   Note that if the later components are fitted to an early gearbox, a later-type modified breather and cap *must* be fitted, to avoid possible fouling of the selector components.

Gearbox casing – modifications
132   From approximately June 1991, an oil deflector has been fitted to the gearbox casing, to improve the lubrication of the 3rd/4th speed synchroniser assembly. Note that the new gearbox casings are interchangeable with the older components, but an oil deflector cannot be fitted to an earlier gearbox.

5th speed synchro assembly – modifications
133   From late 1991, the 5th speed synchro hub is secured using Loctite. This modification affects the dismantling procedure given in paragraphs 25 to 52 of this Section, as follows.

Paragraph 33 – Mark the selector sleeve in relation to the hub. Cover the sleeve with a cloth, to retain the internal balls and springs. Remove the 5th speed sleeve together with the selector fork. Using a suitable three-legged puller, remove the synchro hub with the 5th speed driven gear (see Fig. 13.81). Separate the hub, synchro ring and gear.
Paragraph 34 – Remove from the output shaft the needle bearing, sleeve and thrustwasher.

EARLIER ASSEMBLY   LATER ASSEMBLY

Fig. 13.79 Modifications (a, b and c) to reverse selector components – MA gearbox (Sec 14)

Fig. 13.80 Oil deflector (arrowed) fitted to gearbox casing – later MA gearbox (Sec 14)

Fig. 13.81 Modified 5th speed synchromesh assembly – MA gearbox (Sec 14)

Mark the synchro sleeve (3) in relation to the hub (4)

134   The gearbox reassembly procedure given in paragraphs 101 to 127 of this Section is affected as follows.

> *Paragraph 121 – Coat the internal splines of the 5th synchro hub with Loctite (part No 9733.10 or 9734.41), then engage the selector fork with the 5th synchro unit, and lower them onto the output shaft and selector fork shafts. Make sure that the projections on the synchro ring are aligned with the rockers in the synchro unit.*
>
> *Paragraph 122 – Fit the special lockwasher, then coat the threads of a **new** nut with Loctite, and fit the nut to the end of the shaft finger-tight.*

---

15   Automatic transmission

General description
1   The automatic transmission was introduced in April 1986, and incorporates four forward speeds and one reverse.
2   In the interests of fuel economy, the torque converter is completely bypassed in top (4th) gear and partially bypassed in 3rd; this reduces losses due to torque converter slip.
3   Gearchange is automatic, the transmission responding to changes in speed and load. The usual kickdown facility is provided, for enhanced acceleration when the throttle is depressed fully.
4   Instead of the customary oil cooler mounted in the radiator, cooling is by means of a coolant/oil heat exchanger mounted on the side of the transmission.

Safety precautions
5   The following safety precautions must be adhered to where an automatic transmission is fitted. Whenever the vehicle is parked, or is being serviced or repaired, ensure that the handbrake is fully applied and the selector lever is in 'P'.
6   If it is necessary to tow a vehicle with automatic transmission, the towing speed must be restricted to 30 mph and the distance to 30 miles. If these conditions cannot be met, or if transmission damage is the reason for seeking a tow, the vehicle must be transported on a trailer.

Fluid level – checking
7   This check should be made directly after the vehicle has been used, so that the transmission oil is at its normal operating temperature.
8   With the vehicle parked on level ground and the engine running, move the selector lever through all positions a number of times, then finally leave it in 'P'. The handbrake must be fully applied throughout the check procedure.
9   With the engine still running, remove the transmission fluid dipstick, wipe it clean, reinsert it fully, then withdraw it again and check the fluid level. The fluid level must be between Min and Max levels.
10   If required, top-up the fluid level (but do not overfill) through the dipstick guide tube.
11   Stop the engine and refit the dipstick on completion.

Fluid – draining and refilling
12   Position a suitable container with a minimum capacity of three litres under the transmission (hot). There are two drain plugs to be removed, these being shown in Fig. 13.82. Remove the plugs and drain the fluid, then refit the plugs.
13   Refill, using 2.4 litres of the recommended fluid, through the dipstick guide tube.
14   Recheck the fluid level after a nominal mileage has been covered and, if necessary, top-up the fluid, as described in paragraphs 7 to 11 inclusive.

Kickdown cable (carburettor models) – checking and adjustment
15   The kickdown cable checks and adjustments must be made with the engine at normal operating temperature, the electric cooling fan having cut in, then switched off.
16   Where applicable, check and if necessary adjust the engine idle speed, as described in Section 8 of this Supplement.
17   With the engine switched off, first check the accelerator cable for correct adjustment. Detach the kickdown cable from the cam on the carburettor. Pull the accelerator cable sheath stop pin out, and reposition it to allow a small clearance at 'a' (Fig. 13.84). Depress the accelerator pedal fully, and simultaneously check that the carburettor throttle valves are fully opened.
18   Pull the kickdown cable as shown in Fig. 13.85 until resistance is felt, indicating the start of kickdown. At this point, the stop nipple on the cable must be distance 'x' (39.0 mm) from the end of the cable adjuster.
19   Reconnect the kickdown cable to the cam and fit the clip.
20   In the idle position, check that there is a small clearance between the stop nipple and the end of the cable adjuster (Fig. 13.86) up to a maximum of 0.5 mm. If necessary, reposition the adjuster by loosening the nuts, then re-tighten the nuts.
21   Kickdown cable renewal is best left to your Peugeot dealer, as it involves removal of the valve block.

Kickdown cable (fuel injection models) – checking and adjustment
22   At the time of writing, no information was available regarding adjustment of the kickdown cable on fuel injection models.

Selector control – adjustment
23   Remove the air cleaner, then using a spanner as shown in Fig. 13.87, disconnect the control rod balljoint from the lever on the transmission.
24   Move the lever on the transmission fully forwards to the 'P' position.
25   Inside the car, move the selector lever fully forwards to the 'P' position.
26   The control rod balljoint should align exactly with the coupling ball on the selector lever, so that when reconnected, neither the selector lever within the vehicle nor the selector lever on the gearbox move. Adjust the position of the balljoint on the connecting rod if necessary.
27   If the selector control was adjusted, check the setting by starting the engine and, when it has reached its normal operating temperature, move the selector lever within the vehicle to 'P'. The vehicle should be stationary, and the gearbox parking pawl fully engaged.
28   Now move the lever to 'R' with the handbrake off. The vehicle should move rearwards, the pawl having been released.
29   If either of the checks in paragraphs 27 and 28 is unsatisfactory, unscrew the control rod balljoint one complete turn, and repeat the checks until satisfactory.
30   Refit the air cleaner.

1   Converter housing
2   Main casing
3   End cover
4   Sump
5   Dipstick tube
6   Dipstick
7   Fluid cooler
8   Kickdown cable
9   Breather
10 Inhibitor switch
11 Selector lever
12 Lifting eye
13 Speedometer drive adaptor
14 Final drive left-hand output
15 Final drive right-hand output
16 Final drive drain plug
17 Torque converter
18 Output shaft bearing bolts
19 Brake band adjuster
20 Pressure test points
21 Transmission drain plug

Fig. 13.82 External components of the ZF 4 HP 14 automatic transmission (Sec 15)

Fig. 13.83 Filling the automatic transmission with fluid (Sec 15)

Fig. 13.84 There must be a clearance at (a) on the accelerator cable before adjusting the kickdown cable (Sec 15)

    1   Adjusting ferrule   *2   Stop pin*

Fig. 13.85 Checking the position of the stop nipple (1) on the kickdown cable (Sec 15)

For 'x', see text

Fig. 13.86 Checking idle clearance (a) on the kickdown cable (Sec 15)

    1   Adjustment nuts

Automatic transmission – removal and refitting

31   Remove the bonnet (Chapter 12).

32   Apply the handbrake and loosen the front wheel nuts, then jack up the front of the car and support on axle stands.

33   Remove both front roadwheels.

34   Drain the transmission fluid as previously described.

35   Remove both driveshafts as described in Chapter 7. The driveshafts are the same as fitted to GTI models.

36   Unscrew the dipstick tube nut from the transmission sump.

37   Unbolt the driveplate cover, then unscrew the torque converter bolts while holding the crankshaft pulley bolt with a bar and socket. The pulley may have a plastic cover on it, which must first be removed. The three torque converter bolts are spaced equally around the driveplate.

38   Remove the air cleaner (Chapter 3) and the battery and battery tray (Chapter 12).

39   Disconnect the selector control rod balljoint from the lever on the transmission, then unbolt the cable bracket.

40   Disconnect the fluid hoses from the cooler, and plug them.

41   Unbolt the earth cables.

42   Disconnect the wiring from the inhibitor switch.

43   Disconnect the kickdown cable at the carburettor/throttle body end, wind it into a loose coil and attach it to the transmission.

44   Unbolt and remove the dipstick tube and bracket.

45   Disconnect the speedometer cable, and unbolt the TDC sensor.

Fig. 13.87 Disconnecting the selector control rod balljoint (1) from the transmission lever (2) (Sec 15)

Fig. 13.88 Unscrew the dipstick tube nut (1) and torque converter bolts (2) (Sec 15)

Fig. 13.89 Using an engine support bar (Sec 15)

1   *Left-hand transmission mounting*

Fig. 13.90 Support the weight of the transmission, then unscrew the bolts (1) (Sec 15)

46   Support the weight of the engine. Peugeot recommend the use of a bar as shown in Fig. 13.89; however, a hoist may be used, or alternatively, a trolley jack and suitable cradle from below.
47   Unbolt the left-hand mounting, then lower the engine sufficiently to allow for removal of the transmission.
48   Support the weight of the transmission. A hoist may be used as shown in Fig. 13.90, or a trolley jack and suitable cradle from below.
49   Unscrew the three hexagon and single socket-head bolts securing the transmission to the engine.
50   Separate the transmission from the engine, while making sure that the torque converter remains engaged with the transmission. When clear of the engine, fit a bracket as shown in Fig. 13.91 to hold the torque converter in place.
51   Lower the transmission to the floor, and remove it from under the car.
52   Before refitting the transmission, check the condition of the spigot bush in the rear of the crankshaft, and apply a little grease to aid entry of the torque converter. Also check that the two locating dowels are in place on the engine. Apply a little grease to the differential/driveshaft seals.
53   Make sure that the torque converter is fully engaged by checking the dimension shown in Fig. 13.92. If necessary, rotate the torque converter until it is correctly engaged.

Fig. 13.91 Bracket and bolt (1) for holding toque converter in transmission (Sec 15)

Fig. 13.92 The torque converter is fully engaged if dimension 'x' is more than 7.0 mm (Sec 15)

1   *Retaining bracket and bolt*

16.2A Remove the bolt (arrowed) ...

16.2B ... and withdraw the front suspension lower balljoint for driveshaft removal

16.3 Inserting the right-hand driveshaft protector (arrowed)

16.4 Staking a locking-shoulder-type hub nut

16.5 Lockwasher and spring clip fitted to later-type hub nut

Fig. 13.93 Multi-position lockwasher and spring clip for locking the hub nut on later models (Sec 16)

54   Refitting is a reversal of removal, but tighten all nuts and bolts to the specified torque, and adjust the kickdown cable and selector control as previously described. Fill the transmission as previously described, and bleed the cooling system with reference to Chapter 2, Section 3.

Fault diagnosis – automatic transmission
55   Faults not due to incorrect fluid level or adjustment of the selector and kickdown cables must be diagnosed by a Peugeot dealer or automatic transmission specialist.
56   Do not remove the transmission for specialist repair without allowing the specialist to test it *in situ*. Some faults cannot be diagnosed with the transmission removed.

Modifications
57   From May 1987, the gear ratios have been changed to provide improved performance (see Specifications).

16   Driveshafts

Driveshafts (automatic transmission) – description
1   The driveshafts fitted to automatic transmission models are the same as those fitted to GTI models, as described in Chapter 7, and the following sub-section.

1,5 mm right-hand side
1,0 mm left-hand side

Casing

Seal

Shaft

Correct fitting   **Incorrect fitting**

Fig. 13.94 Correct fitting of modified differential/driveshaft oil seals – BE 1/5 gearbox (Sec 16)

Fig. 13.95 On DBA Bendix disc calipers, the lugs (1) may be ground away from the guide retaining plates (Sec 17)

Driveshafts – removal and refitting
2   On 1988 and later models, the procedure for driveshaft removal and refitting is basically as described in Section 4 of Chapter 7 (photos). Note, however, that paragraph 10 no longer applies for any model produced after early 1985.
3   Always use a plastic protector when refitting the right-hand driveshaft (photo).
4   On later models, a multi-position lockwasher and spring clip is fitted to the hub nut instead of the locking shoulder type of hub nut (photo).
5   After tightening the hub nut to the specified torque, locate the lockwasher over the nut so that the cut-outs in the shoulder are aligned with the hole in the driveshaft stub, then insert the spring clip (photo).

Driveshafts (1.9 GTI) – identification
6   The driveshafts on 1.9 GTI models are strengthened, and are identified by two grooves on the open shaft between the inner and outer joints. There are no grooves on the driveshafts for other models.

Differential/driveshaft oil seals (BE 1/5 gearbox) – modifications
7   During 1988, the differential/driveshaft oil seals were modified. The earlier seals are no longer available, and the revised seals will be supplied as spares for all models.
8   When fitting the later type of seal, **do not** drive the seal fully into the final drive housing, as the seal lip may fail to contact the driveshaft, causing oil leaks.
9   The oil seals must be fitted with the correct protrusion as shown in Fig. 13.94. Note the different protrusions for left and right-hand seals.

---

17   Conventional braking system

Braking system (CTI models) – description
1   The braking system on CTI models is the same as that described for GTI models in Chapter 8.
2   From 1991, ABS is available as an option. The ABS system is described later in this Supplement.

Abrasive disc pads – description
3   From late 1985, genuine Peugeot disc pads have a thin coating of abrasive material, which cleans the disc during the initial applications of the brakes. This coating also removes any disc imperfections which would cause steering vibration.

Fig. 13.96 Front view of DBA Bendix disc calipers fitted with offset disc pads (Sec 17)

4   After fitting these pads, the brakes must be applied lightly and intermittently for the first 3 miles (5 km), then 'bedded-in' for 120 miles (200 km), avoiding heavy or prolonged braking wherever possible.
5   Note that non-genuine disc pads may not have the abrasive coating.

DBA Bendix disc calipers and pads – modifications
6   On early models fitted with the DBA Bendix disc calipers, the lugs on the guide retaining plates can cause misalignment of the guide sleeves, resulting in the outer disc pads wearing quicker than the inner pads. The lugs have been discontinued on later retaining plates, and may be ground off the earlier type if necessary.
7   From September 1987, offset front disc pads may be fitted to some models, to reduce squeal and whistle. It is important to fit these pads in the correct positions as shown in Fig. 13.96. The inner pads with pad wear wires must be located at the top of the caliper.

Girling disc pads – modifications
8   From chassis no 5 600 000, an anti-squeal shim (Fig. 13.97) was fitted between the inner disc pads and the caliper pistons, being located on both upper and lower pad retaining pins. However, as from chassis no 5 957 000, the shim was modified to the shape shown in Fig. 13.98, being located only on the lower pad retaining pin.
9   When fitting the anti-squeal shims, the arrow cut-out must face downwards (ie in the forward rotational direction of the disc).
10   If problems of brake squeal are experienced on models fitted with the early type of shim, the later type should be fitted instead.

Handbrake (models with rear drum brakes) – adjustment
11   On all models from 1988, VIN No 1 285 000 approximately, the handbrake adjustment has been revised.
12   The procedure for adjustment remains as described in Chapter 8, Section 14, but note that in paragraph 2 the handbrake lever should be placed on the seventh notch, and in paragraph 8 the brakes should be fully applied after pulling the handbrake lever up between 7 and 9 notches.

Braking system (1.9 GTI) – description
13   The 1.9 GTI braking system differs from the system fitted to the 1.6 GTI, in that the hydraulic circuit is split diagonally, the Girling front disc caliper is modified, DBA rear disc calipers are fitted, and two rear brake compensators are fitted in the two rear hydraulic circuits.

Fig. 13.97 Anti-squeal shim fitted to early Girling disc pads (Sec 17)

Fig. 13.98 Anti-squeal shim fitted to later Girling disc pads (Sec 17)

17.16 Pad wear warning light wire and connector

Fig. 13.99 Retracting the automatic handbrake adjustment on a 1.9 GTI model (Sec 17)

1   Piston

Front disc pads (1.9 GTI) – inspection and renewal

14   Apply the handbrake, then jack up the front of the car and support on axle stands. Remove the front roadwheels.

15   Viewing through the hole in the caliper, check if the friction material has worn down to 2.0 mm (0.079 in) or less. This is indicated by the central groove in the pads, which will not be visible when the wear limit is reached.

16   To remove the pads, first disconnect the wire for the pad wear warning light (photo).

17   Hold the lower guide stationary with one spanner, then unscrew the bolt (photo).

18   Swivel the caliper upwards, then withdraw the two disc pads from the bracket (photos).

19   Clean away all dust and dirt, but do not inhale the dust, as it may be injurious to health. Check for brake fluid leakage around the piston dust seal and, if evident, overhaul the caliper with reference to Chapter 8. Check the brake disc for wear, and also check that the rubber bellows on the guides are in good condition.

20   Push the piston fully into the cylinder.

21   Clean the backs of the disc pads, and apply a little anti-squeal brake grease. Refit the inner pad (with the pad wear warning wire), then the outer pad.

22   Lower the caliper. Apply locking fluid to the lower guide bolt, insert it, and tighten to the specified torque while holding the guide stationary with another spanner.

23   Reconnect the pad wear warning light wire.

24   Fully depress the brake pedal several times to set the disc pads in their normal position.

25   Check the fluid level in the reservoir, and top-up if necessary.

26   Repeat the operations on the opposite disc caliper.

27   Refit the roadwheels, and lower the car to the ground.

Rear disc pads (1.9 GTI) – inspection and renewal

28   Chock the front wheels, then jack up the rear of the car and support on axle stands. Remove the rear wheels.

29   Release the handbrake.

30   Check the disc pads for wear as described in paragraph 15.

31   To remove the pads, extract the spring clip (photo) and slide out the locking key retaining the bottom of the pads.

32   Withdraw the disc pads using pliers, while pressing down on the upper locating ears (photo).

33   Clean away all dust and dirt, taking care not to inhale it, as it may be injurious to health. Check for brake fluid leakage around the piston dust seal, and if evident, overhaul the caliper using the basic procedure described in Chapter 8. Check the brake disc for wear, and also check that the rubber bellows on the guides are in good condition.

34   The automatic handbrake adjustment must now be retracted, in order to accommodate the new disc pads. To do this, turn the piston using a screwdriver in the grooves (photo), at the same time using a second screwdriver to apply an outward force to the caliper. Do not damage the brake disc while carrying out this procedure.

35   Set the piston so that the mark (Fig. 13.100) is horizontal, and either above or below the piston groove.

36   Apply a little anti-squeal brake grease to the pad contact areas on the caliper.

37   Locate the two disc pads in the caliper, pressing the upper ears fully into position.

38   Slide the locking key into the caliper, and secure with the spring clip.

39   Fully depress the brake pedal several times to set the automatic adjuster and position the disc pads in their normal position.

17.17 Unscrewing the lower caliper guide bolt

17.18A Swivel the caliper upwards ...

17.18B ... and withdraw the disc pads

17.31 Spring clip (arrowed) retaining locking key

17.32 Removing the rear disc pads

17.34 Turning the rear caliper piston with a screwdriver

17.45 Rear caliper brake hose and union

17.46 Handbrake cable attachment at rear caliper

17.57 Rear brake compensator

40 Check the fluid level in the reservoir, and top-up if necessary.
41 Repeat the operations on the opposite disc caliper.
42 Refit the roadwheels and lower the car to the ground.

Rear disc caliper (1.9 GTI) – removal and refitting

43 Remove the disc pads as previously described.
44 Fit a brake hose clamp to the flexible hose connected to the caliper. Alternatively, where possible, remove the filler cap from the brake fluid reservoir, then tighten it down onto a piece of polythene sheeting.
45 Loosen the brake hose union at the caliper (photo).

46 Unhook the handbrake cable from the lever on the caliper, and withdraw the outer cable (photo).
47 Unscrew the two mounting bolts, withdraw the caliper from the disc, then unscrew the caliper from the brake hose. Plug the hose to prevent loss of fluid.
48 To refit the caliper, first screw it onto the brake hose and locate it over the brake disc, so that the hose is not twisted.
49 Clean the mounting bolt threads, and apply a little locking fluid. Insert the bolts together with the anti-rotation plate, and tighten them to the specified torque.
50 Tighten the brake hose union.
51 Insert the handbrake outer cable, and re-connect the inner cable to the lever.
52 Refit the disc pads as previously described.
53 Remove the brake hose clamp or polythene sheeting, and bleed the hydraulic system with reference to paragraph 62.
54 Check and if necessary adjust the handbrake, as described in paragraphs 63 to 70.

Brake discs (1.9 GTI) – removal and refitting

55 The procedure is as given in Chapter 8, Section 6. However, before removing the front disc, the caliper must be unbolted and tied to one side. There is no need to disconnect the hydraulic hose.
56 Refer to Chapter 8, Section 5 when refitting the caliper.

Rear brake compensators (1.9 GTI) – general

57 Two compensators are fitted, since the hydraulic system is split diagonally. Each compensator is located in the rear circuit near the rear wheel (photo). They are of fixed calibration, and not load-sensitive.
58 Removal and refitting procedures are basically as given in Chapter 8, Section 10.
59 From December 1988, modified compensators have been fitted.
60 The modified components can be identified by the letter on the body – see Fig. 13.101. Early components have the identifying letter "F", while later components have the identifying letter "E".
61 The later components can be used to replace the early components, but both compensators **must** be of the same type.

Hydraulic system (1.9 GTI) – draining and bleeding

62 Refer to Chapter 8, Section 12, and proceed as for the diagonally-split system.

Fig. 13.100 Correct final position of piston on a 1.9 GTI rear caliper (Sec 17)

1 Piston   3 Groove
2 Mark

Fig. 13.101 Location of identifying letter on rear brake compensators – 1.9 GTI model (Sec 17)

Fig. 13.102 Handbrake adjustment on 1.9 GTI model (Sec 17)

1   Handbrake operating lever on the caliper   a = 5.0 mm

Handbrake (1.9 GTI) – adjustment

63   Chock the wheels and fully release the handbrake.
64   Apply the brake pedal hard several times.
65   Working inside the car, remove the screw and lift the cover from the handbrake lever.
66   Working beneath the rear of the car, measure the distance between the operating levers on the calipers and the end stops on the inner cables.
67   Inside the car, loosen the nut on the handbrake lever until the distance measured in paragraph 66 is 5.0 mm (0.197 in) on both sides.
68   Check that the operating levers on both calipers move freely and return positively to their stops.
69   Now tighten the nut on the handbrake lever so that the handbrake is fully applied between 7 and 9 notches. Do not over-adjust so that the handbrake is fully applied over fewer notches, otherwise the automatic adjusters will not operate correctly.
70   Refit the cover over the handbrake lever.

Handbrake cables (1.9 GTI) – renewal

71   Working inside the car, remove the screw and lift the cover from the handbrake lever.
72   Unhook the cable from the compensator.
73   Chock the front wheels, then jack up the rear of the car and support on axle stands.
74   Release the cable(s) from the retaining clips, the floor, the fuel tank, the bracket(s), and the caliper lever(s), and withdraw from under the car.
75   Fit the new cable(s) using a reversal of the removal procedure. Finally adjust the handbrake as described previously.

Stop-lamp switch – removal and refitting

76   Remove the lower facia panel from the steering column.
77   Disconnect the two wires (photo).

78   Unscrew the locknut nearest the pedal, and withdraw the switch from the bracket.
79   Refitting is a reversal of removal, but adjust the locknuts so that the distance between the end of the switch threaded body and the pedal (fully released) is 3.5 mm.

18   Anti-lock braking system (ABS)

Warning: *It is strongly recommended that any work involving components of the braking system on a vehicle equipped with ABS is entrusted to a Peugeot dealer, who will have the necessary specialist knowledge and equipment to carry out the work safely and effectively. Before starting any work on the ABS hydraulic system, the battery negative lead must be disconnected, and the brown three-way, brown five-way and green five-way wiring connectors must be disconnected from the regulator unit to prevent the possibility of air entering the system. The connectors must not be reconnected until the hydraulic system has been bled.*

Anti-lock braking system (ABS) – description

1   From 1991, the Bendix anti-lock braking system is available as an option on GTI models.
2   The system is fail-safe, and is fitted in addition to the conventional braking system, which allows the vehicle to retain conventional braking in the event of a failure in the ABS system.
3   To prevent wheel locking, the system provides pressure modulation in the brake circuits. To achieve this, sensors mounted at each front wheel monitor the rotational speeds of the wheels, and are thus able to detect when there is a risk of wheel locking (low rotational speed). Solenoid valves are positioned in the brake circuits to all four wheels, and the solenoid valves are incorporated in the regulator unit, which is controlled by an electronic control unit. The electronic control unit controls modulation of the braking effort applied to each wheel, according to the information supplied by the wheel sensors.
4   Should a fault develop in the system, a self-diagnostic facility is incorporated in the electronic control unit, which can be used in conjunction with specialist diagnostic equipment available to a Peugeot dealer to determine the nature of the fault.
5   The brake components used on models fitted with ABS are similar to those used on models with a conventional braking system. Rear disc brakes are fitted to all ABS-equipped models, and all procedures for the rear brake and handbrake components are as described for 1.9 GTI models in Section 16 of this Chapter. Refer to the following paragraphs for details of the additional ABS components, and the special hydraulic system bleeding procedure to be observed.

17.77 Stop-lamp switch and wiring plug (arrowed)

Fig. 13.103 Schematic layout of ABS system (Sec 18)

1 Brake calipers
2 Master cylinder
3 Rear brake compensators
4 Wheel sensors
5 Regulator unit
6 Electronic control unit

Hydraulic system – draining and bleeding

Warning: *Refer to the warning note at the beginning of this Section before proceeding.*

6   During the bleeding procedure, the following points must be observed.

The hydraulic fluid level must be maintained by topping-up.
Use only clean, bubble-free hydraulic fluid.
Take extreme care to prevent dirt from entering the hydraulic system.

7   If the hydraulic system is to be drained, follow the procedure given in Chapter 8, Section 2, but bleed the system with reference to this Section. If the master cylinder, regulator unit or connecting pipes have been removed, the complete hydraulic system must be bled, and it is recommended that the complete system is bled if a caliper is removed.
8   Bleed the four brake calipers using one of the methods described in Chapter 8, Section 12, in the order given for GTI models.
9   Connect a suitable length of tubing to the bleed screw (1) in Fig. 13.104 on the ABS regulator unit, in a similar manner to that used to bleed the calipers.
10   Have an assistant depress the brake pedal and hold it down.

11   Open the bleed screw, then close the screw and tighten it. Take care not to overtighten the bleed screw (as a guide, the recommended torque wrench setting is 6.5 Nm/5.0 lbf ft).
12   Have the assistant release the brake pedal.
13   Repeat the procedure given in paragraphs 10 to 12 inclusive until hydraulic fluid, free from air bubbles, flows from the bleed screw.
14   Similarly, repeat the procedure for the bleed screw (2) in Fig. 13.104.
15   Proceed as described in Chapter 8, Section 12, paragraph 21 onwards.
16   On completion, reconnect the three wiring connectors to the regulator unit, and reconnect the battery negative lead.

Regulator unit – removal and refitting

17   At the time of writing, no information was available regarding removal and refitting of the regulator unit.

Wheel sensor – removal and refitting

18   The wheel sensors are mounted in the rear of the hub carriers. To remove a wheel sensor, proceed as follows.
19   Disconnect the battery negative lead.
20   Carefully pull the sensor wiring from its retaining clips, and working under the wing, disconnect the sensor wiring connector.
21   Unscrew the securing bolt, and withdraw the sensor from the hub carrier.
22   Refitting is a reversal of removal, but ensure that the front face of the sensor (2) shown in Fig. 13.105 is perfectly clean, and ensure that the wiring is correctly routed. Clean the sensor securing bolt threads, then apply suitable thread-locking fluid and tighten the bolt securely.

Electronic control unit – removal and refitting

23   The electronic control unit is located on the left-hand side of the luggage compartment. To remove the control unit, proceed as follows.
24   Disconnect the battery negative lead.
25   Open the tailgate, and carefully pull the trim from the left-hand side of the luggage compartment to reveal the control unit.
26   Unscrew the securing nuts, and withdraw the cover from the control unit.
27   Disconnect the control unit wiring plug.
28   Unscrew the securing nuts, and withdraw the control unit from its mounting bracket.
29   Refitting is reversal of removal.

Fig. 13.104 Bleed screws (1 and 2) on ABS regulator unit (Sec 18)

Fig. 13.105 ABS wheel sensor (1). Front face (2) must be perfectly clean before fitting (Sec 18)

H.20486

Fig. 13.106 7.0 mm diameter front anti-roll bar guide bar and split clamp (Sec 19)

1   Mounting bolt   x = 101.0 mm
2   Split clamp

19   Suspension and hubs

Front anti-roll bar (non-GTI models) – general

1   On non-GTI models, the front anti-roll bar is located laterally by a guide bar. It is possible for the bar to become dislocated or bent following an impact to a front wheel, resulting in the vehicle pulling to the left or right.

2   The guide bar length must be adjusted as described in Chapter 9, Section 3. Note that a full-circle clamp is fitted to early models with a 6.0 mm diameter bar, whereas a split clamp is fitted to later models with a 7.0 mm diameter bar. On the later type, position the clamp centrally on the turned-back end of the bar before tightening the bolts.

Rear suspension assembly (five-door models) – modification

3   On five-door models manufactured from mid-September 1986 onwards, the seat belt anchorage shown in photo 12.5, Chapter 9 is no longer fitted. However, the anchorage must always be fitted to earlier five-door models, and all three-door models.

Rear hub/drum assembly – modifications

4   Models manufactured from early 1986 are fitted with modified rear hub/drum assemblies which allow the rear hub bearings to be renewed, this not previously being possible. Reference to Fig. 13.107 shows that the oil seal shoulder is removed on the later hub/drum assemblies, in order to allow the use of a special bearing removal tool (Peugeot tool No. 7.052X).

5   Bearing renewal requires the use of a press in conjunction with the special tool to remove the old bearing, and this is best entrusted to your Peugeot dealer (once removed, a bearing is rendered unserviceable).

6   When renewing the oil seal, Peugeot recommended the use of special tool No. 7.052Y to seat the new seal. If unavailable, make a careful note of the position of the original seal before removing it.

20   Power steering system

Power steering system – maintenance

1   A power steering system is fitted as standard equipment to certain models, and is available as a factory-fitted option on others.

2   At the intervals specified in the *Routine maintenance* Section at the beginning of this manual, check the level of the fluid in the power steering fluid reservoir, which is located adjacent to the battery.

3   With the fluid cold, the level must not be below the "MIN" mark. If necessary, top-up with the specified type of fluid.

4   The power steering pump is driven by the alternator drivebelt, and the drivebelt tension should be periodically checked as described in Chapter 12, Section 2.

5   Regularly check all system hoses and unions for signs of damage or leakage.

Fig. 13.107 Early (A) and later (B) rear hub oil seal locations (Sec 19)

Fig. 13.108 Extract the spring clip (6) from the gearchange linkage (Sec 20)

Power steering pump – removal and refitting

6   Remove the alternator as described in Chapter 12, Section 6.

7   Prepare a suitable container, then disconnect the fluid hoses from the pump, and allow the fluid to drain into the container.

8   Unscrew and remove the power steering pump mounting bolts, then withdraw the pump.

9   Refitting is a reversal of removal, but on completion, tension the drivebelt as described in Chapter 12, Section 2, and bleed the power steering hydraulic system as described later in this Section.

Power steering gear – removal and refitting

10   Apply the handbrake, then jack up the front of the vehicle and support securely on axle stands.

11   Prepare a suitable container, then disconnect the fluid pipes from the steering gear, and allow the fluid to drain into the container.

12   Unscrew the track rod end balljoint nuts, then use a separator tool to detach the track rod end balljoints from the hub carriers.

13   Mark the lower column in relation to the pinion on the steering gear.

14   Unscrew and remove the column-to-pinion clamp bolt.

15   Disconnect the three gearchange control rods from the levers on the gearbox.

16   Extract the spring clip ("6" in Fig. 13.108) from the gearchange linkage, then unclip the gearbox selector and engagement rods, and support them in an upright position out of the way, using wire or string.

17   Remove the two steering gear securing bolts, and recover the spacer tubes from the subframe, then disconnect the steering gear pinion from the steering column shaft.

18   Support the front subframe using a trolley jack and interposed block of wood positioned under the subframe crossmember.

19   Refer to Fig. 13.109, and remove the four bolts securing the rear of the subframe to the body, and the two nuts or bolts, as applicable, securing the front of the subframe to the body. Also remove the nut and bolt from the lower engine mounting.

20   Carefully lower the subframe sufficiently to enable removal of the steering gear, ensuring that the subframe is adequately supported.

21   Rotate the steering gear towards the rear of the vehicle, and withdraw the assembly over the rear of the subframe, taking care not to damage the rack bellows.

22   Refitting is a reversal of removal, bearing in mind the following points.

23   Do not forget to fit the spacer tubes to the steering gear securing bolts.

24   Tighten all fixings to the specified torque.

25   Ensure that the marks made on the steering gear pinion and the lower column during removal are aligned.

26   When reconnecting the fluid pipes to the steering gear, the high-pressure fluid pipe (1) in Fig. 13.110 must be vertical.

27   Secure the hose (10) in Fig. 13.110 to the high-pressure fluid pipe (1) using a cable tie.

Fig. 13.109 The front subframe must be lowered to enable removal of the power steering gear (Sec 20)

9   Subframe securing bolts (rear)   11   Lower engine mounting nut
10   Subframe securing bolts (front)

28   Check the gearchange mechanism for correct operation after reconnecting the linkages.

29   On completion, check the front wheel alignment as described in Chapter 10, Section 10, and bleed the power steering hydraulic system as described later in this Section.

Power steering hydraulic system – bleeding

30   Fill the fluid reservoir to within 20 to 30 mm (0.8 to 1.1 in) of the rim with the specified type of fluid.

31   With the engine stopped, turn the steering wheel slowly from lock to lock.

32   Top-up the reservoir.

33   Start the engine.

34   Turn the steering wheel slowly from lock to lock several times, ensuring that the fluid level does not drop below the "MIN" mark on the reservoir.

35   Stop the engine and allow the fluid to cool, then recheck the fluid level and top-up if necessary. With the fluid cold, the level must not be below the "MIN" mark.

Fig. 13.110 Correct refitting of power steering gear (Sec 20)

1   High-pressure pipe   10   Hose secured with cable tie
3   Column-to-pinion clamp bolt

Fig. 13.111 Removing the fixed rear quarterlight glass on Cabriolet models (Sec 21)

Fig. 13.112 Door glass height adjustment screw (1) shown during removal and regulator assembly – Cabriolet model (Sec 21)

21   Bodywork and fittings

Minor body damage – repair
Plastic components

1   With the use of more and more plastic body components by the vehicle manufacturers (eg bumpers, spoilers, and in some cases major body panels), rectification of more serious damage to such items has become a matter of either entrusting repair work to a specialist in this field, or renewing complete components. Repair of such damage by the DIY owner is not really feasible owing to the cost of the equipment and materials required for effecting such repairs. The basic technique in-volves making a groove along the line of the crack in the plastic using a rotary burr in a power drill. The damaged part is then welded back together by using a hot air gun to heat up and fuse a plastic filler rod into the groove. Any excess plastic is then removed and the area rubbed down to a smooth finish. It is important that a filler rod of the correct plastic is used, as body components can be made of a variety of different types (eg polycarbonate, ABS, polypropylene).

2   If the owner is renewing a complete component himself, or if he has repaired it with epoxy filler, he will be left with the problem of finding a suitable paint for finishing which is compatible with the type of plastic used. At one time the use of a universal paint was not possible owing to the complex range of plastics encountered in body component applica-tions. Standard paints, generally speaking, will not bond to plastic or rubber satisfactorily, but Holts Professional Spraymatch paints to match any plastic or rubber finish can be obtained from dealers.

Fig. 13.113 Door glass rear edge adjustment screw (1) on Cabriolet models (Sec 21)

a   Switch wiring

However, it is now possible to obtain a plastic body parts finishing kit which consists of a pre-primer treatment, a primer and coloured top coat. Full instructions are normally supplied with a kit, but basically the method of use is to first apply the pre-primer to the component concerned and allow it to dry for up to 30 minutes. Then the primer is applied and left to dry for about an hour before finally applying the special coloured top coat. The result is a correctly coloured component where the paint will flex with the plastic or rubber, a property that standard paint does not normally possess.

Door trim panel – removal and refitting
3   On certain later models, the radio speakers are located in the doors, and it is therefore necessary to disconnect the speaker wiring during removal of the door trim panel.

Door (Cabriolet) – dismantling and reassembly
4   Remove the trim panel.
5   Where applicable, disconnect the battery, then disconnect the wiring from the regulator motor.
6   Unscrew the nuts and withdraw the regulator from the door.
7   Detach the weatherstrips from the top edge of the door.
8   Raise the door glass, and lift it from the door.
9   Unscrew the mounting nuts, and remove the fixed quarterlight glass through the sliding glass location.
10   Reassembly is a reversal of dismantling, but carry out the follow-ing adjustments. Temporarily refit the window regulator handle, or reconnect the regulator motor wiring, as applicable, then close the window, and if necessary adjust the height of the window by reaching in through the speaker aperture and turning the screw indicated in Fig. 13.112. (The illustration shows the regulator part-removed – with the regulator installed, access to the adjustment screw is possible through the speaker aperture). Close the door, and check that the rear edge of the door glass seals correctly with the hood. If not, remove the cap and turn the screw shown in Fig. 13.113.

Rear quarterlight glass and regulator (Cabriolet) – removal and refitting
11   Fold down the front and rear seats, then open the hood a little way.
12   Fully close the quarterlight.
13   Unbolt the seat belt lower anchor.
14   Note the position of the regulator handle, then remove it using pliers of the type shown in Fig. 13.114 or an alternative similar instru-ment.
15   Using a wide-bladed screwdriver, release the plastic clips and withdraw the trim panel.
16   Pull off the polythene sheet.
17   Unscrew the five bolts securing the regulator mechanism.
18   Remove the casing from the hood hinge.
19   Remove the pad from the quarter glass lower channel.
20   Push in the regulator mechanism, then tilt it and withdraw it through the aperture, complete with the cable. Take care not to damage the seat belt reel.
21   Remove the inner quarter glass weatherstrip and clips.

Fig. 13.114 Using special pliers to remove the rear quarterlight glass regulator handle on Cabriolet models (Sec 21)

1   *Seat belt lower anchor*   2   *Regulator handle*

Fig. 13.115 Removing the rear quarterlight glass regulator mechanism on Cabriolet models (Sec 21)

Fig. 13.116 Plastic rivets (1) securing the stretcher support on Cabriolet models (Sec 21)

Fig. 13.117 Removing the rear quarterlight glass on Cabriolet models (Sec 21)

1   *Guide channel*

Fig. 13.118 Channel position on the rear quarterlight glass – Cabriolet models (Sec 21)

x = 145.0 mm   1   Guide pads

Fig. 13.119 Screw (a) and sleeve (b) for fitting the guide pads to the rear quarterlight glass on Cabriolet models (Sec 21)

Fig. 13.120 Hood opening balance point – Cabriolet models (Sec 21)

Fig. 13.121 Prise off the trim caps (1) and unscrew the hinge cover securing screw (2) – Cabriolet models (Sec 21)

Fig. 13.122 Hood bracket securing bolt (3) and lower hood securing bolts (4 and 5) – Cabriolet models (Sec 21)

Fig. 13.123 Slide off the retaining strips (6) and release the hood lining retaining clips (a) – Cabriolet models (Sec 21)

22   Push the plastic rivet centre pins (Fig. 13.116) and remove the stretcher support.
23   Lift the glass and remove it.
24   Refitting is a reversal of removal. If a new glass is being fitted, position the lower channel as shown in Fig. 13.118. Remove the guide pads from the old glass by drilling out the rivet heads. Fit them to the new glass using the special sleeves and screws obtainable from a Peugeot dealer. Apply a little locking fluid to the screw threads before inserting and tightening them. Unlike the door glass, there are no adjustment points.

Hood and rear window (Cabriolet) – removal and refitting
25   Open the hood to the point where it is in balance, as shown in Fig. 13.120.
26   Working inside the vehicle, prise off the trim caps, and unscrew the hinge cover securing screws.
27   Working outside the vehicle, unscrew the brackets and securing bolts shown in Fig. 13.122.
28   Fold down the rear seats and remove the parcel shelf, then slide off the retaining strips and unclip the edges of the hood lining.
29   Release the three press-studs, prise off the rear hood crossmember trim strip, then extract the crossmember securing screws and withdraw the crossmember.
30   Unzip the rear window, and release the velcro securing strips from the hood, then withdraw the window from outside the vehicle.

Fig. 13.124 Release the three press-studs (7) and remove the crossmember trim strip for access to the crossmember securing screws (8) – Cabriolet models (Sec 21)

Fig. 13.125 Unclip the tensioners (11) and remove the bracket securing bolts (12 and 13) – Cabriolet models (Sec 21)

Fig. 13.126 Remove the remaining hood securing bolts (14) – Cabriolet models (Sec 21)

Fig. 13.127 Refit the lower frame securing bolts (1), then partially unfold the hood and loosely refit the bolts (2) – Cabriolet models (Sec 21)

Fig. 13.128 The hooks (3) must line up with their strikers (4). Note striker locknut (7) – Cabriolet models (Sec 21)

31   Refer to Fig. 13.125, and unclip the tensioners, then remove the indicated bracket securing bolts.
32   Fold the hood down, remove the remaining hood frame securing bolts, then lift the frame from the vehicle.
33   Commence refitting as follows.
34   Place the hood in its compartment, and with reference to Fig. 13.127, refit the lower frame securing bolts (1). Do not tighten the screws at this stage.
35   Partially unfold the hood, then loosely refit the bolts (2) in Fig. 13.127. **Note:** *Ensure that the brackets (11) in Fig. 13.129 are not lodged in the hinges, which may cause scratching of the paint on the rear wings.*
36   Fully unfold the hood, and check that the hooks at the front corners of the hood line up with their strikers – see Fig. 13.128. If the hooks and strikers are not aligned, move the hood support brackets (the securing bolt holes are elongated) until satisfactory alignment is obtained.
37   Open and close the hood a number of times to ensure that it operates correctly, then tighten the lower frame securing bolts.
38   The effort required to operate the handle can be adjusted by loosening the locknuts (7) in Fig. 13.128 and adjusting the length of the hooks to obtain a force at the handle of approximately 5 N (11 lbf).
39   Partially fold the hood, and refit the rear window and the hood rear crossmember and trim strip.
40   Clip the tensioners to their lugs, then refit the bracket securing bolts.

41   Fold the hood completely flat, and check that the stops (12) in Fig. 13.129 are in contact with the rear stretcher. If adjustment is required, loosen the locknuts (13) and adjust the length of the stops as necessary.
42   Partially raise the hood, then clip the edges of the hood lining in place, and refit the retaining strips.
43   Clip the hood lining side strips in place.

Power-operated hood components – removal and refitting
Note: *Whenever any work is carried out which involves disconnecting the hood hydraulic fluid pipes, the hydraulic fluid circuit must be bled. At the time of writing, little information was available regarding this procedure, and it is recommended that the task is entrusted to a Peugeot dealer.*

Hydraulic ram
44   Tilt the rear seat cushion, then pull the weatherstrip from the front edge of the rear passenger compartment side trim panel.
45   Unbolt the rear seat belt lower anchor.
46   Note the position of the window regulator handle, then remove it using a suitable pair of pliers, or a suitable alternative tool – Fig. 13.114.
47   Using a wide-bladed screwdriver, release the plastic clips and withdraw the trim panel.
48   Tilt the rear seat back, then remove the three fasteners, and withdraw the cover from the hydraulic ram.

Fig. 13.129 Hood stop adjustment – Cabriolet models (Sec 21)

10 *Tensioner clip*   12 *Stop*
11 *Bracket*   13 *Locknut*

Fig. 13.130 Power-operated hood hydraulic ram cover (1) and fasteners (6) – Cabriolet models (Sec 21)

Fig. 13.131 Power-operated hood hydraulic fluid pipes – Cabriolet models (Sec 21)

7 *Strap*   9 *Ram lower clip*
8 *Hydraulic fluid pipes* 10 *Ram upper clip*

Fig. 13.132 Removing the power-operated hood hydraulic ram – Cabriolet models (Sec 21)

11 *Hydraulic ram*   13 *Lower fixing*
12 *Lower pin*   14 *Fluid pipe unions*

Hydraulic pump
58   The hydraulic pump is located behind the felt trim on the right-hand side of the luggage compartment.
59   Disconnect the battery negative lead.
60   Carefully prise the trim from the side of the luggage compartment.
61   Unscrew the three bolts securing the pump mounting bracket to the body panel, and withdraw the pump from its location. Note that one of the mounting bracket bolts also secures the hydraulic fluid hose bracket.
62   Cover the boot carpet with plastic sheeting or similar protection, to guard against hydraulic fluid spillage.
63   Identify the fluid hoses to aid refitting, then place the pump over a suitable container (to catch the fluid which will be released) and disconnect the fluid hoses.
64   Disconnect the pump wiring connector, and remove the pump.
65   Refitting is a reversal of removal, bearing in mind the following points.
66   Ensure that the fluid pipes are correctly reconnected, as noted during removal.
67   On completion, the hydraulic fluid circuit must be bled, and the fluid level should be topped-up. It is recommended that these operations are entrusted to a Peugeot dealer.

49   Refer to Fig. 13.131 and cut the strap (7) to free the hydraulic hoses.
50   Release the clip from the bottom of the ram by tilting it upwards, and remove the clip from the top of the ram.
51   Tilt the ram, then pivot the ram to enable removal of the lower pin (12) in Fig. 13.132.
52   Remove the lower fixing, and detach the ram from the body.
53   Cover the seats with plastic sheeting or similar protection, to guard against hydraulic fluid spillage.
54   Identify the fluid hoses to aid refitting, then place the ram over a suitable container (to catch the fluid which will be released), disconnect the fluid hoses and withdraw the ram.
55   Refitting is a reversal of removal, bearing in mind the following points.
56   Ensure that the fluid pipes are correctly reconnected, as noted during removal.
57   On completion, the hydraulic fluid circuit must be bled, and the fluid level should be topped-up. It is recommended that these operations are entrusted to a Peugeot dealer.

Fig. 13.133 Power-operated hood hydraulic pump location –
Cabriolet models (Sec 21)

1	Felt trim	7	Hydraulic fluid pipes
5	Bolt	8	Hydraulic pump
6	Pump mounting bracket bolts	9	Pump mounting bracket

Hydraulic pump supply relays
68 The hydraulic pump supply relays are located behind the felt trim
on the left-hand side of the luggage compartment.
69 Disconnect the battery negative lead.
70 Carefully prise the trim from the side of the luggage compartment.
71 Remove the relevant relay securing screw, then disconnect the
wiring plug, and remove the relay.
72 Refitting is a reversal of removal.

Sunroof glass – removal and refitting
73 Working inside the car, remove the roof console. Then remove the
screws from the sunroof handle and latch.
74 From outside the car, remove the front cover and the corner
screws.
75 Slide off the side covers to the rear, while exerting outward
pressure.
76 Remove the rear stops, then withdraw the sunroof rearwards.
Take care not to damage the top edge of the tailgate.
77 Refitting is a reversal of removal, but lightly grease the guide
channels. Should resonance be a problem when the sunroof is open, a
modified rubber seal or a wind deflector is available to eliminate the
trouble.

*Heater assembly (models from 1986/87) – removal,
dismantling and refitting*
78 It is not necessary to completely remove the facia panel as
described in Chapter 11, Section 23. First remove the gear lever trim and
centre console.

Fig. 13.134 Power-operated hood hydraulic pump supply relay
location – Cabriolet models (Sec 21)

| 5 | Felt trim | 7 | Relays |
| 6 | Relay securing screws | | |

Fig. 13.135 Sunroof handle screws (1) and latch screws (2) (Sec 21)

Fig. 13.136 Remove the sunroof front cover (1) and corner screws (2
and 3) (Sec 21)

Fig. 13.137 Removing the sunroof rearwards (Sec 21)

21.89 Removing a right-hand lower facia panel securing screw

79   Remove the driver's side parcel shelf and lower steering column shroud.
80   Remove the heater side trims by uncoupling the box-section sleeves.
81   Unscrew the heater panel screws, but do not remove the panel at this stage.
82   Clamp the heater hoses inside the engine compartment.
83   Inside the car, protect the carpet from water spillage with a polythene sheet, then remove the heater pipes.
84   Remove the glovebox together with the heater panel.
85   Unscrew the mounting bolts, disconnect the wiring, and withdraw the heater assembly from the car.
86   The dismantling procedure is given in Chapter 11.
87   Refitting is a reversal of removal, but top-up the cooling system if necessary.

Facia panel (models from 1988) – removal and refitting
88   Disconnect the battery negative lead.
89   Remove the screws and withdraw the right-hand lower facia panel (photo).
90   Prise out the instrument panel rheostat, and disconnect the wires.
91   Remove the screws and withdraw the lower steering column shroud (photo).
92   Prise out the coin box and the triangular cover (photos).

93   Pull off the heater control knobs (photo).
94   Remove the screws and withdraw the heater control surround (photos).
95   Remove the screws and withdraw the central vent assembly (photos).
96   Remove the radio (Section 22) or oddments compartment, as applicable.
97   Remove the screws and withdraw the trim quadrants from each side of the facia (photo).
98   Remove the ashtray and disconnect the wiring from the cigar lighter (photos). Identify the wiring.
99   Unclip the clock surround (photo).
100   Insert lengths of welding rod, or similar, into the holes at the top of the switch surround to release the upper clips, then undo the lower screws and remove the surround (photos).
101   Prise the steering column grommet from the floorpan (photo).

21.91 Removing a lower steering column shroud securing screw

21.92A Prise out the coin box ...

21.92B ... and triangular cover

21.93 Removing a heater control knob

21.94A Remove the screws ...

21.94B ... and withdraw the heater control surround

21.95A Removing the central vent assembly upper ...

21.95B ... and lower screws

21.97 Trim quadrant and securing screw

21.98A Remove the ashtray ...

21.98B ... and disconnect the cigar lighter wiring

21.99 Removing the clock surround

21.100A Method of releasing the switch surround upper clips

21.100B Remove the lower screws ...

21.100C ... and withdraw the switch surround

21.101 Steering column grommet partially withdrawn

21.102 Steering column mounting nuts (arrowed)

21.103 Prise out the vent ...

21.104 ... and remove the screw

21.105 Removing the centre console tray

21.106A Remove the screws ...

21.106B ... and slide the surround up the gearstick

21.107A Removing the centre console upper nuts ...

21.107B ... and lower nut

21.109A Front facia panel screws (arrowed)

21.109B Disconnect the switch wiring

21.110A Removing a heater control panel support screw

21.110B Heater control panel mounting screws (arrowed)

21.111 Removing a side vent

21.113 Removing the left lower facia mounting screw

21.114 Removing the glovebox light switch

21.115A Removing the facia lower left screw ...

21.115B ... left mounting nut ...

21.115C ... centre mounting nut ...

21.115D ... and front mounting nuts (arrowed)

21.115E Facia wiring connectors

21.117A Heater motor assembly

21.117B Heater mounting nut (arrowed)

21.117C Heater matrix and supply tubes

102   Unscrew the mounting nuts and lower the steering column to the floor (photo).
103   Prise the small vents from each side of the centre console (photo).
104   Pull back the carpet and remove the screws (photo).
105   Prise the small tray from the centre console (photo).
106   Remove the screws, and slide the surround up the gearstick (photos).
107   Remove the upper and lower nuts, and withdraw the centre console (photos).
108   Unclip the felt cover from under the facia.
109   Remove the screws and withdraw the front facia panel. Disconnect the wiring from the switches (photos).
110   Remove the heater control panel retaining screws (photos).
111   If necessary, remove the side vents (photo).
112   Remove the instrument panel (Section 22) and choke cable, where applicable (Chapter 3).
113   Remove the left lower facia mounting screw (photo).
114   Unclip the glovebox and remove the lighting switch (photo). Also remove the light.

115   Remove the remaining mounting screws and nuts, and withdraw the facia sufficiently to disconnect the wiring. Access to the front mounting nuts is gained by removing the wiper arms and the plastic guard from the plenum chamber in the engine compartment (photos). Identify each wire for location.
116   Unclip the fuse and relay panel, and withdraw the facia panel from the car.
117   With the facia removed, access is gained to the heater and heater control panel (photos).
118   Refitting is a reversal of removal, but on completion check the operation of all electrical components.

Exterior mirror (models from 1988) – removal and refitting
119   Carefully prise the trim cover from the interior mirror control lever (photo).
120   Remove the mounting screws, then feed the rubber grommet through the hole and withdraw the mirror from outside (photos).
121   Refitting is a reversal of removal.

21.117D Heater control panel

21.117E Heater control cable and flap lever

21.119 Removing trim cover from mirror control lever

Bodywork – maintenance
122   Door hinges and safety straps should be lubricated with multi-purpose oil (photo).
123   The bonnet lock should be lubricated with a lithium-based grease (photo).

Front bumper (models with driving lamps) – removal and refitting
124   The procedure is basically as given in Section 10 of Chapter 11, but note the additional details shown (photos).

Front wing (passenger side, 1987-on) – removal and refitting
125   Although the procedure is essentially as described in Chapter 11, Section 9, access to the wing upper fixing will prove difficult on later models, due to obstruction by the glovebox liner.
126   It is possible to gain access to the upper fixing by drilling a hole in the glovebox liner, but this should only be done using a template, which may be available from a Peugeot dealer.

21.120A Remove the mounting screws ...

21.120B ... and withdraw the exterior mirror

21.122 Lubricating a door safety strap

21.123 Lubricating the bonnet lock

21.124A Driving lamp wiring connector

21.124B Front bumper mounting bracket

21.124C Removing a front bumper side bracket nut

21.124D Front wing trim retaining clip

21.124E Using a socket to remove the front bumper centre bolts (viewed from underneath)

21.124F Removing the front bumper side mounting bracket

a	Outside air
b	Outside or recirculated air
c	Fresh and dried air
GHP	High-pressure gas
LHP	High-pressure liquid
GBP	Low-pressure gas
1	Condenser
2	Dehydrator
3	Compressor
4	Expansion chamber
5	Evaporator
6	Pressostat

Fig. 13.138 Air conditioning system (Sec 21)

22.9 Starter motor-to-solenoid cable (arrowed)

22.10 Removing solenoid from starter drive end bracket

22.11 Unscrew the bolt and remove the washers

Air conditioning system – general

Warning: *Components of the air conditioning system may obstruct work being undertaken on other components such as the engine, and it is not always possible to unbolt and move components aside sufficiently, within the limits of their flexible connecting pipes. In such a case, the system should be discharged by a Peugeot dealer or air conditioning specialist. The refrigerant is harmless under normal conditions, but in the presence of a naked flame (or a lighted cigarette) it forms a highly-toxic gas. Liquid refrigerant spilled on the skin will cause frostbite.*

127   From 1993, an air conditioning system is available as an option on GTI and CTI models.
128   A diagrammatic view of the system is given in Fig. 13.138.
129   At the time of wiring, no specific information was available regarding the removal and refitting of the system components.
130   Any faults or problems relating to the air conditioning system should be referred to a Peugeot dealer who will have the necessary specialist knowledge required to carry out work on the system.

22   Electrical system

Alternator (Paris-Rhone) – regulator renewal

1   There are two types of regulator fitted to Paris-Rhone alternators, one having the part number 5761 67 and the other 5761 56. The two regulators differ in that they supply the current to the rotor windings in opposite directions. Due to residual magnetism in the rotor pole pieces, the alternator may not 'self-excite' after replacing one type of regulator with the other. Where this occurs, the following procedure will be necessary.
2   Disconnect the ignition warning lamp wire from the single terminal on the regulator (terminal L).
3   Connect a wire to the battery positive terminal, then touch the free end of the wire on the regulator terminal for approximately three seconds.
4   Disconnect the wire from the battery, and re-connect the ignition warning lamp wires.

Alternator (Valeo) – regulator renewal

5   There are two types of regulator fitted to Valeo alternators, and although they are interchangeable, care must be taken when fitting, as they are of different dimensions.
6   The regulators carry the identifying marks YV or YH on their bodies.
7   The baseplate of the YV alternator is thinner than that of the YH type, and therefore requires shorter fixing screws. If the longer screws from the YH regulator are used to secure a YV regulator, they will foul the rotor and so prevent it from rotating.
8   Screws 20 mm long must be used to secure the YV type regulator, and 30 mm long screws must be used to secure the YH type.

Starter motor (Valeo) – dismantling and reassembly

9   Unscrew the nut and disconnect the motor cable from the solenoid (photo).

10   Unscrew the through-bolts and remove the solenoid from the drive end bracket, at the same time unhooking the solenoid core from the lever (photo).
11   Unscrew the bolt and remove the washers from the commutator end (photo).
12   Unscrew the nuts from the through-bolts, and withdraw the end cover, at the same time extracting the field brush (photos).
13   Remove the thrustwashers from the armature (photo).
14   Mark the yoke and end bracket in relation to each other, then remove the yoke (photo).
15   Prise out the rubber bearing, and withdraw the armature from the drive end bracket (photo).
16   Remove the rubber bearing from the lever.
17   Remove the core and spring from the solenoid.
18   Reassembly is a reversal of dismantling.

Fuses

19   The fuse circuits for later models are changed as shown in the Specifications at the beginning of this Chapter.

Facia switches (models from 1988) – removal and refitting

20   Disconnect the battery negative lead.
21   Open the ashtray.
22   Unclip the bottom of the clock surround (where fitted) and remove it.
23   Remove the screws from the bottom of the switch panel, then insert lengths of welding rod (or similar) into the special holes, and remove the switch panel.
24   The individual switches may now be removed by inserting two small screwdrivers in the slots on each side of the switch, extracting the switch, and disconnecting the wiring.
25   Refitting is a reversal of removal.

Clock (models from 1988) – removal and refitting

26   Disconnect the battery negative lead.
27   Remove the trapezium-shaped coin compartment or cover from the top of the facia by lifting the bottom edge.
28   Pull off the heater control knobs, using card or thick cloth and pliers on the central bars.
29   Remove the screws beneath the control knobs, and withdraw the upper front panel surround.
30   Open and remove the ashtray.
31   Unclip the bottom of the clock surround and remove it.
32   Remove the oddments tray, or if fitted, the radio, as described later in this Section.
33   Remove the screws and withdraw the lower front panel surround by releasing the bottom edge first.
34   Disconnect the wiring plug from the rear of the clock, then release the clock from the lower front panel surround.
35   Refitting is a reversal of removal.

Instrument panel (models from 1988) – removal and refitting

36   Disconnect the battery negative lead.
37   Remove the trapezium-shaped coin compartment or cover from the top of the facia by lifting the bottom edge.

22.12A Unscrew the through-bolt nuts (arrowed) ...

22.12B ... and withdraw the end cover

22.13 Removing thrustwashers from armature

22.14 Removing the yoke

22.15 Withdrawing armature from drive end bracket

38   Pull off the heater control knobs, using card or thick cloth and pliers on the central bars.
39   Remove the screws beneath the control knobs, and withdraw the upper front panel surround.
40   Remove the screws and withdraw the visor from the instrument panel.
41   Remove the screws and withdraw the centre vents.
42   Using a screwdriver through the steering column lower shroud, unscrew the visor locating studs.
43   Remove the side screw, then lift away the visor.
44   Remove the mounting screws from each side of the instrument panel (photo).
45   Tilt the instrument panel and disconnect the wiring plugs, noting their locations (photo).
46   Disconnect the speedometer cable by squeezing the end fitting. Remove the instrument panel (photo).
47   Refitting is a reversal of removal.

Side repeater light and bulb – removal and refitting
48   On early models, reach up behind the front wing, squeeze the plastic tabs together and push out the lamp. On later models, turn the lamp anti-clockwise and withdraw it from the front wing (photos).

49   Disconnect the wiring, remove the end cap, and extract the bulb.
50   Refitting is a reversal of removal, but on the early type, position the lamp so that the location peg enters the hole in the front wing.

Reversing lamp bulb renewal (models from 1991)
51   On models from 1991, a single reversing lamp is mounted in the rear valance, instead of the twin lamps in the rear lamp clusters fitted to previous models.
52   Bulb renewal is as described for the rear foglamp bulb in Chapter 12, Section 19.

Dim-dip lighting – description
53   All models manufactured from late 1986 are fitted with a dim-dip lighting system, which essentially prevents the vehicle from being driven with the sidelights alone switched on.
54   When the ignition is switched on with the sidelights also switched on, the relay is energised, closing the internal contacts and supplying current to the dipped beam circuit via the resistor. This causes the dip filaments in the headlamps to be illuminated at one-sixth dipped beam brightness. The relay winding is earthed through the headlamp main beam filaments, so that the relay is de-energised when the main beam is switched on.

22.44 Removing an instrument panel mounting screw

22.45 Disconnecting the instrument panel wiring plugs

22.46 Disconnecting the speedometer cable (arrowed)

22.48A Removing a later-type side repeater light

22.48B Side repeater light components

22.56 Removing the radio side trims

22.57 Disconnecting the radio wiring plug

22.59 Removing the instrument panel rheostat

Radio (later models) – removal and refitting
55   Disconnect the battery negative lead.
56   Remove the radio side trims (photo), and insert lengths of welding rod or metal dowel into the exposed holes to release the clips. Special tools are available at low cost from motor accessory shops.
57   Withdraw the radio from the facia, and disconnect the aerial and wiring (photo).
58   Refitting is a reversal of removal.

Instrument panel rheostat – removal and refitting
59   Prise the rheostat from the steering column lower shroud, and disconnect the wiring (photo).
60   Refitting is a reversal of removal.

Reversing light switch – removal and refitting
61   Disconnect the wiring and unscrew the switch from the top of the gearbox (photo). Remove the washer.
62   Refitting is a reversal of removal, but renew the washer if necessary.

Clock illumination bulb (models from 1988) – renewal
63   Remove the clock as previously described.
64   Twist the bulbholder to remove it, then extract the bulb (photo).

Heater control panel illumination bulb (models from 1988) – renewal
65   Follow the procedure given in paragraphs 26 to 29.
66   Pull the bulb from the control panel (photo).

Glovebox illumination bulb (models from 1988) – renewal
67   Open the glovebox and prise out the lamp (photo).
68   Remove the festoon-type bulb from the terminals.

Air compressor and horn (1.9 GTI) – removal and refitting
69   Remove the left-hand headlamp as described in Chapter 12, Section 21.
70   Disconnect the air hose and supply wire.

22.61 Removing the reversing light switch

22.64 Removing the clock illumination bulb

22.66 Removing the heater control panel illumination bulb

22.67 Glovebox illumination lamp and bulb

22.71 Air compressor (A) and horn (B) –
1.9 GTI

22.73A Fusebox behind radiator

22.73B Relays on bulkhead

22.73C Headlamp dim-dip system resistor –
1.9 GTI

71   Unbolt and remove the compressor or horn as required (photo).
72   Refitting is a reversal of removal.

Fuses and relays (models from 1988) – general

73   In addition to the fuses and relays above the glovebox, fuses are located behind the left-hand side of the radiator, on the left-hand side of the bulkhead, and near the horn on 1.9 GTI models (photos).
74   Most electrical components and accessories are protected by relays; refer to the wiring diagram key for details.

Vehicle immobiliser (GTI models) – general

75   From 1993, a vehicle immobiliser system is fitted to certain GTI models.
76   The system is activated by locking the car with the PLIP remote control device.
77   A possible fault with the system should not be overlooked if the car cannot be started, and other areas of investigation have failed to locate the cause.
78   Refer to a Peugeot dealer for additional information.

NOTES:

1. All diagrams are divided into numbered circuits depending on function e.g. Diagram 2: Exterior lighting.
2. Items are arranged in relation to a plan view of the vehicle.
3. Items may appear on more than one diagram so are found using a grid reference e.g. 2/A1 denotes an item on diagram 2 grid location A1.
4. Complex items appear on the diagrams as blocks and are expanded on the internal connections page.
5. Not all items are fitted to all models.
6. For fuse information see specifications.
7. Wire identification is not by colour, but by letters or numbers appearing on the wire at each end.

INTERNAL CONNECTION DETAILS

KEY TO SYMBOLS

PLUG-IN CONNECTOR

EARTH

BULB

LINE CONNECTOR

FUSE/ FUSIBLE LINK

FUSE/RELAY BOARD CONNECTOR PIN No.

EARTH POINT

P121C

KEY TO INSTRUMENT CLUSTER (ITEM 64)

a = Oil Pressure Warning Lamp
b = Ignition Warning Lamp
c = High Temp. Warning Lamp
d = Brake Warning Lamp
e = Brake Warning Lamp
f = Direction Indicator Lamp
g = Instrument Illumination
h = Earth
i = Main Beam Warning Lamp
j = Dipped Beam Warning Lamp
k = Instrument Illumination
l = Tachometer
m = Clock
n = +VE Supply
o = Choke Warning Lamp
p = Low Fuel Warning Lamp
q = Fuel Gauge
r = Sidelamp Warning Lamp

KEY TO INSTRUMENT CLUSTER (ITEM 64)
(ADDITIONAL CONNECTIONS XU/TU MODELS ONLY)

s = Direction Indicator Lamp LH
t = Direction Indicator Lamp RH
u = Oil Level Warning Lamp
v = Oil Temperature Gauge
w = Coolant Temperature Gauge
x = Coolant Level Warning Lamp
y = + VE Supply
z = Earth
a1 = Oil Pressure Gauge
a2 = Injection System Warning Lamp

ITEM	DESCRIPTION	DIAGRAM/ GRID REF.
1	Air Flow Sensor	1b/B5
2	Alternator	1/C3, 1a/C3, 1b/B2, 2/C3
3	Ashtray Illumination	2a/H4
4	Auto. Trans. Inhibitor Relay	1/G4
5	Auto. Trans. Inhibitor Switch	1/D5
6	Auto. Trans. Pump Control Relay	1/G6
7	Battery	1/C7, 1a/C7, 1b/C7, 2/C8, 2a/B7, 3/B7, 3a/B7
8	Brake Pad Wear Sensor	1/D1, 1/D8, 1a/D1, 1a/D8, 1b/C1, 1b/C8
9	Central Locking Control Switch	3a/K1
10	Central Locking Motor LH Front	3a/K8
11	Central Locking Motor LH Rear	3a/M8
12	Central Locking Motor RH Rear	3a/M1
13	Central Locking Motor Tailgate	3a/M5
14	Choke Switch	1/J3, 1a/J3
15	Cigar Lighter	2a/H4

Key to wiring diagrams

T.M.MARKE

ITEM	DESCRIPTION	DIAGRAM/GRID REF.
16	Cigar Lighter Illumination	2a/H4
17	Clock	2a/J3
18	Combination Switch – Lighting, Direction Indicators And Horn	2/J3, 2a/G3, 3/G3
19	Combination Switch – Wash/Wipe	3/G3
20	Coolant Temp. Gauge Sender Unit	1a/D5, 1b/G4
21	Coolant Temp. Sensor	1b/D5
22	Coolant Temp. Switch	1/B5, 1a/C5, 1b/G3
23	Cooling Fan Motor	1/A5, 1a/B5
24	Cooling Fan Resistor	1/G8, 1a/A5
25	Cooling Fan Switch	1/A3, 1a/B3
26	Diagnostic Socket	1/D6, 1a/D6, 1b/D2
27	Dim/Dip Relay	2/E5
28	Dim/Dip Resistor	2/E7
29	Direction Indicator Flasher Relay	2a/E7
30	Direction Indicator LH Front	2a/A8
31	Direction Indicator RH Front	2a/A1
32	Distributor	1/E6, 1a/E6, 1b/E5
33	Driving Lamp LH	2/A6
34	Driving Lamp Relay	2/E4
35	Driving Lamp RH	2/A3
36	Electric Window Motor LH Front	3a/J8
37	Electric Window Motor RH Front	3a/J1
38	Electric Window Relay	3a/D6
39	Electric Window Switch LH	3a/H8
40	Electric Window Switch RH (Drivers)	3a/J1
41	Electric Window Switch RH (Passengers)	3a/H1
42	Foglamp Rear	2/M3
43	Foglamp Switch	2/G3
44	Fuel Gauge Sender Unit	1/M5, 1a/M5, 1b/M5
45	Fuel Injection ECU	1b/G6
46	Fuel Injectors	1b/D4
47	Fuel Pump	1/L6, 1b/M6
48	Glove Box/Lamp Switch	2a/J7
49	Handbrake Warning Switch	1/L5, 1a/L5, 1b/K5
50	Hazard Warning Lamp/Switch	2a/F4
51	Headlamp Unit LH	2/A7
52	Headlamp Unit RH	2/A2
53	Heated Rear Window	3/M4
54	Heated Rear Window Relay	3/E6
55	Heated Rear Window Switch	3/H3
56	Heater Blower Motor	3/H4
57	Heater Blower Motor Control Unit	3/C8
58	Heater Blower Motor Speed Control	3/J4
59	Heater/Ventilation Illumination	2a/H3
60	Horn	3/A8
61	Ignition Coil	1/E7, 1a/E7, 1b/E6
62	Ignition Module	1/E7, 1a/E6, 1b/E6

ITEM	DESCRIPTION	DIAGRAM/GRID REF.
63	Ignition Switch	1/J1, 1a/J1, 1b/K1, 2/F1, 2a/G1, 3/E1, 3a/F1
64	Instrument Cluster	1/H3, 1a/H3, 1b/K3, 2/F3, 2a/F3
65	Instrument Illumination Control	2a/F3
66	Interior Lamp	2a/D5
67	Interior Lamp Door Switch LH	2a/C8
68	Interior Lamp Door Switch RH	2a/C1
69	Lamp Cluster LH Rear	2/M7, 2a/M7
70	Lamp Cluster RH Rear	2/M1, 2a/M1
71	Low Brake Fluid Sender Unit	1/E2, 1a/E2, 1b/E2
72	Low Coolant Sender Unit	1b/F8
73	Luggage Comp. Lamp	2a/L4
74	Luggage Comp. Lamp Switch	2a/M4
75	Map Reading Lamp	2a/E5
76	Number Plate Lamp	2/M4, 2/M5
77	Oil Level Indicator Unit	1b/H5
78	Oil Level Sensor	1b/G4
79	Oil Pressure Sender Unit	1b/G3
80	Oil Pressure Switch	1/B5, 1a/C5, 1b/G4
81	Oil Temp. Sender Unit	1b/H4
82	Radio/Cassette Unit	3a/F5
83	Reversing Lamp Switch	2/D5
84	Spark Plugs	1/E5, 1a/E5, 1b/E4
85	Speaker LH Front	3a/C8
86	Speaker RH Front	3a/C1
87	Starter Motor	1/C6, 1a/C6, 1b/B6, 2/B5
88	Stop-Lamp Switch	2a/D3
89	Supplementary Air Device	1b/D5
90	Suppressor	1/C2, 1b/B2
91	Tachymetric Relay	1b/A7
92	TDC Position Sensor	1/C6, 1a/D6, 1b/D3
93	Throttle Switch	1b/B4
94	Washer Pump Front	3/B8
95	Washer Pump Rear	3/M2
96	Wiper Motor Front	3/C3
97	Wiper Motor Rear	3/M5
98	Wiper Relay Front	3/E8, 3/J5
99	Wiper Relay Rear	3/M6

Key to wiring diagrams (continued)

H24481

T.M.MARKE

Diagram 1: Typical starting, charging, ignition, cooling fan, warning lamps and gauges (XV8, XW7, XY8 and XU51C engine models)

Diagram 1a: Typical starting, charging, ignition, cooling fan, warning lamps and gauges (TU1, TU3 and TU9 engine models)

368

Diagram 1b: Typical engine management, warning lamps and gauges (XU5J/JA and XU9JA engine models)

Diagram 2: Typical exterior lighting – reversing lamps, foglamps, sidelamps and headlamps

370

Diagram 2a: Typical exterior lighting – direction indicators and stop-lamps; typical interior lighting and associated circuits

Diagram 3: Typical ancillary circuits – wash/wipe, horn, heater blower and heated rear window

Diagram 3a: Typical ancillary circuits – electric windows, central locking and radio/cassette

373

Supplementary diagram A: Typical engine management (TU3M/Z and TU3FM/L engine models)

KEY TO ITEMS

1 Injection control unit
2 Ignition switch
3 Fuel pump
4 Loadbo sensor
5 Temperature sender
6 Fuel injector
8 Engine speed sensor
9 Canister solenoid
11 Spark plugs
13 Ignition coil
14 Suppressor
15 Battery
16 Positive supply control unit
19 Tachymetric relay
20 Injection supply relay
22 Inlet manifold pressure sensor
23 Idling actuator
24 Starter
25 Throttle potentiometer
26 Inlet air temp. sensor
27 Auto. trans. starter inhibitor switch
28 Starter motor isolator relay
64 Instrument cluster (see internal connection page)

Supplementary diagram B: Typical engine management (TU1M/L and XU5M3/Z/L engine models)

KEY TO ITEMS

1 Injection control unit
2 Ignition switch
3 Fuel pump
4 Lambda sensor
5 Temperature sender
6 Fuel injectors
7 Throttle switch
10 Distributor
11 Spark plugs
12 Ignition control unit
13 Ignition coil
15 Battery
16 Positive supply control unit
17 Flow sensor
18 Supplementary air device
19 Tachymetric relay
21 Lambda sensor fuse
64 Instrument cluster (see internal connection page)

Supplementary diagram C: Typical engine management (XU9J1/Z/L engine models)

Supplementary diagram D: Typical engine management (XU9JA/L engine models)

Index